Mental Causation

Edited by
John Heil and Alfred Mele

CLARENDON PRESS · OXFORD
1993

Oxford University Press, Walton Street, Oxford OX2 6DP
Oxford New York Toronto
Delhi Bombay Calcutta Madras Karachi
Petaling Jaya Singapore Hong Kong Tokyo
Nairobi Dar es Salaam Cape Town
Melbourne Auckland
and associated companies in
Berlin Ibadan

Oxford is a trade mark of Oxford University Press

Published in the United States
by Oxford University Press Inc., New York

British Library Cataloguing in Publication Data
Data available

Library of Congress Cataloging in Publication Data
Mental causation/edited by John Heil and Alfred Mele.
p. cm.
Includes bibliographical references and index.
1. Philosophy of mind. 2. Causation—Psychological aspects.
3. Act (Philosophy) 4. Intentionalism. 5. Mind and body.
I. Heil, John. II. Mele, Alfred R., 1951– .
BD418.3.M45 1993 128'.2—dc20 92—22764
ISBN 0–19–823929–7

Typeset by Pentacor PLC, High Wycombe, Bucks
Printed in Great Britain
on acid-free paper by
Bookcraft (Bath) Ltd.
Midsomer Norton, Avon

Preface

COMMON sense and a long philosophical tradition agree that mind makes a difference. What we do depends not only on what our bodies are made of, but on what we think as well. Criticizing Anaxagoras for contending that 'Mind . . . causes all things' and then adducing only physical causes, Socrates argues:

His position was like that of a man who said that all the actions of Socrates are due to his mind, and then attempted to give the causes of my several actions by saying that the reason why I am now sitting here is that my body is composed of bones and sinews, and that the bones are hard and separated by joints, while the sinews, which can be tightened or relaxed, envelop the bones along with the flesh and skin which hold them together; so that when the bones move about in their sockets, the sinews, by lessening or increasing the tension, make it possible for me at this moment to bend my limbs, and that is the cause of my sitting here in this bent position. Analogous causes might also be given of my conversing with you . . . to the neglect of the true causes, to wit that, inasmuch as the Athenians have thought it better to condemn me, I too in my turn have thought it better to sit here, and more right and proper to stay where I am and submit to such punishment as they enjoin. For, by Jingo, I fancy these same sinews and bones would long since have been somewhere in Megara or Boeotia, impelled by their notion of what was best, if I had not thought it right and proper to submit to the penalty appointed by the State rather than take to my heels and run away. (Plato, *Phaedo*, 98*c*–99*a*)

Aristotle more concisely captures the popular idea that mental states and events drive intentional behaviour in Book 6 of the *Nicomachean Ethics*: 'The origin of action—its efficient, not its final cause—is choice, and that of choice is desire and reasoning with a view to an end' (1139*a* 31–3). Descartes, too, echoes common sense in remarking that 'everyone feels that he is a single person with both body and thought so related by nature that the thought can move the body and feel the things which happen to it' (Kenny 1970, p. 142).

Explaining *how* mind can make a difference has proved challenging, however. In a letter to Descartes, Princess Elizabeth of Bohemia observes that 'it would be easier for me to attribute matter and extension to the soul, than to attribute to an immaterial body the capacity to move and be moved by a body' (Kenny 1970, p. 140). It is usually supposed that the difficulty facing Descartes stems from his conception of mind and body as distinct substances, a conception that would seem to rule out in advance any possibility of causal interaction between minds and bodies. The problem is not confined to Cartesian dualism, however; it has deeper metaphysical roots. So long as we regard the material world as causally closed, and in that respect *autonomous*, Princess Elizabeth's worry survives. Physical accounts of agents' behaviour seem to leave no room for accounts framed in terms of reasons or purposes.

Norman Malcolm considers a potential resolution of the apparent conflict, one according to which purposive and non-purposive, neurophysiological explanations of behaviour 'explain different things': 'Purposive explanations explain actions. Neurophysiological explanations explain movements. Both explain behavior: but we can say this only because we use the latter word ambiguously to cover both actions and movements' (Malcolm 1968, pp. 51–2). Consider a man 'climbing a ladder in order to retrieve his hat from the roof'. In saying that the man climbed the ladder for that purpose, we purport to explain his behaviour in terms of an intention. In contrast, 'a neurophysiological explanation of his climbing would say nothing about his intention but would connect his movements on the ladder with chemical changes in body tissue or with the firing of neurons' (p. 52).

Malcolm notes, however, that while there may be some truth in the notion 'that the different kinds of explanation employ different concepts and, in a sense, explain different things', it is much less clear that the explanations are at base 'independent of one another'. Indeed, 'purposive explanations would be refuted by the verification of a comprehensive neurophysiological theory of behavior' (p. 51). If the man's 'movements on the ladder' were 'completely accounted for by his antecedent neurological states (his "programming"), then it was not true that those movements occurred *because* he wanted or intended to get his hat' (p. 53).

The envisaged neurophysiological theory was supposed to provide *sufficient* causal explanations of behavior. Thus the movements of the man on the ladder would be *completely* accounted for in terms of electrical, chemical, and mechanical processes in his body. This would surely imply that his desire or intention to retrieve his hat had nothing to do with his movement up the ladder. It would imply that on this same occasion he would have moved up the ladder in exactly this way even if he had no intention to retrieve his hat, or even no intention to climb the ladder. Given the antecedent neurological states of his bodily system together with general laws correlating these states with the contractions of muscles and the movements of limbs, he would have moved as he did regardless of his desire or intention (pp. 52–3).

We confront a dilemma. Either we concede that 'purposive', reason-giving explanations of behaviour have only a pragmatic standing, or we abandon our conception of the physical domain as causally autonomous. Although each of these options has its advocates, most theorists have sought a middle way, a route between the horns of the dilemma, one that accommodates both the metaphysical conviction that the physical world is causally closed and the common-sense view that minds make a difference.

The papers that follow—each written expressly for this volume—approach these issues from widely divergent perspectives. Rather than attempting to summarize them, we shall let the authors speak for themselves, motivated, like Socrates, by what we think better.

Donald Davidson graciously made available his contribution, 'Thinking Causes' (Chapter 1), well in advance of our deadline, thus enabling us to include three papers explicitly addressing the arguments Davidson develops in that chapter.

J.H.
A.M.

Davidson College
Davidson, North Carolina

Contents

Part III. Content

Notes on Contributors

ROBERT AUDI is professor of philosophy at the University of Nebraska. He is author of *Belief, Justification, and Knowledge*, and *Practical Reasoning*.

LYNNE RUDDER BAKER is professor of philosophy at the University of Massachusetts at Amherst and at Middlebury College, Middlebury, Vermont. She is author of *Saving Belief: A Critique of Physicalism*.

TYLER BURGE is professor of philosophy at UCLA. He has written on the philosophy of language and the philosophy of mind.

DONALD DAVIDSON is professor of philosophy at the University of California at Berkeley. He is author of *Essays on Actions and Events* and *Inquiries into Truth and Interpretation*.

FRED DRETSKE is professor of philosophy at Stanford University. He has published books and articles on perception, epistemology, philosophy of science, and philosophy of mind. His most recent book is *Explaining Behavior: Reasons in a World of Causes*.

TED HONDERICH is Grote Professor of the Philosophy of Mind and Logic at University College London. He is the author of *Theory of Determinism: The Mind, Neuroscience, and Life-Hopes* and other books and articles, and the editor of several series.

JENNIFER HORNSBY teaches philosophy at Corpus Christi College, University of Oxford. She is author of *Actions*, and of articles in the philosophy of mind and language, and co-editor of *Ethics: A Feminist Reader*.

FRANK JACKSON is professor of philosophy at the Australian National University. He is author of *Perception* and *Conditionals*, and editor of *Conditionals*.

JAEGWON KIM is professor of philosophy at Brown University. He has published papers in the philosophy of mind and metaphysics.

BRIAN P. MCLAUGHLIN is associate professor of philosophy at Rutgers University. He is the author of numerous articles in the philosophy of mind and metaphysics. He is co-editor of *Actions and Events*, *Perspectives on Self Deception*, and editor of *Dretske and His Critics*.

RUTH GARRETT MILLIKAN is professor of philosophy at the University of Connecticut. She is author of 'Thoughts Without Laws', 'Truth Rules, Hoverflies, and the Kripke–Wittgenstein Paradox', 'Biosemantics', 'Metaphysical Antirealism?', and *Language, Thought, and Other Biological Categories.*

H. W. NOONAN is reader in philosophy at the University of Birmingham. He is author of *Personal Identity.*

PHILIP PETTIT holds a personal chair in the Research School of Social Sciences at the Australian National University. He is co-editor (with John McDowell) of *Subject, Thought, and Context*, co-author (with John Braithwaite) of *Not Just Deserts*, and author of *The Common Mind: From Intentional Psychology to Social and Political Theory.*

ERNEST SOSA is professor of philosophy at Brown University.

ROBERT VAN GULICK is associate professor of philosophy and Director of the Cognitive Science Program at Syracuse University. He is co-editor with Ernest LePore of *John Searle and His Critics* and has published on a variety of topics in the philosophy of mind.

PART I

Davidson, Anomalous Monism, and Mental Causation

1

Thinking Causes

DONALD DAVIDSON

In 1970 I proposed a theory about the relation between the mental and the physical that I called Anomalous Monism (*AM*).[1] *AM* holds that mental entities (particular time- and space-bound objects and events) are physical entities, but that mental concepts are not reducible by definition or natural law to physical concepts. The position is, in a general way, familiar: it endorses ontological reduction, but eschews conceptual reduction. What was new was the argument, which purported to derive *AM* from three premisses, namely, (1) that mental events are causally related to physical events, (2) that singular causal relations are backed by strict laws, and (3) that there are no strict psycho-physical laws.[2] The first premiss seemed to me obvious, the second true though contested (I did not present arguments for it), and the third true and worth arguing for. Many readers have found my arguments against the existence of strict psycho-physical laws obscure; others have decided the three premisses are mutually inconsistent. But the complaints have most often been summed up by saying that *AM* makes the mental causally inert. The criticisms are connected: if *AM* makes the mental causally inert, then *AM* apparently implies the falsity of the first premiss and hence the inconsistency of the three premisses. The third premiss seems to many critics the relevant offender, so they urge that it should be dropped.

In this paper I attempt three things: first, to defend *AM* against misunderstandings and misrepresentations. This will involve some clarification, and perhaps modification, of the original thesis. Second, I want to maintain that the three premisses from which I argue to *AM* are consistent when taken together, and so *AM* is a

[1] Davidson 1970.

[2] This summary simplifies the original thesis and argument. Those not familiar with 'Mental Events' should consult it for caveats and additional assumptions.

tenable thesis (it is weaker than the premisses). Third, I shall say why I do not think *AM* makes the mental causally powerless. I do not plan here to argue for the truth of *AM* or the premisses on which it rests.

In 'Mental Events' (Davidson 1970) I endorsed the idea that mental concepts[3] are supervenient, in a sense I explained, on physical concepts. I thought this would make it clear that, contrary to first impressions, *AM* and its entailing premisses were after all consistent. So what I am defending in this paper is in effect not only *AM* itself, but *AM* in conjunction with the three premisses and the doctrine of supervenience. (In what follows, I shall abbreviate the expression 'anomalous monism conjoined with premisses (1)–(2)' by '*AM+P*'; '*AM+P+S*' will mean supervenience in addition to *AM+P*.)

When I wrote 'Mental Events' I thought I knew that G. E. Moore had used the word 'supervenience' to describe the relation between evaluative terms like 'good' and descriptive terms like 'sharp' or 'inexpensive' or 'pleasure-producing'. Moore's idea seemed clear enough: something is good only because it has properties that can be specified in descriptive terms, but goodness can't be reduced to a descriptive property. In fact, Moore apparently never used the word 'supervenient'. I had probably found the word in R. M. Hare's *The Language of Morals* (1952), and applied it, as he had, to Moore. (Hare has since complained that I got the concept wrong: for him supervenience implies a form of what I call nomological reduction.[4]) In any case, the idea I had in mind is, I think, most economically expressed as follows: a predicate *p* is supervenient on a set of predicates *S* if and only if *p* does not distinguish any entities that cannot be distinguished by *S*.[5] Supervenience so understood

[3] In the present paper I do not distinguish concepts from properties or predicates, except to the extent that I allow that physics may well come to require predicates not now available.

[4] Hare (1984, p. 3) says, '. . . supervenience brings with it the claim that there is some "law" which binds what supervenes to what it supervenes upon . . . what supervenience requires is that what supervenes is seen as an instance of some universal proposition linking it with what it supervenes upon.' But so far as I can see, Hare's characterization of supervenience, on the page before the one from which the above quotation is taken, does not imply the existence of laws or law-like generalizations linking what supervenes to what it supervenes on. Hare compares his version of supervenience with Kim's 'weak' supervenience, but Kim himself (correctly, I think) finds my version of supervenience very close to his 'weak' supervenience, and as not entailing connecting laws.

[5] In 'Mental Events' I said the supervenience of the mental on the physical 'might

obviously applies in an uninteresting sense to cases where *p* belongs to *S*, to cases where *p* is explicitly definable by means of the predicates in *S*, and to cases where there is a law to the effect that the extension of *p* is identical with the extension of a predicate definable in terms of the predicates in *S*. The interesting cases are those where *p* resists any of these forms of reduction. I gave as a non-controversial example of an interesting case the supervenience of semantic predicates on syntactical predicates: a truth predicate for a language cannot distinguish any sentences not distinguishable in purely syntactical terms, but for most languages truth is not definable in such terms. The example gives one possible meaning to the idea that truths expressible by the subvenient predicates 'determine' the extension of the supervenient predicate, or that the extension of the supervenient predicate 'depends' on the extensions of the subvenient predicates.

How can the possibility of a supervenient relation between the mental and the physical help to show that *AM* (or *AM+P*) is consistent, since supervenience says nothing about causality? The answer is simple: supervenience in any form implies monism; but it does not imply either definitional or nomological reduction. So if (non-reductive) supervenience is consistent (as the syntax-semantics example proves it is), so is *AM*. But supervenience is also consistent with premisses (1) and (2), which are not implied by *AM*, since (1) and (2) concern causality, and supervenience says nothing about causality.

It is difficult, then, to see how *AM+P* together with supervenience can imply a contradiction. So it surprised me to read in a recent article by Jaegwon Kim that not only are the premisses of *AM* inconsistent with one another, but 'the notion of supervenience Davidson favours' is also inconsistent with the first premiss of *AM* (Kim 1989*b*, p. 6).

Let us look at these supposed inconsistencies. According to Kim,

> The fact is that under Davidson's anomalous monism, mentality does no causal work. Remember: on anomalous monism, events are causes only as

be taken to mean that there cannot be two events alike in all physical respects but differing in some mental respect'. I intended this to be equivalent to the present formulation, but apparently it is easily misunderstood. In answer to a question about 'Mental Events', I gave an unambiguous definition of supervenience which is clearly equivalent to the present one: a predicate *p* is supervenient on a set of predicates *S* if for every pair of objects such that *p* is true of one and not of the other there is a predicate in *S* that is true of one and not of the other. I suggested that it is a common fallacy in philosophy (of which the naturalistic fallacy is an example) to switch the order of the quantifiers in this formula. See Davidson 1985, p. 242.

they instantiate physical laws, and this means that an event's mental properties make no causal difference. And to suppose that altering an event's mental properties would also alter its physical properties and thereby affect its causal relations is to suppose that psycho-physical anomalism, a cardinal tenet of anomalous monism, is false.

Of course, if 'mentality does no causal work' means that mental events do not enter into causal relations, the first premiss of *AM* is false, for it says mental events cause, and are caused by, physical events. This is not enough to prove *AM* itself inconsistent, but it certainly would show the three premisses of *AM* inconsistent with one another. And if Kim's last sentence quoted above is correct, then *AM* is inconsistent with any form of supervenience.

Why does Kim think *AM+P+S* is inconsistent? At least part of the answer is contained in the sentence in which Kim asks us to 'remember' what he thinks is a feature of *AM+P*; and here I believe Kim speaks for many of the critics of my position. What Kim asks us to 'remember' is that 'on anomalous monism, events are causes only as they instantiate laws'. This is not anything I have claimed. I could not have claimed it, since given my concept of events and of causality, it makes no sense to speak of an event being a cause 'as' anything at all. *AM+P+S* is formulated on the assumption that events are non-abstract particulars, and that causal relations are extensional relations between such events. In his article, Kim does not dispute these two theses. But there is then no room for a concept of 'cause as' which would make causality a relation among three or four entities rather than between two. On the view of events and causality assumed here,[6] it makes no more sense to say event *c* caused event *e* as instantiating law *l* than it makes to say *a* weighs less than *b* as belonging to sort *s*. If causality is a relation between events, it holds between them no matter how they are described. So there can be descriptions of two events (physical descriptions) which allow us to deduce from a law that if the first event occurred the second would occur, and other descriptions (mental descriptions) of the same events which invite no such inference. We can say, if we please (though I do not think this is a happy way of putting the point), that events instantiate a law only as described in one way rather than another, but we cannot say that an event caused another only as described. Redescribing an event

[6] This view is spelled out in detail in the articles in the second part of Davidson 1980.

cannot change what it causes, or change the event's causal efficacy. Events, unlike agents, do not care how what they cause is described: an agent may kill a bird because she wanted to perform an action that could be described as 'my killing of that bird'. But her killing of the bird might have been identical with her killing of the goose that laid the golden egg though 'My killing of the goose that laid the golden egg' may have been the last description she wanted to have describe an action of hers.

Kim thinks that *AM+P* cannot remain consistently anomalous if it holds that altering an event's mental properties would also alter its physical properties. This seems to be a mistake. *AM+P+S* (which includes supervenience) does hold that altering an event's mental properties would also alter its physical properties. But supervenience does not imply the existence of psycho-physical laws. To see this, it is only necessary to recognize that although supervenience entails that any change in a mental property *p* of a particular event *e* will be accompanied by a change in the physical properties of *e*, it does not entail that a change in *p* in other events will be accompanied by an identical change in the physical properties of those other events. Only the latter entailment would conflict with *AM+P*.

The definition of supervenience implies that a change in mental properties is always accompanied by a change in physical properties, but it does not imply that the same physical properties change with the same mental properties. Supervenience implies the first, because if a change in a mental property were not accompanied by a change in physical properties, there would be two events distinguished by their mental properties that were not distinguished by their physical properties, and supervenience, as I defined it, rules this out. Kim says supervenience 'is best regarded as independent' of the thesis of *AM+P*. This is true in the sense that neither supervenience nor *AM+P* entails the other. But it is not true that the consistency of supervenience is irrelevant to the consistency of *AM+P* since, as I just argued, supervenience helps not only in showing that *AM+P* is consistent, but also that there is a version of *AM+P* that gives a plausible picture of the relation between the mental and the physical. Kim may have made this remark because he mistakenly thinks that my 'weak' version of supervenience entails that 'the removal of *all* mental properties from events of this world would have no consequence whatever on how physical properties are distributed over them' (Kim 1989*b*, p. 35, n. 8). In fact supervenience entails the reverse. For consider two events with the same physical properties, but one with some mental property and the other with that property removed. These cannot be the same event, since one has a property the other lacks. But then contrary to the definition of supervenience, mental properties would distinguish two events not distinguished by their physical properties.

But the point seems clear enough whatever one wants to say about supervenience: if causal relations and causal powers inhere in particular events and objects, then the way those events and objects are described, and the properties we happen to employ to pick them out or characterize them, cannot affect what they cause. Naming the American invasion of Panama 'Operation Just Cause' does not alter the consequences of the event.

So far I have said little about laws because laws are not mentioned in the definition of supervenience, and the logical possibility of supervenience is important in establishing the consistency of *AM+P*. But of course the thesis that there are no strict psychophysical laws is one of the premisses on the basis of which I argued for *AM*. So even if *AM* is consistent, there is a question whether the denial of such laws somehow undermines the claim that mental events are causally efficacious. I say 'somehow' since it would seem that the efficacy of an event cannot depend on how the event is described, while whether an event can be called mental, or can be said to fall under a law, depends entirely on how the event can be described.

Let me digress briefly. The second assumption from which I argued to *AM* was that if two events are related as cause and effect, there must be a law that covers the case. In 'Mental Events' I explained in some detail what I meant by a law in this context, and what I meant by 'covering'. A law (formulated in some language) covers a case if the law, conjoined with a sentence that says the event (described appropriately) occurred, entails a sentence that asserts the existence of the effect (appropriately described). I made clear that what I was calling a law in this context was something that one could at best hope to find in a developed physics: a generalization that was not only 'law-like' and true, but was as deterministic as nature can be found to be, was free from caveats and *ceteris paribus* clauses; that could, therefore, be viewed as treating the universe as a closed system. I stressed that it was only laws of this kind (which I called 'strict' laws) that I was arguing could not cover events when those events were described in the mental vocabulary. I allowed that there are not, and perhaps could not be expected to be, laws of this sort in the special sciences. Most, if not all, of the practical knowledge that we (or engineers, chemists, geneticists, geologists) have that allows us to explain and predict ordinary happenings does not involve strict laws. The best descriptions we are able to give of most events are not descriptions that fall under, or will ever fall under, strict laws.[7]

There are two reasons for reminding those interested in *AM* (or *AM+P* or *AM+P+S*) of these facts. The first is simply that much of the criticism of *AM+P* has ignored the distinction I painfully spelled out in 'Mental Events' between the 'strict' laws I think exist covering singular causal relations and the less than strict laws that can be couched in mental terms. Thus Kim, in the article I mentioned, begins by saying correctly that *AM+P* denies that there are precise or strict laws about mental events, but goes on to criticize *AM+P* for maintaining that 'the mental is anomalous not only in that there are no laws relating mental events to other mental events but none relating them to physical events either'(Kim 1989*b*, p. 33). In fact I have repeatedly said that if you want to call certain undeniably important regularities laws—the familiar regularities that link the mental with the mental (as formulated, for example in decision theory) or the mental with the physical—I have no objection; I merely say these are not, and cannot be reduced to, *strict* laws.

Because he ignores the distinction between strict laws and other sorts of regularities, it is by no means clear that Kim really holds views at odds with *AM+P*. Kim maintains, plausibly it seems to me, that any satisfactory account of the relation between the mental and the physical must permit appeal to 'local correlations and dependencies between specific mental and physical properties'. But then he adds, 'The trouble is that once we begin talking about correlations and dependencies between specific psychological and physical properties, we are in effect talking about psycho-physical

[7] Davidson 1970/1980, pp. 216–23. There I said, 'I suppose most of our practical lore (and science) is heteronomic [i.e. not in the form of strict laws, and not reducible to such]. This is because a law can hope to be precise, explicit, and as exceptionless as possible only if it draws its concepts from a comprehensive closed theory', p. 219. Also see Vermazen and Hintikka 1985, pp. 242–52, and Pettit, Sylvan, and Norman 1987, pp. 41–8.

laws, and these laws raise the specter of unwanted physical reductionism. Where there are psycho-physical laws, there is always the threat, or promise, of psycho-physical reduction.' (Kim 1989*b*, p. 42.) But if the laws are not strict, the threat is averted, and the promise false. Kim offers no reason to think the laws can be strict; I have given arguments (which he does not mention or discuss in this article; see Kim 1989*b*, p. 42) why I think they cannot. It is not clear that Kim has come to grips with *AM+P*.

Kim is by no means the only critic of *AM+P* to fail to notice the crucial importance of the distinction between strict and non-strict laws. Thus J. A. Fodor writes that he is going to defend the view that intentional (mental) properties are 'causally responsible' and that there are 'intentional causal laws . . . contrary to the doctrine called "anomalous monism"'. His defence is that in common sense and in many (all?) of the 'special' sciences, there are plenty of laws that are far from strict. He cites as an example of a law in geology that mountains are apt to have snow on them; it is *because* Mt. Everest is a mountain that it has snow on it.[8] But as I have just pointed out, this defence of the causal efficacy of the mental is consistent with *AM+P*.

It is a question whether others who have attacked *AM+P* have taken the distinction between types of regularity fully into account. Fred Dretske, who has also maintained that *AM+P* makes the mental causally inert, has never claimed that there are strict psycho-physical laws (see Dretske 1989). There is thus no clear reason to believe that the sort of account he wants to offer of how the mental causes the physical is itself inconsistent with *AM+P*. I don't think his account succeeds; but that is another matter. Dagfinn Føllesdal has also thought there must be psycho-physical laws; but he gives as an example of such a 'law', 'Any severely dehydrated person who drinks water will improve' (Føllesdal 1985, p. 321). *AM+P* does not

[8] See Fodor 1989. The argument Fodor gives there is, though he does not realize it, a *defence* of *AM*, since he argues that although there may be no strict laws in geology, this does not show that such properties as being a mountain are not causally efficacious. As he says, to suppose that the lack of such strict laws makes geological properties epiphenomenal is absurd: 'there are likely to be parallel arguments that *all properties are inert excepting only those expressed by the vocabulary of physics*.' I think this is exactly right if one adds, 'expressible in the vocabulary of physics or in a vocabulary definitionally or nomologically reducible to the vocabulary of physics'. The same point is made in Fodor 1987, pp. 5–6. There the example is 'A meandering river erodes its outer banks unless, for example, the weather changes and the river dries up'.

rule out such laws, for such a law is obviously far from strict, and it is not likely that it can be made truly exceptionless.

The second reason for paying attention to the distinction between the laws of an ideal physics and other generalizations (whether or not we call them laws) has to do with the logic of the argument that leads from the premisses to *AM*. The argument does not depend on the claim that there are no psycho-physical laws: the argument demands only that there are no laws that (i) contain psychological terms that cannot be eliminated from the laws nor reduced to the vocabulary of physics and (ii) that have the features of lacking *ceteris paribus* clauses and of belonging to a closed system like the laws of a finished physics. In other words, I argued from the assumptions that mental events are causally related to physical events, and that all causally related events instantiate the laws of physics, to the conclusion that mental events are identical with physical events: thus monism. The extent to which mental concepts fall short of being reducible to physical concepts measures the degree of anomaly. As far as I can see, the positions of both Kim and Fodor on the relation between the physical and the mental are consistent with *AM* and *AM+P*, and it seems to me possible that the same is true of Dretske and Føllesdal.

There remains an issue, however, that separates my views from Kim's and perhaps also from Fodor's. Fodor holds that mental (or intentional) concepts can't be reduced to the concepts of a finished physics, so in this respect his position is that of *AM+P*. Kim, on the other hand, believes in reduction. But he may simply have different standards for reduction than I do; if this is so, our difference on this point may be mainly verbal. But behind what may be merely a verbal point there lies a substantive issue: both Fodor and Kim seem to think that unless there are psycho-physical laws of *some* sort, the mental would have been shown to be powerless. I think the reasoning that leads them (and others) to this conclusion is confused.

Let's be clear about what is at stake. At this point I am not concerned with the question whether or not there are psycho-physical laws. In the sense in which Kim and Fodor think there are laws linking mental and physical concepts, I also think there are laws; what I have claimed is that such laws are not strict, and that mental concepts are not reducible by definition or by strict 'bridging' laws to physical concepts. But unlike my critics, I do not think it would prove that the mental is causally inert even if there were no psycho-physical laws of any kind.

Suppose I create a table in which all the entries are definite descriptions of one sort or another of events. I refer to the events by giving the column and the row where the description is to be found: column 179 row 1044 for example is the event of my writing this sentence. Let us call the events listed in the table 'table-events'. The vocabulary needed to describe (needed to provide a definite description of) each event is just the vocabulary needed to pick out the column and row. These events have their causes and effects: for example event 179–1044 caused a certain rearrangement of electric flows in the random access memory of my computer. There are, I imagine, no interesting tablo-physical laws whatever, that is, laws linking events described in the table language and events described in the vocabulary of physics. Yet this fact does not show that table-events are not causally efficacious.

It will be retorted that it is simply irrelevant to the causal efficacy of table-events that they are table-events—that they are described in the table vocabulary. This is true. But it is also irrelevant to the causal efficacy of physical events that they can be described in the physical vocabulary. It is *events* that have the power to change things, not our various ways of describing them. Since the fact that an event is a mental event, i.e. that it can be described in a psychological vocabulary, can make no difference to the causes and effects of that event, it makes no sense to suppose that describing it in the psychological vocabulary might deprive the event of its potency. An event, mental or physical, by any other name smells just as strong.

The point seems so simple and so clear that it is hard to see how it can be doubted. Suppose Magellan notices that there are rocks ahead, an event that, through the intervening events such as his uttering orders to the helmsman, causes the ship to alter course. Magellan's noticing is a mental event, and it is causally efficacious. That event is also a physical event, a change in Magellan's body, and describable in the vocabulary of physics. As long as the predicates used to describe the mental event are not strictly reducible to the predicates of physics, all this is in accord with $AM+P$.

Yet according to Kim and others, $AM+P$ implies that the mental is causally inert: Kim asks 'What role does mentality play on Davidson's anomalous monism?', and he answers, 'None whatever'.

Why does he think this? We get a hint when he says 'on anomalous monism, events are causes or effects only as they instantiate physical laws.' The same idea is expressed by the phrase 'in virtue of': mentality is causally effective only if events are causes *in virtue of their mental properties* (see Kim 1989*b*, p. 43). 'Because of' has been recruited to express the same idea. Kim has even implied that it is my explicit view that 'it is only under its physical description that a mental event can be seen to enter into a causal relation with a physical event (or any other event) by being subsumed under a causal law' (Kim 1984*b*, p. 267). Those who are familiar with the literature will recognize other ways of putting the point: on *AM*+*P* (so one reads) the mental does not cause anything *qua* mental; the mental is not efficacious *as such*. This is the vein in which Ernest Sosa writes that 'The key to [Davidson's] proposed solution . . . is the idea that mental events enter into causal relations *not* as mental but only as physical' (Sosa 1984, p. 277). Sosa does at least recognize that this is not my way of putting things, but he does not realize that I couldn't put things this way. For me, it is events that have causes and effects. Given this extensionalist view of causal relations, it makes no literal sense, as I remarked above, to speak of an event causing something as mental, or by virtue of its mental properties, or as described in one way or another.

But might it not happen that the mental properties of an event make no difference to its causal relations? Something like this is what critics have in mind when they say that according to *AM*+*P* the mental is inert. Of course, the idea that mental properties make no causal difference is consistent with the view that there are no psycho-physical laws (strict or not) and with the supposition that every singular causal relation between two events is backed by a strict (physical) law; it is also consistent with the thesis that mental events (i.e. events picked out by mental properties) are causally related to physical events. So *AM*+*P* is *consistent* with the (epiphenomenalist) view that the mental properties of events make no difference to causal relations. But this is not enough to discredit *AM*+*P*, for it does not follow that *AM implies* the causal inertness of the mental. What critics must show is that *AM* (or *AM*+*P*) implies the impotence of mental properties, and this I see no way of establishing.

Another way of putting the point is this: we have the makings of a refutation of *AM*+*P* provided it can be shown that *AM*+*P* is inconsistent with the supervenience of mental properties on physical properties. The refutation would consist, not in showing *AM+P* inconsistent, but in showing it inconsistent with supervenience, and so with the supposition that the mental properties of an event make a difference to its causal relations. For supervenience as I have defined it does, as we have seen, imply that if two events differ in their psychological properties, they differ in their physical properties (which we assume to be causally efficacious). If supervenience holds, psychological properties make a difference to the causal relations of an event, for they matter to the physical properties, and the physical properties matter to causal relations. It does nothing to undermine this argument to say 'But the mental properties make a difference not *as* mental but only because they make a difference to the physical properties'. Either they make a difference or they don't; if supervenience is true, they do.

How might one try to show that *AM+P* is inconsistent with supervenience? Kim, as we noted, thinks my version of supervenience implies that all mental properties could be withdrawn from the world and this would make no difference to causal relations; but this supposition turned out to be incompatible with my understanding of supervenience. He subsequently argues that there is no plausible way to understand my brand of supervenience because there is no plausible way to reconcile the demands that the mental be irreducible to the physical and yet be 'dependent' on it (Kim 1989*b*, pp. 39–41). But clearly supervenience gives a sense to the notion of dependence here, enough sense anyway to show that mental properties make a causal difference; so unless it can be shown that even weak supervenience is inconsistent with *AM+P*, it has not been shown that *AM+P* makes the mental causally inert.

Kim does have a point. Supervenience as I define it is consistent with the conjunction of *AM+P* and the assumption that there are no psycho-physical laws whatever, strict or not. It is not even slightly plausible that there are no important general causal connections between the mental and physical properties of events. I have always held that there are such connections; indeed much of my writing on action is devoted to spelling out the sort of general causal connections that are essential to our ways of understanding, describing, explaining, and predicting actions, what causes them, and what they cause. But why should the importance and ubiquity of such connections suggest that psychological concepts must be reducible to physical concepts—*strictly* reducible? Yet the failure of strict reducibility is all that is required to establish *AM*.

Why have there been so many confusions and bad arguments in the discussion of *AM*, *AM+P*, and supervenience? The main source of confusion, I think, is the fact that when it comes to events people find it hard to keep in mind the distinction between types and particulars. This in turn makes it easy to conflate singular causal connections with causal laws, and invites neglect of the difference between explaining an event and simply stating that a causal relation holds.

Of course those who have commented on *AM+P* cannot have failed to notice that the argument hangs on the distinction between particular events and types of events. But the distinction has nevertheless proved easy to overlook. Kim, for example, asks whether the identity of mental events with physical events solves the problem of the causal efficacy of the mental. It does not, he says, because what is at issue is 'the causal efficacy of *mental properties* of events *vis-à-vis* their physical properties. Thus the items that need to be identified are properties—that is, we would need to identify mental properties with physical properties' (Kim 1989*b*, p. 45). But prop-erties are causally efficacious if they make a difference to what *individual* events cause, and supervenience ensures that mental properties do make a difference to what mental events cause. So why is the identity of *properties* required to make mental properties causally efficacious? It isn't; but one might think so if one were confusing individual events with classes of events, i.e. all those that share some property.

I sense a similar slippage in the argument when Kim introduces what he calls 'the problem of causal-explanatory exclusion'. This is the problem, he says, that 'seems to arise from the fact that a cause, or causal explanation, of an event, when it is regarded as a full, sufficient cause or explanation, appears to *exclude* other *independent* purported causes or causal explanations of it' (Kim 1989*b*, p. 44). The idea is that if physics does provide such 'full, sufficient' explanations, there is no room for mental explanations unless these can be (fully, strictly?) reduced to physical explanations. What can this strange principle mean? If we consider an *event* that is a 'full, sufficient' cause of another event, it must, as Mill pointed out long ago, include everything in the universe preceding the effect that has a causal bearing on it, some cross-section of the entire preceding light-cone; and even then, if we take 'sufficient' seriously, we must assume perfect determinism. How can the existence of such an event 'exclude' other causes? It can't, since by definition it includes everything that could be a cause. Given supervenience, such an event would include, as proper parts, all relevant mental events. What has all this to do with explanation? Well, if we ever had the laws of physics right, and we had the appropriate physical description of an event *and* of some cross-section of the preceding light-cone, we might be able to give a full and sufficient explanation of the second event. How could this exclude any other sort of explanation? It might *preclude* less complete physical explanations, in the sense that we would lose interest in them. But if mental concepts are not reducible to physical concepts, there is no reason to suppose we would lose interest in explanations in mental terms just because we had a complete physical explanation. What is true, of course, is that psychological explanations are never full and sufficient; like most explanations, they are interest-sensitive, and simply assume that a vast number of (unspecified and unspecifiable) factors that might have intervened between cause and effect did not. This does not mean they are not causal explanations, nor that physical explanations exclude them. It is only if we confuse causal relations, which hold only between particulars, with causal explanations, which, so far as they are 'sufficient' must deal with laws, and so with types of events, that we would be tempted to accept the principle of 'causal-explanatory exclusion'.[9]

Let me give one more example of what I take to be error brought on by not taking seriously the distinction between particular events and their types. I draw the example from an article by Ernest Sosa; but similar examples can easily be found in the writings of Kim, Dretske (1989), Føllesdal, Honderich (1982), Achenstein (1979), Stoutland (1976), and Mark Johnston (1985) (for additional references, see LePore and Loewer 1987). Suppose, Sosa argues, that someone is killed by a loud shot; then the loudness of the shot is

[9] Kim says a full, sufficient cause or explanation excludes other *independent* causes or explanations; in my discussion, I may seem to have neglected the condition of independence. I have, because dependence means entirely different things in the cases of events and of explanation. Events 'depend' on one another causally, and the failure of psycho-physical laws has no bearing on the question of whether mental and physical events are causally related. Explanation, on the other hand, is an intentional concept; in explanation, dependence is geared to the ways in which things are described. There is no reason why logically independent explanations cannot be given of the same event (as Socrates points out in Plato's *Phaedo* 98 ff.).

irrelevant to its causing the death. 'Had the gun been equipped with a silencer, the shot would have killed the victim just the same' (Sosa 1984, p. 278). In the same way, Sosa thinks, $AM+P$ entails that mental properties are irrelevant to what the events that have the properties cause. Such examples, whether about mental causation or physical, do not establish the conclusion. The crucial counterfactual is fatally (sorry) ambiguous. Had the gun been equipped with a silencer, a quiet shot, if aimed as the fatal shot was, and otherwise relevantly similar, would no doubt have resulted in *a* death. But it would not have been the *same* shot as the fatal shot, nor could the death it caused have been the same death. The ambiguity lies in the definite description 'the shot': if 'the shot' refers to the shot that would have been fired silently, then it is true that that shot might well have killed the victim. But if 'the shot' is supposed to refer to the original loud shot, the argument misfires, for the same shot cannot be both loud and silent. Loudness, like a mental property, is supervenient on basic physical properties, and so makes a difference to what an event that has it causes.[10] Of course, both loud and silent (single) shots can cause a death; but not the same death.

[10] It is sometimes suggested that if we cannot make sense of the idea of an event losing its psychological properties while remaining the same event, we are stuck with the idea that *all* of an event's properties are 'essential'. I have no theory about which properties of an event, if any, are essential, but it seems clear that to serve the purposes of my argument, mental properties need supervene on only those physical properties that are required for a complete causal account of the universe (i.e. that suffice for the formulation of a closed system of 'strict' laws).

2

Can Supervenience and 'Non-Strict Laws' Save Anomalous Monism?

JAEGWON KIM

In 'Thinking Causes', Donald Davidson proposes to defend his doctrine of 'anomalous monism' (*AM*) against 'misunderstandings and misrepresentations' of his critics, myself included, who have called attention to its epiphenomenalist tendencies.[1] Although part of what I am going to say will be in direct reply to Davidson's specific points, I believe that several points of more general interest will emerge.

1. Have the Critics of *AM* (or *AM* + *P*) Charged it with Inconsistency?

AM is the claim that, although mental properties are irreducible to physical ones, mental events are in fact physical events; and *P* is the conjunction of 'the three premisses', as Davidson calls them, of *AM*: (1) mental events cause, and are caused by, physical events; (2) causally related events instantiate 'strict' laws; and (3) there are no 'strict' psycho-physical laws. Davidson quotes me as having said that 'under Davidson's anomalous monism, mentality does no causal work' (Kim 1989*b*, p. 35), and he apparently takes this remark to contradict (1) and hence *AM* + *P*. What he says is this:

> If 'mentality does no causal work' means that mental events do not enter into causal relations, the first premiss of *AM* is false, for it says mental events cause, and are caused by, physical events. This is not enough to prove *AM* itself inconsistent, but it certainly would show the three premisses of *AM* inconsistent with one another. (p. 6)

[1] 'Thinking Causes', Chap. 1, above, p. 3. Page references to this paper are entered parenthetically.

I don't dispute any of this. What is curious, though, is that Davidson does not defend, or even explicitly affirm, the reading of 'mentality does no causal work' suggested in the first sentence of this quotation. Thus it is puzzling why he is so certain that I have characterized *AM* + *P* as inconsistent; the paragraph in which my offending sentence occurs makes it abundantly clear, I dare say, that by 'mentality' I was referring to mental properties, not individual mental events.[2] In the context of *AM* + *P*, the claim 'Mental events cause physical events' only comes to the assertion, which is not disputed by his commentators, that events with some mental property or other are causes of events with some physical property or other. The difficulty that has been voiced by the many critics whose names Davidson cites, and with an impressive if unsurprising unanimity, is precisely that the truth of this assertion does not ensure the causal efficacy of mental properties (compare: 'These orange pills will relieve your headache').

2. Have the Critics of *AM* Made an Error in Claiming that *AM* + *P* is a Form of Epiphenomenalism?

It must be admitted that Davidson's commentators have not always been careful to distinguish between the following two claims: (1) *AM* + *P* entails the causal inertness of mental properties, and (2) *AM* + *P* fails to provide mental properties with a causal role. According to Davidson, (1) is false; and in this he is arguably right.[3] However, this does not necessarily absolve *AM* + *P* of the charge of epiphenomenalism; for if something that purports to be a theory of mental causation assigns no causal role to mental properties—if it has nothing to say about the causal powers of mental properties while saying plenty about those of physical properties—the theory can, it seems to me, reasonably be said to be epiphenomenalistic

[2] The sentence that immediately precedes the one in question reads as follows: 'For anomalous monism entails this: the very same network of causal relations would obtain in Davidson's world if you were to redistribute mental properties over its events any way you like; you would not disturb a single causal relation if you randomly and arbitrarily reassigned mental properties to events, or even removed mentality entirely from the world' (Kim 1989*b*, pp. 34–5).

[3] I believe Brian McLaughlin was the first to argue this point; see his 1989 article.

with regard to mental properties. Plainly (2) is true, and has never been seriously disputed; and the defenders of *AM* have focused, by and large, on extending *AM* by adding a positive account of the causal efficacy of mental properties.[4] In fact, that is Davidson's own approach in 'Thinking Causes': he wants to supplement *AM* + *P* with supervenience (*S*), and perhaps also with 'non-strict laws', to restore causal efficacy to mental properties, tacitly acknowledging that within the framework of *AM* + *P* mental properties have no causal role to play.

3. Have the Critics tried to Turn the Causal Relation into a Multi-Termed, Description-Dependent, Intensional Relation?

Throughout 'Thinking Causes', Davidson complains that his critics have tried to turn the binary relation of causation, '*c* causes *e*', into a multi-termed (that is, more than binary), possibly non-extensional, relation by employing such expressions as '*c qua P* causes *e qua M*', '*c* under description *D* causes *e* under description *D**', etc.[5] He is anxious to defend causation as an extensional binary relation whose relata are concrete events ('no matter how described'). But none of this has much to do with the main issue on hand, and getting rid of these admittedly inelegant locutions will not make it go away. The issue has always been *the causal efficacy of properties of events—no matter how they, the events or the properties, are described*. What the critics have argued is perfectly consistent with causation itself being a two-termed extensional relation over concrete events; their point is that such a relation isn't enough: we also need a way of talking about the causal role of properties, the role of properties of events in generating, or grounding, these two-termed causal relations between concrete events.

To talk about the role of properties in causation we don't need to introduce the '*qua*' locution or any other multi-termed causal

[4] e.g. McLaughlin 1989; LePore and Loewer 1987. See also Horgan 1989; MacDonald and MacDonald 1986. The strategies that have been tried include the use of non-strict laws and certain causal counterfactuals.

[5] Davidson includes me among those who have used such expressions, on the basis of my writing 'on anomalous monism, events are causes only as they instantiate laws'. The culprit in Davidson's light is the word 'as'; I used it in the sense of 'because' or 'since', but Davidson apparently takes it in the sense of '*qua*' or 'in the role of', which is a bit curious, given that 'as' in my sentence functions as a grammatical conjunction, not a preposition.

relation, although I see nothing in principle objectionable about them; all that is necessary is the recognition that it makes sense to ask questions of the form 'What is it about events *c* and *e* that makes it the case that *c* is a cause of *e*?' and be able to answer them, intelligibly and informatively, by saying something like 'Because *c* is an event of kind *F* and *e* is one of kind *G* (and, you may add if you favour a nomic conception of causality, there is a law of an appropriate form connecting *F*-events with *G*-events)'. This is only to acknowledge that the causal relation obtains between a pair of events *because they are events of certain kinds, or have certain properties*. How could anyone refuse to acknowledge this—unless, that is, he believed that causal relations were brute facts about events, having nothing to do with the kinds of events that they are? In fact, Davidson himself acknowledges in the end that it makes sense to discuss the causal relevance of properties; for, after all, he offers an account of it, based on supervenience and non-strict laws.

4. Can you have Psycho-Physical Supervenience without Psycho-Physical Laws?

Well, that depends on what sort of supervenience you have in mind (see Kim 1984*a* and 1990*a*). Davidson says that I made an error about the logic of supervenience in closely associating supervenience with laws; according to him, 'supervenience does not imply the existence of psycho-physical laws', because 'although supervenience entails that any change in a mental property *p* of a particular event *e* will be accompanied by a change in the physical properties of *e*, it does not entail that a change in *p* in other events will be accompanied by an identical change in the physical properties of those other events' (p. 7). So far so good. But he goes on to add, 'only the latter entailment would conflict with *AM* + *P*'. Here, Davidson is plainly looking for the wrong kind of law; when the question of law is discussed in connection with supervenience, it almost always concerns laws *from* the base (or subvenient) properties *to* the supervenient properties (thus, physical-to-mental laws), not laws going in the opposite direction (mental-to-physical laws). Thus, assume that two systems are in the same total physical state (at the same or different times); psycho-physical supervenience implies this: *if the systems change in some identical physical* *respect Q, they must change in an identical psychological respect M.* In fact, mind–body supervenience (and supervenience in general) can be explained in terms of the existence of generalizations from the subvenient to the supervenient, thus: whenever anything has mental property *M* there is some physical property *Q* such that it has *Q* and everything that has *Q* has *M*. On certain plausible assumptions concerning property compositions, this formulation is demonstrably equivalent to the usual definition of supervenience in terms of indiscernibility in respect of supervenient and base properties (see Kim 1984*a* and 1987). There is of course a question as to whether the kind of supervenience Davidson says he has in mind, which appears to be equivalent to what I have called 'weak supervenience', can impart to these generalizations an appropriate nomic force; but that isn't a question Davidson raises, and there is in any case a doubt as to whether weak supervenience can provide the kind of dependency relation that most philosophers want to associate with supervenience (see Kim 1984*a*).

5. Does *AM* + *P* + *S* (that is, Davidsonian Supervenience) Provide a Satisfactory Account of the Causal Relevance of Mental Properties?

On this question, Ernest Sosa makes a number of cogent points in his reply, 'Davidson's Thinking Causes' (Chapter 4, below), with which I am by and large in agreement. So I will make just one point.[6] 'Causal relevance' may be one thing; 'causal efficacy' another. An epiphenomenalist may argue, mimicking Davidson, that on his view mental properties are indeed causally relevant, since, according to his doctrine, what mental properties an event has makes a difference to what physical properties it has, and physical properties are causally efficacious. But that doesn't mean that he contradicts himself in refusing to allow causal efficacy to mental properties. If this is right, supervenience can at best show that mental properties are causally relevant, not that they are causally efficacious. And it would seem that to sustain the kind of position

[6] I have myself given an account of mental causation on the basis of supervenience; see e.g. Kim 1979 and 1984*b*. My account is based on a supervenience relation stronger than Davidson's. I am inclined to think, however, that even this stronger supervenience relation may not be strong enough for a fully adequate account of mental causation.

he has argued for in 'Actions, Reasons, and Causes' (1963), Davidson may very well need causal efficacy, not just causal relevance, for mental properties. Mere causal relevance seems too weak to support the causal-explanatory 'because' in rationalizing explanations. And it seems to me that most philosophers who believe in mental causation would want efficacy, not just relevance.

6. What then of *AM* + *P* + *NS* (the Existence of 'Non-Strict' Psycho-Physical Laws)?

From the text of 'Thinking Causes', I am not certain that Davidson wants to embrace non-strict psycho-physical laws to account for the causal efficacy of mental properties, although that is the impression one gets. In any case, I think there are some serious difficulties with this approach for anyone who accepts *AM* + *P*. Whether *NS* can comfortably fit in with *AM* + *P* is a question that has to wait until we are in possession of a clearer account of just what the 'non-strictness' of non-strict laws consists in, or just what the much-bandied phrase '*ceteris paribus*' means when it qualifies a law. Davidson says that his position is consistent with Fodor's defence of mental causal efficacy based on non-strict laws hedged by '*ceteris paribus*' clauses. But it would be ill-advised for the anomalous monist to buy into Fodor's notion of '*ceteris paribus* law'. For, according to Fodor, such a law has something like this form, 'There exist conditions $C_1, \ldots, C_m$ such that when they are satisfied, *F*-events cause *G*-events'; and when the C_i's have been identified, that will give us a strict law of the form 'Under $C_1^*, \ldots, C_m^*$, *F*-events cause *G*-events', where each C_i^* is some value of the variable C_i that satisfies the open inner sentence (Fodor 1989, pp. 75–6). Thus, on this account, a non-strict law is simply a strict law with some of its antecedent conditions existentially quantified. But that means that *where there is a non-strict psycho-physical law, there must be a strict psycho-physical law waiting to be discovered*. I think it obvious that the anomalous monist must reject this notion of non-strict law.

Moreover, it seems to me that, however the non-strictness of non-strict laws is explained, non-strict laws *are* laws and must carry an appropriate nomological force; given this, it isn't obvious that Davidson's fundamental argument against psycho-physical laws can allow even non-strict laws between the mental and the physical. As I understand it (Kim 1985), the gist of the argument is something like this: the mental domain and the physical domain are each governed by their own special synthetic a priori constitutive constraints (principles of rationality, in the case of the mental), and the existence of psycho-physical laws with their strong nomic force would ultimately bring these two sets of constitutive principles into conflict or at least jurisdictional disputes. Hence, if each domain is to retain its own integrity, there cannot be laws connecting them. It isn't clear why this argument, if it succeeds in banning strict psycho-physical laws, doesn't banish non-strict ones as well; at least, an explanation is called for. I have always thought that the power of the Davidsonian argument for mental anomalism is seen in the fact that, if it works at all, it should work against laws of all kinds—for example, statistical laws as well as deterministic ones (after all, the only strict laws we have may be statistical). Remember: non-strict laws, whatever they are, are supposed to be laws!

7. Are there Other Reasons for being Wary of *NS* ('Non-Strict Laws') if you are an Anomalous Monist?

Yes, there are. First, if you accept non-strict laws as nomological grounds of causal relations, you will need a convincing rationale for retaining Davidson's strict law requirement on causation. It can be seen, in fact, that having laws of both kinds ground causal relations opens up a serious new problem, 'the problem of exclusion' (see Kim 1989*a*). Suppose a mental event, *m*, causes an event *e* (which can be either mental or physical); *m*, as a mental event, must have some mental property, *M*, and let's assume that *M*, in virtue of a non-strict psycho-physical law relating it to some physical property of *e*, is causally efficacious in *m*'s causation of *e*. But, given the strict law requirement, *m* must also have a certain basic physical property *P* which is connected, by a strict law, to some property (presumably, another basic physical property) of *e*, and this fact grounds the causal relation between *m* and *e*. Thus, *m* turns out to have two properties each of which is causally efficacious in *m*'s causation of *e*, and, on *AM*, *M* and *P* are irreducibly distinct. We now face this question: given that the causal relation from *m* to *e* is grounded in the basic physical properties of *m* and *e* and a strict law relating them, what causal work is there for *M* to do?[7] *M*'s precise causal role in this picture—exactly what contribution *M* makes in the causation of e—is in need of an explanation. There are various moves one can make at this point, but the problem is there, especially for the adherents of *AM*.

The exclusion problem is a general problem with mental causation, something most of us have to contend with. There is, however, a further specific problem with *NS* that Davidson and friends of *AM* seem not to have recognized. It is this: *NS* may put anti-reductionism in serious jeopardy. One can still hold on to Davidson's claim that psychology is not reducible, by strict law, to some underlying physical theory. But why insist on reduction by strict laws only? *What's wrong with non-strict psycho-physical laws as 'bridge' laws*? This is not an idle question; nor is it merely a verbal issue. For there seems to be a general consensus, among those who speak of the 'strictness' of laws, that there are no strict laws outside basic physics, and Davidson seems to agree.[8] If this is correct, *there isn't going to be, and there has never been, any reduction anywhere in science—that is, if you insist on reduction via strict laws*. You are going to find strict laws only in basic physics, and you aren't going to reduce basic physics to basic physics! (At least, you are not going to find reductions outside basic physics.) This surely cannot be a sense of reduction that holds serious philosophical interest for us. If psychology is reducible by the same standards that apply to the best cases of theory reduction in the sciences (pick your favourite examples), why isn't that reduction enough? There has been a tendency, among some current anti-reductionists, to base their arguments on an unrealistically stringent and idealized model of reduction, thereby weakening their conclusions.

I think 'non-strict laws' are bad news for anomalous monists. In embracing them they may end up losing anomalism from anomalous monism.

[7] LePore and Loewer (1989) raise a similar difficulty with respect to Fodor's account of mental causation in terms of *ceteris paribus* psychological laws. There is a brief discussion of this issue in 'Thinking Causes'.

[8] Davidson says, 'I made clear that what I was calling a law in this context was something that one could at best hope to find in a developed physics' (above, p. 8). Others who hold a similar view include Fodor, and LePore and Loewer. I am not sure I understand what Davidson means by 'developed physics'; whatever it is, it follows that Davidson isn't going find any reductions outside 'developed physics'.

3

On Davidson's Response to the Charge of Epiphenomenalism

BRIAN P. McLAUGHLIN

IN recent years, Donald Davidson has been widely charged with commitment to epiphenomenalism.[1] He responds to the charge in 'Thinking Causes', Chapter 1, above. In what follows, I will examine the charge and his responses to it.

Davidson seems to find the charge puzzling. He has, he points out, long insisted that mental events cause physical events; and he has, he argues, espoused no views that commit him to denying this (see above, pp. 3–4).[2] He reminds us, moreover, that much of his work in action theory is devoted to spelling out the role of mental events in the causation of actions (which he takes to be certain sorts of bodily movements, and, so, physical events) (above, p. 14).

The charge that Davidson is committed to denying that mental events cause physical events would indeed be puzzling. Moreover, it would be completely unwarranted. He has espoused no views that commit him to such a denial. There is, however, no need to linger over this. For none of Davidson's critics charge that he is committed to such a denial. Whether he can hold that mental events cause physical events is not the issue. Critics concede that he can hold that. When they charge that he is committed to epiphenomenalism, they do not mean that he is committed to denying that mental events cause physical events. They mean, rather, that he is committed to the view that when mental events cause physical events, they do so in virtue of falling under physical types, and not in virtue of falling under mental types.

[1] See Honderich 1982; Sosa 1984; Stoutland 1985; Johnston 1985; Kim 1984*b*, 1989*b*; Fodor 1989; and Dretske 1989.

[2] Unless I indicate otherwise, all page references are to 'Thinking Causes' (Chapter 1, above).

I will elaborate. Two types of epiphenomenalism can be distinguished:

Token Epiphenomenalism. Physical events cause mental events, but mental events cannot cause anything.

Type Epiphenomenalism. (*a*) Events cause other events in virtue of falling under physical types, but (*b*) no event can cause anything in virtue of falling under a mental type.

Davidson's critics recognize that he can (and does) deny token epiphenomenalism (hereafter, token-*E*). They charge that he is, however, committed to type epiphenomenalism (hereafter, type-*E*).[3] That he is not committed to token-*E* has no bearing on whether he is committed to type-*E*; for type-*E* does not imply token-*E*. Token-*E* is false if all physical events cause physical events, and mental events are physical events. But even if mental events cause physical events, the question remains whether they do so in virtue of falling under mental types. Critics charge that Davidson holds doctrines which commit him to denying that mental events cause physical events in virtue of falling under mental types. On his view, they claim, the mental *qua* mental is causally inert.

More specifically, critics claim that Davidson's *principle of the nomological character of causality* implies that (i) events can cause other events only in virtue of falling under physical types cited in strict laws; and that his *principle of the anomalism of the mental* implies that (ii) no mental event-type is a physical event-type cited in a strict law.[4] The critics recognize that (i) and (ii) are consistent

[3] Type-*E* has been a topic of concern for many years in discussions of 'non-reductive materialism'. Nearly seventy years ago, C. D. Broad said that the claim that the mental is epiphenomenal may be taken to assert 'that mental events either (*a*) do not function at all as causal-factors; or that (*b*) if they do, they do so in virtue of their physiological characteristics and not in virtue of their mental characteristics' (1925, p. 473). He held a doctrine he called 'Emergent Materialism', according to which every particular is physical, and mental properties are distinct from, but emerge from, physical properties. Broad pointed out that on his view mental events are causes, but he struggled over whether they might count as causes only in virtue of their physical properties. He never resolved the issue. See McLaughlin 1989.

[4] For the purposes of this paper, it will not matter what, exactly, a strict law is. The important point is just that Davidson maintains that all strict laws are physical laws. I should note, however, that in 'Thinking Causes' Davidson seems to characterize a strict law simply as 'a generalization that [is] not only "lawlike" and true, but [is] as deterministic as nature can be found to be, and [is] free from caveats and *ceteris paribus* clauses' (p. 8). (A general statement is law-like on his view if and only if it is confirmable by its positive instances, and such that if it is true, it supports counterfactuals.) Since this characterization of strict laws is gaining currency, it

with the claim that mental events cause physical events. For it is consistent with (i) and (ii) that mental events cause physical events in virtue of falling under physical types. Thus, (i) and (ii) do not imply token-*E*. But, they claim, (i) and (ii) imply type-*E*: (*a*) events cause other events in virtue of falling under physical types, but (*b*) no event can cause anything in virtue of falling under a mental type.

Davidson is, of course, well aware of the charge of type-*E* (though he does not mention it by that name), and he emphatically denies it. While he readily concedes conjunct (*b*) of type-*E*, he denies conjunct (*a*). No event, he concedes, can cause anything in virtue of its mental properties.[5] So, (*b*) is true. But, he insists, no event can cause anything in virtue of its physical properties either. For events are not causes or effects in virtue of their properties, mental or physical. Thus, (*a*) is false; and so type-*E* is too.

Critics go wrong, according to Davidson, in thinking that the principle of the nomological character of causality implies that events can cause other events only in virtue of their physical properties.[6] For, claims Davidson, the principle does not imply that events cause other events in virtue of any of their properties, physical or mental. Indeed, Davidson holds that type-*E* 'makes no literal sense' given his views about causation. 'For me', he says, 'it is events that have causes and effects. Given this extensionalist view of causal relations, it makes no literal sense, as I remarked above, to speak of an event causing something . . . by virtue of its . . . properties' (p. 13).[7] If this indeed 'makes no literal sense' given the

deserves comment. Given this characterization, 'All human beings are mortal' would count as a strict law and 'All sentient creatures are mortal' would count as a strict psycho-physical law: They are true, counterfactual-supporting generalizations, confirmable by their positive instances, free from caveats and *ceteris paribus* clauses, and are 'as deterministic nature can be found to be'. (Of course, if quantum mechanics can be trusted, the laws arguably won't quite have a probability of unity, but neither will any other law.) But these laws would not have counted as strict laws on Davidson's earlier characterization. (Note 7 of 'Thinking Causes' contains a quotation with a brief, partial statement of his earlier characterization of a strict law). Presumably, Davidson does not intend, in 'Thinking Causes', to be stating a sufficient condition for a law's being strict. (The notion of a strict law is discussed in McLaughlin 1985 and 1989.)

[5] Nothing turns on the shift from talk of types to talk of properties. The properties in question are those of falling under event-types. For example, if *M* is a type of mental event, then the relevant mental property would be the property of being an *M*.

[6] I argue for this same point in McLaughlin 1989, but I offer different reasons from those Davidson offers. I reject his reasons below.

[7] He also denies that it makes literal sense 'to speak of an event causing something

views in question, then neither does type-*E*. For type-*E* implies that events cause other events in virtue of at least some of their (physical) properties.

Immediately after this protest, however, Davidson asks: 'But might it not happen that the mental properties of an event make no difference to its causal relations? Something like this is what critics have in mind' (p. 13). Then, he goes on to acknowledge that, of course, certain physical properties 'make a difference' to (singular) causal relations. He acknowledges, moreover, that his principles of the nomological character of causality and of the anomalism of the mental 'are consistent with the (epiphenomenalist) view that the mental properties of events make no difference to causal relations' (p. 13). He denies, however, that the principles imply that mental properties 'make no difference' to causal relations. None the less, he recognizes that one may wonder how mental properties could 'make a difference' to causal relations, given the principles in question. And he tries (for the first time) to offer an account of how mental properties make a difference to causal relations.

By Davidson's lights, then, it makes perfect sense to claim that properties 'make a difference' to whether events are causally related, but no literal sense to claim that events are causally related 'in virtue of' their properties. Davidson would have to acknowledge that if two events are causally related in virtue of certain of their properties, then those properties make a difference to whether the events are causally related. But he denies that properties can make *that* sort of difference to causal relations. For, he says, causal relations are extensional.

I will turn, in due course, to Davidson's account of how mental properties make a difference to causal relations. First I want to examine in detail his claim that given his extensional view of causal relations, it makes no literal sense to speak of an event causing something in virtue of any of its properties.

Davidson's claim is mistaken. His extensionalist view of causal relations can be expressed as follows:

(C1) The *relata* of the causal relation are non-abstract, particular events; and if event *c* caused event *e*, and $c = d$, then *d*

as mental . . . or as described in one way or another' (p. 13). Indeed, it makes no literal sense on his view to speak of an event causing something 'as described in one way or another'. But Davidson's critics do not claim it does. When they speak of 'an event causing something as mental', they just mean that the event causes something in virtue of falling under some mental type. Whether that makes literal sense given Davidson's extensional view of causation will be discussed below.

caused *e*; and if *c* caused *e*, then there is something that caused *e*.[8]

He is mistaken in holding that *C*1 is inconsistent with

(*C*2) If event *c* caused event *e*, then *c* caused *e* in virtue of certain of *c*'s properties.

Claim *C*2 can be literally true even if *C*1 is true. Consider Davidson's own example of an extensional relation between non-abstract particulars, the weighs-less-than relation (p. 6).[9] Notice that the following claims are consistent:

(*W*1) The relata of the weighs-less-than relation are non-abstract, particular substances; and if *a* weighs less than *b*, and $a = c$, then *c* weighs less than *b*; and if *a* weighs less than *b*, then there is something that weighs less than *b*.

(*W*2) If substance *a* weighs less than substance *b*, then *a* weighs less than *b* in virtue of certain of *a*'s properties.

A proponent of *W*2 will hold that if *a* weighs less than *b*, then this is so in virtue of something about each, namely, their weights. Such a proponent can hold without fear of inconsistency that the weighs-less-than relation is an extensional relation between non-abstract particulars (substances). Similarly, a proponent of *C*2 can hold without fear of inconsistency that the causal relation is an extensional relation between non-abstract, particular events. A proponent of *C*1 can hold that if an event, *c*, causes an event, *e*, then this is so in virtue of something about each; and, so, in virtue of something about *c*.

I will elaborate. Consider claim *W**: If *a* weighs less than *b*, then *a* has some weight, w_1, and *b* has some weight, w_2, w_1 is less than w_2, and *a* weighs less than *b* in virtue of this. To shift the discussion from the material to the formal mode: claim *W** does not imply that to be true, a statement asserting that one substance weighs more than another must contain predicates that ascribe weights to the

[8] I have stated the view in the material mode. In the formal mode, it can be stated as follows: In singular causal statements containing 'cause', 'cause' is a two-placed relational predicate that is flanked by singular terms which purport to refer to non-abstract, particular events; 'cause' creates a linguistic context that is subject to substitutivity of identicals and existential generalization.

[9] The points below can be made without reifying relations; but I prefer to write in the material mode.

substances. 'Tom weighs more than Mary' may be true, though no weight is ascribed either to Tom or to Mary. That it may be true is obviously compatible with *W**. If Tom weighs more than Mary, then they are so related however they are described. None the less, if Tom weighs more than Mary, then they are so related in virtue of the fact that Tom has some weight, w_1, Mary, some weight w_2, and w_2 is less than w_1. Consider, then, claim *C**: If *c* causes *e*, then *c* is of some type, *X*, and *e* is of some type, *Y*, *X* and *Y* are appropriately related, and *c* causes *e* in virtue of this.[10] Claim *C** does not imply that a singular causal statement is true only if it describes *c* and *e* in terms of the types in question. Rather, *C** implies that if a singular causal statement is true, then the event-tokens cited in the statement must fall under appropriately related types. But the singular causal statement itself need not describe the events in terms of such types, or provide even a clue as to what the relevant types are. For if *c* and *e* are causally related, they are so related however they are described. Indeed, if *c* caused *e*, and if we dub *c* 'Tom' and *e* 'Mary', then 'Tom caused Mary' will be true. That is compatible with *C** (and, so, compatible with *C*2, since *C** implies *C*2).

That causal relations are extensional relations between events is straightforwardly compatible with the claim that when events are causally related, they are so in virtue of something about each. Indeed, typically, when a particular bears an extensional relation to another particular, the particulars are so related in virtue of something about each.

While *C*1 and *C*2 are consistent, one could, of course, maintain *C*1 and deny *C*2. And that appears to be what Davidson does in 'Thinking Causes'. He appears to claim that when an event causes another, there is nothing about the events in virtue of which this is so. But that claim seems quite implausible. Suppose that events *c* and *e* are causally related, but that events *f* and *g* are not. There must, then, it seems, be some difference between *c* and *e*, on the one hand, and *f* and *g*, on the other hand, in virtue of which *c* and *e* count as causally related and *f* and *g* do not. One could, of course, deny this. One could say that *c* and *e* count as causally related and that *f* and *g* do not, and that is that. But that two events count as

[10] There is, of course, some controversy over what type–type relations are appropriate. Some claim that only certain kinds of nomological relationships are appropriate; some claim that certain kinds of counterfactual relations are appropriate; and there are other proposals. Davidson's critics think that he holds that only strictly nomological relationships are appropriate. But of that, more later.

causally related seems an implausible candidate for a brute fact that admits of no explanation. In any case, Davidson has given us no reason to think otherwise. For to say that events count as causally related because of something about each is compatible with the view that causal relations are extensional.[11]

Why does Davidson hold that *C*1 and *C*2 are incompatible? Apparently, he thinks that the claim that event *c* causes event *e* in virtue of *c*'s having *F* implies that *c*'s having *F* causes *e* (or that *c* causes *e* under the description 'the *F*'[12]). And since *C*1 implies that causes are events, *C*1 and *C*2 are, he thinks, incompatible. He also offers a diagnosis of why his critics hold *C*2. They have, he maintains, confused causation with causal explanation. Events causally explain other events only when they are typed in certain ways (or only 'under descriptions'). Citing that the shot was loud, for instance, might causally explain something that merely citing that the shot occurred would not. But causation should not be confused with causal explanation. Events themselves are causes and effects: if events are causally related, they are so however they are typed (or described). Davidson also suspects that his critics may have thought that certain examples support *C*2 because they have confused event-tokens with event-types. While a loud shot is a different type of event from a shot, a shot could be a loud shot. And if a shot is a loud shot, then the shot caused whatever the loud shot caused. Though, again, citing that the shot was loud might causally explain something that merely citing that the shot occurred would not.

All this would be fair enough if the claim that *c* caused *e* in virtue of *c*'s having *F* implied that *c*'s having *F* caused *e* (or that *c* caused *e* under the description 'the *F*'). But it does not. In fact, *C*2 implies that events themselves are causes. Consider, again, the weighs-less-than relation. That *a* weighs less than *b* in virtue of weighing 10

[11] I should mention that the statements we have considered that employ 'in virtue of' can all be paraphrased by statements employing 'because'. For example, *a* weighs less than *b* in virtue of weighing 10 lbs if and only if *a* counts as weighing less than *b* because *a* weighs 10 lbs. (Quine has remarked that 'in virtue of' 'is almost "because of"' 1973, pp. 8–9.) See McLaughlin 1989 for further discussion.

[12] Davidson often paraphrases talk of events having properties by talk of events 'under descriptions'. This paraphrasing is intended to avoid purported reference to such entities as events having properties. An entity consisting of an event having a property would, presumably, be a state of affairs. The points I make below about states of affairs could all be recast, Davidsonian style, in terms of particulars under descriptions.

pounds, does *not* imply that *a*'s weighing less than 10 pounds weighs less than *b*. *A*'s weighing less than 10 pounds is a state of affairs, and states of affairs have no weight. Thus, to be sure, *a*'s weighing less than 10 pounds does not weigh less than *b*; for that is nonsense. But if *b* weighs (say) 11 pounds and *a* weighs 10 pounds, then *a* weighs less than *b* in virtue of weighing 10 pounds. And this implies that *a* itself weighs less than *b*. Moreover, if *a* weighs less than *b*, then *a* does so however *a* and *b* are typed (or described). Similarly, a non-abstract, particular event's having a property is, presumably, a state of affairs. The claim that event *c* caused event *e* in virtue of *c*'s having *F* does not imply that the state of affairs consisting of *c*'s having *F* caused *e*. A proponent of *C2* can consistently claim that states of affairs are never causes (or effects), that only events are causes and effects.[13]

Why, then, does Davidson think that the claim that *c* caused *e* in virtue of *c*'s having *F* implies that *c*'s having *F* caused *e* (or that *c* caused *e* under the description 'the *F*')? It is hard to know, for he does not say. In any case, as we have seen, the claim has no such implication.

A proponent of *C2* can accept *C1*, Davidson's distinction between causation and causal explanation, and his account of events. Davidson's charge that in asking how events can cause other events in virtue of having mental properties, his critics confuse causation with causal explanation and event-tokens with event-types is unwarranted.[14] These charges are based on a misunderstanding of what it means to say that events cause other events in virtue of certain of their properties. Because of this misunderstanding, Davidson argues at cross-purposes with his critics.

Critics hold that Davidson himself is committed to the view that events cause other events in virtue of certain of their properties by his principle of the nomological character of causality. For they think that this principle implies that events are causally related in

[13] Indeed, one who held that when events are causally related, they are so in virtue of something about each could even deny that there are states of affairs. Such a person need not countenance the existence of entities consisting of events having properties.

[14] His charge that some critics treat causation as a three- or four-placed relation is also unwarranted (p. 6). They treat causation as a two-placed relation. The view that when two events are causally related they are so in virtue of something about each (say e.g. their instantiating a law) is compatible with the claim that causation is a two-placed relation. Indeed, two-placed relations are *typically* such that when two particulars are so related, they are so in virtue of something about each.

virtue of having properties that are cited in strict laws (or, to speak in the formal mode, in virtue of falling under descriptions under which they are subsumed by some strict law). Davidson would deny this interpretation of the principle. He would deny that events are causally related in virtue of falling under strict laws. His denial, however, is based on a misunderstanding. He mistakenly thinks that this implies that events are causes and effects only relative to falling under certain types or only 'under descriptions'; and that singular causal statements are true only if they describe (type) events by descriptions under which they are subsumed by a strict law. The claim that events are causally related in virtue of falling under a strict law does not have these implications however; it is straightforwardly compatible with the claim that if events are causally related, they are so related however they are described (or typed).

As we saw earlier, Davidson acknowledges in 'Thinking Causes' that physical properties 'make a difference' to causal relations; and he acknowledges that it is consistent with his principles of the nomological character of causality and the anomalism of the mental that mental properties 'make no difference' to causal relations. It should now be apparent that type-*E* is consistent with the principles in question too.

Whether the principles of the nomological character of causality and the anomalism of the mental imply type-*E* is, of course, quite another matter. As we have seen, Davidson's reason for holding they do not is mistaken, for type-*E* is consistent with his extensional view of causal relations. But he may well be right, nonetheless, in holding that type-*E* is not implied by the principles in question. If he is right, then it is open to him to try to provide an account of how events can cause other events in virtue of having mental properties that is consistent with the principles. I will not pursue this here, however, since I have done so at considerable length elsewhere (McLaughlin 1989). I will instead continue to focus on what Davidson actually says in response to his critics, rather than on what I think he should say to them.

Let us turn now to Davidson's account of how mental properties make a difference to causal relations. He claims that mental properties make a difference to causal relations because they supervene on physical properties that make a difference to causal relations, namely 'those physical properties that are required for a complete causal account of the universe (i.e. that suffice for the formulation of a closed system of "strict" laws)' (n. 10). And he defines 'supervenience' as follows:

> a predicate (property) *P* is supervenient on a set of predicates (properties) *S* if and only if *P* does not distinguish any entities that cannot be distinguished by *S*.[15]

As he correctly points out, this notion of supervenience is 'close to' Kim's notion of weak supervenience (Kim 1984*a*, 1987). Indeed, on some fairly uncontroversial assumptions, Davidson's version of supervenience and Kim's weak supervenience are logically equivalent. So, let us follow Davidson in calling his supervenience relation 'weak supervenience'. (I will, however, strictly follow Davidson's definition, rather than Kim's, when speaking of weak supervenience.) Davidson maintains, then, that the weak supervenience of mental properties on physical properties that make a difference to causal relations (hereafter, 'weak psycho-physical supervenience') ensures that mental properties make a difference to causal relations.

Davidson anticipates that his critics will try to argue that weak psycho-physical supervenience is incompatible with the conjunction of the principles of the nomological character of causality and the anomalism of the mental. But I anticipate no such response from his critics. For it is quite obvious that the supervenience thesis is compatible with the principles in question. I anticipate that his critics will, instead, deny that weak psycho-physical supervenience implies that mental properties make a difference to causal relations that makes any difference to the issue of whether Davidson is committed to type-*E* or any difference to their concerns. Consider Davidson's only other example of weak supervenience, the supervenience of the truth predicate on the syntactic properties of (eternal) sentences. Consider also the following extensional relationship between two non-abstract, particular (eternal) sentences: 'having exactly the same syntactic structure as'. When two sentences participate in this relation, they do so in virtue of weak supervenience base properties for their truth-values.[16] But the sentences

[15] In note 5 of 'Thinking Causes', Davidson says that this supervenience thesis is equivalent to the one stated in Davidson 1985, p. 242; and he repeats that thesis. But the theses are not equivalent. Notice that the supervenience thesis in the body of the text contains the modal term 'cannot', while the earlier thesis (repeated in n. 5) does not. The former thesis implies the latter, but not conversely. The supervenience thesis in Davidson 1985 expresses a *de facto* relation which lacks modal force.

[16] See Kim 1984*a* for a discussion of the notion of a 'supervenience base' property.

will not participate in the relation in virtue of their truth-values. There is, likewise, no reason whatsoever to think that if mental properties weakly supervene on physical properties in virtue of which events are causally related, then those mental properties are ones in virtue of which the events are causally related.[17] Of course, Davidson does not purport to be providing an account of how events can participate in causal relations in virtue of their mental properties, but rather just of how mental properties can 'make a difference' to causal relations. But consider, again, the weak supervenience of the truth predicate on the syntactic properties of sentences. One wonders what sort of difference the truth-values of two sentences make to whether they have the exactly the same syntactic structure. Whatever sort of difference that is, it is hard to see how the fact that mental properties make *that* sort of difference to causal relations will answer any of the critics' concerns.

Let us look at Davidson's response to the critic who receives the bulk of his critical attention in 'Thinking Causes'. Perhaps that will help us see how, according to Davidson, psycho-physical weak 'supervenience ensures that mental properties make a difference to causal relations'. In commenting on a remark of Kim's, Davidson says:

> Kim may have made this remark because he mistakenly thinks that my 'weak' version of supervenience entails that 'the removal of *all* mental properties from events of this world would have no consequence whatever on how physical properties are distributed over them' (Kim 1989*b*, p. 35, n. 8). In fact supervenience entails the reverse. For consider two events with the same physical properties, but one with some mental property and the other with that property removed. These cannot be the same event, since one has a property the other lacks. But then contrary to the definition of supervenience, mental properties would distinguish two events not distinguished by their physical properties (pp. 7–8).

But Kim does not mistakenly think that Davidson's weak version of supervenience entails that 'the removal of all mental properties from events of this world would have no consequences whatever on how physical properties are distributed over them'. Rather, Kim thinks that Davidson's weak version of supervenience is consistent

[17] While I lack the space to argue the point here, even strengthening the supervenience condition to strong supervenience (Kim 1984*a*, 1987) would not be enough. Even if mental properties strongly supervene on the physical properties in virtue of which events participate in causal relations, it would not follow that the events participate in causal relations in virtue of those mental properties.

with its being the case that 'the removal of all mental properties from events of this world would have no consequences whatever on how physical properties are distributed over them'. Of course, Davidson would contend that that claim too is false. But he fails in the passage in question to provide reasons that justify this contention. Davidson is absolutely right in claiming that weak psycho-physical supervenience implies:

(*D*) If one event has a mental property that another event lacks, then the events cannot have exactly the same physical properties.

But Kim's point is, of course, that weak psycho-physical supervenience is consistent with the following claim:

(*K*) Events could have had all of their physical properties and yet lacked all of their mental properties.

Davidson's claim *D* and Kim's claim *K* are consistent. So, that weak psycho-physical supervenience implies *D* has no bearing on whether such supervenience is, as Kim holds, consistent with *K*.

Davidson also says in response to Kim that weak psycho-physical supervenience implies that an event cannot alter in any mental respect without altering in some physical respect. He claims that if an event were to alter in some mental respect, then there would be at least one physical property of the event such that the event had the property at one time *t* and then lacked the property at another time *t'*. Davidson is quite correct in claiming that this is implied by weak psycho-physical supervenience (across time). Given weak psycho-physical supervenience, if an event at *t* differs in some mental respect from itself at *t'*, then the event at *t* must be different in some physical respect from itself at *t'*. For suppose that the event altered (in the sense in question) in a mental respect but remained the same in every physical respect. Then, a mental property would distinguish the event at *t* from itself at *t'*, but no physical property would distinguish the event at *t* from itself at *t'* (p. 6). And that contradicts weak psycho-physical supervenience. So, psycho-physical weak supervenience (across time) indeed implies:

(*D'*) If an event has a mental property at one time *t* and lacks the property at another time *t'*, then the event cannot have exactly the same physical properties at *t* that it has at *t'*.

But notice that *D′* is compatible with *K*, the claim that: events could have had all of their physical properties yet have lacked all of their mental properties. So, that weak psycho-physical supervenience implies *D′* simply has no bearing on whether such supervenience is consistent with *K*. Moreover, notice, for instance, that someone who held that the causal powers of an event at a time are determined only by the physical properties of the event at that time could readily accept *D′*.

Kim is right that *K* is compatible with weak psycho-physical supervenience. And here, in a nutshell, is Kim's concern based on this. Davidson holds that mental properties of events weakly supervene on 'those physical properties that are required for a complete causal account of the universe (i.e. that suffice for the formulation of a closed system of 'strict' laws)' (n. 10). Given this, the fact that no mental property is cited in a strict law, and the fact that weak psycho-physical supervenience is consistent with *K*, Kim wonders how mental properties make any difference to causal relations. Davidson has not adequately addressed this concern. Pointing out that weak psycho-physical supervenience implies *D* and *D′* fails to do so.

I want now to turn to a different line of thought that Davidson briefly pursues in 'Thinking Causes'. He points out both that some of his critics provide accounts of how mental properties are relevant to causal relations and that their accounts are compatible with the anomalism of the mental (see pp. 10–11). For example, Fodor (1989) maintains that two events are causally related if they fall under a non-strict law, and that mental properties figure in non-strict laws. This, he claims, makes mental properties relevant to (singular) causal relations. Davidson correctly points out that this account is consistent with the anomalism of the mental. For while the anomalism of the mental implies that there can be no strict psycho-physical or psychological laws, it allows that there can be non-strict psycho-physical and psychological laws (pp. 8–9). Davidson seems to suggest also that it is at least open to him to accept Fodor's account of how mental properties are relevant to causal relations (pp. 10–11).[18] But, while plainly compatible with the anomalism of the mental, Fodor's account is compatible with the principle of the nomological character of causality only if a certain quite contentious strict-law thesis is true. The thesis is that when events fall

[18] Of course, he denies, however, that mental properties must figure in laws, strict or non-strict, to be causally relevant (pp. 11–12).

under a non-strict law, they must fall under some strict law or other. (For on Fodor's account, subsumption under a non-strict law is a sufficient condition for causation.) Fodor would deny this strict-law thesis; though it is none the less consistent with the letter of his account. The point to note for present purposes, however, is that Davidson can accept Fodor's account of the causal relevance of mental properties without repudiating the principle of the nomological character of causality only if the thesis in question is true.[19] Davidson has never offered any reason to believe the thesis. Nor, as he readily admits, has he ever argued for the principle of the nomological character of causality.

A related point in closing: Davidson says that many critics think he should reject the anomalism of the mental; that principle, he says 'seems to many critics the relevant offender, so they urge that it should be dropped' (p. 3). Perhaps. But when critics appreciate that the anomalism of the mental is consistent with the existence of non-strict psychological and psycho-physical laws, they will, I predict, take the principle of the nomological character of causality to be the culprit.

[19] See McLaughlin 1989 for a discussion of related points.

4

Davidson's Thinking Causes

ERNEST SOSA

AGAINST anomalous monism (*AM*) I have drawn an analogy between the relevance of mental properties to the causal efficacy that *AM* grants to mental events and the relevance of loudness to the causal efficacy of a loud shot. Neither the mentality of mental events nor the loudness of the loud shot is causally relevant to the respective relevant effects. The point seems clear in the case of the shot:

> A gun goes off, a shot is fired, and it kills someone. The loud noise is the shot. Thus, if the victim is killed by the shot, it's the loud noise that kills the victim. . . . Yes, in a certain sense the victim is killed by the loud noise; not by the loud noise as a loud noise, however, but only by the loud noise as a shot, or the like. . . . [The] loudness of the shot has no causal relevance to the death of the victim; had the gun been equipped with a silencer, the shot would have killed the victim just the same. (Sosa 1984, pp. 277–8.)

Yet Davidson objects at just this point to my argument from the loud shot. We are told that:

'(*a*) both loud and silent (single) shots can cause a death; but not the same death' (Davidson, above, Chapter 1, p. 17).

But two shots, one loud, one silent, one per temple, can, together, cause the same death. Is the point then rather this:

(*b*) if (i) s causes d and s is a loud shot and no other shot causes d, and (ii) s' causes d' and s' is a silent shot and no other shot causes d', then (iii) not-($d=d'$)?

This is true enough but trivial and uncontroversial, and has no evident bearing on what effects a silent shot *would* have had if it had occurred in place of a loud one. The point then must be rather this:

This paper grew (slightly) from my commentary on Davidson's 'Thinking Causes' (Chapter 1, above) at the Bielefeld conference on mental causation in March 1990.

(*c*) If (i) *s* causes *d* and *s* is a loud shot and no other shot causes *d*, then (ii) if there had been some shot *s′* that had caused a death *d′* and *s′* had been silent and no other shot had caused *d′*, then *d′* would have been distinct from *d* (i.e. *d′* would not have been numerically the same shot that *d* is).

This would give a kind of causal efficacy to the loudness of *s*, of course, since if either *s* had been silent rather than loud, or if a silent *s′* had taken the place of *s*, then *d* would *not* have been caused after all, not by any *silent* shot anyhow.

But why should we accept (*c*)? Is it assumed that every event—such as death *d*—has its every property essentially? This *would* explain why *d′* must be distinct from *d*, since it would be caused by a silent shot, unlike *d*, which is caused by a loud one. Only some such essentialism of events seems a plausible basis for (*c*). But if *this* is the way the mental is efficacious, then the mental seems no more efficacious than a speck of dust on the butt of a murder gun. For any death *d′* caused by a dustless gun would have to be different from a death *d* caused by the gun with the speck, all of which shows the speck to be surprisingly efficacious.

Davidson's response to that objection would apparently involve the following claim: 'to serve the purposes of my argument, mental properties need supervene on only those physical properties that are required for a complete causal account of the universe (i.e. that suffice for the formulation of a closed system of "strict" laws)' (see Davidson above, Chapter 1, p. 17, n. 10). But even if mental properties supervene thus on only such physical properties, the speck of dust on the butt of a gun would still make a difference to what a shot from that gun causes (since between any particular case of speckedness and any particular case of specklessness there must be differences in terms of the physical properties required for a complete physical account of the universe). Is it only in so weak a sense that *AM* can allow mental properties to 'make a difference'?

Davidson's apparent willingness to countenance modality, or at least counterfactuals—in the case of the loud shot—is surprising and unusual, in the present paper at least. Earlier in the paper he seems to avoid it studiously. It is this, perhaps more than anything else, that accounts for the impasse between Davidson and his critics. For example, when Kim says that Davidson's weak supervenience allows that the removal of *all* mental properties leave the physical intact and unaltered, this seems best interpreted *not* as a mere temporal point—the way Davidson apparently takes it—but as a modal point. Davidson seems to take it as the point that there could come a time in the course of history when all mentality would be stripped off the brains of all creatures, and off the universe entirely, leaving bodies to run unminded, but otherwise the same. Against this Davidson protests, of course, that weak supervenience (across time) rules it out, since you might then have psychologically distinct but physically indistinguishable cross-sections of history. But Kim's point is rather to be interpreted as follows: that you might have two whole possible worlds (their entire histories included), one minded just as ours, the other bereft of mentality but otherwise the same; and that weak supervenience would allow this if it works world by world, saying of each that in it the physically indistinguishable must be psychologically alike.

If Davidson is right, we can avoid these issues of modality, anyhow, for it is his view that the critics of anomalous monism are making a simple mistake whose explication and correction requires no appeal to modality. The main lines of his reasoning seem to be these:

1. We are warned that when critics accuse *AM* of making the mental inert, they must be supposing *AM* to be incompatible with the supervenience of the mental on the physical; yet the critics have never proved this.
2. Why must the critics be making that unproved assumption? Because if the mental does after all supervene, even weakly, then the mental properties of an event can be shown to make a difference to its causal relations, and *not* to be inert after all. How would the argument go? Apparently like this (where we restrict our universe of discourse to events):
   (*a*) Mental properties supervene on physical properties: i.e. no events *e* and *e′* differ mentally without differing physically (by assumption).
   (*b*) Mental properties of events therefore make a difference to their physical properties (from (a)).
   (*c*) Physical properties of events make a difference to their causal relations (by assumption).
   (*d*) Mental properties of events therefore make a difference to their causal relations (from (*b*), (*c*)).

Troublesome here is the expression of the form '*P* properties of entities *E* make a difference to their *R* relation(s)'. Take the set *E* of positive integers. And let the *R* relation be the greater than relation (>), and the *P* properties: being even, being odd. Do the *P* properties here 'make a difference' to the *R* relation over the set *E*? I suppose that for Davidson they do, and I hazard that his meaning is as follows:

(*P*/*R*) properties (P_1, P_2, . . .) make a difference to relation *R* over set *E* iff (for all *x*, *y*, *i*) { [(*x* and *y* belong to *E*) & (*x* has P_i but *y* lacks P_i)] only if (for some *z*)[(*z* belongs to *E*) & [not-(*xRz* iff *yRz*) or not-(*zRx* iff *zRy*)]] }(That is: entities in set *E* that are *P*-distinct must be differently related by relation *R* to some entity in *E*.)

What is more, in the sense given of 'making a difference', the argument above may be seen to be valid, when supplemented as follows:

(*Q*/*P*) *Q* properties (Q_1, Q_2, . . .) make a difference (in the supervenience way) to *P* properties (P_1, P_2, . . .) over a set *E* iff (for all *x*, *y*){ (*x* and *y* belong to *E*) only if [(for all *i*)(*x* has P_i iff *y* has P_i) only if (for all *j*)(*x* has Q_j iff *y* has Q_j)] } (That is: entities in set *E* that are *Q*-distinct must be *P*-distinct.)

Under this interpretation, the argument from (*a*) to (*d*) above seems clearly valid, and can be put as follows:

(*a′*) Mental properties of events supervene on their physical properties: i.e. no mental difference without a physical difference (assumption).
(*b′*) Mental properties of events make a difference to their physical properties: i.e. events that are mentally different must be physically different (from *a′*).
(*c′*) Physical properties of events make a difference to their causal relations: i.e. events that are physically different must be differently causally related to some event (assumption).
(*d′*) Mental properties of events make a difference to their causal relations: i.e. events that are mentally different must be differently causually related to some event (from *b′*, *c′*).

Since *b′* follows from *a′*, and *d′* follows from *b′* and *c′*, we have here a valid argument based on assumptions *a′* and *c′*. Does this answer the critics?

If in the sense given physical properties make a difference to causal relations over the set of events, then presumably locational properties (which specify the coordinates of an event in space and time) will likewise make a difference to causal relations. However, suppose that events e and e' are distinct iff e and e' are differently located in space or time. If so, then every conceivable property of events weakly supervenes on the locational (coordinate) properties of events. Hence every conceivable property of events 'makes a difference' (in the sense above) to the causal relations of events. To say that in *that* sense mental properties 'make a difference' is therefore not to say very much, and it is doubtful that the critics will be satisfied.

However, perhaps it is not true that events e and e' are distinct iff e and e' are differently located in space or time. Consider then once more an arbitrary set of events E: $\{e_1, \ldots, e_i, \ldots\}$. And define relative to E the set πE: {Being identical with e_1, . . . , Being identical with e_i, . . . }, or in a simpler notation: $\{[x=e_1], \ldots, [x=e_i], \ldots\}$. Two things are worth observing about E and πE:

1. Any conceivable set of properties Ω, pertinent to E, would necessarily supervene (in Davidson's sense, weakly) on πE, for there could not possibly be any difference in respect of any property whatsoever between any two entities in E without there being a difference in respect of the properties in πE between these two entities.
2. πE properties of the events in E do make a difference to their causal relations, since events in E could not be different in respect of their πE properties without being differently related causally to some event. In other words, different events could not have absolutely all their causes and effects in common. (This thesis is famously advanced by Davidson himself in other writings.)

But given 1 and 2 and the earlier account of what it is for a set of properties to make a difference to the causal relations of events, it follows that any conceivable set of properties Ω must make a difference to the causal relations of events. It is only in so weak a sense of making a difference that, through the argument under consideration, Davidson allows for mental properties of events to make a difference to their causal relations. And that is clearly not enough to satisfy his critics who allege that *AM* makes mental properties inefficacious, and that for *AM* the mental is in that sense inert and makes no difference.

Turning now to another aspect of anomalous monism, I find puzzling the combination of:

(*a*) an extensional relation of causation *C* between events, one not subject to intensional explanation or analysis, and
(*b*) principle *U* of the 'universalizability' of causation:
(*U*) the causal relation cannot relate events *e* and *e'* unless these events fall under a strict (physical) law when appropriately described.

Of course, we might allow an extensional relation of causation *C*(*e*,*e'*), which nevertheless gave us the basis for an explanation of principle *U*. Thus suppose:

(*AC*) *C*(*e*,*e'*) iff (for some *D* and *D'*)(*D* covers *e*, *D'* covers *e'*, and there is a strict law appropriately connecting *D* and *D'*)

In order to connect *D* and *D'* appropriately, the strict law in question must be of the right sort, NB, since for one thing not every strict law is a causal law. Accordingly, *AC* would need to be supplemented with a positive account of the requirement for a law to be 'of the right sort'. In any case, if we can accept this account, *AC*, of the causal relation, as a general principle, then *C*(*e*,*e'*) would remain an extensional relation, since the principles:

C(*e*,*e'*) & (*e*=*e''*) only if *C*(*e''*, *e'*)
C(*e*,*e'*) & (*e'*=*e''*) only if *C*(*e*,*e''*)

would still hold with full generality. Yet we would have an explanation of principle *U*. On the basis of *AC* we would be able to see that the causal relation is not a fundamental relation, but necessarily supervenes on other properties and relations and how these combine lawfully.

However, we would *also* have a natural sense in which *e as D* causes *e' as D'*—which, incidentally, may be seen to be compatible with *e as* D_1 also causing *e' as* D_1'.

Moreover, the very definition, or analysis, or general account of the causal relation would then make the causal relation *dependent* on laws connecting the properties (descriptions) of the events in question. And this would also make available a clear sense in which events would be causally efficacious *because* of their physical properties only and not at all because of their mental properties. (Of course, this would leave open the possibility that there be *another* sense in which some events might still be causally efficacious because of their mental properties. Indeed, some consequences of taking this option will be explored below.)

In order to remove suspicion that *AM* makes the mental inert, therefore, the anomalous monist would do well to make public the basis for the universalizability of causation, principle *U*. If principle *U* is defensible without need to rely on any analysis or account such as *AC*, that would provide crucial support to *AM*.

The public defence of principle *U* is necessary, I think, in order to clear *AM* of suspicion that it makes the mental inert. But it is not sufficient. For we have seen already why we must reject the positive explanation of the causal efficacy of the mental offered on behalf of *AM*. Therefore, the anomalous monist must not only defend *U* without thereby making available a clear notion of inertness usable in a persuasive thesis that *AM* entails mental inertness; in addition to defending *U* under those constraints, the anomalous monist would then need some positive defence for the claim that *AM* does *not* make the mental inert, some positive defence to take the place of the one in terms of weak supervenience already questioned above. Surely this would involve introducing some *stronger* sense in which mental concepts make a difference to causal relations, stronger than the one above. For according to the one above *all* possible concepts would likewise make such a difference.

What is more, *AM* must make room for our mental properties to make a causal difference not just to something or other but to our behaviour specifically. So far we have no inkling of how this requirement could be met, except by countenancing conditionals or unstrict laws connecting mental properties and behavioural properties.

This whole project of finding some stronger sense in which the mind can matter has been actively pursued in recent years. So far the results in every case postulate a stronger sense that involves either modality, or subjunctives, or unstrict laws connecting the mental and the physical — and sometimes all three.

Note now a threat to *AM* in this project: namely, that once we admitted that stronger sense in which the mental can make a difference to the physical, it would threaten to take over; that it would offer a sense in which causation can supervene on something *other* than strict laws; and that it would hence offer a *rival* to *AC*. This could be fatal to *AM*, for two reasons: first, because the rival, positive proposal would suggest that causation can relate events *e* and *e′* even when the operative properties of *e* and *e′*—namely *P* and *P′*—are connected *not by strict law but only in the alternative way*, the way in which the mental can be connected with the physical, which might be just through some relation of modality or conditionality or unstrict law; and, second, because rejecting *AC* would leave principle *U* entirely without support.

In conclusion, I would like to step back and reflect more generally on the status that anomalous monism allows to the mental. Either *AM* accepts properties or it does not. If it does, then is not *AM* committed essentially to property dualism? Does it not stand together with the phenomenological view according to which there are fundamental psychological or phenomenological properties not reducible to the physical? Consider the roundness of a billiard ball in reality, such that the billiard ball is in itself round; this primary quality of roundness is not a property generally reducible to other properties (or if one accepts reducibility to points equidistant from a centre, then let us say more cautiously that presumably there are some irreducible primary qualities that are physical). For the *AM* token physicalist who accepts properties there are also psychological qualities that apply to a subject of experience and consciousness with just as little possibility that these qualities should reduce to physical properties. Indeed these qualities are not even related by any general unrestricted laws to any physical properties. So there they sit, these psychological qualities—for example the property of aching that might apply to someone with a headache—beyond the reach of strict physical law. And this seems clearly to be a property dualism that makes the advocate of *AM* only half a physicalist—only a physicalist with regard to particulars, to the particular, token events allowed into their view of reality, but *not* a physicalist with regard to the properties allowed, since some of these would be irreducibly mental, and not even connected with physical properties by strict physical laws, much less by the necessary principles required for strong metaphysical supervenience.

Alternatively, *AM* may reject properties (along with facts in virtue of which or corresponding to which any true sentences would be true). In this case, reality may be in itself homogeneously physical, since all particulars, all particular token events, would be physical. This seems a more radical and interesting, a truly monistic physicalism. Reality on this view seems physical through and through. Consider again a particular headache *h*, and its being an aching. *AM* is not going to deny the existence of the *sentence* '*h* is an aching', surely, nor its truth. But in that case one may well wonder why *h* is an aching, or anyhow why there is an aching there then. For almost any other view of the mind, there is the *possibility* of an illuminating and explanatory answer. With more information about the property of aching and its nature and its relationship to other physical properties present in the context, one could (or at least God could) devise an explanation that would answer the question in an illuminating way. Once again the anomalous monist seems to stand with a particular sort of property dualist in holding that no such explanation is possible, not just because matters are too complicated for limited humans, apparently, but because there simply are no principles, whether metaphysically necessary or scientific, no principles that enjoy strict generality, to connect mental predicates with physical predicates. Thus, if we may assume that any illuminating explanation of why that aching takes place would have to appeal to physical factors in the circumstances, factors like a blow on the head, or indigestion, or nervous tension, or the like, we seem forced to the view that the nature of things precludes any illuminating explanation of that mental phenomenon (as mental)—of *why there is an aching there and then*, in any case. What differentiates the eliminativist from the anomalous monist is apparently a restriction on what they are willing to countenance in reality: apparently, for the eliminativist if there really is an aching there and then, it must be subject to the possibility of scientific explanation, a possibility to be realized only in the millennium perhaps, but a real possibility nonetheless; whereas for the anomalous monist there can be such an aching even if there is no such possibility of its being explained scientifically at all, there being no strict generalizations that could appropriately be invoked in such explanation, there being, in the nature of things, no such generalization to be discovered.

It might be replied that *AM* does admit the possibility of a kind of explanation even for achings and other such experiential states. For *AM* does admit the existence of *non-strict* generalizations connecting mental properties, or at least predicates, with physical ones.

But, again, if we allow that an interesting *because* of explanation, as in 'the headache occurs because of the blow on the head', can be based on and legitimated by non-strict generalizations, as in 'blows on the head normally lead to headaches', then it becomes highly problematic what our basis can be for insisting that *e* cannot *cause e'* unless there is a *strict* law connecting *e* and *e'* under suitable descriptions. Our ordinary and philosophical vocabulary of *explanation*, *understanding*, *cause*, and *because* seems to me just not refined enough to allow such subtle distinctions, and the relevant requirement of *strictness* for *causation* has all the appearance of almost pure and arbitrary stipulation, an appearance that will be dispelled only through a convincing argument, one that at present remains to be seen.

PART II

Causation and Explanation

5

Mental Causation: Sustaining and Dynamic

ROBERT AUDI

THE causal power of the mental is at once pervasively presupposed in common-sense thinking and widely disputed among philosophers. In everyday life we constantly talk about doing things because of what we want or believe; we even explicitly dub as 'causes' such mental phenomena as suspicion, anger, and pain. There are, however, non-causal uses of 'because', as where a syllogism is said to be invalid because it has two negative premisses; and clearly the question of the causal power of mental phenomena cannot be settled by mere terminological observations. To make the issue tractable, I propose to consider only one major domain: that of propositional attitudes and closely related mental elements. Even here, my main concern will be beliefs, desires, and intentions. These, after all, seem to be the basic mental elements crucial in everyday explanations of human action; and if cognitive psychology is to provide a broadly scientific understanding of our actions, it is presumably these or quite similar mental states that must play the central role.

Among the sources of doubt about the causal power of the mental, four in particular will concern me: first, the view that reasons—which, paradigmatically, include beliefs and desires—cannot be causes; second, the related view that the explanatory relevance of psychological states such as beliefs and intentions derives from their content, which is abstract and so not a candidate for a causal role; third, the idea that if the mental supervenes on the physical, then what really explains our actions is the physical properties determining our propositional attitudes, and not those attitudes themselves; and fourth, the thesis that since there are no laws linking (intentional) mental states to actions, those states

I particularly want to thank John Heil and Alfred Mele for helpful comments; the paper has also profited from discussions with Joseph Mendola and Barbara von Eckhardt.

cannot be genuine causes of action. Sections 1–4 will critically assess these sources of doubt about the causal power of the mental; Section 5 will sketch a positive account of what seem the two main causal roles played by mental factors in the explanation of action.

1. Reasons and Causes

In discussing reasons and causes, it is essential to distinguish two kinds of reason. Consider my reason for telephoning (as opposed to writing to) an employer about a job candidate. Asked why I did so, I might say that I wanted to get my supporting statement there before the deadline, or simply: to get my support there before the deadline. Strictly speaking, the reason I had for my action is expressed by the phrase, 'to get my support there before the deadline'; but what this phrase expresses is *my* reason only because I am suitably motivated: I am in a reason-state, namely, wanting to get the support there before the deadline.[1] It is only reason-states—especially wants, beliefs, and intentions—and not reasons strictly so called, that are serious candidates to be causes. The former are abstract contents of propositional attitudes; the latter are psychological elements that presumably play a motivational role in producing action.[2] That the former, reasons proper, are not causes is widely believed; but if that point is the force of denying that reasons are causes, we should wonder why there has been so much debate about the issue. Let us assume, then, that the issue concerns the causal power of reason-states.

If reason-states can motivate, why (apart from confusing them with reasons proper) would philosophers deny that they are causes? For one thing, reason-states are not events, at least in the usual sense in which the occurrence of an event entails that of a change;

[1] Here and in most of what follows I speak of wanting rather than desiring. The former term seems broader, but nothing of substance in the paper will turn on this assumption. I have explicated wanting in this broad sense in my 1973 paper.

[2] Particularly when the contents can be specified only through using an indexical, such as 'my', accounting for them is problematic. But the points I am making do not seem to depend on any particular resolution of this difficulty and are neutral with respect to the question whether (*de dicto*) beliefs are understood as relations to propositions or in some other way, e.g. as certain kinds of representational state. Such '*de se*' attitudes as believing that I myself must have (say) forgotten the key have been extensively discussed by Hector-Neri Castañeda (e.g. in his 1967), and by John Perry (e.g. in his 1983 and 1990).

they are dispositional states (this contrasts them with occurrences, but does not imply that, as logical behaviourism would have it, they admit of dispositional analysis or any kind of analysis in terms of counterfactuals). It has also seemed to those who deny that reasons are causes that the former justify (or tend to justify) as well as explain the actions for which they are reasons, whereas the proper role of causes, on the view in question, is at most to enable us to explain and predict. Still another claim is that the relation between reasons (and here reason-states are often cited explicitly as examples of what is meant by 'reasons') and the actions they explain is non-contingent, whereas the relation of causes to their effects is contingent. Let us consider these arguments in turn.

First, even if causes are events, *sustaining causation* may explain, as where the leaning position of a shrub is explained by the pressure of a parked car whose bumper has pushed it over and holds (sustains) it in that bent position. Indeed, without appeals to sustaining causation, there is much in and beyond human behaviour that cannot be explained: it seems required for any comprehensive explanation of why a (non-event) state obtains, or why some process or activity continues over time. My deciding to telephone, which is itself an event, may be explained by another event, say my being told that today is the deadline; but my talking for three minutes straight, which is an ongoing process, must be explained by such things as my standing belief that several points remain to be communicated before I am through. Processes, which are unlike dispositions in being 'composed' of events, may also be sustaining causes, as where heating produces evaporation; but the main sustaining causes of interest here are dispositional, since this is the category to which propositional attitudes apparently belong.

Second, there is prima-facie good reason to take the 'because' in 'I telephoned because I wanted to get my supporting statement there before the deadline' to be in some sense causal. Indeed, where it is not so taken, this purported explanation, if regarded as honestly offered, would be considered only a rationalization.[3] Granted that the apparent causal connection is not mechanical and is arguably not even physical (an issue to which we will return), there is no plausible non-causal account of the kinds of explanations in question.

[3] This claim is defended in Audi 1985, but is surely independently plausible.

Third, if any 'non-contingent connection' can be established between, say, my wanting something and the action it explains, there are causal analogues of that sort of 'logical connection', such as the relation between bringing a magnet to iron filings and their gravitating towards it, which seem similarly close: this is, after all, a 'definitive' causal connection. To use a phrase common in writings which attack the causal conception of explanations that appeal to propositional attitudes, 'part of what we mean by' 'being a magnet' is 'tending to attract iron filings' (this is argued in detail in Audi 1971).

There are, to be sure, further issues underlying the reasons–causes debate. But having addressed this elsewhere (and in view of the large literature supporting a causalist position on propositional attitudes), I shall not extend the sketch just provided.[4] The views developed below, especially in Section 5, will indicate further lines of reply.

2. Mental Contents Versus Mental Causes

One might accept the distinction between reasons proper and reason-states and still deny that the latter have causal power. For one might argue that it is the reasons as contents of propositional attitudes that do the explanatory work which may seem to be done, causally, by the states themselves, as internal causal elements. Or, perhaps more plausibly, one might argue that since the states explain *by virtue of their content*, their explanatory role is not causal and we thus have no good reason to ascribe causal power to them. What explains my telephoning, on this conception, is that it is required for my goal of supporting my candidate for the position: the action is made intelligible by being exhibited as a means to a normal end. This is not a causal, genetic, or dynamic account, but a purposive explanation rooted in a particular culture.

I agree that the content of propositional attitudes is essential to their action-explaining power, and I grant, at least for the sake of argument, that contents themselves are not causes. But I reject the idea that if content is essential to explaining an action, then the

[4] My own effort to refute the 'logical connection' thesis about reasons and causes is summarized in Audi 1973 and 1985, and much relevant literature is referred to there, including Davidson 1963, and Goldman 1970. For a more recent, brief treatment of some of the issues see Dretske 1989.

states expressing it do not causally explain that action. Traditionally (and quite plausibly), propositional attitudes are individuated in terms of their content; for example, wanting to support the president's policy would not be the state it is apart from its content, and so even when, by convention, the president is identical with the chief executive, wanting to support the president's policy is different from wanting to support the chief executive's policy. Why not say, then, that while content itself is not a cause, it plays a causal role in explaining action because the reason-states which causally explain action do so in part *by virtue of their content*? The action is explained, after all, *qua* type, say as a vote; the content of the explaining attitudes, e.g. wanting to promote a policy, together with believing that voting for it is required to do so, determines what action-type is appropriate. A weaker view would be that even if this explanatory role of reasons as contents is not itself causal, reason-states can still play a causal role, and hence mental factors can have causal power.

To explain just how propositional attitudes, say beliefs and wants, explain by virtue of their content requires a major theory. What is needed here is simply a sketch of a key part of such a theory. Recall the telephoning. It is explained *qua* telephoning and not, say, as lifting a receiver and pushing buttons, which is another correct description of the action. The telephoning, as an action for a reason, is a discriminative response to the agent's reason-states, not a mere effect of them: the want to communicate support sets my goal; the belief that telephoning is required—together with background beliefs and related perceptions—guides my behaviour. I go to what I take to be a free phone; I dial the number I believe to be correct; I redial or adjust my behaviour in other ways if necessary; and (barring a new goal's overriding this one) I normally continue in the service of the goal set by my want until my information, recorded partly in beliefs, indicates a match between the goal I want to realize and my behaviour subordinated to that goal. Very roughly, my relevant beliefs provide a cognitive map; my governing want indicates a destination on that map; and my action is explained as an effort to reach that destination.[5] Even physical causes can have direction as well as energy. The natural analogy here is to beliefs as

[5] This picture is suggested, and in some aspects, refined and defended, in Audi 1986. The map metaphor is intentionally reminiscent of Tolman 1948, but I am not here trying to follow Tolman's account of behaviour.

providing, with the help of perception, the direction of behaviour, and wants providing its energy: the direction requires a kind of instrumental content; the energy requires a conceptualized goal to which that content is connected.

The notion of a propositional attitude I presuppose is internalist and the associated notion of content is, in a corresponding sense, narrow. Certainly believing, *of* a telephone, that it is a means to reach another city, implies the existence of a telephone. But it is my believing *that* using a telephone will suffice which—together with certain external factors—is crucial in explaining my behaviour. Imagine an atom-for-atom duplicate of me who has been exposed not to telephones but to 'telepaphones'—devices perceptually indistinguishable from telephones but working by causing a telepathic transmission of thoughts.[6] In precisely my circumstances we would (I believe) expect my double to exhibit the same *de dicto* beliefs and, largely for that reason, the same behaviour. If he were in a world like mine apart from the different kind of phone, our *de re* beliefs would be different, mine being of (and in that sense about) a telephone, his being of a telepaphone; and different externally phrased explanations can be given for our matching behaviour: I picked up the telephone because I caught sight of it just as I was ready to recommend the candidate; he picked up the telepaphone because he caught sight of it just as he was ready to recommend the candidate. But our behaviour-explaining intentional attitudes are the same.[7]

Nothing said here precludes the existence of a non-causal kind of explanation which reasons as contents can provide. There is a sense in which a goal, considered in the abstract, makes intelligible, and at

[6] If their working on such a principle is not possible given the atom-for-atom identity, the example can be varied either by restricting the extent of their identity or by changing the difference between the two phones.

[7] This does not imply that 'meaning is in the head' if that is taken to entail that our beliefs are 'about' the same things in the two worlds. Roughly, it is the internal attitudinal content, not the referential content, of our beliefs that is the same when our environments are perceptually indistinguishable. For a related discussion, see Fodor 1991*b*. He says e.g. 'To have a water thought *just is* to have a thought that is connected to water in the right way, and to have a twater thought [one similarly related to the Twin Earth counterpart of water] *just is* to have a thought that is connected to twater in the right way. So it is not the case that my being connected to water rather than to twater is a difference in my causal powers in virtue of its responsibility for my having water thoughts rather than twater thoughts' (pp. 20–1); and 'there are *no* taxonomically relevant differences consequent upon broad-content differences as such. . . . So individualism is true and local supervenience preserved' (p. 25).

least in that way explains, an action which is a good means to it. Thus, suppose a (hypothetical) movement of troops is queried in a strategy discussion; self-defence may be said to explain it, and one could explicate how it does this without going into the psychology of any particular agents. To be sure, more commonly, if no causal relation is taken to hold between the relevant reason-states and the action, the natural thing to say is that the former 'would explain' the latter. Still, that the movement of troops is a good means to self-defence provides, given that goal, an explanation of the movement, considered as a type. We are in effect provided with a schematic practical argument that a reasonable agent might use, and act on, which favours such a movement of troops. We might even speak here of a *type–type explanation*, one that explains the appropriateness of an action-type by connecting it to a suitable set of want- and belief-types.

A type of action, then, may be reasonable, and in that way understandable, in terms of instrumental propositions and (types of) goals to which those propositions indicate means. This point may underlie some of the inclination to deny that everyday intentionalistic explanations of action are causal. The point is important: certainly action-types can be appropriate, intelligible, and reasonable in the light of the contents of beliefs and wants. But it is action-tokens whose explanation is in question, for we are considering particular deeds. Now even if the type of thing I do, such as telephoning for a candidate, is rendered intelligible by the contents of my beliefs and wants, what I do, my particular telephoning here and now, is explained only by something that in some way produces the action. Explanation of tokens, as opposed to mere rationalization, requires a causal connection (this is argued in detail in Audi 1985). The relevant practical argument, one might say, must be realized in the agent's psychology and not merely constructable in the abstract from the contents of propositional attitudes therein.

There is no need, then, to deny that contents of propositional attitudes have, as such, a kind of non-causal explanatory power, and they surely play some role in the apparent causal explanatory power of the states whose contents they are. If, however, considerations about the content of propositional attitudes do not show that they have no causal power, facts about their basis may yet show that.

3. The Supervenience of the Mental

Another source of doubt about the causal power of the mental comes from reflection on the significance of its apparent supervenience on the physical. There is considerable difficulty about how supervenience should be analysed, but for my purposes the following rough formulation should suffice: to say that mental properties supervene on physical ones is to affirm a relation such that (1) no two things can share all their physical properties and differ in their mental properties (if they have any) and (2) a thing having a mental property has that property in virtue of one or more physical properties it possesses.[8] If the modality in (1) is nomic, we may speak of nomic supervenience; if it is conceptual, of conceptual supervenience, and so on. In broad terms, the worry I have in mind is this: if my mental states are determined by my physical ones (say by certain brain-states), why should we attribute causal power to the former rather than to just the latter? The physical states are more basic, and it seems natural to suppose that mental ascriptions are simply our common-sense way of referring to underlying states and events which carry the real causal power. This is not to deny that actions are explained when intentionalistic explanations are given; the claim is that the real explanatory, or at least causal, work—as far as the action-token is concerned—is done by the properties underlying the beliefs, wants, or intentions to which we ignorantly refer in appealing to the latter.[9]

It is instructive here to consider an analogy in which the supervenience base properties are more clearly candidates for the real causal factors underlying the relevant explanations. Consider moral explanations, realistically construed, i.e. explanations of concrete phenomena by appeal to instances of moral properties.[10] It might be said, for example, that in the end it was because Richard Nixon was morally corrupt that he was run out of office. This

[8] I take the relation to be non-reductive, in the sense that it does not entail reducibility, not in the sense that it precludes it. For a related (though non-equivalent) characterization of supervenience and a statement of some problems of the kind I approach in this section, see Kim 1989*a*, 1989*b*, and 1990*a*.

[9] The suggested view is a kind of epiphenomenalism. For interesting recent discussion see Bieri 1992. In what follows I shall be implicitly replying to some of Bieri's points.

[10] In this and the next few paragraphs I draw on Audi 1992.

explanation is plausible, but if it is successful then such moral properties as corruption seem to have causal power. May we take it at face value?

As already suggested, the supervenience of moral on natural properties reflects an 'ontic dependence': even if moral properties are not themselves natural, their possession presupposes that of certain natural properties as their basis. This is how, for any plausible moral realism, moral properties are anchored in the world. Now the moral epiphenomenalist, as we may call the ethical counterpart of the epiphenomenalist concerning the mental, suggests that certain of the base properties in fact do the explaining that the moral properties seem to do. To be sure, this raises the question whether we should ever attribute explanatory power to supervening properties, unless they can be plausibly claimed to be identical with sets of base properties not themselves supervenient on other properties. But is there good reason to think that any explanatory properties are ultimately irreducible or do not even supervene on others? Perhaps there is, at least if it is reasonable to believe that—assuming anything is genuinely explainable—there cannot be a regress of explanations. Suppose, then, that some properties meet this condition. Still, there are supervenient properties, such as temperature, magnetism, and elasticity, which, in their own right, apparently do have explanatory, even causal, power.

This line of reply to moral epiphenomenalism has limited force, however, once we appreciate a difference between moral supervenience and the kind important in science. Unlike, say, magnetism, temperature, and elasticity, moral properties are not only ontically dependent, but also epistemically dependent, on their base properties: roughly, knowing a particular to have a moral property depends on knowing it to have one or more of a certain range of base properties, and justifiedly believing it to have a moral property depends on justifiedly believing it to have one or more base properties in this same range.[11] One might also say that our descriptive and explanatory uses of moral properties exhibit this epistemic dependence, but nothing maintained here will turn on

[11] This concerns what might be called primary knowledge (and justification): I do not deny that one might know a thing to have a moral property on the basis of testimony, or that one might know that there is an injustice from a pattern of events plausibly considered to be its effects. But surely no one can know of injustice in these ways except by virtue of someone's knowing of it through one or more of its base properties.

which formulation we choose. My point is that if there is such a dependence, then whenever we explanatorily invoke a moral property, it will be in part on the basis of, or at least in the light of, some belief or presupposition to the effect that one or more natural properties is playing an explanatory role in relation to the phenomenon being explained. We are thus in a position to rely—often unselfconsciously, to be sure—on those other properties to do the explanatory work, and it is arguable that they, and not any moral property, are in fact what does it. Let me illustrate.

Recall the possibility of citing moral corruption to explain why Nixon was run out of office. One cannot know (and normally would not even believe) that there is such corruption except through some awareness of, say, lies, hypocrisy, and cover-ups. But these are just the sorts of non-moral (social-psychological) factors that, in their own right, we suppose (on the basis of our general knowledge of social forces) can perfectly well explain an official's being forced to resign. They also seem to have causal power in a quite intuitive sense. We understand quite well, for example, how lies, when discovered, lead their victims to retaliate. Perhaps it is on the basis of pragmatic reasons—for instance, out of a desire to combine explanation with moral assessment—that we cite the moral factor as cause. Notice also that when we invoke a moral factor in giving an explanation, we are generally willing to say how it explains, and in explaining how it does we always tend to appeal to the relevant base properties. We are indeed expected to be able to indicate, in this way, how the factor explains, on pain of giving up our explanatory claim. Suppose John asserts that corruption explains Nixon's being ousted but is unable to say, in terms of the sorts of factors I have cited, how it does so, or even how it might do so. We would not accept the purported explanation. Nor, I think, would we be likely to cite moral factors in explanations of events if we could not, at least in a general way, see causal connections between the base properties and the event to be explained.

These points do not entail that moral properties cannot in their own right explain events; but there seems to be better reason to think that it is the base properties which do the real explanatory work when moral properties appear to provide explanations. Our understanding of how ascription of moral properties can explain seems wholly derived from our understanding of how the relevant base properties can do so.[12] Indeed, given an explanation of, say, a

[12] One might go further. As Warren Quinn (1986, p. 531) puts it in explicating

resignation by appeal to such things as lies and hypocrisy, it is not clear what one would add to the explanation of why the resignation occurred by pointing out that these things constituted governmental injustice. This is an appropriate moral comment, but it does not seem to add to the explanation—unless it is taken to imply subvening variables other than those cited in giving the original explanation, or, more likely, it implies that, say, people believed an injustice was done and wanted to take counter-measures. Here, however, it is additional psychological variables, not moral ones, that are contributing to the explanation.[13]

There is, then, at least one sort of case in which we have reason to think that the supervenience of a kind of property implies that, while it has a significant role in explanation, it lacks causal power. But the moral cases (like the other normative ones, I believe) are quite different from the mental cases. There are at least three major disanalogies. First, the ontic dependence of any particular mental property on some physical subvenient property is not a priori, in the sense that it is knowable through reflection on the relations among the properties in question. It is presumably an empirical truth that mental properties supervene on physical ones at all. It may be plausibly argued that a being which has mental properties must also have physical ones, but this is a quite different point—and very controversial. Second, whereas moral properties are epistemically dependent on natural ones, mental properties are not epistemically dependent on physical ones: far from it, there is much non-inferential knowledge of many mental properties in one's own

Gilbert Harman's line of argument, 'The better explanations that may always replace our moral explanations can . . . be fashioned from concepts that the intelligent moral explainer must already have because his own application of moral principles depends on them. Moral theory, in presupposing a rich supply of naturalistic concepts, contains the full-blown means by which its own explanations may be put aside.' This paper as a whole is a helpful treatment of the controversy between Harman and Nicholas Sturgeon; for that see Harman 1985 and Sturgeon 1985. My point is that moral properties seem to be only indirectly explanatory of concrete events, and that moral explanations, spelled out, depend on appeal to natural properties. But the explanations are not put aside, or even replaceable, as somehow inadequate; indeed (as Harman would perhaps not deny), pragmatically, they may be indispensable.

[13] Granted, there could not be beliefs with this content unless someone had moral concepts; for this reason explanations by appeal to such beliefs might be said to be indirectly moral. Such cases show another way in which the moral plays a role in explaining events, but not that a moral property is a causal variable in any explanatory generalization or that some moral phenomenon, as such, has explanatory power.

case,[14] and where one does know a person to possess a mental property on the basis of physical ones, it is normally not through knowledge of the base properties of the former, but rather through knowledge of behaviour which is normally taken to manifest, rather than underlie, the relevant mental property. The very fact that we identify mental properties in this way is best explained as indicating a presupposition of their having causal power. Third, as these points suggest, in the case of the mental, the candidates for base properties are not conceptually constitutive of the mental ones. Indeed, if there are good candidates for natural properties conceptually constitutive of mental properties, say behavioural tendencies, their relation to the mental is probably even more complex than that of, say, lies and hypocrisy to corruption. This is a major lesson of the collapse of logical behaviourism.

These disanalogies do not, of course, show that mental properties have causal power. But they do serve to rebut one source of argumentation against that view and to forestall some misunderstandings that might suggest an epiphenomenalist conclusion. Does supervenience outside the normative domain suggest any positive reason to think that mental properties do have causal power? Here it is useful to recall the scientific analogy. The parallel point is plausible for, say, a physical property like a magnet's ability to attract iron filings and its physical base properties. Note that if a subset of the latter properties can explain the movement of iron filings towards the magnetic bar, and its magnetism supervenes on that set, we would expect that its magnetism can also explain the movement, presumably in a broadly causal sense. For one thing, the presence of magnetism reliably indicates the presence of the base properties; for another, the generalization linking magnetism to the movement of the iron supports counterfactuals, is confirmed by its instances, and has predictive power, which jointly suggest a law-like connection discoverable even apart from the supervenience relation. Here, then, a supervenient property adds explanatory power.

There is a further disanalogy to the moral case. The supervenience here is causal, or at least nomic: it is a nomic, not a conceptual, truth

[14] This implies a kind of 'privileged access', but not infallibility. For an interesting attempt to show that the relevant kind of access supports a kind of individualism about the mental, see McKinsey 1991. For a contrasting view see John Heil's 1988 case for the compatibility of privileged access and externalism.

that magnetism depends on a certain physical constitution. We would also expect a nomic relation between, say, the brain properties on which believing supervenes and the relevant beliefs.[15] In the moral case, by contrast, the supervenience relation is surely not causal or nomic: it is some kind of conceptual truth, and not a causal or nomic truth, that moral corruption depends on (indeed is in a way constituted by) such things as lying and hypocrisy. Now whatever supervenience relation obtains in the mental case is, like the physical instance, also presumably causal or nomic. Perhaps, then, the mental elements inherit causal power from the base elements, as the magnetism of iron, say, apparently inherits its causal power from the base properties in virtue of which it is magnetic. Let me develop this idea.

On the assumption that causation is a transitive relation, if certain physical events cause certain mental ones, and the latter apparently cause certain further events, both mental and physical, it would be natural to think there is a causal chain. Granted, epiphenomenalism, taken to be roughly the view that mental events are effects of physical events but causes of nothing, cannot be ruled out a priori; but its a priori implausibility is matched or exceeded by the implausibility of supposing that physical events produce events which themselves have no causal power. Indeed, there are surely no clear examples of any concrete events that have no causal power; and such models of causation as we best understand seem to involve what it is natural to call transfers of power or energy from cause to effect: think of pushing, pulling, heating, freezing, colouring, wetting, crushing, and inflating. Not only is something affected in these cases; it also acquires or at least retains causal power (not all of these relations are transitive, of course, but a non-transitive relation can imply a transitive one). When we add to this that it is partly by virtue of its content that the mental plays the role it does in explaining action, we can see how the mental might be a crucial link in any causal chain from the physical to action: through the map

[15] There is of course a dispute about whether believing does supervene on brain properties or any properties belonging to what is inside the organism. Supposing that it does not, (*a*) it might still supervene on some complex physical properties or (*b*) there might still be some partial dependence of the sort indicated here or (*c*) a kind of believing, 'narrow believing', with a crucial role in explaining certain actions might supervene on brain properties. For general discussion of this issue see Baker 1987, Horgan 1989, and (particularly for discussion of the causal power of belief even taken to have broad content) Heil and Mele 1991.

provided by their content, mental factors give direction to physical forces that, so far as we can tell, would otherwise be blind. Granted that mental factors might have no causal power apart from their non-mental bases, they might both exercise the power they derive from the latter and, in so doing, direct that power. An inheritance may not be earned, but it is owned.

It might be argued that there remains a significant disanalogy: we can describe the movement of the iron filings in the same physical vocabulary that expresses the properties on which magnetism supervenes; but we cannot, e.g., describe voting in the neural vocabulary expressing the properties on which intentional attitudes supervene. Suppose this is so. It would show that a kind of reduction of generalizations linking intentional elements to action would not be possible; it would not show either that the former have no explanatory power or that they have no causal power. Granted, one of the best ways to show that a generalization has explanatory (or causal) power is to reduce it to, or even deduce it (with suitable auxiliary assumptions) from, one already acknowledged to have it. But the impossibility of such a reduction does not imply that the generalization lacks explanatory power. The unifiability of science is not a condition for explanation in its several domains. In any case, it is surely not self-evident that there cannot be a way to describe voting in an enriched physical language—in a sense of 'describe' that does not imply that the concept of voting is itself physical. It is even further from being self-evident that there are no mental properties reducible to certain (e.g.) neurobiological ones, and in that case we would have to grant the former the same causal powers as the latter.

Since much of what is said above links causal and explanatory power, I should stress that I am not equating them. For one thing, not all explanations are causal. But causes seem by their very nature to promise some degree of explanation, at least in the sense that if one knows a cause of an event one is warranted in assuming that there is at least one pair of descriptions of the two such that citing the cause under the former can provide an explanation of the effect under the latter. Moreover, there is good reason to think that the interest of the concept of causation largely depends on this promise—together with the similarly promised predictive value of causal knowledge, a value that on some views is necessary for, and perhaps a main reason for, the relevant explanatory power. If, as I believe, mental properties have both explanatory and predictive power, this is immensely significant even if there should remain an important sense in which they lack causal power.

4. The Covering Law Problem

Nothing said so far establishes that mental events actually have causal power. To be sure, given sceptical problems about causation, perhaps there is no establishing that anything has causal power. This is one reason I have stressed the analogy between the mental and certain apparently supervenient physical explanatory properties and the disanalogy between mental and moral properties, for which the special features of their supervenience on the natural does suggest reason to doubt their having causal power. If, however, there should be broadly causal laws linking mental properties to the actions they explain, we could treat the mental as more like the physical and construe the associated explanations as backed by these laws. Let us pursue this.

It is notoriously difficult to say what constitutes a law (of nature), and not all laws are causal. Intuitively, laws are general—though not necessarily universal—propositions that are testable (in principle) and support subjunctives and counterfactuals. If there are laws to which we tacitly appeal in explaining actions, they are presumably of this sort: if an agent, *S*, wants something, *x*, and believes that *A*-ing is necessary for realizing *x* (or that it is a good way to realize *x*), then, given the ability and opportunity to *A*, *S* tends to *A*. The tendency qualification is required because there are (as is well known) inhibitors, for instance (i) wanting *y*, which *S* believes incompatible with *x*, as much or more; (ii) believing that *B*-ing would be better than *A*-ing as a way to get *x*; and (iii) believing that one lacks the ability to *A* or that one lacks the opportunity to *A*. The reference to opportunity implies that some instances of this nomic schema are mixed laws, in the sense that they essentially refer to both psychological and non-psychological (including non-behavioural) variables such as physical enabling conditions. This implies that some 'psychological' generalizations are conceptually heterogeneous; but if such generalizations pose any problem for the case made here, it should be noted that there are purely psychological instances of the schema, such as generalizations linking wants, beliefs, and thoughts to volition. This may be in part why some action theorists take volition to be basic action and construe physical actions as performed only by virtue of volition. In any case, the main question here is not whether generalizations instantiating the suggested schema are psychological, but whether they could be genuine causal laws.

One view is that this sort of generalization is analytic and hence not a candidate to be a law; another is that it is simply too imprecise to be one; and still another is that if we do not idealize scientific laws, and particularly if we take seriously models from the social sciences, then we may consider such generalizations to be a kind of law. I have defended the latter view against the former two, arguing that such generalizations have a measure of predictive power as well as much explanatory power.[16] This difficult issue cannot be reviewed here, but one point is particularly relevant: the availability of precise, universal covering laws is neither a condition on the explanation of events in general nor even a requirement on causal explanation. We may take exposure to poison ivy as an adequate explanation (and a cause) of someone's breaking out in a rash when we neither have, nor even assume there exist, precise universal laws of the kind in question, e.g. laws that specify a sufficient condition for a rash in terms of type and length of exposure to a certain sort of leaf and relative to a certain sort of skin etc., to contraction of a specific type of rash. Why should the standards for nomicity or causation be more restrictive in the mental case than they are here?[17]

If mental properties can figure in laws of a kind that (arguably) underlie our apparently successful practice of intentionalistic explanation of action, this is excellent ground for taking them to have explanatory power. I am aware of no good reason to deny them such power, and I tentatively conclude that on this point the

[16] See Audi 1973; I have replied to criticism of the view described here in Audi 1980. For a conception of physical laws that supports a view of them favourable to according nomic status to the kind of tendency generalization in question, see Hempel 1988. Interesting doubts about conceptions like mine are raised by Stephen Schiffer (1991). Some of these doubts are answered in Audi 1973, and Jerry Fodor (1991*b*) replies to others of them.

[17] Thus, I can agree with part of what Davidson says about causality: 'where there is causality, there must be a law: events related as cause and effect fall under strict deterministic laws'. See Davidson 1970/1980, p. 208. I do not see, however, why causal relations must be backed by strict deterministic laws, and this seems applicable to causal connections between mental and behavioural variables as well as to those between physical and mental variables.

common-sense view is correct. However, it is far from self-evident that even a nomically backed explanation of an event must be a causal explanation. Whether the mentalist explanations we are considering are causal is a further matter, to which I turn in the next section.

5. Intentionalistic Explanation and the Dynamics of Action

There is much plausibility in the view that only events—in the usual sense in which their occurrence entails change—are causes, or at least, only events are causes of other events. To be sure, non-events are referred to as causes: flat tyres, old age, brittleness—and beliefs, desires, and intentions—may all be cited as causes of one thing or another. But upon analysis in the context, some event usually emerges as 'the cause' more properly speaking. For example, the peeling off of the flattened tyre turns out to be the key event that caused the skid. Now although the formation of, say, a belief or want is an event, beliefs, desires, and the other main action-explaining propositional attitudes—at least the ones we think of as 'reasons'—are dispositional mental states. There is this much truth in the view that reasons are not causes. What, then, of our conclusion in Section 4, that certain generalizations linking reason-states to actions are plausibly considered laws? Are these non-causal laws?

The notion of a causal law is too vague to make a decisive answer possible. The best course here is to distinguish sustaining causation from event causation and treat the standard action-explaining generalizations, in a broad sense, as causal in virtue of expressing the former and, in a narrow sense, as non-causal in virtue of omitting the latter from their explicit scope. The word 'explicit' is important here. For just as, when a non-event is correctly cited as the (or a) cause of an event, there is some causative event to be found by suitable inspection of the context, so when a dispositional mental state is correctly cited as explaining an action, a similar causative event can be found. Indeed, dispositions surely do not produce anything without such an event, as, apart from an impact, brittleness does not produce shattering. This leads to at least two questions. Are there such triggering events in the case of the relevant mental dispositions? And if so, are these events mental? If the answer to the first question is no, then there is something odd about mental causation even as sustaining causation. If the answer to the second is no, then we have yet to find candidates for mental causes in the full-blooded sense in which causes of events—as actions surely are—are themselves events.

Regarding the first question, at least typically there are causative events to be found in the context of actions explainable by appeal to reasons. Intentions, for instance, do not execute themselves. I have a reason to telephone a prospective employer when, given my intending (and thereby wanting) to help a job candidate, I discover (hence come to believe) that the deadline is today. But the mere having of a reason for action does not produce action. I act for a reason when, say, I decide that now is a good time to get through, and have my phone ready before me and pick it up in order to fulfil my intention. Indeed, I believe that in giving intentionalistic explanations, we normally presuppose a *principle of the differential temporality of causation*, to the effect that there is an intimate relation between temporal properties of the cause or causal explainer and of the effect (where this is an event), such that the time at which the cause occurs, or the causal explainer is activated, explains why the effect occurs when it does.[18] Thus, where oily rags left inside a sunlit window burst into flames from the heat, what explains the time of their ignition is the time at which the temperature reached the kindling point for the oil. And where I telephoned because I wanted to help my candidate, what explains why it was at, e.g., 1.30 that I did so is that it was then that (in hospitable circumstances) I decided the time was right. In cybernetic terms, an intention is like a feedback system ready to be triggered; its energy is supplied by the motivational (want) component, its direction by the cognitive (belief) component, and its activation by any of a number of conscious perceptual events.

If this line of thinking is correct, then not only are reason-states sustaining causes, they are also standardly conceived as operating in connection with events that are dynamic causes: dynamic in triggering the dispositions constituted by the propositional attitudes in question and in providing both event (partial) causes of the relevant actions and (in the context) 'complete' causes (or at least causal explanations) of their occurring when they do.[19] It appears,

[18] This is a variant of the principle I proposed, under the same name, in Audi 1989, p. 128. See also Mele 1992.

[19] This phrasing of the point may suggest that there is an event distinct from the

then, that far from being epiphenomena, mental elements are in many cases sustaining causes of action and, in many others, event causal factors in their timing: in the former case they explain the action *simpliciter*, e.g. why one telephoned at all; in the latter they provide contrastive explanations that can answer the question why the action occurred at the time it did rather than some other, say why one telephoned just then rather than earlier or later.[20]

We are now ready to pursue the second question: given that the intentional sustainers do have associated triggering events, are the latter mental? That these causative events are sometimes mental has already been illustrated by the case of my *deciding* that now is the time to phone. Similarly, I might have *judged* that I must phone at the earliest time possible and *noticed* that it is now. The judging caused the formation of a dispositional state; the noticing triggered it. This triggering event might, in turn, be caused by the perceptual one: catching sight of what I take to be a free telephone.

It might be objected that the causal work in these cases is done by the physical base properties on which judging, for instance, supervenes: it is they that cause the instantiation of my telephoning. I do not deny that this causal work is done; but it does not follow that the judging itself does no causal or explanatory work. Indeed, it is not clear that my action can be explained (even just causally explained) *qua* telephoning without appeal to some mental property. This point can be brought out by noting that my telephoning might equally well be triggered by my catching sight of a free telepaphone. This is a different perceptual event having a different object; but even here the event's ability to trigger action will depend on an internal match: I must perceive the telepaphone in such a way that it satisfies my instrumental belief. What this way is will depend crucially on its perceptible properties (those with a suitable internal

agent's *A*-ing at *t*. But the claim need not be so read: the crucial point is that the fact that *S A*-ed at *t* (as opposed to some other time) can (and sometimes needs to be) be explained. Usually, it does not matter why *S A*-ed at one exact time rather than another, and it is thus not noticed that everyday explanations of actions in terms of reason-states do not normally explain this while mental event explanations of actions typically do. If mental events do explain it, this surely indicates a kind of causal power.

[20] Not just any other time can be specified; I mean the explanandum here to be stated just as it is, since I am individuating explanations finely: even if *p* and *q* are logically equivalent, it does not follow that explaining *p* is identical with explaining *q*. Presumably the standard is precisely as fine as the one that individuates why-questions, which, in turn, appears to be the one appropriate to sameness of propositional content (at least for explanations of general propositions).

sensory representation) in relation to my beliefs and conceptual framework, not its intrinsic nature. That the causal power of this perceptual event in producing my action depends on this match is a truth underlying individualism (a kind of internalism) about psychological explanation; that its causal power to put me in contact with an actual telephone (as opposed to a telepaphone) depends on its (broad) content (which depends on what it is about in the *de re*, external sense of 'about') indicates a truth underlying externalism.

There are other kinds of behavioural triggering. Musing about two incompatible options I want, such as riding to the concert with Ella and riding to it with Elbert, I might suddenly come to want one of the options more and as a result immediately pursue it. Notice that what explains why, given my plan to ride with one or the other, I ride with (say) Ella is that I wanted her company more; but what explains why I get into her car when I do is that, given my already believing that riding with her requires entering her car, I just then come to want her company more. As in the other examples, we have a sustaining cause of the action, one or more propositional attitudes expressing a reason for that action, and a dynamic trigger which is a mental factor eliciting the action at a particular time. To be sure, the usual trigger in such a case might be a thought, e.g. that I can talk to Elbert, but not Ella, later. But such a thought still works as a trigger by strengthening one want over the other; and my point is that this crucial change can occur without such a thought. It is a mental event in the sense that it is a change in one's mental condition; but it is not an ordinary intentional event, such as a judging or even the acquisition of a belief.

With the issue of covering laws in mind, one might wonder whether the dynamic mental causal relations I have illustrated are backed by laws. I see no reason to doubt this, though here we must be more speculative. Consider the generalization that when, at time *t*, *S* has the ability and opportunity to *A* and decides to *A*, *S* tends to *A*. This seems confirmed by experience; and given that normally we do not decide to *A* unless we want to *A* more than to do anything we believe incompatible with doing it, it should be expected that decisions are backed by the appropriate motivation. We do not (at least apart from weakness of will) normally decide to do something if we are not motivated, on balance, to do it. Similarly, given, at *t*, a standing intention to *A* (which typically implies wanting to *A* more than to do anything one believes incompatible with *A*-ing), if, at *t*, *S* sees an apparent opportunity to *A*, then, at *t*, *S* tends to *A*. Refinement of such generalizations is the business of both psychology and (in different ways) the philosophy of action; but commitment to something like them is a pervasive element in our standard action-explaining practices.[21]

If epiphenomenalism is the view that although mental events are effects, they do not have causal power, then the dynamic cases just described refute it. To do this, I take it, they need not even causally 'explain actions' in the usual, overall sense, i.e. explain why they occur *simpliciter*; even to explain, in the way they do, the timing of actions, i.e. why they occur when they do, would exhibit some causal power. Quite apart from such cases, however, the spirit of epiphenomenalism would be refuted by the existence of mental sustaining causes. For mental factors, even if in virtue of their supervening on physical ones, would causally matter to the course of the world and could provide explanations backed by laws. Granted, physical events, such as the removal of a barrier on which one is pushing, can also explain why one acts when one does—say begins chasing a runaway dog. But the possibility of mental factors producing action only in conjunction with certain physical elements need not be denied by defenders of the causal power of commonsense psychology. Indeed, even if there are physical triggers, mental ones may be indispensable: it may be that for every intentional action there is not only at least one reason-state as a sustaining cause, but some mental event as a causal factor, even if only a trigger.[22] Volitionalism entails the latter; but even if there need be no volitional event, there may still be an appropriate thought or judging or perception or other mental element not equivalent to volition.[23]

6. Conclusion

We have examined some grounds for doubting that mental properties have causal power, i.e. can play a causally explanatory role in broadly causal generalizations. None of these grounds

[21] Further discussion of the dynamics of action is given in Audi 1989, chap. 6.

[22] A limiting case here might be a want–belief pair's existing only at the moment of their formation and simultaneously yielding action; this would be a case in which the formation of the dispositional elements could perhaps serve as their own trigger.

[23] For a plausible recent defence of a volitionalist view see Ginet 1990.

justifies that negative conclusion. In showing this, we have stressed two major distinctions. One is between reasons as abstract contents and reason-states. The other is between sustaining causation, which may obtain between dispositional states and actions as well as between events or processes and other events or processes, and dynamic causation, which is a productive or at least eliciting relation between causative events and other events, those constituting their effects. That intentional dispositions, notably reason-states, play the first kind of role and that mental events, such as judgements and perceptions, play the second kind of role best explains the relevant data, including the apparent success of our everyday explanatory and predictive practices concerning human action. There are even presumptive laws that seem to underlie the relevant mentalistic explanations. To be sure, there are many questions about the relation between the mental and the physical which this paper does not address; the assumption of a supervenience relation between the former and the latter certainly leaves open many interesting possibilities. But if our results are correct, then the view that in some way the mental has explanatory and indeed causal power should at least be taken both as a prima-facie constraint on an overall account of the relation between the mental and the physical and as a presumption for psychological inquiry.

6

Metaphysics and Mental Causation

LYNNE RUDDER BAKER

DOES what we think ever affect what we do? The answer to this question may seem obvious: of course, having the thoughts that we have leads us to do what we do. But philosophers have recently cast doubt on the relevance of what we think to what we do. Mental causation—the causation of what we do by what we think—becomes a problem against a particular metaphysical background. My aim is twofold: first, to root out the metaphysical assumptions that generate the problem of mental causation and to show that they preclude its solution; second, to dissolve the problem of mental causation by motivating rejection of one of the metaphysical assumptions that give rise to it.

There are three features of this metaphysical background picture that are important for our purposes. The first concerns the nature of reality: all reality depends on physical reality, where physical reality consists of a network of events.[1] The second concerns the nature of causation: causation is conceived of as 'objective', a 'real relation' in nature, instances of which are independent of anyone's explanatory interests.[2] The third concerns the conception of behaviour: behavi-

I am grateful to Derk Pereboom and Hilary Kornblith for helpful conversations and critical comments. Pereboom gave patient advice on multiple drafts.

[1] Terminology is a problem in the literature. Although the term 'event' is prominent in the writings of both Donald Davidson and Jaegwon Kim, the two philosophers have in mind different things. Davidson takes an event to be a concrete particular, with a particular spatio-temporal location. Kim takes an event to be an instantiation of a property at a time. When discussing Davidson, however, Kim sometimes engages in what seems to be a hybrid use: e.g. Kim charges that on Davidson's anomalous monism, 'an event's mental properties make no causal difference' (Kim 1989*b*, p. 35). I shall follow Kim in this hybrid use. A Davidsonian may replace talk of what properties an event has by talk of what descriptions an event has. A Kimian may replace talk of events as items having properties by talk of objects.

[2] On such a view, 'every event has a unique and determinate causal history whose character is entirely independent of our representation of it' (Kim 1988*a*, p. 230).

our is to be understood in terms of events with certain kinds of internal causes.

The internal events that cause behavioural events (are thought to) have various kinds of properties, some physical and some intentional. The intentional (or mental) properties are what I shall call 'content-properties': a desire to get a beer from the refrigerator, a belief that Summer Squall will win the Kentucky Derby. As I am using the term, 'content-properties' are e.g. those properties in virtue of which beliefs are themselves true or false.[3] When we explain behaviour in terms of a person's reasons, what we cite in explanations are various content-properties—properties determined by what she believes, what she desires, and so on. In this picture, these content-properties are attributed to the person's internal events that cause the behaviour.

In the wake of these assumptions, suspicion about mental causation comes naturally: assuming that a bit of behaviour is an event caused by internal events that have content-properties (such as a belief that you left your keys on the counter), it may well be that content-properties of the cause are causally inert. To borrow an example from Fred Dretske (1989), the soprano may be making meaningful sounds when she hits the glass-shattering high C, but the meaning is irrelevant to the properties (e.g. amplitude) of the sound that causes the glass to shatter. The fear concerning mental causation is that all content-properties may be like those of the soprano's high C.

Understood against this background, the question with which we started, 'how can what we think affect what we do?', is recast as this question: 'how can content-properties of internal events be causally relevant to producing behavioural events?' The problem of mental causation is to answer this question.[4]

A widespread assumption about the nature of explanation produces a corollary to the problem of mental causation. The thesis about explanation is that an explanation of a behavioural event

[3] I am not concerned here with some alleged narrow component of beliefs.

[4] Jaegwon Kim gives an account of mental causation in terms of the intrinsic properties of the agent. Since, arguably, content-properties depend in part on the agent's embedding in an environment, content-properties seem not to be intrinsic but relational. Hence, Kim declines to include content-properties in his account—an account which he restricts to properties like having a pain: having a pain may be a supervenient cause of quickly removing one's hand from a fire. As we shall see, however, the distinction between intrinsic and relational properties is less clear than it may at first seem.

mentions a causally relevant property of an internal event that causes the behaviour. Given this thesis and the background picture, if content-properties are causally irrelevant, then they are also explanatorily irrelevant. In that case, the shattering of the glass cannot be explained by what the high C meant. Moreover, if content-properties turned out to be causally, and hence explanatorily, irrelevant to behaviour, then (again, in light of the background picture) we should conclude that reasons, identified by content-properties, have never explained anything that anyone has ever done. It would not be just that putative explanations by reasons turned out to be second-class explanations; rather, they would not be explanatory at all.

What I want to show is that, given this metaphysical picture, the problem of mental causation is insoluble.[5] We simply have no answer to the question 'How can mental events, in virtue of having mental properties, make a difference to behaviour?' because the very assumptions that generate the question render it unanswerable. Moreover, I want to show that the metaphysical assumptions with which we began inevitably lead to scepticism not only about the efficacy of contentful thought, but about macro-causation generally. But if we lack warrant for claiming that macro-properties are generally causally relevant, and if we take explanations to mention causes, then most, if not all, of the putative explanations that are routinely offered and accepted in science and everyday life are not explanatory at all. So, I shall argue, we have an impasse: we must either give up (part of) the metaphysical background picture or give up almost all explanations that have ever been offered for anything. Since the generalization of the problem to macro-causation depends only on the theses about reality and causation, I shall here neither examine the conception of behaviour as events with internal causes nor the conception of beliefs as internal states.[6] Rather, I shall focus on the theses about reality and causation, and suggest that we stick with the explanations that have proved their worth and let the metaphysical chips fall where they may.[7]

[5] Kim (1989*a*, 1989*b*) goes some distance in this direction. Although I want to extend his arguments, my motivation is somewhat different from his: whereas Kim finds the background picture attractive, I do not.

[6] I consider these conceptions of behaviour and of belief in 'What Beliefs Are Not' (in preparation).

[7] NB, the metaphysical chips will not fall into two neat piles—mental and physical.

1. The Metaphysical Background

There are two obstacles to an affirmative answer to the question 'Is the fact that an event has a content-property causally relevant to behaviour?' First, since content-properties are arguably relational properties that depend on an agent's embedding in an environment, the proponent of mental causation must show how relational properties can be causally relevant to behaviour.[8] Since this issue is already under discussion,[9] and since the other obstacle to solving the problem of mental causation seems to me both more fundamental and more intractable, I shall say nothing more about providing a causal role for relational properties. Rather, I shall focus on the second obstacle: namely, that the metaphysical background picture itself contains elements that call into question mental causation.[10]

Two metaphysical theses, both of which are parts of the background picture, generate the problem of mental causation. The first is the thesis of materialism (roughly, the thesis that every property-instantiation supervenes on physical property-instantiations), and the second is the thesis of the 'causal closure of the physical' (roughly, the thesis that every physical property-instantiation that has a cause at *t* has a complete physical cause at *t*). Let us consider the import of these theses in order to formulate them more precisely.

On the intended interpretation, the thesis of the causal closure of the physical entails that 'if we trace the causal ancestry of a physical event, we need never go outside the physical domain'.[11] I take this to mean that the occurrence of the event, and its having a particular physical property, both have sufficient causes wholly in the physical domain. Thus, for any event that has a physical property—whether

[8] For arguments that content-properties depend on environment, see Burge 1979, Van Gulick 1989, and Baker 1987.

[9] For example, see Dretske 1988 and Millikan 1989*g*. At least some relational views of content-properties have internal difficulties, I believe. See Baker 1989, 1991*a*, 1991*b*.

[10] Philosophers who are concerned with similar metaphysical issues include McLaughlin 1989, and LePore and Loewer 1989. Fodor tries to bypass these issues (Fodor 1989).

[11] Kim 1989*b*, p. 43. The discussion of non-reductive materialism borrows heavily from Kim.

or not it has mental or other properties—there are sufficient physical conditions for its occurrence and for its having all of its physical properties.

Now, what is a physical property? Often, philosophers speak as if neurophysiological properties were physical properties. But are they physical in the sense needed for the causal closure of the physical? No. If we interpreted the causal closure of the physical to imply that every neurophysiological event that has a cause at *t* has a complete neurophysiological physical cause at *t*, then the thesis would be obviously false. For not every neurophysiological event at *t* has a complete neurophysiological cause at *t*: neurophysiological laws will themselves be hedged by *ceteris paribus* clauses. 'Lower-level' phenomena at the molecular or even quantum level will interrupt neurophysiological processes that are otherwise governed by neurophysiological laws (cf. Fodor 1981*b*). So, there is no causal closure at the neurophysiological level. A system is causally closed if and only if the elements of the system interact causally *only* with other elements of the system; there is no causal influence from 'outside' the system. Since the notion of causal closure of the physical applies only at the lowest level of micro-physics, the only sense of 'physical' in which the causal closure of the physical has a chance of being true is micro-physical, where 'micro-physical' is a name for whatever turn out to be basic physical particles and their properties. So, let us formulate the thesis of the causal closure of the physical like this:

CCP Every instantiation of a micro-physical property that has a cause at *t* has a complete micro-physical cause at *t*.

Now let us turn to the thesis of materialism: every instantiation of a property supervenes on instantiations of micro-physical properties. How are we to understand the relation of supervenience? First and foremost, the supervenience relation is to be a relation of dependence or determination. On the intended interpretation, materialism is supposed to capture the idea that everything that happens depends on, or is determined by, what happens at the micro-physical level. Some philosophers have tried to formulate the relevant sense of supervenience as 'global supervenience':

GS Two possible worlds that are indiscernible in all micro-physical respects are indiscernible in all respects.[12]

[12] The usual formulations of global supervenience refer to physical, not to

But GS alone does not entail that the micro-physical determines the mental and hence by itself is insufficient to support materialism.[13] For it entails nothing about the ways that properties are distributed over individuals within possible worlds. It is consistent with GS, for example, that there be two individuals in physically similar environments within a given world who have all the same physical properties, but who differ mentally. For GS, unsupplemented by connective laws, is silent about the relation between micro-physical and higher-level (e.g. mental) properties within a given world. GS is not violated as long as all other physically indiscernible possible worlds also have two individuals who are physically alike but mentally different.[14]

Thus, GS does not even imply that an individual's mental properties (relational or not)[15] are determined by her micro-physical properties. Since what is needed for materialism is a stronger notion of supervenience, I shall adapt Kim's construal of 'strong supervenience' for the purpose of explicating Materialism:[16]

SS Necessarily, for any instantiation of any property, *F*, there is an instantiation of a micro-physical property, *G*, and, necessarily, anything that has *G* has *F*.

Although I believe that SS captures the basic idea that everything that happens is determined by what happens at the micro-physical

micro-physical, properties. But I formulate GS with reference to micro-physical properties to make GS parallel to CCP. Anyway, I believe that, for purposes of materialism, it is assumed that two worlds are physically indiscernible if and only if they are micro-physically indiscernible. For (however one construes 'physically') if two physically indiscernible worlds were micro-physically discernible, then the physical world would not encompass the micro-physical; and if two micro-physically indiscernible worlds were physically discernible, then the physical would be determined by something other than the basic micro-physical elements—i.e. the materialism would not 'go all the way down'.

[13] This point is made forcefully in Kim 1989*b*.

[14] John Post has constructed a model to show that supervenience does not entail the existence of connective laws. Granted, but without connective laws, supervenience is compatible with the falsity of 'all truth is determined by physical truth', as we have just seen. See Post 1990, 1987. Petrie (1987) has a similar example, which is criticized by John Heil 1992.

[15] The point applies whether or not mental properties are taken to be relational, as long as relational properties are construed in such a way that (e.g.) 'being in a world with *n* electrons' does not count as a relational property in the relevant sense.

[16] Kim 1984*a*. Kim defines strong supervenience as an abstract relation between families of properties, but it is unclear to me that all properties are naturally sorted out into families. (See my comment about 'levels' below.) For my purposes, I want to formulate strong supervenience as a substantive thesis about the nature of reality.

level, SS still requires some elaboration. For even if content-properties ultimately depend on micro-physical properties, they do not directly depend on micro-physical properties. Presumably, content-properties are determined by neurophysiological properties and the relations of the neurophysiological properties to other (e.g. environmental) properties, and neurophysiological properties depend on molecular biological properties, which in turn depend on chemical or physical properties, and so on down to the micro-physical level. The 'levels' metaphor makes most sense in scientific contexts. For those properties for which the 'levels' metaphor is apt, however, let us replace SS with a definition that allows for intermediate 'levels':

> SS* Necessarily, for any instantiation of a property F at level i ($i = 1, \ldots, n$), there is an instantiation of a property G at level j ($0 \leq j < i$), and necessarily, anything that has G has F; and all properties at level 0 are micro-physical properties.[17]

Since I do not think that we have a well-defined idea of 'levels' that is sufficiently general to accommodate the supervenience of all properties (e.g. the property of 'being three feet from an ocean', or of 'being a bachelor'), I prefer SS, and introduce SS* only as an elaboration.

Several features of the intended interpretation of SS deserve mention. The first four may be stated briefly. The fifth requires explanation.

1. SS is a metaphysical, not an epistemological thesis; we may never discover the relevant micro-physical properties on which higher-level properties supervene. So, SS does not imply reducibility in any epistemological sense.
2. SS does not require that *G* be a 'well-behaved' micro-physical property mentioned in the laws of fundamental physics. *G* may be hideously complex, a Boolean combination of properties that occur in the laws of fundamental physics (and their relations—see below). So, there is no assumption that the supervenience base *G* is a natural kind.
3. SS also allows for 'multiple realization' of higher-level properties: the property of being a desire to go to the beach, for example, may be realized in any number of different micro-physical properties (and their relations).

[17] The necessity required for SS* need not be as strong as metaphysical necessity. For purposes here, 'necessarily' may be read as 'it is a law that'.

4. The bearers of the micro-properties are not the same as the bearers of the macro-properties: Jill has a pain; the particles in Jill's body have spin; but Jill doesn't have spin even if the pain ultimately supervenes on the spin of the particles.[18]
5. If the bearers of the micro-properties are micro-parts of, say, medium-sized objects, then, for supervenience to hold, the micro-parts' relational properties must be included in *G*. For example, consider a ball's property of being round. This property instantiation supervenes on the properties of the ball's micro-parts; but the micro-parts' intrinsic properties do not suffice as a supervenience base for the ball's roundness. For something having micro-parts with exactly the same intrinsic properties may fail to be round, because the micro-parts have different relations to each other. For suppose that there are two qualitatively similar round balls. The object that is the mereological sum of the upper hemisphere of one ball and the lower hemisphere of the other has micro-parts with the same intrinsic properties as either of the balls, but this new object is not round. Therefore, *G* is not only a perhaps infinitely complex property, but is itself composed of relational properties. The ball's intrinsic properties supervene on its parts' intrinsic and relational properties.

So, we must admit that the micro-properties in the supervenience base *G* are relational. But from the micro-perspective, we have no distinction relevant to supervenience between the relational properties whose relata are micro-particles of the same macro-object, and relational properties whose relata are micro-particles of different macro-objects. Since the supervenience base, *G*, includes micro-particles' relations to micro-particles of different macro-objects anyway, then the macro-property *F* that supervenes on *G* may itself be a relational property. The intrinsic–relational distinction at the macro-level is simply irrelevant to the metaphysics of supervenience. For example, the ball's property of 'being three feet from the basket' supervenes on the ball's micro-parts' properties and their relations as much as the ball's property of 'being round'. Indeed, according to general relativity theory, the property

[18] On Kim's formulation, *x*'s having *F* supervenes on *x*'s having *G*, where *F* may be a macro-property and *G* a micro-property. It would be more accurate to say that *x*'s having *F* supervenes on *x*'s having parts that have *G*. Kim takes up this issue in his 1988*b*.

expressed by '*x* is three feet away from *y*' supervenes not only on the properties of the smallest spatio-temporal region that includes objects so related, but also on the distribution of matter in other parts of the universe. So, SS is comprehensive in the sense that it grounds all properties—any higher-level object's relational as well as intrinsic properties—in micro-physical properties, relational and non-relational.

In the light of these features, I believe that SS and SS* provide the weakest notion of supervenience that can underwrite materialism.[19] So, I shall take the metaphysical background picture to require CCP and SS (or SS* wherever the 'levels' metaphor is appropriate.)

2. The Problem of Mental Causation

To see how CCP and SS* generate the problem of mental causation, suppose that, at a certain auction, Jill wanted to make a bid, moved her eyebrow in a certain way and thereby made a bid. According to CCP, there is a complete micro-physical cause of Jill's eyebrow's moving—say, a brain-event's having parts with micro-physical property *p*, where *p* may be a heterogeneous disjunction of properties and their relations. Let us suppose also, via SS*, that there was a neurological event that was sufficient for her eyebrow's moving. Then, we have:

(*a*) The event that caused Jill's eyebrow to move did so in virtue of having neurophysiological property *N*.

The question is whether or not Jill's wanting to make a bid is also causally relevant to her eyebrow's moving. Assuming that (*a*) is not only true, but also gives the complete cause of the eyebrow movement, then Jill's desire to make a bid is causally relevant to her eyebrow's moving just in case the following is also true:

(*b*) The event that caused Jill's eyebrow to move did so in virtue of being a desire to make a bid.

Now, given that (*a*) is true, is there any reason to think that (*b*) is also true? We are assuming that the neurological event that sufficed for the eyebrow movement also had (or realized) the property of

[19] Even proponents of what is called 'non-reductive materialism' should endorse SS, if they are really materialists. For a defence of non-reductive materialism, see Pereboom and Kornblith 1991.

being a desire to make a bid. But, of course, it does not follow from its being a desire that it was causally relevant to the behaviour. As we have seen, not every property of an event is causally relevant to what the event causes. For suppose that later Jill gave an interview to the *New York Times*, which mentioned her desire to make a bid. As it happened, her desire to make the bid was the first event referred to on page 27 of the *Times* on 12 September 1990. Then, since her desire to make the bid had the property of being the first event referred to on page 27 in the *New York Times* on 12 September 1990, on Davidsonian views at least, the first event referred to on page 27 of the *Times* on 12 September 1990 caused Jill's moving of her eyebrow. But causal relevance concerns properties (or descriptions) of events, and no one would hold that being the first event referred to on page 27 was causally relevant to Jill's moving her eyebrow. (For one thing, the desire acquired the property of being the first event referred to on page 27 days after Jill made the bid.)[20] So, we cannot conclude that the desire was relevant to the eyebrow movement simply because the relevant neurophysiological event that produced the eyebrow movement had the property of being a desire.

So, what would entitle one to conclude that the desire to make a bid was causally relevant to the eyebrow movement? If there were a law that any instantiation of N is sufficient for a desire to make a bid, then it may be thought that Jill's desire to make a bid is causally relevant to her eyebrow movement. More generally, one could try to secure the causal relevance of the desire by invoking this principle:[21]

> P If an instantiation of property G at t is a complete cause of an instantiation of H at t' ($t' > t$), and, necessarily, any instantiation of G at t is sufficient for an instantiation of F at t, then the instantiation of F is causally relevant to the instantiation of H at t'.

Using P, we may argue as follows: by assumption, the instantiation of property N is a complete cause of the eyebrow movement;

[20] This example is a variation on the kind of example that Davidson (1970) advanced.

[21] I am adding references to times here to avoid obvious counter-examples to P in which the instantiation of G is a common cause of two later events that instantiate H and F, respectively. The need for the reference to times was pointed out by Alexander Rosenberg.

so if, necessarily, all instantiations of *N* are desires to make a bid, then, by Principle *P*, the desire to make a bid is causally relevant to the eyebrow movement. Let us assume for the moment that, necessarily, all instantiations of *N* are desires to make a bid.[22] (Such an assumption is, in fact, false since someone could be in neurological state *N* in a world without auctions or conventions for bidding, in which case the instantiation of *N* would not be a desire to make a bid. But this problem is irrelevant to the illustrative purpose of the example.) So—it may be claimed—by *P*, Jill's desire to make a bid is causally relevant to her eyebrow's moving.

However, this argument is problematic because *P* is subject to counter-examples. According to *P*, properties that intuitively are not causally relevant get counted as causally relevant. Here are a couple of examples:

(i) Suppose that a certain woman's having measles during her pregnancy was a complete cause of an instance of a birth defect, and suppose that, necessarily, anything that has measles at *t* has red spots at *t*. Then it would follow from *P* that having red spots was causally relevant to the baby's having a birth defect. In that case, it is in virtue of the mother's having red spots that the baby had a birth defect. But the only relevance of having red spots is that red spots are a symptom of measles; it is not in virtue of, or because of, the woman's having red spots that the baby had a birth defect. Symptoms are just the sorts of things that we want to rule out as having causal relevance to the effects of disease.

(ii) Suppose that Moby Dick's being a large whale at *t* was the complete cause of Captain Ahab's interest in him at *t′*, and suppose that necessarily, anything that is a whale at *t* is a mammal at *t*. Then, it would follow from *P* that Moby Dick's being a mammal at *t* was causally relevant to Ahab's interest at *t′*. Then, it would be in virtue of Moby Dick's being a mammal that Moby Dick caused Ahab to become interested in him. But, intuitively (I should check with Melville about this), Moby Dick's being a mammal played no causal role in Ahab's interest.

These examples render *P* problematic and hence not available to secure the causal relevance of Jill's desire. Given CCP, SS* and (*a*), we need some warrant for (*b*). Principle *P* looked promising, but seems subject to counter-examples. The fact (if it were a fact) that

[22] But not, of course, conversely, if we allow for multiple realization.

Jill's desire supervened on instantiations of physical properties would not be enough to show that the desire—in addition to the physical properties on which it supervened—was causally relevant to the eyebrow movement. In light of the background picture, then, we need an independent reason to think that content-properties are causally relevant.

I am not claiming that we always need a principle in order to make any distinction in a non-*ad hoc* way. We may have no line that determines when a fetus is a person, say; yet it is clear that a fertilized egg that is not yet attached to the uterine wall is not a person, and that an adult human being is a person. But there are at least two salient differences between the person case and the case of causally relevant properties, where we do require a principle. (i) There is a continuous process from the fertilized egg to the adult; but whether or not a property is causally relevant to behaviour has nothing to do with drawing a line in a continuous process. (ii) We have clear cases of adult human beings that are persons; the only problem in the person case is where to draw the line, not whether there is something on one side of it. But what is at issue in the case of the causal relevance of content-properties is not where to draw the line, but whether or not there is a line to be drawn. So, to claim that the failure of *P* calls into question the causal relevance of content-properties is not to suppose that we need some principle to warrant making every distinction.

To sum up the discussion so far: all significant versions of materialism (I think) are committed to CCP and SS; yet, given CCP and SS, there seems no way to avoid the unhappy conclusion that content-properties have never explained any behaviour, and hence that no explanation of behaviour in terms of an agent's reasons has ever been correct. We seem to be at an impasse. On the one hand, CCP and SS (or similar theses) are well-entrenched metaphysical views; on the other hand, they render the problem of mental causation insoluble.

3. From Mental Causation to Macro-causation

Before looking for ways out, let us consider the extent of our metaphysical predicament. The problem of mental causation is generated without any assumptions about intentionality, without any assumptions about the existence or non-existence of belief/

desire laws or of any psycho-physical laws, and without any assumptions about the nature of a correct theory of behaviour. All that is needed to generate the problem of mental causation are the two widely held metaphysical assumptions CCP and SS (or SS*).

In fact, the difficulty is worse than it may appear, for the problem of mental causation generalizes to a comprehensive problem of macro-causation. The idea underlying CCP and SS is that what happens at the micro-level determines everything else that happens: every instantiation of every property supervenes on an instantiation of some micro-physical property, and every instantiation of every micro-physical property (that has a cause) has a complete micro-physical cause. The general problem is this: since every property of every event supervenes on a property that has a complete cause in terms of micro-physical properties, we need some warrant to hold that any macro-physical properties are causally relevant to anything. If every instantiation of every property has a complete micro-physical cause, what room is there for macro-causation?

One may try to avoid the sceptical conclusion by holding that the explanatory success of the special sciences is itself warrant to take macro-physical properties to be causally efficacious. In the context of the purely metaphysical argument given so far, however, appeal to the explanatory success of the special sciences is to no avail. For, on the metaphysical picture, causation is metaphysically prior to explanation. So when SS and CCP call into question the causal efficacy of macro-properties, they *ipso facto* call into question the explanatory success of explanations that mention macro-properties. Given SS and CCP, the apparent explanatory success of the special sciences may well be just that: apparent, not genuine. If one wants to retain SS and CCP without scepticism about macro-causation generally, then one needs a metaphysical account that shows how macro-causation is possible.

Jaegwon Kim has offered an account of macro-causation which, he says, respects the closed causal character of the physical. The idea is that macro-causation reduces to micro-causation. If *F* and *G* are macro-causal properties, the macro-causal relation of *x*'s having *F* and *y*'s having *G* is reduced as follows: '*x*'s having *F* supervenes on *x*'s having *m*(*F*), *y*'s having *G* supervenes on *y*'s having *m*(*G*), where *m*(*F*) and *m*(*G*) are micro-properties relative to *F* and *G*, and there is an appropriate causal connection between *x*'s having *m*(*F*) and *y*'s having *m*(*G*)'.[23]

[23] Kim, 1984*b*, p. 262. According to Kim's schema, the same individual that has *F*

Let me show why I believe that this account accords no causal efficacy to macro-properties. In light of CCP and SS, what we need is a warrant for taking macro-causation to be more than a 'mere chimera'. But what Kim has provided cannot be that warrant, because causally related micro-properties have the same relation to non-causally related macro-properties as to causally related macro-properties. So, postulating causally related micro-properties on which macro-properties supervene is insufficient to establish that the macro-properties are causally related. Therefore, Kim's picture cannot account for genuine macro-causation. In greater detail, if Kim's schema for reducing macro-causation is correct, then *P′* should be true:

P′ If an instantiation of a micro-physical property *m*(*F*) is a complete cause of an instantiation of micro-physical property *m*(*G*), and necessarily, for every instantiation of *m*(*F*), there is an instantiation of *F*, and necessarily, for every instantiation of *m*(*G*), there is an instantiation of *G*, then the instantiation of *F* is causally relevant to the instantiation of *G*.

Now *P′* would allow instantiations of non-micro-physical properties to be causally relevant to instantiations of other non-micro-physical properties. But is *P′* acceptable? First, notice that all the causal work allowed by *P′* is done by instantiations of micro-physical properties. Non-micro-physical properties are deemed causally relevant by fiat. Second, *P′*, like *P*, seems susceptible to counter-examples.

Let *m*(*F*) be micro-physical properties of a certain sample of sulphur, and *m*(*G*) be micro-physical properties of the dying of a certain bush. Let *F* be an instantiation of the characteristic yellow colour of sulphur (where we assume colour to be a spectral reflectance property, not a property of experiences), and *G* be the death of a certain bush. Now suppose that the instantiation of *m*(*F*) was a complete cause of an instantiation of *m*(*G*). Then, according to *P′*, the instantiation of the yellow colour caused the death of the bush. That just seems false: although the instantiation of the yellow colour is a major clue to the cause of the death of the bush, it is a clue only because it is a sign of the presence of sulphur. Intuitively, what caused the death of the bush was the presence of sulphur; the

also has *m*(*F*). As noted above, however, the bearers of the micro-properties are not the same as the bearers of the macro-properties. This can be remedied by taking *x*'s having *F* to supervene on *x*'s having micro-parts that have *m*(*F*).

instantiation of the yellow colour was causally inert with respect to the death of the bush.

Or consider a different kind of case: suppose that a person exercising in front of a mirror jumps up and comes back down. Let $m(F)$ be micro-physical properties of the space-time region that includes the mirror and the exerciser as she goes up, and $m(G)$ be micro-physical properties of the space-time region that includes the mirror and the exerciser as she comes down; let F be some macro-properties of the reflection in the mirror as the exerciser goes up, and G be some macro-properties of the reflection of the exerciser as she comes back down. Necessarily, anything that has $m(F)$ has F, and necessarily, anything that has $m(G)$ has G. Therefore, by P', the instantiation of the properties of the reflection in the mirror as the exerciser went up caused the instantiation of the reflection's properties as she came down. But, again, intuitively, the reflection has no causal efficacy.

So, the same kinds of causal micro-processes underlie non-causal macro-processes as underlie causal macro-processes. Therefore, even assuming SS, the existence of causal micro-processes cannot provide the warrant to take macro-properties to be causally relevant to anything.

One may try to block the radically sceptical conclusion by claiming that Kim's account is not intended to allow us to infer anything about macro-causation from micro-causation; rather, the direction of fit may only go the other way. Given that we have a case of macro-causation, we can give an account of it in terms of micro-causation. However, since the problem was that CCP and SS seemed to leave no room for macro-causation, one needs a reason to believe that macro-causation exists. If the existence of micro-processes on which macro-processes supervene is compatible with the macro-processes' not being causal at all, then Kim's account is insufficient. It certainly cannot supply any warrant for taking macro-causation seriously in the face of CCP and SS.

If we need a warrant which we lack, many would counsel scepticism about the causal relevance of macro-physical properties generally. In that case, the implications for explanation are equally disastrous. For, as mentioned earlier, another background assumption is that correct explanations cite only causally efficacious properties. So, if macro-physical properties are never causally efficacious, then we also have no warrant to hold that any explanation in terms of macro-physical properties is correct.[24]

[24] In the 'one philosopher's *modus ponens* is another philosopher's *modus tollens*' vein, let me anticipate by suggesting that macro-properties generally (and content-

The conclusion that macro-properties lack causal efficacy is cognitively devastating. The same reasoning that precludes solution to the problem of mental causation leads to scepticism about explanations in the special sciences and much of physics. On the metaphysical picture, even 'the acidity of the liquid caused the litmus paper to turn pink' is unwarranted. The actual causal transaction—the 'real relation in nature'—took place at the micro-physical level. On Kim's account of macro-causation, the acidity of the liquid no more caused the litmus paper to turn pink than the smoke of the fire caused the ceiling to collapse.

Indeed, none of the paradigmatic core cases, which originally define our concept of cause, would turn out to be genuine cases of causation. (Perhaps I am not alone in considering this consequence a *reductio ad absurdum* of the metaphysical assumptions.) The irony is that philosophers take the metaphysical background picture from which CCP and SS are derived to be 'the scientific world-view'. On the contrary, the metaphysical picture seems to undermine most of science as well as almost all of common sense.

4. A Modest Proposal

We have a choice: either we give up one or more of the metaphysical theses, or we give up (almost) all of our causal understanding of the way the world works. Many philosophers think that the metaphysical picture from which the theses stem has much to recommend it. Without emphasizing (or perhaps even recognizing) the consequences of theses like CCP and SS, they think that the picture is required by a rigorous scientific outlook. I hope to have shown that not only does the picture render unwarranted any attempt to explain what we do by what we think, not only does it subvert our ordinary causal notions that are constitutive of law, morality, and everyday life, but also that it makes a mockery of the causal claims and explanations in the special sciences.

These consequences seem to me sufficient motivation to give up at least part of the metaphysical picture. But what part? Although there are three aspects of the picture—conceptions of reality,

properties specifically) are explanatory, and hence causal. To take this line is to abandon the metaphysical picture; for, as we have seen, we have no way to fit content causation and macro-causation into the metaphysical picture.

causation, and behaviour—that generate the problem of mental causation, I have focused, and shall continue to focus, only on the conceptions of reality and causation. It is not that I think that the conception of behaviour is innocent, but that the conceptions of reality and causation by themselves give rise to a comprehensive problem about macro-causation generally.

The trouble caused by the conjunction of SS and CCP can be avoided by rejecting CCP and rethinking the notion of causation. Although I believe SS to be logically consistent with my proposal, I think that it is a gratuitous bit of metaphysics whose role is primarily to fulfil a need for a totalizing thesis. I would simply point out that SS has less to do with science than with the central realist intuition, which I do not share. The intuition is that metaphysics can be done in total isolation from epistemology: we can say what, of metaphysical necessity, is the case without regard to how we might come to know it apart from metaphysical reasoning. It is doubtful that we will ever be able to ascertain the micro-physical supervenience base of macro-property instantiations generally. For example, the micro-physical properties in virtue of which the thing that I am sitting on is a chair are vast; they include not only the properties of the particles that compose the chair, but the properties of particles on which our conventions and intentions supervene. Something is a chair in virtue of the use to which it is put, the intentions of its maker, and so on, not in virtue of the properties of its constituent parts. Since I do not believe that we will ever be in a position to trace very many (if any) property instantiations to any micro-physical base, SS seems to me to be idle speculation.[25] So, let us leave SS alone and turn to CCP, which is the real culprit for causation.

CCP is founded on the idea that causation is an 'objective relation' between events in the following sense: 'that it is instantiated does not entail anything about the existence or non-existence of any intentional psychological state—in particular, an epistemological or doxastic state—except, of course, when it is instantiated by such states' (Kim 1988*a*). This seems to me an unacceptably narrow characterization of causation. On this view,

[25] Indeed, SS suggests an inverse of the Great Chain of Being. Whereas in the original Great Chain of Being, the 'higher' in the chain the greater the degree of reality; in the contemporary Great Chain of Being, the 'lower' in the chain, the greater the degree of reality.

'taking a deduction for the office in your home caused you to be audited by the IRS', would seem to be false. For the relata do entail that there are intentional psychological states, yet the relation is not instantiated by any such states. For example, if no one ever had had any intentional psychological state, 'being audited by the IRS' would not denote anything, but neither your being audited by the IRS, nor the relation between deducting your home office and being audited by the IRS, is instantiated by anybody's intentional psychological state.

There are endless further examples of intuitive causal connections that seem unproblematic and that are not instantiated by intentional psychological states, yet are not wholly independent of anybody's having epistemological or doxastic states either: Smith's failing French caused him to be ineligible to play NCAA Division I basketball; Milken's purveying of junk bonds weakened the US economy. None of these events—failing French, being ineligible to play NCAA Division I basketball, purveying junk bonds, or weakening the US economy—nor the relations between them, are instantiated in any intentional psychological state; yet, they could not occur if there were no intentional psychological states.[26] Therefore, on the conception of causation that underwrites CCP, the claim that there is a causal relation between, say, Smith's failing French and his ineligibility, is false. Since intuitively there is a causal connection, I do not think that the conception of causation that underwrites CCP is what we want anyway. So, let us reject that conception.

How, then, are we to understand causation? My suggestion is to take as our philosophical starting-point, not a metaphysical doctrine about the nature of causation or of reality, but a range of explanations that have been found worthy of acceptance. These include, pre-eminently but not exclusively, scientific explanations. They also include commonplace explanations that explain the phenomena that we encounter in everyday life—answers to questions like: 'Why is the traffic so snarled today?' 'Why is General Sherman's statue so shiny?' 'Why didn't you bring more beer?'[27] Construing explanations as answers to 'why' questions, with

[26] Eliminative materialists like Stich (1983) recognize that intentional action is as much at stake as belief and desire.

[27] For a defence of the explanatory worth of such explanations, see Baker (1987) and 'The Cognitive Status of Common Sense', in preparation.

perhaps some constraints on what can count as an adequate answer, my proposal is to begin with explanations that earn their keep, rather than with the metaphysics, which seems to me a freeloader that just interferes with real work.

Let me suggest that causes are the sorts of things that are cited in explanations of events. Let us understand '*c* caused *e*' in this (loose and intuitive) way: (i) If *c* had not occurred, then, other things being equal, *e* would not have occurred, and (ii) given that *c* did occur, then other things being equal, *e* was inevitable (cf. Haugeland 1983). Whether one thing caused another, then, depends on what 'other things' get held constant; and in different explanatory contexts, it is appropriate to hold different 'other things' constant.

If we put aside the metaphysical picture and begin with the explanations that work, causation becomes an explanatory concept. This presents a sharp contrast to the metaphysical picture, which subordinates explanation to causation, where causation, in turn, is conceived as an 'objective relation' in nature. According to the metaphysical picture, causal power flows 'upward'—to put it metaphorically (how else can it be put?)—from subatomic particles through atoms and molecules through simple organisms through intermediate configurations up to persons with beliefs and other intentional states. There is no 'downward' causation. In the metaphysical picture, the font of all causality remains at the bottom.

If we reverse the priority of explanation and causation that is favoured by the metaphysician, the problem of mental causation just melts away. We began with the question: Does what we think ever affect what we do? Then, in light of the metaphysical picture, the question was recast as this: How can content-properties of internal events be causally relevant to producing behavioural events? With the reversal of priority of cause and explanation, the metaphysical version of the question just does not arise, and the original question has an easy answer. For example, when Jill returns to the bookstore to retrieve her keys, what she thinks is that she left her keys on the counter and that she wants them back. What she thinks affects what she does in virtue of the following explanatory fact: if she hadn't thought that she had left her keys, then, other things being equal, she wouldn't have returned to the bookstore; and given that she did think that she had left her keys, then, other things being equal, her returning was inevitable.

If we take our ontological cue from our successful explanatory and predictive practices, then, admittedly, we end up with an ontological hodgepodge: statements concerning statutory laws, social roles, political, economic, and biological facts, as well as reasons, find their way into successful explanations and predictions. We make our reductions where we can, but on my proposal, we do not hold successful explanations hostage to ultimate assimilation into science. Unity is merely desirable, not inevitable.

My proposal, then, is to dismantle the problem of mental causation by rejecting the metaphysical background picture that generates it. If we accept paradigm cases of explanation in the sciences and in everyday life, and if we take the notion of explanation to be prior to that of causation, then the idea of a 'complete cause' in CCP hardly makes sense.

What we are left with is not dualism, nor materialism, nor any other comprehensive metaphysical doctrine. These doctrines do not earn their keep. Explanations do, in particular, explanations of what we do in terms of what we think. We could have almost none of the kinds of institutions and interactions that we have without such explanations. As for psychology, our relaxed attitude places no a priori constraints on the taxonomy of psychology. Indeed, different psychological theories, equally well-confirmed, may have different taxonomies, and thus systematize and explain different ranges of reality. Systematic explanatory success, in either science or everyday life, stands in need of no metaphysical underpinning.

5. Conclusion

Given standard metaphysical and methodological assumptions, not only has the problem of mental causation proved to be intractable but even worse: the same reasoning that leads to scepticism about mental causation also leads to scepticism about almost all supposed 'upper-level' causation, and hence to scepticism about explanations that mention 'upper-level' properties, including explanations offered by the special sciences and much of physics. Of course, pointing out such sceptical conclusions, even of this magnitude, is not a refutation of the metaphysical assumptions that generate them. But sceptical consequences may well be a motivation for taking a different philosophical tack.

Much of contemporary philosophy simply assumes the adequacy

of a metaphysical picture, and then takes the task of philosophers to be to determine what fits in and where it belongs in the picture. (We get all the news that fits.) Anything that resists such packaging is deemed unreal or illusory. But who said that reality had to be tidy? My proposal is to perform a methodological about-face. Instead of beginning with a full-blown metaphysical picture, we should begin with a range of good explanations, scientific and commonsensical. In the spirit of G. E. Moore, I think that our grounds for the claims that reasons sometimes explain behaviour are much stronger than any grounds for a metaphysical premiss that would lead to a contrary conclusion. And I am equally confident that our grounds for claims that macro-physical properties sometimes explain events and their properties are much, much stronger than any grounds of a metaphysical picture that would lead to a contrary conclusion.

Although my proposal has a strong pragmatic cast, it is by no means an anti-realist suggestion. I am not equating what is real with what is needed for explanations and predictions. The point is, rather, that we have no better access to reality than what is required for cognitive success, construed broadly enough to include what is cognitively required for achieving goals in both science and everyday life. Start with successful explanatory practices and let the metaphysics go. At least, we can avoid the insoluble problem of mental causation.

7

Mind–Body Causation and Explanatory Practice

TYLER BURGE

In recent years a number of philosophers have worried about whether we can reasonably believe that mental properties are causally efficacious. They are concerned whether the intentional 'aspects' or qualitative 'aspects' of mental events are epiphenomenal—that is, lacking in causal power and irrelevant to causal transactions. They typically assume that mental events themselves are causes. But this is supposed to be ensured by the prior assumption that mental events are physical events. Individual mental events are assumed to be instantiations or tokens of physical event-kinds. The doubt is whether the mental 'aspects' of these states and events play any significant role in causal processes.

I think that these worries can be met within the materialist metaphysical framework in which they arise. I will say a little about what I think is wrong with some of the more prominent sorts of argument that lead to epiphenomenalism. But what interests me more is the very existence of the worries. I think that they are symptomatic of a mistaken set of philosophical priorities. Materialist metaphysics has been given more weight than it deserves. Reflection on explanatory practice has been given too little. The metaphysical grounds that support the worries are vastly less strong than the more ordinary grounds we already have for rejecting them.

I shall first outline the worries about epiphenomenalism, and identify some of the weak spots in the arguments for them. Then I shall explain why I think that the starting-point for the worries is itself dubious. Finally I shall generalize a little about the misguided priorities (as I see them) that engender these worries.

I am grateful to Ned Block for several suggestions.

1

The picture that leads to the worries about epiphenomenalism begins with a plausible idea. It is that certain non-intentionally described states or events that 'underlie' mental states and events participate in causal processes that are instances of physical laws that do not mention mentality. I want to leave open what 'underlie' is to mean here. I will assume, however, at least that mental states and events would not occur if some 'underlying' physical states and events did not occur. There are no gaps in these physical chains of events. So, for example, there are underlying, gapless neural processes that are instances of laws of neurophysiology; and the mental events would not occur if some such processes did not occur. I have no serious doubts about this view.

These physical states and events are usually thought to 'underlie' the mental states and events in a more specific sense. They are held to be token-identical with them. I do not accept this materialist claim. But it is widely accepted, largely because of its supposed virtues in clarifying mental causation. From the time of Descartes it has often been thought that there is some mystery in how mental and physical events can interact. This and other materialist views purport to dispel the mystery by holding that there is only one sort of causation—a relation between physical events. In this section, I will accept this ontology, though only for the sake of argument.

The worry about epiphenomenalism arises by considering that some properties of events (or states) are relevant to their causal relations, while others are not. The property of being the third large explosion in a given county during the last ten years may be irrelevant to that explosion's causing certain damage, whereas the heat of the explosion would be relevant. The question is whether mentalistic properties are causally efficacious, or whether mentalistic descriptions of properties are relevant to understanding causation. Many philosophers have developed more confidence in the causal efficacy of the underlying neural properties than in that of the 'intentional aspects' of mental events. If those neural processes are going on, the body's movements, and hence what we count as behaviour, will depend on the properties of those processes. The intentional or phenomenal 'aspects' of the mental events might, they think, be irrelevant or at best quite derivative and indirect—epiphenomenal on the real underlying causal processes.

A comparison of mental properties to properties like phenotypes in biology is typical. There are regular, even—assuming richly filled-in background conditions—loosely nomological, relations between the phenotypes of parents and phenotypes of their immediate offspring. But the phenotypes of the parents are causally inefficacious in producing those of their offspring. The real causal efficacy derives from the parental genotypes. Some philosophers appear to be seriously concerned that intentional kinds are, like phenotypes, part of a nomologically describable system, but not causally efficacious in their own right.

What motivates these worries? Broadly and crudely speaking, it is the picture that the underlying processes are occurring anyway and that the mental events really derive their causal efficacy from the physical properties which are the real agents of causation. This picture leads to the idea that the mental properties are superfluous. Even if the mental properties were not separable from the physical properties (because they necessarily supervened on them), they would be in a sense along for the ride, since the primary mechanisms of causation are located in the underlying physical properties.

Let us cast this sort of motivation into an argument. One could assume: (*A*) that mental event-tokens are identical with physical event-tokens; (*B*) that the causal powers of a physical event are determined only by its physical properties; and (*C*) that mental properties are not reducible to physical properties. From these assumptions, it may seem to follow that a mental event's mental properties play no role in determining its causal powers.

Here is another argument for the picture: Assume (*a*) that the world of physical events and properties is a complete and closed system, in the sense that physical events can be caused only by virtue of physical properties of other physical events; (*b*) that mental properties are not reducible to physical properties. It may again seem to follow that no physical events can be caused by virtue of mental properties, even if these mental properties are properties of physical events. The argument does leave open the possibility that mental properties of mental events are causally efficacious with respect to other mental properties of mental events. But if mental causation has no outlet among physical events, it is surely a peculiarly limited sorted of causation.[1]

[1] For a discussion of such arguments with which I have some sympathy, see

Let us begin with the first argument. As is common in arguments for epiphenomenalism, the key phrases leave much clarity to be desired. 'Is determined by' is a case in point. It could mean 'supervenes on', 'is explained by', or 'is individuated by'. For reasons that will emerge, I need not choose among these readings. (*B*) is problematic on all of them.

It is also not clear what is to be included in the notion of a physical property. In particular, it is unclear whether various relations to the environment count among the physical 'properties'. If they do not, the premiss is difficult to defend. I will assume that a very broad notion of physical property is intended—one that encompasses relations to the environment which are described in non-mentalistic, non-intentional terms.

The fundamental unclarity lies in the notion of causal power.[2] The causal powers of a kind of event are to be understood in terms of the patterns of causation that events of that kind enter into. Such patterns are identified as explanatory in causal explanations. And the properties that 'determine' the causal powers of an event are those that enter into causal explanations. The second premiss is plausible only insofar as one considers the causal powers of a physical event to be got only through patterns of properties described in the physical sciences, or in other common-sense explanations in physical terms. The sense in which only physical properties determine the causal powers of a physical event is just that within the patterns of causation described in the physical sciences and common-sense physicalistic discourse, physical properties suffice to provide a basis for the existence and understanding of the causal powers of physical events; and no other properties enter in. Both the chains of causation and the patterns of explanation are in no need of supplementation from outside the realm of physical properties or physicalistic discourse. This is a tempting and plausible interpretation of the second premiss. But on this interpretation the conclusion will not follow.

If physical events have mental properties, one is not entitled to the view that only physical properties (properties specified in the

Robert Van Gulick, 'Who's in Charge Here? And Who's Doing All the Work?' (this volume, Chap. 13). My criticisms of these arguments differ from his, but are for the most part compatible.

[2] Cf. my 1989*a* for a detailed account of my understanding of causal power.

physical sciences or in ordinary physicalistic discourse) determine all the causal powers of a physical event (as opposed to merely all the causal powers associated with physicalistic explanations of the physical event), unless one can show that mentalistic explanation is either non-causal or fails to describe patterns of causal properties. For the causal powers of a physical event that is mental might include possible effects that are specified in mentalistic explanation. No one has shown that mentalistic explanation is either non-causal or non-descriptive. Nor is either view plausible.

Normally we consider an entity's causal powers relative to the kind in terms of which the entity is specified. For example, in asking for the causal powers of the heart, we implicitly expect physiological patterns of properties to be cited. We do not expect citation of powers that would be studied by physics. Pumping blood is usually considered relevant; squashing a bug if dropped from a ladder is not. If we were to specify the heart as a physical object of such and such physical dimensions, the latter property would seem relevant. The second premiss (*B*) of the argument attracts an interpretation that is plausible but insufficient for the argument because the mental events are specified as physical. Then mental properties seem irrelevant to its causal powers. But if it is specified as mental ('What are the causal powers of a thought that it is raining?'), the idea that only properties specified in the physical sciences are relevant to determining the causal powers seems outlandish. Thus one cannot just take the second assumption of the argument as a generalized self-evident metaphysical principle.[3] Interpreted in a way that leaves the argument valid, the premiss is either false or question-begging.

[3] Sometimes the second premiss is stated, 'The causal powers of a physical event are *completely* determined by its physical properties'. This premiss has substantially the same difficulties as the one I discuss. This premiss is, however, weaker in that it allows the possibility that although the physical properties completely determine the causal powers of a physical event, mental properties may also play a role in determining those powers. To complete the argument, one needs a premiss excluding 'over-determination'. Issues about 'over-determination' are fairly similar to those that I am discussing. I might say, however, that I find the term extremely misleading inasmuch as it assimilates different levels or ranges of causal interaction to ordinary cases in which (say) physical causes occur simultaneously and each is sufficient unto itself for their common effect. There are deep differences in the two cases.

I might add here that in all these arguments, a materialist must have some explanation for regarding mental properties as material in character. Their existence must not be seen as incompatible with the materialism. I think that this is not an easy problem, but there are various solutions that seem to satisfy many materialists. And since I am accepting materialism in this section for the sake of argument, I shall not pursue the matter.

Let us turn to the second argument. Problems with the second argument lie in the first premiss, (*a*). The claim that physical events can be caused only by virtue of physical properties of other physical events has problems entirely analogous to those that beset the first argument. The existence of a closed system reflects a pattern of causal relations and of causal explanation that needs no supplementation from the outside. There are no gaps. It does not follow from this that such a system excludes or overrides causal relations or causal explanation in terms of properties from outside the system. Indeed, if it did follow, as has often been pointed out, there would be no room for causal efficacy in the special sciences, even in natural sciences like chemistry and physiology. For there is no gap (other than perhaps quantum gaps) in the causal relations explained in terms of the properties of physics. But few are tempted by the idea that physical events cannot be caused in virtue of physiological properties of physical events.

Is the causal efficacy of properties cited in chemistry and physiology dependent on the reducibility of the properties cited in these fields to those cited in physics? That seems almost equally outlandish. It is a wide-open empirical question whether properties of these special sciences are reducible to those cited in physics. In fact, it seems very unlikely that general reduction is possible. The causal relevance of the properties of these special sciences seems independent of questions of reducibility.

Weaknesses in the foregoing arguments are widely known. But there remains a sense of unease. Many seem disturbed by the picture of mental properties supervening on physical properties and just going along for the ride. Thus there have been various attempts to state what kind of supervenience relations would 'allow' mental properties to be causally efficacious even though they supervene on physical properties (Kim 1984*b*, Sosa 1984).

These projects can be interesting. But in my view, the worries about epiphenomenalism have an air of make-believe. It is much surer that epiphenomenalism is false than that the various assumptions (even including the materialist assumptions) that have been thought to lead to it are true. It is also much surer that epiphenomenalism is false than that the various attempts to show it false or avoidable by appeal to counterfactuals, accounts of laws, or supervenience, are true. Epiphenomenalism is often taken as a serious metaphysical option. But it is better seen as at best a source of pressure for clarifying our common conceptions. It is rather like one of the less plausible scepticisms, which can be used as an instrument for philosophical clarification, but which has little real persuasive force. I think that a different, less metaphysical attitude in thinking about the problem would be more realistic and fruitful.

The irony is that by trying to clarify mentalistic causation, many materialists have come to believe that there is a serious metaphysical issue whether mentalistic characterizations have any causal relevance at all. I think that this is tantamount to admitting that materialism has failed to illumine mental causation. But such illumination has been advertised as materialism's chief selling-point. Although materialism is not forced to accept epiphenomenalism, the very fact that the view is taken so seriously as a metaphysical option suggests that something has gone wrong in the search for clarification.

One cannot understand mentalistic causation (causation involving mentalistic or intentional properties) and mental causal powers by concentrating on properties characterized in the physical sciences. Our understanding of mental causation derives primarily from our understanding of mentalistic explanation, independently of our knowledge—or better, despite our ignorance—of the underlying processes. Materialist accounts have allowed too wide a gap between their metaphysics of mental causation and what we actually know about the nature and existence of mentalistic causation, which derives almost entirely from mentalistic explanations and observations.

2

So far I have not questioned the materialist metaphysics that helps ground the worries about epiphenomenalism. In this section I want to advance reasons for doubting the most common form of materialism and its centrality in understanding mental causation.

There is certainly reason to believe that underlying our mental states and processes are physical, chemical, biological, and neural processes that proceed according to their own laws. Some such physical processes are probably necessary if intentional (or phenomenal) mental events are to be causes of behaviour. They seem necessary even for the mental events to exist. But, in my view, the nature of the relation between mental events and these physical processes is thoroughly unclear. The most widely accepted account of the relation is the materialist token-identity theory.

Some years ago I gave an argument against a significant version of the materialist token-identity theory (Burge 1979, pp. 109–13). The version I had in mind holds that each mental-state instance and event-token is identical with a physical-state instance or event-token that instantiates a physical natural kind specified in some actual natural science, or specifiable in some reasonable extension of the natural sciences as we now know them. Different mental event-tokens of the same mental event type may be tokens of different physical natural kinds.

The requirement that the physical event-token instantiate a physical kind specifiable in a natural science (physics, chemistry, biology, neurophysiology, and so on) is meant to ensure that the materialist utilize a non-question-begging identification that is not only uncontroversially physical, but plays some role in explanation of physical causation. I think that there are materialist views that are less committal than this one. My argument does not defeat these views. I shall remark on some of them later.

The argument against this sort of token-identity theory is partly based on Twin Earth thought experiments that I shall presume are familiar.[4] According to these thought experiments, it is possible for a person's body, considered in isolation from its relations to the environment, to be physiologically and molecularly the same even if the person were to think thoughts that have different intentional content. The difference in content depends on dif-ferences in the individual's historical relations to his or her environment. For example, it is possible for a person who has borne some historical relation (perhaps through vision or interlocution) to aluminium or arthritis to think that aluminium is a light metal or that arthritis is a painful disease, even though the person has no dispositions that would enable him to discriminate aluminium or arthritis from all other actual or possible metals or diseases—except by thinking of it as aluminium or arthritis. Counterfactual environments are possible in which one of these other 'look-alike' metals or diseases plays the

[4] Burge 1979, 1982*a*, 1986*b*, 1986*c*, 1989*b*. The thought experiments use the methodology set out in Putnam 1975*a*.

same role in the acquisition and production of thoughts that aluminium and arthritis actually do. In such counterfactual environments the person might, for all intents and purposes, have a body that is a chemical and physiological duplicate of the actual person's body. Yet the person would be thinking thoughts with different content. The person would not be thinking that aluminium is a light metal or that arthritis is a painful disease.

I shall take it for granted that these thought experiments are sound, as so far described. The first premiss of the argument against the token-identity theory is strongly suggested (though not entailed) by the thought experiments:

(1) It is possible for a person to think thoughts with different contents even though all event-tokens that occur in the individual's body, that are plausible candidates for identification with mental events, and that are specifiable by physical sciences such as physics, chemistry, and neurophysiology, are the same.

The second premiss is less specifically related to the thought experiments:

(2) No occurrence of a thought could have a different intentional content and be the very same token-event or event-particular.

Now take any physical event-token *b* in the individual's body that is a plausible candidate for being identical with the individual's occurrent thought (mental event-token) *a* that aluminium is a light metal (or that arthritis is a painful disease). By (1), there are possible situations in which the same token *b* occurs, but in which there occur only thoughts (mental event-tokens) with different intentional content. By (2), none of these thought occurrences is the very same token event as *a*. So since *b* could occur without *a*'s occurring, *b* cannot be identical with *a*.

This argument has been criticized by Donald Davidson. Davidson accepts the second premiss, calling its denial 'not merely implausible but absurd. If two mental events have different contents, they are surely different events.' He does not squarely confront the first premiss. But he appears to reject it. He thinks that the relevant thought experiments show that 'people who are in all relevant respects similar . . . can differ in what they mean or think. . . . But of course there is *something* different about them, even in the physical world; their causal histories are different.'[5]

I find this response unconvincing. There certainly are physical differences between actual and counterfactual situations in the relevant thought experiments. The question is whether there are always physically different entities that are plausible candidates for being identical with the different mental events or state-instances. The different physical causal histories are not plausible candidates. These histories do not have the same causes or effects that the relevant mental events (states) do. Moreover, it is doubtful that relevantly described causal histories instantiate explanatory natural kinds in any of the physical sciences.

One might think that since, in the counterfactual situation, there are differences at least in the remote causal ancestry of every relevant physical event in the individual's body, every such event would be a different event-token from any event-token in the actual situation. Events are, on this view, different just by virtue of having some difference in their causal histories.[6] But this seems an extremely implausible view of event identity. It seems to me clearly possible to consider the same event-token in an individual's body in a counterfactual situation, without being committed to the view that every event in the causal ancestry of that event, however remote, remains token- (or type-) identical. Much counterfactual reasoning about events depends on not being so inflexible. We frequently talk about a particular event under counterfactual suppositions in which it is not assumed that every prior event in the history of the world that is causally linked with it is the same.[7]

[5] The quotations are from Davidson 1986, p. 452. Davidson has helpfully confirmed his rejection of premiss (1) in private communication.

[6] This may be a consequence of Davidson's criterion for individuating events; cf. Davidson 1969. But since the criterion is not formulated modally, it is not clear that Davidson intends to apply the criterion in all counterfactual situations. He does, however, consider at least one counterfactual situation in discussing it.

[7] Davidson (1986, pp. 451–3) concedes that events in the individual's body can be type-identical in the relevant actual and counterfactual situations. But he gives no reason for thinking that events in the individual's body cannot be token-identical—the same individual events—between actual and counterfactual situations.

There is an unexplained suggestion, p. 453, that he thinks that 'essentialist' assumptions might be playing a role in my argument. I do not mind being committed to some types of essentialism. But my argument does not depend on essentialism. All modal claims (including the one in the second premiss) can be interpreted as supported by the best available methods of individuation. In the first premiss I have not made a claim about essence or necessity at all, only one about possibility. To counter this claim, Davidson would have to appeal to a certain impossibility. He

Suppose I get my thoughts about aluminium from reading books. In the counterfactual situation I see identical-looking print. The salient difference lies at the end of a long causal chain: the counterfactual chain goes back to some other metal; the actual one goes back to aluminium. On the view we are considering, every event in the two chains must be different, a different particular. So the physiologically characterized events in my brain caused by reading the print cannot be token-identical in the two cases. What is objectionable about this view is that it makes the individuation of brain events depend on matters that are irrelevant to the physiology of the brain. I know of nothing in our explanatory practices that would support such a metaphysical view.

As far as I can see, in numerous cases it is possible for all physical (token-) events that are candidates for identification with intentional mental events to remain the same in counterfactual situations while the relevant mental events, the thoughts, differ. I do not see the slightest plausibility in the idea that there are always physical events — identifiable with the mental events and specifiable in the natural sciences—whose identity will, under all possible counterfactual circumstances, vary exactly when the mental events vary. At any rate, objections of the sort Davidson raises need to show, in the light of the thought experiments, what differences in physical events might plausibly be token-identical with the different mental events.

There is another element in Davidson's resistance to my argument. He holds that an appreciation of the external factors that enter into our common ways of identifying mental states does not discredit a token-identity theory. He cites sunburn as an example of a state whose identification is environmentally dependent. Davidson thinks, plausibly, that a particular sunburn is token-identical with a particular state of the skin. And he thinks that mental states and events are broadly analogous to sunburn.

would have to deny that it is possible that an event could be the same token event if, counterfactually, its causal ancestry differs in any of the ways needed to yield different thoughts. This denial would itself seem to me to suggest an extreme form of essentialism about individual events. It suggests that the entire causal ancestry of an event is always part of the essence of that event. The denial could be reparsed in terms of methods of individuation (cf. above), but it seems to me to have no support in our actual explanatory practices. Davidson does think that events are the same if and only if they have the same causes and effects (cf. note 8). But for the present purposes, he needs to hold that it is impossible for an event to have been the same if it had had any differences in causal history. As far as I know, he has not defended this modal thesis. I suspect that it is indefensible.

I think the sunburn example irrelevant to my argument. My argument does not claim that no non-individualistically characterized states or events can be identified with states or events in the individual's body. It claims only that some mental states and events cannot be.[8] The state of being sunburned is, I agree, token-identical with a physiologically specifiable state (instance) of the skin. But the state of being sunburned is relevantly unlike a state of belief, or a thought-event. In the first place, we know how to identify sunburned states of the skin in systematic and explanatory ways that are completely independent of the fact that they are sunburns. That is part of what makes plausible the identification of a sunburn with a physiological state of the skin. We can see the effect of the sun on the skin, and give a chemical or physiological account of that effect. Significantly, this account need not make any assumptions about whether a celestial body caused that effect. We have no such ways of identifying states of the body that (putatively) are beliefs, independently of assumptions about the beliefs. I think that this difference reflects our ignorance of the relation between beliefs and states of the body. It is not incompatible with an identity theory, but it renders questionable the easy analogy to cases where identities are obvious.

In the second place, the analogue of my argument would not work for sunburns in the way the argument works for thoughts. The analogue of the first premiss seems true for sunburn. That is, the very same (instance-identical) state of the same skin, specifiable in physiological terms, could (metaphysically could) have been caused by something other than the rays of the sun. This seems true because there are uncontroversial and obvious ways of identifying sunburns with physiologically specifiable states (state-instances) of the skin. These specifications are deeply explanatory and seem to be

[8] Davidson (1986, p. 452) says I may make the mistake of thinking that the thought experiments by themselves are incompatible with the token-identity theory. His further discussion seems to suggest that I do make this mistake. I have never thought this, and I have never written anything that entails it. In a later paper (Davidson 1989), he says that the argument behind my denial of the token-identity theory 'assumes that if a state or event is identified (perhaps necessarily, if it is a mental state or event) by reference to things outside of the body, then the state or event itself must be outside the body, or at least not identical with any event in the body'. I do think that certain mental events that are necessarily individuated by reference to things outside the body are not identical with any event in the body describable via kind terms of the physical sciences. But I have never taken this view as an assumption. I have argued for it. Davidson's discussion does not go to the heart of our disagreement. What follows should make the point clearer.

individuatively relevant. Yet they do not presume anything about those states' deriving from the sun's rays.[9]

On the other hand, the analogue of premiss (2) seems to fail for sunburn. I think that we have no grounds to think that if a physiologically specifiable state (instance) of the skin had not been a sunburn, it would have been impossible for it to have been the same state (instance) as one that is. Again, our ability to identify states of the skin with sunburns and fit them into a systematic, individuatively relevant scheme of explanation that prescinds from anything about the sun supports this view. The kind *sunburn*, by contrast, fits into a much less systematic, informative, and important explanatory scheme—if it fits into any such scheme at all. Its claim to individuate state-instances across counterfactual situations is far less strong than the physiological scheme. Similarly, its claim to provide a fundamental form of individuation (as premiss (2) claims for intentional contents) is substantially less strong than the claim of mental kinds. The failure of analogy, in these respects, between sunburn and thoughts makes the example incapable of undermining my argument.

Whereas Davidson doubts premiss (1) of the argument, some token-identity theories have been taken as denying premiss (2). It is common to hold that intentional states and events can be type-identified with functional states and that these states could be realized by a variety of physical states or events. The realizing physical states and events are supposed to be instance- or token-identical with the mental states or events. This view does not entail a denial of (2). But it is usually also assumed, at least implicitly, that the identity of the underlying physical states and events is

[9] In my view, therefore, the sunburn example does not line up very well with Davidson's criticism of my argument—since he wishes to deny premiss (1). Davidson very likely denies that the analogue of (1) holds for sunburn. Cf. his 1986, pp. 451–5, where he concedes only that the state of the skin might remain type-identical. But he gives no reason for holding that an instance-identical state of the skin could not have been caused by anything other than the sun. Perhaps he thinks that states are analogous to events in (necessarily) being instance-identical only if they have the same causes (cf. note 6). But I see no metaphysical or even physiological impossibility in thinking of a given state-instance as having been arranged by light rays with exactly the same physical powers and vectors as the sun's which, however, did not emanate from the sun. Whether Davidson holds the analogue of premiss (2) for sunburn is unclear to me. It appears, however, that he probably would hold that no state-instance of a sunburn could be caused by something other than the sun and be the very same state-instance. As noted below, I find this implausible.

independent of their exact functional role in a given system. If this is assumed, then this sort of theory would be committed to denying (2).

Such a theory seems very unpromising. There is little in our explanatory practice to encourage identification of intentional mental types with non-intentionally specified functional types.[10] The identification of intentional mental tokens with tokens specified in the natural sciences has, I think, even less clear support in explanatory practice. But what I want to centre on is the main reason for accepting (2).

The system of intentional content attribution is the fundamental means of identifying intentional mental states and events in psychological explanation and in our self-attributions. In fact, we have no other systematic way of identifying such states and events. Davidson holds that (2) is intuitively obvious and denials of it are absurd. I agree. But I think that it can also be justified by noting that it is our only way of individuating intentional mental events that provides systematic understanding, description, and explanation of mental events and intentional activity. Such cognitive practices are our most reliable way of knowing the nature of what exists.

I know of no plausible or even serious arguments against (2).[11] But failure to hold it firmly in mind is a major source of the misguided worries about epiphenomenalism. In so far as one allows oneself to think that intentional contents are only contingently associated with a thought-event, one is in a position to imagine that one can hold constant a neural event supposedly identical with a mental event, while imagining the mental/physical event to have a different content. Supposing that the causal laws connecting the neural processes are sufficient for their effects, one is led to wonder wherein the intentional properties are causally relevant. This conceit can naturally be seen to lie behind the view that the intentional content of mental states and events is a mere epiphenomenal 'aspect' of those events—the view that I noted in the first paragraph of this paper.

[10] For a recent discussion of reasons for this charge, cf. Putnam 1988.

[11] I have heard it suggested that although (2) is not true, it is true that there could not be two events that are mentally the same if they had different contents. (2) is still denied because the same physical event could allegedly be identical with a mental event that had one content, in the actual situation, or with a mental event that had another content, in the counterfactual situation. It is not the same thought content, but it is the same thought/neural event. This subtlety does not seem to me to count for much in defending opposition to (2). The remarks in the preceding paragraph still seem to apply.

But in fact, such content is the explanatory and identificatory centre of those events. We have little else to go on in talking about the causal powers and ontology of the mental. Systematic, informative, important explanatory schemes—like our mentalistic one—usually (there are special cases) make the strongest claim for providing individuating descriptions that indicate what is essential to the identities of individuals, particulars, or instances.[12] It seems to me that any metaphysical theory that seeks to illumine mental causation or the ontology of mental events that denies (2) is hopelessly misdirected.

As I have been noting, systematic, informative, important explanatory schemes of events and states are also our strongest indications of causal relevance. The idea that the causal relations described in psychology are really or most fundamentally causal only under some other description seems extremely tenuous and doubtful. I see no reason to think that there is anything in the idea, now common among philosophers, that in some sense the 'real' causal work is being done at a lower level. I also see no reason to think that we can understand mentalistic causation through some analysis of supervenience (although I think that understanding the sense in which mental events supervene on the physical is an important enterprise). Our understanding of mental causation derives not primarily from re-descriptions in physical terms.[13] It derives primarily from our understanding of mentalistic explanation. This understanding is largely independent of reference to the underlying processes.

Davidson's profoundly stimulating argument for a token-identity theory seems to me flawed by a subtle analogue of the tendency to

[12] Again, one can reparse talk about essence into talk about the most fundamental method for identifying individuals and re-identifying them under counterfactual considerations; cf. note 7.

[13] Or worse yet, in syntactical terms. One might well grant that many psychological states and events involve operations on syntactic entities. One may also see such inner mental syntactic items as expressing intentional content. But the idea that the brain is sensitive only to syntactic shape, not to content, seems to me a misleading metaphor. The brain is sensitive to neural forms. One may think of there being causal relations among syntactic entities, but this is already to describe causation at a higher level of abstraction than that of brain physiology. If causation can be described at that level, it can also be described at the level of intentional content. I see little ground for seeing the syntactic properties as prior to intentional properties in the order of causal relevance. Syntax is attributed to serve explanations that are fundamentally intentional. In my view, there is no non-artificial sense in which syntax is ontologically or causally more secure.

underrate the centrality of cognitive practice in understanding mental causation and ontology (Davidson 1970). The argument partly relies on the premiss that causal relations between events must be backed by (entail the existence of) laws of a complete, closed system of explanation, where the predicates of these laws are true of the events that are causally related. Davidson conjoins this premiss with the assumption that there are causal relations between mental and physical events and the assumption (for which he argues) that mentalistic explanations cannot themselves be part of a complete, closed system of explanation. From these three premisses he concludes that mental event-tokens must fall under predicates of physical laws that do form part of a complete, closed explanatory system. As far as I can see, these must be the laws of physics.

I think that we do not know, and cannot know a priori, that causal statements entail the existence of laws or explanatory systems that have such specific properties. We cannot know a priori this much about the form of the laws of nature, described by any science. Nor can we know a priori the relations among the ontologies and causal schemes of the various sciences. That is, we cannot know a priori that the laws, or nomological generalizations, of psychology describe events that have any very specific relation to events that fall under the laws of any other science. I think that there is no reason, much less any a priori reason, to accept Davidson's first premiss. Thus we cannot know a priori that mental events that are causes fall under any other (non-mentalistic) sort of law.

Our best guide to the nature of mental causation and ontology lies in understanding our best means of explaining and describing mental events. Our actual cognitive practice lends little credence to the idea that intentional mental events fall under exceptionless physical laws, or instantiate physical descriptions of the most fundamental natural science.

Let us return to the argument against the form of token-identity theory that I described at the outset (a form that Davidson's argument was intended to support). Since premisses (1) and (2) seem strongly plausible and free of serious counter-arguments, the argument seems to me forceful and sound. The most common metaphysical ground for worries about epiphenomenalism seems on weak ground.

There are less committal forms of materialism about mental events. All such forms must take mental event-tokens to be physical event-tokens that are not instances of kinds described by any of the natural sciences. Perhaps this is not an intrinsically implausible claim. Particular wars, avalanches, thunderstorms, meal-cookings may not fall under any natural event-kind describable in any natural science. I doubt that there is ever any one definite token event that instantiates kinds of a natural science, even physics, with which an event-token of these kinds can be identified. Yet they are clearly physical events. Maybe mental events are like that.

On the other hand, these analogies seem merely hopeful. The relevant descriptions are uncontroversially physical. The problem with identifying them with events described in physics lies merely in their complexity and in the fact that they fall into patterns that are salient for macro-decriptions, but not particularly useful for systematic explanation. By contrast, psychological states do fall into systematic patterns which explanation can make use of. But these patterns do not seem to involve ordinary physical properties (like mass, energy, composition, and so on) that physical explanations and descriptions make use of.[14] So the view that these are, in the ordinary sense, physical patterns seems doubtful.

In any case, such forms of materialism provide little new insight into mental causation, as long as the relevant physical events with which the mental events are supposedly token-identical remain unidentified in non-mentalistic terms. There is little in current cognitive practice to encourage the view that any such descriptions of central intentional state-instances or event-tokens are forthcoming. So even if such a liberalized version of materialism were true, it would offer little help in understanding mental causation.

3

The problem about mental causation that is usually raised as a means of motivating an appeal to materialism is that of explaining a

[14] The composition relation is probably the critical one. There are forms of materialism that maintain that all objects are decomposable into inorganic physical particles. Apart from the fact that these forms do not apply very well to properties or events (not to speak of objects like numbers, intentional contents, methods), they make a claim for the relevance of physical composition to our understanding of mental entities that seems to me (so far) quite unsupported by anything that we know.

mechanism that would make possible causal interaction between two such different things as a physical event (or substance) and a mental event (or substance). Materialists hold that the problem disappears if mental events are seen as physical. This problem was posed by Descartes; and he professed himself baffled by it. The problem was acute for Descartes because he viewed mental and physical entities as substances in the old-fashioned sense—entities that were not dependent on anything else for their nature or existence. But mental events and other mental entities like minds are not substances in the old-fashioned sense. So there is for us no antecedent problem of admitting various sorts of constitutive and existential dependency of the mental on the physical. It is not obvious, however, that this dependency need involve material constitution—the mental events being identical with or made up of physical events.

I have no satisfying response to the problem of explaining a mechanism. But I am sure that there is less reason to think it a decisive consideration in favour of materialism than is often thought. What is unclear is whether the question is an appropriate one in the first place. Demanding that there be an account of mechanism in mind–body causation is tantamount to demanding a physical model for understanding such causation. It is far from obvious that such a model is appropriate. It is not even obvious why any model is needed. The argument I have just cited presents no clearly formulated problem about mental causation that need force us to embrace materialism, including the computer model's version of materialism, as a solution. The demand for a mechanism is tantamount to an implicit demand for a materialist solution.

A better articulated argument for materialism along similar lines goes as follows. Physical effects are caused by prior physical states or events according to approximately deterministic physical laws. Mental causes bring about physical movements of our bodies. If such causation did not consist in physical processes, there would be departures from the approximately deterministic physical patterns described by physical laws. It would interfere with, alter, or otherwise 'make a difference' in the physical outcomes. But there is no reason to think that this happens. Physical antecedent states suffice for the physical effects. Appeal to mental causation that does not consist in physical causation appears, on this reasoning, to require us to doubt the adequacy of current forms of physical explanation, even within the physical domain. So such appeal should be rejected.

This reasoning seems to me to have some force. But I think that it is not as forceful as it may appear. Why should mental causes alter or interfere with the physical system if they do not materially consist in physical processes? Thinking that they must, surely depends on thinking of mental causes on a physical model—as providing an extra 'bump' on the effect. The idea seems to be that a cause must transfer a bit of energy or exert a force on the effect. On such a model, mental causes would deflect a physical effect off the course a physical cause alone would set it on. Cases where the mental cause and the physical cause yield the same physical outcome—cases of 'over-determination'—will be seen, on such a model, as coincidences that must be abnormal. So appeals to over-determination by mental causes and physical causes will seem unattractive as a gloss on the general failure of mental causes to interfere with or alter the physical outcomes expected on purely physical grounds.

But whether the physical model of mental causation is appropriate is, again, part of what is at issue. As we have seen, one can specify various ways in which mental causes 'make a difference' which do not conflict with physical explanations. The differences they make are specified by psychological causal explanations, and by counterfactuals associated with these explanations. Such 'differences' made by psychological causes do not require that gaps be left in physical chains of causation. They do not seem to depend on any specific assumptions at all about the physical events underlying the mental causes.

I think that we have reason, just from considering explanatory goals and practice—before ontology is even considered—to think that mentalistic and physicalistic accounts of causal processes will not interfere with one another. Part of the point of referring to mental states lies in explaining intentional activity that involves (or is identical with) physical movement. A man's running to the store is explained by his believing that his child would suffer without the needed medicine and by his decision not to wait on a doctor. We think that the man's running is caused by the formation of his belief and by his decision.

It would be perverse to think that such mental events must interfere with or alter, or fill some gap in, the chain of physiological events leading up to and including the movements of his muscles in running. It would be perverse to think that the mentalistic explanation excludes or interferes with non-intentional explanations of the physical movement. I think that these ideas seem perverse not because we know that the mental events are material. They seem perverse because we know that the two causal explanations are explaining the same physical effect as the outcome of two very different patterns of events. The explanations of these patterns answer two very different types of inquiry. Neither type of explanation makes essential, specific assumptions about the other. So the relation between the entities appealed to in the different explanations cannot be read off the causal implications of either or both types of explanation. The perversity of thinking that mental causes must fill gaps in physical chains of events probably has its source in traditional dualism, or in libertarian worries about free will. But the perversity remains regardless of its source.

The upshot of this reasoning is that we have no ground for assuming that the failure of mental causes to interfere in the physical chain of events must be explained in terms of mental causes' consisting in physical events. Interference would be surprising, given antecedent assumptions about mental and physical explanation. So non-interference is in no need of explanation in ontological terms.

There are surely some systematic, even necessary, relations between mental events and underlying physical processes. We have good reason to believe that mental processes depend on underlying physical processes. By probing or damaging parts of the brain we can bring about, affect, or ruin mental states and processes. But the relations of identity and physical composition are relations that have specific scientific uses. For example, we explain the behaviour of a molecule in terms of the behaviour of its component parts. It is far from clear that these compositional relations have a systematic scientific use in bridging psychology and neurophysiology (cf. note 15). They are guesses about what sorts of relation might obtain. But they seem to me just one set of possibilities for accounting for relations between entities referred to in these very different explanatory enterprises. What form an inter-level account might take seems to me to be an open question.

I find it plausible to believe in some sort of broad supervenience thesis: no changes in mental states without some sort of change in physical states. But the inference to materialism is, I think, a metaphysical speculation which has come, misleadingly, to seem a relatively obvious scientific or commonsensical bromide.

As long as mentalistic explanation yields knowledge and understanding, and as long as that explanation is (sometimes) causal, we can firmly believe that mind–body causation is a part of the world. The primary way of understanding such causation is by understanding mentalistic causal and explanatory statements in the ordinary, non-philosophical sense of 'understanding'. How much more illumination philosophy or neuro-psychology can offer remains to be seen. At any rate, mentalistic explanation and mental causation do not need validation from materialist metaphysics.

It seems to me that philosophers should be more relaxed about whether or not some form of materialism is true. I think it a thoroughly open—and not very momentous—question whether there is any point in insisting that mental events are, in any clear sense, physical. Maybe science will never make use of anything more than limited correlations with the lower, more automatic parts of the cognitive system. Maybe identities or part–whole relations will never have systematic use. Maybe the traditional idea of a category difference will maintain a presence in scientific practice. What matters is that our mentalistic explanations work and that they do not conflict with our physicalistic explanations. As philosophers, we want a well-founded understanding of how these explanations, and their subject-matters, relate to one another. But it serves no purpose to over-dramatize the conflict between different ontological approaches or the merits of the materialist approach.

The flood of projects over the last two decades that attempt to fit mental causation or mental ontology into a 'naturalistic picture of the world' strike me as having more in common with political or religious ideology than with a philosophy that maintains perspective on the difference between what is known and what is speculated. Materialism is not established, or even clearly supported, by science. Metaphysics should venture beyond science with an acute sense of its liabilities.

4

I have argued that epiphenomenalism need not be seen as a serious metaphysical option even if materialism is true. The probity of mentalistic causal explanation is deeper than the metaphysical considerations that call it into question. I have also argued that materialist metaphysics is not the most plausible starting-point for reasoning about mind–body causation. Explanatory practice is.

I think it more natural and fruitful to begin by assuming, defeasibly perhaps but firmly, that attributions of intentional mental events are central to psychological explanation both in ordinary life and in various parts of psychology. We may also assume that intentional mental events are often causes and that psychological explanation is often a form of causal explanation. Given these assumptions, the 'worry' about epiphenomenalism seems very remote. For if intentional mental events are type-individuated in terms of their intentional 'aspects'—if those aspects are the fundamental explanatory aspects—and if such events enter into causal relations and are cited (in terms of those aspects) in explanations, then there seems to be every reason to conclude that those aspects are causally efficacious. None of the metaphysical considerations advanced in current discussion seem to me remotely strong enough to threaten this conclusion.[15]

I shall conclude by mentioning a further reason for thinking that intentional events are, as such, causally efficacious. Why is it that philosophers who discuss epiphenomenalism are worried about it? Why should one not take a more disinterested attitude?

Part of the answer lies in the fact that many philosophers instinctively feel that if epiphenomenalism were a consequence of their metaphysics, their metaphysics would be in trouble.[16] This is good philosophical sense. Outside our philosophical studies, we all know that epiphenomenalism is not true.

But there is a deeper reason why epiphenomenalism should seem intellectually unattractive. Much of the interest of psychological explanation, both in psychology and in ordinary discourse, lies in helping us understand ourselves as agents. Causal implications are built into our intentional concepts and intentional modes of explanation. We think that we make things happen because we

[15] The fact that intentional mental events are appealed to, as such, in explanations by itself differentiates them from phenotypes. Phenotypes are explananda in biology, but intentional mental events are part of causal explanations in psychology and everyday life—not simply the explananda for explanations. It is a mark of much of the discussion in this area that such simple differences in explanatory status are not so much as mentioned. The metaphysics of the situation is often discussed in virtual isolation from explanatory practice.

[16] Cf. Block 1990 for a clear statement of this view.

make decisions or will to do things. We think that we make assertions, form theories, and create cultures, because we think certain thoughts and have certain goals—and we express and fulfil them. In this context, we identify ourselves primarily in terms of our intentional mental aspects—our wants, our thoughts, our values. Our agency consists in our wants', willings', thoughts', values' as such (under these 'aspects') having some sort of efficacy in the world. Our mental events' having the intentional characters that they have is, in individual instances, what we define our agency in terms of.

Most of our intellectual and practical norms and evaluations presuppose that we are agents. If our willing or deciding made something happen, but that event's being a willing or deciding were not causally efficacious (so that the efficacy resided in some underlying neural property), then the agency would not be ours. If our theoretical deliberations were not ours to control, we could not see ourselves as being the authors of our theories; nor could we criticize ourselves as deliberators. Most normative evaluations of our intellectual and practical activities would be empty.

If intentional psychological explanation 'made sense' of what we did, 'rationalized' it, but did not provide insight into the nature of any causal efficacy, it would lose much of its point. It would provide no insight into the various forms of agency that give life its meaning and purpose, and psychology its special interest.

I am not here asserting that it is inconceivable that psychological explanation could break down—or at least be very much more limited than we conceive it as being. I think that the question of conceivability is quite subtle and complex. The point is that this form of psychological explanation has not in the least broken down. It works very well, within familiar limits, in ordinary life; it is used extensively in psychology and the social sciences; and it is needed in understanding physical science, indeed any sort of rational enterprise. We have reason to believe that it provides explanatory insights. But then as I have noted, there is a deep connection between intentional psychological explanation and the view it provides of ourselves as agents, on one hand, and the attribution of some sort of causal efficacy to intentional mental states and events as such, on the other.

I think that these are not the only reasons for this form of attribution. But even if they were, it would leave the attribution so deeply entrenched that there is no real hope that epiphenomenalism could become a credible view. Epiphenomenalism is better seen as an instrument, like scepticism, for clarifying our most deeply held beliefs. It seems to me, however, that the traditional scepticisms about agency, will, and responsibility are more penetrating tools for this purpose.

8

Mental Events as Structuring Causes of Behaviour

FRED DRETSKE

CAUSAL explanations are context-sensitive. What we pick out as the cause of *E* depends on our interests, our purposes, and our prior knowledge. Almost any event, *E*, depends on a great variety of other events in such a way as to make any one of them eligible, given the right context, for selection as the cause in a causal explanation of *E*.[1] My purpose in this paper is not to dispute this doctrine, but rather, by assuming its validity, to describe a difference between two kinds of cause—what I call a triggering and a structuring cause—and to exhibit the usefulness of this distinction for understanding two ways of causally explaining the behaviour of systems. I will, finally, by way of illustration, suggest that the difference between psychological and biological explanations of animal behaviour is fundamentally a difference of this kind: psychological explanations provide structuring causes of behaviour, while biological explanations provide triggering causes of behaviour.

1. Triggering and Structuring Causes

An operator moves the cursor on a screen by pressing a key on the keyboard. Pressure on the key is the triggering cause of cursor

My thanks to Fred Adams, Martin Eimer, and Lynne Rudder Baker for helpful criticism.

[1] I will not try to say how an event must depend on an earlier event to make this earlier event eligible (given appropriate interests, purposes, and prior knowledge) as 'the cause' of the later. I am, however, sympathetic to the analysis proposed by David Lewis (1973). My purpose in this essay is not to analyse the general notion of cause, but, assuming we already have a workable notion of cause, to make a distinction in different types of cause and, hence, types of causal explanation. For this reason I also

movement.[2] The movement would not have occurred if the key had not been pressed. Pressure on this key makes the cursor move. In conditions that exist at the time the key is pressed, pressure on the key (this type of event) is regularly followed by cursor movement (that type of event). It is this kind of causal arrangement, the sort characteristic of a triggering cause, that allows us to speak of the operator himself as moving the cursor by pressing the key.

On the other hand, we sometimes speak of the events that produced hardware conditions (actual electrical connections in the computer) and programming (software) as the cause of cursor movement. This is especially evident when cursor movement (in response to pressure on a certain key) is unexpected or unusual. Imagine a puzzled operator, watching the cursor move as he pokes the key, asking: 'Why is the cursor moving?' Since the operator knows that pressure on the key is making the cursor move (that, in fact, is what he finds puzzling), a different explanation of cursor movement is being sought. The operator is looking for a structuring cause. He wants to know what brought about or caused the machine to occupy a state, to be in a condition, in which pressure on the key has this effect. He knows, or can easily be assumed to know (after a few presses of the key) that *E* (cursor movement) is being caused by *T* (pressure on the key). What he wants to know is why it is. Who or what made *E* depend on *T* in this way?

A terrorist plants a bomb in the general's car. The bomb sits there for days until the general gets in his car and turns the key to start the engine. The bomb is detonated (triggered by turning the key in the ignition) and the general is killed. Who killed him? The terrorist, of course. How? By planting a bomb in his car. Although the general's own action (turning on the engine) was the triggering cause, the

ignore complications having to do with over-determination and causal pre-emption, probabilistic causal relations, and so on. These complications, though relevant to getting clear about the general idea, are not (because they apply equally to both sorts of cause I distinguish) relevant to the distinction I seek to make.

[2] Mackie (1974, p. 36) uses the term 'triggering cause' and contrasts it with what he calls a 'predisposing cause'. This is close to, but not quite the same as, my own distinction. For Mackie the predisposing cause is part of (what he calls) the 'field' for the triggering cause, part of the existing background (standing) conditions relative to which the trigger becomes necessary (and often sufficient) for its effect. The spark is a triggering, while the presence of inflammable material is a predisposing, cause of the explosion. A shift in interest and purposes could promote the standing condition, the presence of inflammable material, to a triggering cause. A structuring cause, as I use the term, is best understood as a triggering cause of one of Mackie's predisposing causes (i.e. one of the standing conditions).

terrorist's action is the structuring cause, and it will be his (the terrorist's) action, something he did a week ago, that will certainly be singled out, in both legal and moral inquiries, as the cause of the explosion that resulted in death.[3]

Specifying the structuring cause of an event yields quite a different kind of causal explanation than does specification of its triggering cause. The two causes exhibit a much different relationship to their effect. For those accustomed to thinking of causal relationships in a Humean way, in terms of constant conjunction, *T*, the triggering cause, produces *E* in a familiar way: in the circumstances that exist at the time of its (*T*'s) occurrence, events of type *T* are regularly followed by events of type *E*. A triggering cause of *E* merely tops up[4] a pre-existing set of conditions, a set of conditions that, together with *T* (but not without it), are sufficient for *E*. Since these conditions exist at the time of *T*'s occurrence, triggering causes of *E* give rise to causal regularities of the following sort: Whenever *T* occurs in *these* conditions (the conditions existing at the time of *T*'s occurrence) *E* occurs. Structuring causes, however, occur in conditions that, generally speaking, are (even together with *S*) in no way sufficient for *E*. Later events, events that are independent of *S*, must conspire to convert *S* into a structuring cause of *E*, and these later events may or may not occur. Unlike a triggering cause, therefore, there are no regularities between a structuring cause and its effect of the form: 'When *S* occurs in these conditions (conditions existing at the time of *S*), *E* also occurs'. Tom rewires the computer so that pressure on a certain key will move the cursor, but no one ever decides to press that key. Still, if they had pressed that key, Tom's action would have been the structuring cause of the resulting movement.

There is another important difference between structuring and triggering causes. The structuring causal relationship is a one–many relation while the triggering causal relationship is one–one. Each

[3] By changing the constellation of intentions and knowledge on the part of the bomber and victim, we can, without changing any of the causal dependency relations, change the context in such a way that the victim's actions become the cause of death. Imagine an unsuspecting mechanic wiring what he takes to be an emission-control device to a car's engine. Unknown to the mechanic, but known to the car's owner, the device is actually a bomb. The suicidal owner, pleased by this convenient development, waits until the bomb is wired, climbs in the car, starts the engine and blows himself up. In this case, the owner causes his own death—kills himself. In this case the triggering, not the structuring, cause is the cause of death.

[4] This is Jonathan Bennett's language; see his 1988.

(token) movement of the cursor is produced by a distinct (token) press of the key. Distinct causes produce distinct effects, and distinct effects are produced by distinct causes. But if Tom's activities yesterday are the (structuring) cause of this movement of the cursor, then they, the very same activities, are the structuring cause of that movement of the cursor. Tom doesn't have to re-wire the computer again and again. Once will do. Once he's done it, his (token) action becomes the structuring cause of the many (token) movements that are triggered by distinct key presses.

Our terrorist example is unsuitable to illustrate this difference since, of course, the explosion of the bomb destroys the condition the terrorist created, the condition that made turning on the ignition trigger an explosion. But consider a similar case in which this condition persists. I wire a switch to a light so that I can—again and again—turn on the light by throwing the switch. The structuring cause of the light's going on on Tuesday is the same as its going on on Wednesday—namely, my wiring the switch to the light on Monday. The triggering causes are different each time the light goes on, of course, since Tuesday's flip is different from Wednesday's flip. The structuring cause of each lighting, however, is the same: my activities on Monday.

Some may object to this way of describing things. They may prefer to say that what I am calling the structuring cause of *E* is not a cause *of E* at all. It is, rather, a cause (a good old-fashioned cause) of those background or standing conditions (call them *B*) in which *T* causes *E*. So instead of having two different types of cause (triggering and structuring) for *E*, we have one sort of cause, a triggering cause, for different effects: *T* (what I am calling the triggering cause of *E*) causes *E*, but *S* (what I am calling the structuring cause of *E*) causes *B*, the conditions (or one of the conditions) in which *T* causes *E*. *S*, if you like, is the cause, not of *E*, but of *T*'s causing *E*.

I have no objection to this way of putting things. Quite the contrary. For certain purposes, this is the way I prefer to describe matters. For these special purposes, structuring causes of *E* are *best* thought of as causes, not of *E*, but of conditions, *B*, in which certain other events (what I am calling a triggering cause) cause *E*. From this vantage point, the designers, builders, and programmers of word processors, *qua* designers, builders, and programmers, do not cause individual (i.e. token) movements of the cursor. Keyboard operators do that. Instead, as designers, builders and programmers, they cause the machine to be in a condition that allows, or enables, an operator to move the cursor by pressing a key. Structuring causes (of *E*) are, in reality, causes of more or less persisting conditions (*B*) which make (events of type) *E* depend on (events of type) *T* in such a way that tokens of *T* (if and when they occur) cause tokens of *E*.

None the less, although I think that, for certain purposes, this is a better way to describe the relation of a structuring cause to its 'effect' I will continue to speak of structuring causes as causes of *E* out of deference to those (and I think this is most of us most of the time) who think that a cause of *E* is an earlier event on which *E* is counterfactually dependent in the right way,[5] a way which allows us (given a suitable context) to single it out as the cause of *E* in causal explanations of *E*. For (as the above examples are meant to show) it seems clear that structuring causes of *E* are earlier events on which *E* depends in the right way (if it isn't the right way, then it isn't clearly the wrong way). The cursor would not have moved (just now, when the operator pressed the key) if the wires hadn't been changed earlier. Hot water would not have flowed from the shower-head just now (when I turned on the cold water tap[6]) if a plumber, working in the basement yesterday, hadn't made a mistake. The general would still be alive today if the terrorist had not planted that bomb. So, in deference to these facts, I propose to continue speaking of events which 'configure' circumstances so as to make (tokens of) *T*, when (and if) they occur, cause (tokens of) *E*, events which (in this sense) cause *T* to cause *E*, as themselves causes of *E*.

[5] 'In the right way' because we want to rule out 'backtracking' counterfactuals that make two events 'depend' on each other (counterfactually) when they are related, not as cause to effect, but as common effects of a single cause. When *B* and *C* (slightly later than *B*) have a common cause, *A*, and we allow a backtracking interpretation of the counterfactual (expressing the dependency between *B* and *C*), we can say that if *B* hadn't happened, then (since that would mean—and here we are backtracking—that its cause, *A*, didn't occur) *C* wouldn't have happened. Once again, I ignore these complications as irrelevant to the point I am making. Both triggering and structuring causes are causes. So we need to require (or assume) that, in both cases, the dependency relations (whatever, exactly, they are) are right.

[6] These parenthetical clauses (when I turned on the water, when the operator pressed the key) serve merely to specify which event is the effect in question (which—of the perhaps many—cursor movements or flows of water). They are not to be interpreted as (part of) what is being caused. On the present interpretation of a structuring cause, the structuring cause (of cursor movement, say) causes a particular cursor movement. It does not cause something conditional in nature—e.g. a-movement-when-the-key-is-pressed. It is possible, however (see below), to interpret a structuring cause as the cause of a disposition in a system (to do *E* when *T*) or as the cause of one thing (*T*) causing another (*E*).

There is some danger in speaking this way, a danger of confusing causes of different (sorts of) things with different (sorts of) causes of the same thing, but as long as one is aware of just what I am calling a structuring cause of E, and just how it differs from a triggering cause, this way of talking will (I hope) do no harm.[7]

Fig. 8.1 summarizes the main points. For any event E that has a causal explanation, there exists a chain of triggering causes stretching from the proximal, T_1, to the remote (T_2. . .). There is also a chain of structuring causes—once again going from proximal, S_1, to the remote—for the condition, B, on which the causal relation between T_1 and E depends. The vertical arrow between B and the causal relationship (→) between T_1 and E is meant to signify this dependency relation: S_1, we might say (and in *Explaining Behavior* I often did say), causes T_1 to cause E by creating the conditions (or one of the conditions) on which the causal relationship between T_1 and E depends. B is a condition whose onset necessarily occurs before T_1 and whose termination is (typically) after E.[8]

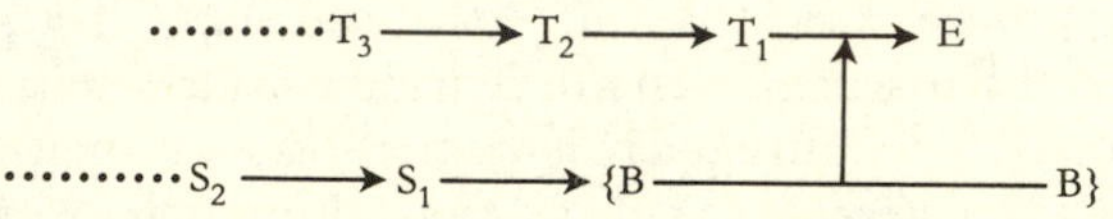

FIG. 8.1. The triggering and structuring causes of an event

To keep things simple, I have indicated only a single chain of triggering causes and one chain of structuring causes, but there is

[7] In *Explaining Behavior* (1988) I identified behaviour with a causal process (some internal event, C, causing bodily movement, M). A causal explanation of behaviour was then a description of (what I am now calling) the structuring cause of M: the earlier event or state that caused the system to be in the condition (B) in which tokens of C cause tokens of M.

As I have already indicated, I still think this is the right and proper way to proceed. Behaviour, what it is we invoke mental states to explain, is a causal process ($C \rightarrow M$) having (typically) bodily movement (M) as its product, not the bodily movement (M) itself. Hence, to explain behaviour, why C is causing M, we need to find the cause (or explanation) for C's causing M or what I am now calling the structuring cause of the movements, M, that (in part) constitute the behaviour.

But I don't want to argue about it in this paper. I avoid the need to argue about it by distinguishing types of causes of M (triggering and structuring). My present argument that mental explanations of behaviour are attempts to specify structuring causes of bodily movement M (what I earlier called 'output' to distinguish it from genuine 'behaviour') is, then, equivalent to my earlier argument that mental explanations are attempts to specify the cause of the 'process' ($C \rightarrow M$) having such movements or output as its product.

[8] This, incidentally, is another respect in which structuring causes differ from triggering causes. In the causal chain between S and E there is a link (namely, B)

nothing to prevent there being several (converging) chains of triggering causes, each with its associated structuring cause, and different structuring causes for each of the causal links in the triggering chain (i.e. a different structuring cause for the possibly different *B* conditions associated with $T_3 \rightarrow T_2$, $T_2 \rightarrow T_1$, etc.)[9] Also, we can have different structuring causes for each of the distinguishable conditions (existing at a given time) on which the (triggering) causal relationship depends. That is, *B* might, in fact, be a composite of different sub-conditions, B_1, B_2,. . . , each of which has a distinct cause. Getting hot water from the shower-head (*E*), an event that is (given the messed-up plumbing) triggered by turning on the cold water tap (*T*), depends, not only on the hot-water pipe being connected to the cold-water tap (B_1), something the plumber did yesterday (S_1), but also on the proper functioning of the hot-water heater (B_2), adequate water pressure (B_3), and so on, each of which has its own causal history (both triggering and structural). Given the right context (e.g. recent repair of the hot-water heater), any one of these earlier events could be cited as the cause of *E* in an explanation of why *E* occurred.

B itself is a persisting condition or state of affairs, not really the sort of event-like occurrence or happening that we are accustomed to picking out as a cause. Besides (more of this in a moment), as Fig. 8.1 indicates, *B* typically extends beyond the effect (*E*) for which we are seeking a cause. As a result, in picking out structuring causes, *B* is generally disqualified (or simply ignored) in favour of those events (typically actions) that occur (wholly) before *E* and help bring it about by creating the conditions (*B*) on which the triggering of *E* depends. Hence, the most recent structuring cause can occur in the very remote past. S_1, the most proximal (recent) structuring cause of *E*, may have occurred years before its effect. What transmits its influence, so to speak, is the persisting background condition it brought about (*B*).

One final point about the distinction before we attempt to apply it. Triggering and structuring causes, although always distinct, may

which (typically) exists (goes on existing) after *E*. This is not true of the chain of triggering causes. Each link in the triggering chain expires before the occurrence of its successor (including the effect *E*).

[9] It is for this reason that we should always understand a structuring cause to be relative to some specified triggering cause. The structuring cause of T_1 causing *E* may be quite different from the structuring cause of T_2 (the cause of T_1) causing *E*.

sometimes appear to 'fuse'. Suppose a dim-witted terrorist forgets he planted a bomb. Or he forgets which car it was in which he planted a bomb. A few days later, needing a car, he steals the 'wired' car and blows himself up. Is the terrorist both triggering and structuring cause of his own death? He created the conditions that enabled him to (unintentionally) blow himself up, yes, but that only means that one and the same person was involved in both causes. It doesn't show that the causes are the same. What he did to trigger this outcome is different from what he did to structure it. It was his turning on the ignition that triggered the explosion; it is was his wiring the bomb to the ignition (a week ago) that structured it. Though both events (actions) involve the terrorist, they are quite different.

Just as different actions of the same person can operate as triggering and structuring causes, different states of the same object (a single object having different properties) can function in the same way. *O*'s possession of P_1 might be the triggering cause of E while its possession of some quite different property, P_2, say, can be the structuring cause of the same effect. It is important to keep this possibility in mind when thinking about events occurring in the nervous system and the way these events help determine behaviour. For, as I hope to show, there is reason to think that it is the brain's possession of certain electrical and chemical properties that is effective in triggering bodily behaviour while its relational (including historical) properties are relevantly involved in structuring the same output.

2. Psychological vs. Biological Explanations

This brings us to the next topic of this paper: the alleged difference between biology and psychology. If the claim is that psychological explanations of behaviour provide structuring, and biological explanations triggering, causes of behaviour, then, to avoid trivializing the thesis, some independent specification is needed of the difference between a biological and a psychological explanation of behaviour.

This, of course, is a tall order, and too much for me to satisfy in the space of a few pages. Yet, in order to fulfil my earlier promise, something has to be said. So excuse me while I execute a little time-saving (perhaps even face-saving) manœuvre.

Objects have a variety of properties, some intrinsic, others extrinsic. Extrinsic properties are relational properties, ones that consist of the object's relations to other things. A piece of paper—a $10 bill, for instance—has a certain shape, texture, colour, and size (intrinsic properties), but it also has monetary value, an extrinsic property having to do with its manner and place of origin: where, and under whose authorization, it was printed. Change these historical facts, give the paper an origin in Clyde's basement, say, and you change its legal status and, in this sense, its monetary value. Likewise, printed words have a characteristic set of properties (mainly having to do with shape) by means of which we identify them (as tokens of the same type). They also have a meaning. This, of course, is what makes them words. And, just as in the case of legal currency, the meaning of a word (token) is an extrinsic property of the word. Even if there was a different meaning for every mark, and vice versa (no synonymy or ambiguity), we should still have to distinguish the mark (and the intrinsic properties that made it that mark) from its meaning.

There may be little agreement among philosophers about which properties constitute the meaning of a word, but everyone seems to agree that whatever they are, they are extrinsic to the objects having that meaning. Since we can, as we all know, use the same marks and sounds to mean something different, or nothing at all, their meaning must be extrinsic.

If materialism is really true (as I will assume it is for the sake of this paper), and we nonetheless remain realistic about the mind (as I will)—if, in other words, we think there are such things as beliefs, desires, intentions and purposes, material states having a content or meaning—it not implausible to suppose that these material states, just like words, derive their meaning or content from their relations to other things. Beliefs, intentions and desires may be in the head, but what-we-believe, what-we-intend, and what-we-desire, the content of the belief, intention, and desire is surely not there. It is no more in the head (where the beliefs are) than is the meaning of words, what-words-mean, in the books where the words are.

Beliefs and desires are not words, of course, not part of any natural (or, for that matter, artificial) language. As long as we remain realistic about beliefs (or, if not beliefs, then at least internal representations—whatever we choose to call them), then content, what is believed (represented) when something is believed (represented) to be so, is not conventional in the way the meaning (of words) is. So we cannot expect that the system of relations from which internal representations (beliefs and their ilk) derive their meaning is the same as that from which the words in a language derive their meaning. If Grice is right, words get their meaning from the intentions of their users, but intentions certainly don't get their meaning, their intentional content, from the intentions of their users. They don't, in the same sense, have users. None the less, from wherever they get it, theorists seem to agree it is extrinsic.

It is hard to see how this could fail to be true. It is a certain set of relations that makes a picture a picture of my cousin George and represents him as, say, getting bald. In the case of photographs, this relation is presumably causal. In the case of paintings and drawings, it may also have to do with the intentions of the artist. But in any case, an identical-looking piece of paper or canvas, one sharing all the same intrinsic properties, is not a picture of George, nor does it represent George as getting bald, if it fails to stand in these relations, causal and otherwise, to George. Its being a picture of George, and its representation of him as getting bald, has to do with the aetiology of the picture, with its history, with just how the marks came to be where they are. This being so, it seems only plausible to suppose that what makes a thought, some material process in a brain, a thought about George—the thought, say, that he is getting bald—is likewise relational. It has to do with how the person's brain in which that thought occurs is (or was) related to George, to baldness, or whatever else is needed to make it represent George as getting bald.

If anyone really wants to dispute this, he or she may as well stop reading because I'm not going to argue about it. I am going to execute the little time-saving manœuvre I mentioned earlier by simply assuming it. I am going to assume, without argument, and because it strikes me as so utterly obvious, that if there are beliefs, internal states that not only represent, but can also misrepresent, the state of the external world, and if these states are material states of the believer, then they derive their representational content—and, hence, their identity as beliefs—from their extrinsic relations to other things.

I am going to assume, furthermore, that this distinction between intrinsic and extrinsic, even if it doesn't exhaust the distinction between the mental and the physical,[10] is none the less a fundamental

[10] As it certainly doesn't, since some extrinsic properties of the brain have nothing to do with the possessor's psychological or mental properties.

component in the contrast between what is mental and what is physical. I shall assume, therefore, that we will have gone some distance towards demonstrating a causal relevance of the mind (to the behaviour of any system possessing a mind) if we can make plausible the idea that although it may be a brain's intrinsic properties that are instrumental in triggering bodily behaviour, it is its extrinsic properties that are relevant to structuring this same behaviour. If nothing else, this will at least show that there is nothing about the extrinsicness of the mental that disqualifies it from playing a causal role in the explanation of behaviour. This is no small matter. For much of current thinking in the philosophy of mind (in particular, that centring on methodological solipsism) traces the causal impotence of the mental to precisely this feature—the fact that the mental does not supervene on, and is therefore extrinsic to, the body.[11]

3. Extrinsic States as Structuring Causes

Having taken so long to describe the pieces of this puzzle, I can, I hope, be much briefer in assembling them into a coherent picture of mental causation.

I shall describe a system *Q* whose internal states make it behave in various ways. One particular state—I will label it *R*+ to suggest a positive representational state—is such that tokens of it cause movements of type *M*. *R*+ is to be understood as an intrinsic state: a state defined by *R*'s possession of certain intrinsic properties, P_i (that is, *R*+ = *R*'s having P_i). *R*+ also has certain extrinsic properties, P_e. When *Q* is a living system, the intrinsic properties

[11] For an eloquent recent expression of this dilemma, see McGinn 1989. The basic idea is that since causality is a local (i.e. intrinsic) affair, meanings, being extrinsic, cannot be causally relevant. Incidentally, this conventional wisdom does not deny the causal efficacy of extrinsic properties. Having had a certain history (extrinsic) can cause me to be a certain way (intrinsic). This, in fact, is precisely what the government tries to do with legal currency: it tries to devise a printing process which gives real money (money that has the right history) a distinctive appearance.

No, in saying that extrinsic properties are causally (and, hence, explanatorily) irrelevant, what is usually meant is that their causal relevance is screened off by an object's intrinsic properties. Extrinsic differences in O make a difference in what O does here and now only if they operate through (i.e. cause) intrinsic differences in O. Extrinsic differences that are not reflected in (do not supervene on) the material composition of a system are epiphenomenal (causally irrelevant to explaining the system's behaviour).

are chemical, electrical, and so on. The extrinsic properties of $R+$ can be anything: causal, informational, functional, historical—anything, in fact, that might plausibly be taken to underlie $R+$'s representational content (thereby qualifying Q as inhabiting an appropriate mental state—e.g. believing so-and-so).

My task is to show that M, the output or behaviour of Q, can have, as (part of) its causal explanation, R's possession of extrinsic property P_e (or, if one prefers the language of facts rather than states, the fact that R has property P_e). That is, Q's behaviour can be causally explained by the fact that Q is in a state (like a belief) having a certain intentional (in this case representational) content. I will illustrate how this works by using particular extrinsic properties—those connected with $R+$'s status as an indicator or sign—as the basis for R's content, but others (having different theories of representational content) can (if they can make it work) use their own favourite property.

Suppose that system Q is wired so that $R+$ is tokened when, and only when, an object of type O appears nearby. That is, R registers O's presence by going into its + state—an internal sign or indicator that an O is nearby. O's presence causing a token of $R+$ in Q can be thought of as Q sensing (perceiving) O.[12] Suppose, furthermore, that Os are dangerous and, being dangerous, Q learns to avoid them. Learning to avoid them is a developmental process in which evasive movements, M, come to be produced when Os are nearby. The only way such movements can be co-ordinated with the presence of an O (so that Q engages in these movements when, but—generally speaking—only when, an O is nearby) is if an internal sign or indicator of O—in this case $R+$—is *itself* made into a cause of those evasive manœuvres. The way to co-ordinate M with O is to make O, via $R+$, a cause of M. So, as a result of learning, $R+$, the internal sign of O, becomes a cause (a triggering cause) of M.

Imagine that you know none of this, but that you observe Q (in the wild, as it were) avoiding O. At least you observe Q exhibiting movements M, and you want to know why. Why is Q doing M?

There are two possible answers—one corresponding to the triggering cause of this behaviour, the other corresponding to its structuring cause.

[12] This isn't yet enough to qualify as genuine perception, of course, but it will do no harm to use these suggestive terms in describing the causal relationships in question.

Triggering Causal Explanation: *Q* is running because it saw (perceived, sensed) an *O*—because an *O* approached (and *Q* saw it). This is a triggering causal explanation because one is merely citing a link in the triggering causal chain (e.g. T_2 in Fig. 8.1). The approach of *O* caused, in *Q*, an event (we are calling it *R*+) which, in turn, produced *M*. Knowing nothing of the intrinsic nature (i.e. the neurobiological character) of this internal triggering event, an observer is forced to specify the triggering cause of behaviour *M* by 'backing up', so to speak, to the cause of the triggering cause (which is itself, of course, a triggering cause). The approach of *O* made *Q* run by causing in *Q* an event (*R*+) which triggered movement *M*. We normally compress this into the simple: *Q* ran because it saw an *O* approaching.

Though this gives us the triggering cause, we may still have a problem about understanding why *Q* ran. Perhaps we don't know that *O*s are dangerous to *Q*. Or perhaps though we know that *O*s are dangerous (to *Q*), we don't know whether *Q* knows it. *Q* saw an *O* (a predator) approaching, yes, and that event triggered flight. But why did it trigger flight? Did *Q* recognise the predator as a predator? Could *Q* not only see the predator, but see that it was a predator? These are questions about the way *Q* classifies, the way it represents, *O*. They are questions, not about what *Q* sees, but about what *Q* knows (or believes) about what it sees. They are questions the answer to which will tell us why *Q* ran from the *O* it saw. After all, as we all know, two animals may both avoid *O* (the approach of *O* is triggering cause for both), but do so for much different reasons—one because it represents *O* as an enemy, the other because it represents *O* as a friend, a friend, as it turns out, to whom a favour is owed. So seeing *O* approaching can be the triggering cause for both their behaviours, but the reason they run, the structuring cause of this behaviour, can be quite different.

Structuring Causal Explanation: In supplying the animal's reasons for running from the (external) triggering cause of its flight we are, I submit, providing structuring causes of flight. Just as with our keyboard operator who knew that this key was controlling cursor movement and wanted to know why it was, the observer of *Q* may (after watching *Q* long enough) know that what is triggering *Q*'s behaviour is the sight of *O*. What he doesn't know is why the sight of *O* (the internal *R*+ which registers the presence of *O*) causes *M*: evasive movements.

A structuring cause is needed: some causal explanation for why seeing *O* makes *Q* run. What is it that configured *Q* so as to make *R*+ (the internal perceptual registration of *O*) a cause of movements of type *M*? Before learning occurred the approach of *O* caused *R*+ in *Q*. Before learning to run, before learning that they were dangerous, *Q* could see *O*s approaching. It could see predators before it learned to recognize them as predators. But, at this time, *R*+ did not cause *M*. Now it does. Now *Q* runs from the *O*s it sees. Why?

This question about *Q*'s reasons is, I submit, a question about the structuring cause of *Q*'s behaviour, and in the little scenario I have constructed, its answer obviously has to do with *Q*'s learning history. What explains why, during learning, *R*+ was recruited as, made into, a cause of *M* is the fact that *R*+ was a sign of *O* and the organism had a need to co-ordinate behaviour—in this case evasive movements *M*—with the presence of *O*. *R*+ was somehow (and here I leave neurobiological details of learning—what we know of them—to the experts) made into a cause of *M* because, by signalling the presence of *O*, *R*+ 'told' the animal what it needed to know (viz. when to produce *M*) to escape harm. Hence, the internal sign of *O*, *R*+, was made into a cause of *M*—solving, at one stroke, the co-ordination problem. If, in order to survive, you have to do *M* when *O*, then you have to make some internal sign of *O* into a cause of *M*. There is no way learning can occur unless it happens, unless *R*+, an internal indicator of *O*, is recruited as a cause of *M*. That, indeed, is why animals need internal representations.

The important point to notice is that when behaviour is the result of learning of this sort,[13] the structuring cause of the behaviour is *R*'s possession of an extrinsic property (or, if you prefer, the fact that *R*+ has this extrinsic property). It is the fact that tokens of *R*+ (whatever, intrinsically, they may be like) are signs of *O*, indicators of *O*, carriers-of-information about *O*, that explains why a change was wrought in *Q* so as to make (future tokens of) *R*+ causes of *M*. Since being a sign of *O*, an indicator of *O*, a carrier-of-information

[13] And I believe (though I won't now take the time to argue it) that the only behaviour we invoke reasons (beliefs and desires) to explain is behaviour that is—in one way or another—the result of such learning. We don't need reasons to explain instinctive behaviours (reflexes, tropisms, etc.)—behaviours in which the connections are hard-wired. For an example of hard-wired (innate) connections, see Ewert 1987. Ewert calls *R* the 'releasing mechanism' and the stimulus that triggers it a 'sign-stimulus' (p. 337).

about *O*, are all extrinsic to the internal tokenings of *R*+ that trigger *M*, the structuring cause of *Q*'s behaviour is an extrinsic fact about *Q*'s internal states.[14] It may seem (recall our example of the terrorist) as though one and the same state—namely, *R*+—is both triggering and structuring cause of *M*, but this is mistaken. It is R's having the intrinsic, neurobiological properties defining *R*+ that is the triggering cause of *M*; it is the fact that *R*+ indicates *O*, an extrinsic fact about *R*+, that explains why *Q* was reconfigured to make *R*+ into a cause of *M*. *R*'s having P_i is the triggering cause of *M*; *R*'s having P_e is the structuring cause.

We can see this sort of explanation at work when we look at the 'behaviour' of various connectionist systems (see Rummelhart and McClelland 1986). Such systems are networks of interconnected nodes which can, by gradual re-weighting of excitatory and inhibitory connections between nodes, 'learn' to produce a desired output in response to variety of different inputs. The strengths between nodes are re-weighted during learning (in accordance with a certain rule) by supplying feedback about the difference between the output at any stage of learning and a 'desired' output. Once the system has learned to produce the desired output—call it *M*—the explanation of why it (now) produces *M*, why it now behaves this way, is (or can easily be regarded as) a question about the process that resulted in the present configuration of weights between nodes (a condition that we earlier labelled *B*: see Fig. 8.1). This explanation adverts to extrinsic properties of the system: the external event or process that caused the present configuration of inter-nodal weights that structure current output.

If we embed *Q* into a radically different environment, a world or habitat in which internal tokenings of *R*+, although the same in every intrinsic respect, do not indicate the presence of an *O* (i.e. they have different extrinsic properties), then even if they still cause *M*, the structuring cause (and, hence, the explanation) of this behaviour will be quite different. Perhaps in this different world, tokens of *R*+ cause *M* because they indicate (or indicated) the presence, not of *O*, but of twin-*O*, a much different sort of predator or, perhaps, not a predator at all but just a creature that *Q*, for

[14] In order to allow for (possible) misrepresentation (*Q* doing *M* because it mistakenly thought there was an *O* nearby) the token of *B* that triggers *M* need not itself be a sign or indicator of *O*. It will, however, be a token of a type earlier tokens of which were signs (indicators) of *O*. And being of this type *is* an extrinsic property of the current token.

reasons of its own, has a need (or desire) to avoid. In this possible habitat, *Q*, given time enough and luck, learns to avoid twin-*O*. The causal explanation of *Q*'s behaviour in this novel environment, though it is (in one respect) identical to the behaviour of *Q* in the normal habitat (in both places *Q* avoids or flees from *O*-looking creatures) is quite different. In one case *Q* runs because of its past interaction with *O*s (because his internal *R* indicates the approach of an *O*); in the other case *Q* runs because of its past interaction with twin-*O*s (because, in this different environment, *Q*s internal *R* indicates the approach of a twin-*O*). On certain theories of representational content (including my own) *Q*'s internal states have a different representational content in these two worlds. The behaviours, described in one way, are the same, but they are none the less causally explained by different content. Meanings don't have to be in the head to do their job—even when the job they are doing is the same.

9

The Union Theory and Anti-Individualism

TED HONDERICH

THERE is something called psychoneural intimacy. Hence what you may now recollect, the mental or conscious event *M* of your intending to turn to this page, was bound up with a simultaneous neural event *N*—certain activity in a certain neural locale. More precisely, there was some necessary and direct connection between *M* and *N*. This conviction of psychoneural intimacy is an assumption of neuroscience, and denials of it are rare enough to be strange. There is also something called mental indispensability. Hence *M* is an indispensable part of what explains your action *A* of having turned to this page. More precisely, taking explanations of *A* which include only events at the time of *M*, none is complete without *M*, and, taking complete explanations of *A* after *M*, all include something explained partly by *M*. The conviction of mental indispensability, which concerns the explanation not only of actions but of many mental events, is a denial of epiphenomenalism. The conviction has hardly ever been questioned by philosophers. It is not explicitly or implicitly questioned in the practice of neuroscience, mainly since neuroscience does not seek complete explanations. Nor is the epiphenomenalism which turns up in neuroscientific philosophizing the real thing.[1]

The two convictions are constraints on what we can label philosophies of mind. Those, applied to the example, tell us how *M* is related to the simultaneous *N*, what the explanatory antecedents of *M* are, and what explains *A*. Another possible constraint is

I am most grateful for comments on this paper to Tim Crane, Marcus Giaquinto, Paul Noordhof, Ingmar Persson, Jane O'Grady, Gabriel Segal, Barry Smith, Jerry Valberg, and Arnold Zuboff. We are not in perfect agreement.

[1] This like much else in the first part of this paper, which sketches three philosophies of mind, is defended in Honderich 1988 and 1990.

mental realism: an acceptance of the intrinsic and distinctive nature of mental events. These, although spatio-temporal, and hence physical by that good test, have a nature different from neural events. Mental realism excludes the true identity theory which is eliminative materialism, and also functionalism, taken as purporting to give a complete or basic account of mental events by looking not at them but elsewhere, to their causal or logical relata. (I agree with Tyler Burge (1979, pp. 105–6), at whose views we will be looking later, that functionalism has been more slogans and projects than a single determinate view.) If the constraint of mental realism has been a matter of some philosophical and perhaps scientific orthodoxy, we have had to put up with significant dissidents. Mental realism and psychoneural intimacy will for a while be assumptions here, and will then be reconsidered along with a good deal else in the light of certain objections. Mental indispensability will go unquestioned.

Reflection on these three constraints has or might have issued in certain identity theories or token-identity theories so-called, different from eliminative materialism.[2] Do not the theories satisfy the constraints? They are to the effect that *M* was *N*, but with that claim curiously understood. Let us have in mind what I shall call just the Identity Theory. In terms of *M* and *N*, and with respect to the relation between them, it includes only this: (1) *MP* was a mental property of that single event—*M* or *N*—which also had *NP* as a neural property, (2) that event was a cause of *A*, (3) there was no nomic connection between the event's having *MP* and its having *NP*, but (4) *MP* in a way supervened on *NP*.[3]

Does the Identity Theory, whatever its promise, in fact satisfy the constraint of psychoneural intimacy? It would do so pyrrhically if it asserted that in *M* and *N* we had one thing and it was only neural, but eliminative materialism is certainly not what we have in (1). Intimacy, if it is achieved by the Identity Theory, will be a matter of the relation between the two properties *MP* and *NP*. We just have it that *MP* and *NP* were properties of one thing. Could an advocate suppose that for *any* two properties of a thing, their being such makes them intimate in the way we take the mental and the neural

[2] At several points in what follows here, although my concern is not exactly Anomalous Monism, I have had in mind Donald Davidson's paper in this volume, of which he most kindly let me have an advance copy.

[3] One thing that stands in the way of this being Anomalous Monism (Davidson 1970) is that I take it to presuppose mental realism. The latter, although maybe consistent with what is said of the mental in Anomalous Monism, is no explicit part of it.

to be intimate? Obviously not. My being a cyclist is not intimate with my being hopeful. Nor would it help if, as may be intended, MP and *NP* were the sole properties of the event which had them.

Is intimacy threatened by (3), the denial of psycho-neural nomic connection? Is it in fact secured by (4), what is called supervenience? One's view of these issues, and others, is at least affected by one's view of more general matters.

Causal connection of the fundamental kind, as it seems to me, typically holds between what we can carelessly call a set of events or conditions or a circumstance *CC*, and another event *E*. The first is a complete explanation of the second—which is not to say, certainly, that the first is the full causal history of the second. The connection, roughly and in a first approximation, was that *CC* preceded *E*, and that if or since *CC* occurred, whatever else were the case, *E* would still have occurred. That is, *E*'s occurrence was independent of the context of *CC* and *E* and would have been independent of changes in that context. This fundamental causal connection *is* a species of nomic or lawlike connection. It is distinguished from other species, which also involve context-independence, in part by *CC*'s being before *E*. Another species of nomic connections are of things simultaneous but otherwise similarly connected. They can be dubbed nomic correlates and they will be of interest to us shortly.

Anyone taking this view or one relevantly like it—certainly there are others—takes it that causal and nomic connections are both connections between events, often the very same connections. If someone else tries to make a difference between causal and nomic connection by saying causality is a relation between events, but laws are linguistic or conceptual (see Davidson 1970/1980, p. 215), the reply will be that *statements* of causal connection are linguistic or conceptual too, but both causal and nomic connection is in the extra-linguistic world. And, most relevantly at the moment, an *absence* of nomic connection will also be taken precisely as much a matter of fact of the extra-linguistic world.

I conjecture that a doctrine about nomic connection and its absence which somehow tends to subtract them from the world, from real properties in real heads, has obscured several facts. The one relevant now is that the Identity Theory's denial of psycho-neural nomic connection (3) does indeed tend to threaten psycho-neural intimacy. It detaches or distances real properties. What it pulls apart, so to speak, is not merely linguistic or conceptual.

But is psychoneural intimacy nevertheless secured by supervenience? For *MP* to supervene on *NP* in the intended sense—the term 'supervenience' is variously used—is for it to be true that if there occurs another event with a property qualitatively identical with *NP*, it will also have a property qualitatively identical with *MP*. Also, if *MP* supervened on *NP*, then if *MP* had been different in a way, *NP* too would have been different in a way—but the relation is such that that an identical change in the property *MP* of a second mental event might accompany a different change in the property *NP* of that event. I thus take it, too, that if *MP* of our original event had been different in just the way supposed, and *NP* was also different in a way, it might have been different in some other way.

Psychoneural supervenience of this kind remains fundamentally obscure, and certainly no light is thrown on *it* by, say, the supervenience of semantics on syntactics. *Why* are properties like *NP* always accompanied by properties like *MP*? *Why* would a change in *MP* be accompanied by some change or other in *NP*? Davidson once answered by saying that these connections are a matter of universal material conditional statements.[4] But that amounts to allowing that the connections are *accidental*, that what we have are generalizations of fact or accidental generalizations rather than anything that deserves the name of law.

I do not pretend that the conviction of psychoneural intimacy is so precise as to allow for more than a *judgement* as to whether this intimacy is preserved by the Identity Theory. Taking into account (1), (2), and (4), my own judgement is that other philosophies of mind do a lot better. We will come to them.

Does the Identity Theory in fact respect the conviction of mental indispensability? A lot is said amplifying proposition (3) that the event which had the properties *MP* and *NP* caused the action *A*. It is said that any event is to be understood as a particular entity having a number of properties. It is said, also, that causal connection is extensional in the sense that statements of it are not affected in their truth-value by an event's being picked out by way of a particular property. It is said, finally, that the event *M* would not have been the event it was if it lacked *MP*, but a different event. As can be seen,

[4] At University College London on 6 June 1978.

none of that precludes or answers a certain question. In virtue of what did *M* cause *A*? Or: What about *M* makes it true that *M* caused *A*?

(*a*) The mentioned view of events as many-propertied entities, rather than precluding the question, invites it.

(*b*) Of course the way we pick out or describe events doesn't affect what they cause—but that doesn't entail that they are not causal in virtue of particular properties of them. So with nomic connection, by the way. It seems clear to me, as implied already, that the way we describe events doesn't affect their nomic connections—but that doesn't entail they are not nomically connected in virtue of particular properties of them.

(*c*) Certainly *M* (or *N*) would not have been the event it was in the absence of MP. But that does not entail that we cannot ask the question of what it was about *M* that made it causal with respect to *A*.

The three possible answers seem to be: *MP* together with *NP*, *MP*, and *NP*. The first two are excluded if it is asserted, with Davidson, that there are no nomic connections into which mental properties enter. We are left with the third, that *NP* alone was causal with respect to *A*. Evidently, if more cannot be said, the Identity Theory fails to secure mental indispensability, as many have agreed.[5] *M* is no more explanatory of *A* than the colour of a thing is explanatory of effects of its weight.

So much for the defence of the Identity Theory which is an attempt to burke the question. There is also a defence, seemingly inconsistent with the first, which *does* allow that we can, as we ordinarily do, distinguish causally relevant properties. It is that the theory secures mental indispensability via the given supervenience of *MP* on *NP*, and just the latter's being taken as causal with respect to *A*. What has been said already of the obscurity of this supervenience makes this unpromising. Further, this supervenience as it has been described leaves it possible that *MP* could have existed as it did without its being the case that *NP* existed as it did. (This is implied by the proposition that if *MP* had been different, *NP* would

[5] Dretske 1989, Fodor 1989, Horgan 1989, Kim 1984*b*, McLaughlin 1989, Robinson 1982, Sayre-McCord 1989. Two of my papers on the issue are Honderich 1982 and 1991.

have been different *in some way or other*.) But then *is* it the case that *MP* is part of a complete explanation, at the time of its occurrence or thereafter, of the occurrence of *A*? No more, it seems, than the pattern of knitting on my mittens helps to keep me dry, since the pattern isn't required for their being waterproof. On the Identity Theory, were you *lucky*, there being no psychoneural nomic connection, that having intended to turn to a page, there occurred a neural event such that you *did* turn to it?

Mutual incomprehension, or anyway my incomprehension, may be one reason for not considering this theory further. A better one is that two different philosophies of mind have the support of what is most relevant to our problems. That is not physics or the philosophy of language or anything other than neuroscience. These philosophies of mind, that is, include psychoneural nomic correlation. If this is what is had in mind by some of who speak of supervenience, it is distinct from the supervenience we have been considering. It reflects the attitude among others that theoretical considerations imported from distant subject-matters do little damage to the hypothesis that *M* and *N* were nomic correlates.

The first of these philosophies of mind is the Theory of Psychoneural Nomic Correlation with Neural Causation. It is suggested by some neuroscientific philosophizing, by which I mean philosophizing by neuroscientists. It is in part to the effect that: (5) Since *N* occurred, *M* also occurred, and hence in the absence of *M*, *N* would not have occurred—with this nomic connection understood along the lines sketched earlier, having to do with independence of context, (6) *N* was the effect of a wholly non-mental causal sequence, (7) *N* was a cause of *A*, and part of a wholly non-mental causal circumstance for *A*.

This picture of the mind is no more dualistic, in any significant sense, than the Identity Theory. It might be so couched as to include what is consistent with it, the particular identity claim (1) in the Identity Theory. Since that claim serves no noticeable purpose, it is disregarded. With respect to what is asserted of the psychoneural relation, it would be very mistaken to suppose that neuroscience offers to us complete specifications of neural correlates of simultaneous mental events. It no more aspires to detail these than it aspires to detail complete explanations of later actions. In this it is like most science. However, it is not philosophically profitable to fasten on the partial specifications it does provide and ignore their import. That, unquestionably, is that the psychoneural relation is as nomic as the relations studied elsewhere in science.

Psychoneural Nomic Correlation with Neural Causation, by way of (5), gives us psychoneural intimacy. It is not too much to say, perhaps, that the conviction of intimacy resolves into the conviction that *M* and *N* were truly identical, or in logical or conceptual connection, or were nomic correlates. It is by excluding all three that the Identity Theory does not do well in this connection. Is the success of the present theory the less because (5) does not include the claim that since *M* occurred, *N* also occurred, but rather allows for one–many psychoneural relations, thereby recalling the earlier supervenience? Those not satisfied with having this sort of nomic connection may wish to consider whether neuroscience as it stands would allow the further claim of one–one psychoneural relations.

Does the theory in fact give us mental indispensability? That it does so is in fact an illusion, bound up with its disaster, that it is inconsistent. This can be seen either by way of ordinary and intuitive ideas of causation or by way of more clarified ideas. We have it in (6) that *N* was the result of a wholly non-mental causal sequence. Any slice through that sequence gives us, to speak in ordinary ways, something that *guarantees* the occurrence of *N*, something such that *N* had to happen. But if it guarantees *N*, then *M* is not required for *N*—it is not something which has to be on hand in order for *N* to occur. That it *is* required is asserted by (5). To make the same point by reverting to the clarified view of causation mentioned earlier, any slice of the non-mental causal sequence for *N* gives us a causal circumstance for it: something of which it is true, roughly and in a first approximation, that since it occurred, whatever else were happening, *N* would still have occurred. But then *N* would have occurred in the absence of *M*. Just this is denied by (5). The trouble with Psychoneural Nomic Correlation with Neural Causation, put yet another way, is that in securing mental indispensability by (5), it denies neural causation (6), or, in asserting neural causation, it denies mental indispensability. Let us consider something else.

The Union Theory, applied to the example, is this: (8) since *N* occurred, *M* also occurred, and hence without *M*, *N* would not have occurred, with this nomic connection understood in the way already indicated, (9) *M* and *N* constituted a psychoneural pair, which is mainly to say a single effect, (10) *M* and *N* were causal with respect to *A*. (Fig. 9.1, below, models the theory, for purposes to which we are coming.)

The Union Theory too is no more dualistic than the Identity Theory: certainly it is consistent with *M* and *N* being taken as properties of one thing. Also, it is no more embarrassed by a certain residual problem than the Identity Theory or other contemporary philosophies of mind which have the virtue of asserting or presupposing mental realism. That is the problem of interaction between the neural and the mental, with the latter taken as also physical but distinctive. The problem is a more manageable descendant, of Descartes's problem of interaction between the physical and the mental, with the latter taken as non-physical.

The Union Theory's principal distinction is that, by (9), it denies that anything caused either *M* or *N* taken separately. The only effect in question is the pair *M and N*. Psychoneural pairs are not in this way unique or, on reflection, surprising. What is true of them is true of any entity which has nomically-related parts. The theory is distinctive, as well, in clearly assigning causal efficacy to both *M* and *N* with respect to *A*. The first and principal distinction of the theory saves it from the disaster of its predecessor, inconsistency.

The Union Theory secures psychoneural intimacy by nomic connection between the simultaneous mental and neural. It secures mental indispensability in the most direct way, by making *M* causal and in fact causally necessary to *A*. Further, with respect to the indispensability constraint taken as relating not to actions but to mental events, we have it that explanations of *M* include, along with environmental and other events, previous psychoneural pairs.

Still, almost everything about it is wrong if a certain group of objections can be sustained. Much is wrong too about the other two philosophies of mind, and many others, and also about the three constraints of psychoneural intimacy, mental indispensability, and mental realism. Let us look at the objections — or rather, for clarity and because life is short, two objections.[6]

M was a mental event, an event within consciousness. As such, it had an intrinsic and distinctive character different from neural

[6] My concentration on Putnam's original paper and Burge's series of papers in what follows implies no want of awareness of the daunting arguments of other philosophers for anti-individualism. See in particular McDowell 1984 and 1986. For an acute discussion of these, see Segal 1989.

events and indeed all non-mental events—that is the assumption of mental realism. (Mental *dispositions* are of course different. The account given of them in the Union Theory is in terms of neural structures, and more particularly neural structures which are parts of causal circumstances for mental events.) We have also been assuming, or should have been, that *M* was a personal event. That is, roughly, it was an event within the history of a person, in this case you. Suppose that all talk of events, made more careful, is talk of a token property or relation or token properties or relations of an entity or entities for a time. Then our assumption has been, in taking *M* as an event within your history, that *M* was a token property for a time of but one entity—the person you are, and more particularly your central nervous system (CNS).

Let us now suppose further of *M*, your intending to turn to a page, that *it involved the meaning of the word 'page'*. That supposition is irresistible, or can be made so by specifying *M* further. Needless to say, it is also obscure. Reflection on it will be part of considering the objection to which we now turn.

What is the meaning of 'page'? Consider the conception owed to Hilary Putnam and derived in part from his wonderfully fertile Twin Earth speculations (1975 *b*, pp. 266–71, 247–52). According to it, a description of the meaning of 'page', and not only of natural-kind terms, has at least four components: (i) syntactic markers that apply to the word, such as 'noun', (ii) semantic markers, such as 'artefact', (iii) a description of further stereotypical ideas of a page, which is to say ordinary or conventional descriptions of a page, perhaps of what it looks like and is for, and (iv) a description of the extension of the word. That is to say that *the meaning* of 'page', as distinct from a description of the meaning, has at least four components or parts, of which one is extension. Let me call this, which of course has antecedents in the work of Frege and Carnap, the *four-component conception*.

Into what kind or kinds of things do the first three components fall? The third, and perhaps the first two, are said to consist in 'ideas'. It is remarked that in the parts of the meaning of 'page' which constitute a stereotype (iii and ii?) we have the sole element of truth in part of a discarded conception of meaning. It is that part which speaks of an intension, concept, or psychological state, but also an abstract entity (Putnam 1975*b*, pp. 249–50, 218). However, it is not clear how small and indeed what that element of truth is, since 'ideas' go unexplained. Into what kind of things does the fourth component fall? Well, we are repeatedly told the extension of any term consists in the set of things of which the term is true. The answer to our question, it appears, is therefore nothing other than *pages*, all the pages that there are. Let us assume that for a while.

We now have the makings of a first objection which, if it succeeds, will indeed destroy the Union Theory and much else.[7] Stated in terms of the Union Theory, it is as follows. (11) *M* involved the meaning of the word 'page'. (12) For *M* to have involved the meaning was for the meaning to be a component or part of *M*. (13) The meaning of 'page' in turn has as a part or component the set of all pages. (14) Therefore *M* cannot have been, as assumed, a personal event, more particularly a property of your CNS. (15) Further, all three hypotheses of the Union Theory seem no less than absurd: *M*, all of it, cannot possibly have been necessary to *N*, and, more generally, psychoneural nomic connection is out of the question; *M* and *N* cannot possibly be a single effect; it would be strange indeed to take all of *M* as causal with respect to *A*, your turning to a page.[8] (16) *M* does not have only the intrinsic and distinctive character assigned to it by mental realism, since in part it is pages. What is to be said of this objection?

There is no one thing that is the meaning of 'page'. That is not to say that 'page' is ambiguous or vague, but that the description (*D*) 'the meaning of "page"' can be and is variously used, anyway by philosophers. In the story of meaning we are considering, it is allowed that there is a common-sense conception of meaning, which pertains to a certain subject-matter. Hence there is such a common-sense conception of the meaning of 'page'. That is, the description (*D*) can be used in a common-sense way, of a certain limited subject-matter. Does the meaning of 'page', so understood, where it may be said to be how the word is used or what is conveyed by it or understood by it, include pages as a component or part? It does not, since the meaning of 'page' so understood will not alter or be decreased if all pages are burned, and since you cannot write on this meaning. That is, we can count on commonsensical speakers insisting, after all the pages are burned, that their

[7] It is suggested by much of what Putnam says (e.g. 1975*b*, pp. 220–1, 271) but not everything (e.g. 1975*b*, pp. 224, 227). Those who think his reflections should be limited to natural-kind terms can of course change the example.

[8] Crane 1991 contains a forceful retort to the objection based on the premise that mental events have certain causal roles in virtue of their intrinsic properties.

lamentations are as meaningful as their apprehensions were beforehand. And we know they never own up to having put notes in the margins of meanings or of any parts of them.

Can the Union Theory make use of this commonsense conception of meaning—what theory doesn't use such notions at some point?—without suffering the embarrassments specified in the objection? Can it escape them, that is, by denying (13) that the meaning of 'page' includes pages? Well, depending on exactly what is taken to be in the commonsense conception, the Union Theory might still be in trouble, related but different trouble, if it allowed as in (12) that the meaning of 'page' was a component or part of *M*. This component, even if it does not include pages, might for a start be of such a kind as to obstruct psychoneural nomic connection.

But (12) is deniable. The common-sense conception of meaning can readily be taken as to the effect that *M*, partly in virtue of the meaning of 'page', was about a particular page, but that *M* did not have the meaning as component or part. It seems undeniable (11) that *M* involved the meaning, but in fact very deniable that *M* included the meaning as a part. The meaning of the word stood to *M*, perhaps, as the way the gun was aimed stood to the gun.

Consider now developed theories of meaning, having the same subject-matter as the common-sense conception. These assign to the description (*D*) 'the meaning of "page"' roughly this sense: syntactic, semantic, and perhaps other rules for the use of 'page'. Suppose the Union Theory uses this conception. Do we have reason to think, before more is said, that this conception will embarrass the Union Theory? Well, if rules were or included print in real dictionaries, and if rules were involved in *M* as parts, that would again be disastrous. But evidently it is possible to deny both antecedents of the conditional. With respect to the first, rules might indeed be so conceived as still to exist after the burning of all the dictionaries.

These brisk reflections might be granted by an objector of the kind we are considering, certainly at some cost. It might hopefully be said, however, that the reflections serve to focus us on what is fundamental to the objection. It is that the four-component conception of meaning, which *does* embarrass the Union Theory, has some unique recommendation. It is when 'the meaning of "page"' is so understood that we get what has a unique recommendation. What is it?

Might it be said that the conception, despite what was asserted five paragraphs back, is the best clarification of our commonsense idea? It is hard to take this seriously, and it is not seriously claimed. The conception is claimed, differently, to be unique in being true to or of something else, or to have some truth-related property, perhaps that it will advance psychology with respect to this other thing. Let me speak just of truth. The claim of truth, given a correspondence or realist idea of truth, does indeed presuppose an identified subject-matter, that of which the conception is true. What is this subject-matter?

It must be safe to say, given what is asserted of it, that the intended subject-matter is this: whatever it is in virtue of which a word means something, *and* what the word means. (The particular subject-matter of whatever it is in virtue of which 'page' means something, and what it means, can also be taken as falling under (*D*) 'the meaning of "page"'. Certainly we are free and easy in our use of such descriptions as (*D*).) It is not going to be possible, I think, to find a description of the identified subject-matter which is more distinct or distant from the account given of it in the four-component conception.

Let us grant, for purposes of argument, that the four-component conception is true of its subject-matter. Does it then follow that the conception of meaning in terms of rules, mentioned a moment ago, is false or incomplete? This follows if the four-component conception is true and the rules conception has the same subject-matter. But it does not have the same subject-matter. It pertains only to a part of the subject-matter of the four-component conception. It pertains to the subject-matter of the first three components: in short, what it is in virtue of which a word means something. The rules conception may be regarded as coming to much the same as the first three components, in different language.

If it is not truth that gives to the four-component conception a unique recommendation, what then? It might have the recommendation of relevance. That is, it might be the subject-matter which has first claim on our attention if our purpose is a certain inquiry, the answering of certain questions. What are our questions? They are those to which a philosophy of mind, in the sense indicated earlier, gives answers. In terms of the example, how is *M* related to the simultaneous *N*, what are the explanatory antecedents of *M*, and what explains *A*?

But if this is our inquiry, it seems plain that what is relevant is just the subject-matter which is the concern of the rules conception and the first three components of the four-component conception. To say that what is relevant to the philosophy of mind is the limited subject-matter is not to beg any question about any problem of meaning, and in particular not to rule out the four-component conception as a description of its subject-matter. Nor need the philosopher of mind, in the restricted sense, be troubled by conceding that meaning has to do with more than mental events, that the philosophy of mind does not deal with all the facts of meaning. I can think of no argument to the effect that conclusions within the philosophy of mind are endangered by this. The philosophy of mind, to speak too quickly, has in particular no concern with the *truth* of mental events, and extension is exactly a matter of their truth. It is of interest to recall at this point that Putnam rightly remarks that only the first three components, and not extension, have to do with the linguistic competence of an individual speaker or language-user (1975*b*, p. 269).

To glance back, it has been assumed for the sake of argument that (*D*) 'the meaning of "page" ', being an elastic description, can be used to convey the four-component conception of the meaning of 'page', which is true of a certain subject-matter. It has been denied that that conception or a consideration of all of its subject-matter is necessary to the philosophy of mind as defined, or has a unique recommendation with respect to it. To make that point with reference to the objection, what we have denied is (13) that the meaning of 'page' must be taken to include pages. We have also concluded that if, using the rules conception, we are still in trouble, we can escape it by denying (12) that for *M* to have involved a meaning was for it to have the meaning as part.

That is not all. Let us reflect a bit more on the four-component conception of meaning, and in particular on extension. We have so far assumed extension to be the set of things of which a term is true, as we are repeatedly told in Putnam's story of meaning. The extension of 'page' is all the pages that there are. That is the foundation of the objection we have been considering. Still, the story of meaning has another theme, indeed a fundamental theme.

This theme has the clear consequence that an extension could not be conveyed to someone in a certain way: by a complete list of things identified only spatio-temporally. There may also be other successful identificatory descriptions which will not convey the extension. Rather, it is fundamental to Putnam's story that the extension of our natural-kind term 'water' is H_2O, and, to speak quickly, that extensions in general are determined by science. It thus appears that the extension of 'page' is not merely the set of things of which the word is true, but a set of things with certain properties, perhaps a set of things with properties given by chemical formulae, perhaps properties which are the micro-structure of pages. More briefly, the extension is now *a set of things with certain scientific properties*.

This is not clear. Consider what has just been said. What *is* picked out by the description (*E*) 'a set of things with certain scientific properties'? What *is* picked out by it if what it picks out cannot also be picked out, as just noticed, by (*F*) 'a set of things with certain spatio-temporal locations', which latter description is true of the very same things? We must wonder if it is the case that (*E*) gives us what can be called a set of things thought of in terms of certain properties. Does it then give us a certain thought of a set of things? Does it give us a property-mentioning rule which limits the use of the word to a set of things?

Those ideas certainly conflict with much of what is said about meaning and in particular extension. Try another idea then. Is the extension of a term certain scientific properties of things of which the term is true? That conflicts with all the usages in the story, to the effect that a word's extension is the set of things or the stuff of which the word is true. Further, it is not properties *however identified* that could possibly be the extension. It would have to be properties identified and thought of in certain ways—we come back to the same sort of difficulty as with things.

Putnam's story of meaning, then, involves the proposition that extension in so far as it is part of meaning is a certain thought of a set of things or, certainly different and better, a rule specifying a set of things by way of certain of their properties. The thought or rule, whatever it is, is not the things. It seems to me he is committed to the proposition, and moreover that something like it is true. There is no difference in kind between the first three components and the fourth component of his view. It is notable that quite independently of his H_2O theme he at least touches on the idea that what is part of meaning is not extension in the sense of a set of things (Putnam 1975*b*, pp. 218, 223–4, 245).

We have here a further reply to the objection we have been considering, more particularly a further reason for denying its premiss (13) that the meaning of 'page' has as a part or component the set of all pages. It is not just that the meaning of 'page' need not be understood in the four-component way, and that that understanding has no unique recommendation, but that if it is adequately understood in that way, we do not get pages included in the meaning of 'page'. What is said in amplification of the four-component conception transforms it into something which does not at all challenge the Union Theory, etc.

Is there a general argument, independent of Putnam's considerations having to do with scientific properties, against an extension's being part of the meaning of a word and being just the things of which the word is true? Consider a time t before the word existed. There *did* exist, we suppose, a certain set of things, say undiscovered particles. At this time, that set was the extension of nothing. It was not an extension—not a denotation, referent, or application. This is so since extensions are *of* something, and, what is connected and more important, an extension is a *discriminated* set—what Putnam calls a somehow determined set. Later on, at t_1, a mark by explicit definition or other means became the word—for the particles. At that time, there came into existence the extension of the word. Evidently this extension cannot *be* the set of particles. The set of particles did not come into existence at t_1. If the meaning of a word includes extension, therefore, this must be extension where that is other than the set of things of which the word is true.

That argument-sketch, if something can be made of it, cannot have attention here. Let us turn instead to another objection to the Union Theory etc. This objection also rests on the idea that mental events are somehow not personal or individual events—not token properties of a person or individual. It is owed to the striking and engrossing work of Tyler Burge, which needs little introduction.

We are asked to think of an episode in our actual world W_1 and then of one in a possible world W_2. In our actual world, we are to suppose, a man at some time thinks he is getting arthritis in the thigh—there occurs mental event M_1. We can suppose there also occurs in him the simultaneous neural event N_1. His thought *is* about arthritis, we are to accept, for the reasons among others that he uses the word in it and that he does have various true beliefs about arthritis, such as that stiff joints are a symptom. But his thought that he is getting arthritis in the thigh is false, since in English 'arthritis' means an inflammation of only the joints.

We now imagine the possible world W_2, different in that 'arthritis' means an inflammation not only of the joints. The dictionaries say so, and other facts of W_2 are consistent with this. The linguistic or social environment is in this way different from that of W_1. However, everything else is the same as in W_1, including our man's life-history neurally described. At a time he thinks what he expresses by saying that he is getting arthritis in his thigh — that is, there occurs mental event M_2. Simultaneously there occurs neural event N_2.

In accordance with the supposition about sameness between the worlds, N_2 is identical with N_1. That is, as we can say, the two neural events are identical in being tokens of the same type. To come to the fundamental point, is M_2 of the same type as M_1? We are to see that it is not. This thought, which is not about arthritis, is different from the thought in W_1, which is. The W_2 thought may be not false but true.

These reflections and their conclusion may be taken to refute the Union Theory, on the assumption that N_1 and N_2 are what it designates to be the neural correlates of M_1 and M_2. Since N_1 and N_2 are in the given sense identical, and M_1 and M_2 are not identical, neither pair (M_1N_1 or M_2N_2) can consist in psychoneural correlates.

More generally, we are instructed that a person's mental events stand in a crucial relation not to personal or individual facts, but to environmental facts of a linguistic or social kind: dictionaries, conventions, standards, institutions, community, minds and activities of others, relations the individual bears to his social environment. The crucial relation is one of some kind of dependency. With environmental change, and no neural change, goes change in mental events. If so, the Union Theory and much else is hopeless. Let us look at it all more closely.

One thing so far unmentioned is that this anti-individualism for good reason tolerates the idea that *something* which is mental *is* a matter only of what happens in the brain. Such a mental event is not in the dependency-relation with environmental facts. In the case of the actual-world episode, the man does at the given time have an idea that reflects his deviant understanding that arthritis is an inflammation of more than the joints (Burge 1979, pp. 92, 94,

95–6, 100–1; cf. p. 78). Theoretical consistency—consistency in one's theory—requires that there also be such an idea in the possible-world episode. It too reflects the understanding that arthritis is an inflammation of more than the joints, a correct understanding. We can refer to these two items as *personal mental events*, and label them PM_1 and PM_2. We leave it entirely open how they are related to M_1 and M_2.

It will help to have models of the Union Theory's supposedly refuted account of the two episodes and of the very different account given by what I shall call Anti-Individualism. Perhaps it is as true to say that the second model is of my difficulties with Anti-Individualism.

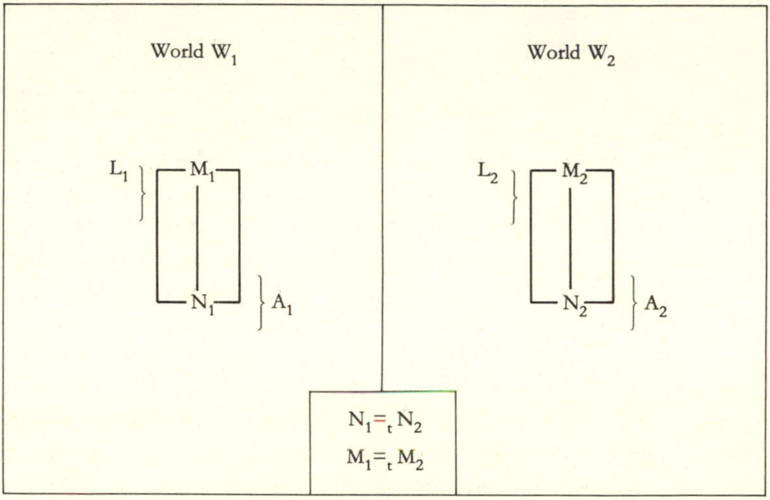

FIG. 9.1. Union Theory

Fig. 9.1 gives the Union Theory's account. L_1 in the actual-world episode is our man's locale, that particular part of the linguistic and social environment which has actually impinged on him in the ordinary way. L_1 is shown as part of a causal circumstance for the psychoneural pair consisting in M_1 and N_1. The latter two events are of course in nomic connection, as shown by the unbroken line joining them, and a single effect, as shown by the bracketing. The psychoneural pair in turn is a part of a causal circumstance for an action A_1. The possible-world episode is similarly represented. Finally, the token events N_1 and N_2 are type-identical ($N_1 =_t N_2$). So are M_1 and M_2.

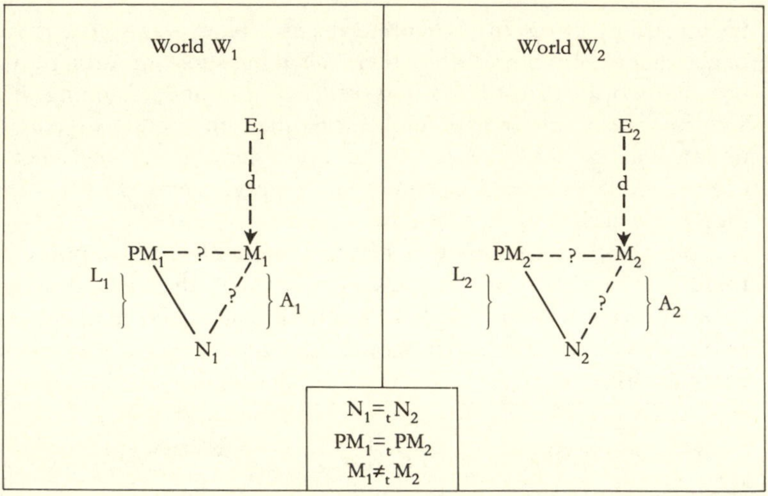

FIG. 9.2. Anti-Individualism

Fig. 9.2 gives my understanding of the anti-individualist account of the two episodes. Taking the actual-world episode, the personal mental event PM_1 is shown in nomic correlation with N_1. It is also in some unspecified relation with M_1. This relation between PM_1 and M_1 could be token-identity, or their being parts of some whole, or anything else. We have it, further, that M_1 stands in the dependency relation *d*, whatever it is, to the set of environmental facts E_1, and in an unspecified relation to N_1. With respect to the first causal connection, the parts of the causal circumstance other than L_1 and also the exact effect are left unspecified, as are the exact parts, other than M_1, of the second causal circumstance. Finally, the token neural events N_1 and N_2 are type-identical, as are PM_1 and PM_2. But, crucially, M_1 and M_2 are not.

The dependency-relation *d* is referred to by a plethora of differing descriptions, often cheek by jowl. What is it?

(I) It is said that mental events are *individuated* by way of owner, time, and content (Burge 1979, p. 111), and very often said that content is *individuated* partly by environment (Burge 1982*b*, p. 286, 1986*a*, pp. 16–17, 1986*b*, pp. 118–19, 1986*c*, p. 697, 1988, p. 650). Further, individuation by way of something is sometimes distinguished from causation by something (Burge 1986*a*, p. 16). Certainly there *is* a common sort of individuation of events by reference to what does not determine them, where determination of an event by something is for that thing to be the answer or part of the answer to the question of why the event occurred. Most of us will take this to reduce to the proposition that there is individuation of events by what does not cause them and is not in nomic connection with them.

But if Anti-Individualism were the hypothesis that E_1 helped to individuate M_1 in the common non-nomic way, it would fail absolutely in its ambition. The anti-individualist models of the two hypotheses could consistently replace the mysterious relation between N_1 and M_1 (and N_2 and M_2) by nomic connection. Evidently Anti-Individualism cannot be the hypothesis in question. The very essence of the doctrine is the denial that the two mental events, being different, are neurally determined or the like.

(II) Is the relation *d* of E_1 to M_1 such that a reference to the first is essential to a full description or interpretation of the second? The very first statement of our Anti-Individualism is indeed that it stresses social factors in descriptions of an individual's mental phenomena (Burge 1979, p. 84, 1986*a*, p. 20). Also, we are told that it is in interpreting a person's words that we need to take account of his community (Burge 1979, p. 84). Further, it is our attribution to a person of a mental event that rests to a fair degree on his having a certain responsibility to communal conventions and conceptions (Burge 1979, pp. 90, 114–15, 116, 1986*a*, p. 25; cf. 1986*c*, pp. 697–8).

This is, so to speak, a linguistic rendering of what can be put more directly. To say that it is impossible to give a full as distinct from an individuating description of M_1 without mentioning E_1 is to say that E_1 is in some relation to M_1, and of course it is such a relation, between these latter terms, that is asserted to hold.

But not all relations which must be represented in full descriptions are determinative relations. My action becomes a killing when my victim dies, and a certain bicycle is mine. Neither the death nor the ownership is determinative. Is there a full description of an answer in an examination which does not mention the examiner's classification of it? If there isn't, that does not make the classification determinative of the answer. If relation *d* were of this undeterminative kind, it would again allow Anti-Individualism to include what it denies, i.e. psychoneural nomic connection.

(III) Is light shed by the mention of a person's responsibility to communal conventions in the last passage referred to above? Could the idea be that a speaker in certain circumstances may be held responsible for what he says, which thing is fixed by what the environment makes his words mean? No doubt that is true, but it does not make *d* into a determinative relation. Also, this idea of responsibility implies a difference between what he says and what he may have had in mind. To talk of *holding* our man in W_1 to having said something false about arthritis is precisely to imply what is denied, that he may not have been thinking of exactly arthritis. If not, was M_1 in fact *identical* with M_2, and is Anti-Individualism deprived of its essential premise and foundation?

(IV) It is conceivable that a different idea of relation *d* is conveyed when it is implied that what environment is needed for is our *understanding* of others' mental events, or the explication of them (Burge 1982*a*, pp. 99, 98). Perhaps there is an isolable truth here, but we have no reason to think that what gives us understanding is also determinative of a mental event in the required way.

(V) Can we then suppose, despite the firm distinction between individuation and causation made above in (I), that relation *d* somehow *does* involve determination of M_1? Other things that are said about the relation might tempt a careless or forgetful reader just to accept that idea. We have it already that with environmental change, and no neural change, goes change in mental events (Burge 1979, p. 79). That is not all. Thoughts are not fixed wholly by neural events, but partly by environment (Burge 1979, p. 104). They depend on environment (Burge 1979, p. 85), and are a product partly of it (Burge 1982*a*, p. 102). They are what they are because of environment (Burge 1988, p. 652) and supervene on it (Burge 1982*b*, p. 286, l986a, p. 4). They are partly determined by it (Burge 1986*b*, pp. 122, 125).

That might indeed suggest that in Anti-Individualism's model of the W_1 episode, what we have is that E_1 simply is part of what causes M_1—and the relation between N_1 and M_1 can be as desired—the first is merely somehow contributory with respect to the second. This causal interpretation of *d* would make trouble for the model, in connection with E_l and L_1, and send us back to the drawing-board.

There is no need for that, it seems. Despite the usages just reported, we are reassured that it is plausible that events in the external world causally affect the mental events of a subject only by affecting in an ordinary way the subject's bodily surfaces (Burge 1986*a*, pp. 15, 17). The model is correct in conveying that the only inward causation is from what was called our man's locale, which is evidently only a part of his environment. (If, in W_1, he had been affected by *more* of his environment, he presumably would have got 'arthritis' right.) Further, we are reassured that any alarmed supposition that the dependency relation amounts to action at a distance by E_1, or special forces or anything of the sort, is out of the question (Burge 1986*a*, p. 20). Putting aside the reassurances, we can conclude for ourselves that Anti-Individualism would simply be incredible if it included causation of my thoughts but not by way of my head.

(VI) Could it be that the dependency relation *d* itself somehow depends on the causal connection between L_1 and—somehow—M_1? 'Information from and about the environment is transmitted only through proximal stimulations, but the information is individuated partly by reference to the nature of normal distal stimuli. Causation is local. Individuation may presuppose facts about the specific nature of a subject's environment' (Burge 1986*a*, p. 17; cf. p. 16). It is remarked that it is non-intentionally that the sensory intake in W_1 and W_2 is the same, that input is non-intentionally identical (Burge 1979, pp. 77–8, 107). Are we to understand that relation *d*, which certainly has to do with mental events as intentional or representative, is itself a matter of the causal relation involving L_1? Again we would have to go back to the drawing-board. But again there is no need. If the dependency relation worked through, so to speak, the causal connection between L_1 and M_1, the end result would be individualist determination of the mental. There would be no effective difference between the Anti-Individualist and Union Theory models.

(VII) What remains? Is there some determinative relation different from what we have had in mind and for good reason rejected? Well, there may be suggestions to that effect. 'Individualism is a view about how kinds are correctly individuated, how their natures are fixed' (Burge 1986*a*, p. 3). Is that one proposition or two? Also, individualism is a denial that there is a 'necessary or deep individuative relation' between environment and mental events (Burge 1986*a*, p. 4, 1986*b*, p. 119). It is also a denial that mental events 'depend essentially' on environment (Burge 1986*b*, p. 119).

Can it be that the dependency relation *d* is one such that E_1 *in* correctly individuating M_1 fixes its nature? Does deep individuation also determine? Is one thing's essential dependence on a second a way of the first thing's being determined but not caused by the second? To these questions, I have no answers, but only the response that the dependency relation, *if* it has a peculiar nature gestured at by these usages, is left unclear, and that if it is made clear, it will surely again make for trouble.

The burden of these reflections, broadly speaking, is that *d* is a merely individuative and non-nomic relation, in which case Anti-Individualism has no reason to deny psychoneural nomic connection, or *d* is a direct determinative connection, and Anti-Individualism is unbelievable, or *d* somehow involves locale and local causation, which is as bad.

The doctrine is an enviably rich one, fully developed, about which only a little more can be said here. The thought-experiment, the reflection on W_1 and W_2, is the premise from which the conclusion about the dependency relation is drawn. My response has been not in the main to examine the premise, but the conclusion. The failure of the conclusion puts into question the premise. I finish with some remarks, no doubt anticipated by others, about the premise taken separately. They are no more than opening cards.

(i) It can be allowed that the W_1 thinker's utterance of his thought is false, or perhaps presupposes a falsehood, and that this is not so in W_2. What might follow from this has been a matter of much philosophical doctrine and dispute. Let me say that there is no easy transition to the conclusion that M_1 is not identical with M_2, as Burge agrees, perhaps unlike some of his readers (Burge 1982*a*, p. 110). My several reflections that the wine in the cellar is cool do not differ because somebody started a fire in the time between them.

(ii) Evidently a difference between M_1 and M_2 can be made by taking words in them as conventionally understood—as understood in W_1 as against W_2. This seems of little significance. Mental events depend for their identity on words used as and however the event's owner uses them. What is non-substitutable is uses, words as used. That is not to deny that the interpretations of both correct and deviant uses in a way depends on convention. The truth does not give us Anti-Individualism.

(iii) To consider the Anti-Individualist model of the W_1 episode, it is impossible to suppose that our thinker had two thoughts, the PM_1 thought and the M_1 thought. He wasn't double-thinking. He had a thought which either did or did not reflect his understanding that arthritis is an inflammation of more than the joints. (That truth may perhaps be missed by running together mental events with mental dispositions.) To opt for the second would be to give *no* effect to our irresistible conviction that he thought of arthritis or the like in a certain way. We are surely driven to PM_1, and its neural correlate.

(iv) Given the causation of M_1, somehow, by the initial causal circumstance including L_1, and the supposition that the environmental relation *d* is a determinative relation, we appear to have an inconsistency like that in the second philosophy of mind discussed earlier—neural causation and psycho-neural nomic connection. Environment is made necessary to what is already guaranteed.

It is to be agreed that a philosophy of mind must be tested by total plausibility (cf. Burge 1979, pp. 92, 97). I think the Union Theory wins over Anti-Individualism.

10

Agency and Causal Explanation

JENNIFER HORNSBY

1. Introduction

SOME philosophical problems about agency can be put in terms of *two points of view*. From the *personal* point of view, an action is a person's doing something for a reason, and her doing it is found intelligible when we know the reason that led her to it. From the *impersonal* point of view, an action would be a link in a causal chain that could be viewed without paying any attention to people, the links being understood by reference to the world's causal workings. We might take it for granted that there are truths available to be discovered from each of these points of view. The problems about agency surface when we start to wonder whether the impersonal point of view does not threaten the personal one.

We might think that a full understanding of everything that happens when there is an action could be had without anyone's knowing who did what thing for what reasons. But then, if the whole truth about an action and its causal past and future can be given in viewing it as a manifestation of the world's causal workings, the impersonal point of view can seem to displace the personal one. Of course the personal point of view might still be adopted, even if it seemed redundant from another point of view. But two lines of thought may be used to make it seem redundant *tout court*. First, there is the thought, which Thomas Nagel has made especially vivid, that it is essential to our conceiving of our ourselves as agents that we take our actions to be completely accounted for in the terms that we use as agents; the possibility of treating actions from the impersonal point of view would then subvert our ordinary conception of ourselves.[1] Second, there is the thought, which is

[1] Or, again, free agency, if not agency itself, may be thought to be subverted: it is said that the impersonal point of view, insofar as it treats actions as happenings, and treats any happening as inevitable of occurrence, exposes freedom as an illusion.

My immediate concern is with with the problem that Nagel discusses under the

familiar in contemporary philosophy of mind, that the impersonal point of view is more 'objective', or for some other reason has better credentials, than the personal one. In order for the personal point of view to be metaphysically sound, then, it would need to be subsumed under the other one; but the possibility of such subsumption may be doubted.[2]

Both these lines of thought introduce rivalry between the two points of view, and suggest that the impersonal one may triumph. Either the personal point of view is supposed to be undermined, by being revealed to rest on an assumption that the possibility of taking an impersonal view shows to be false; or it is supposed to be refuted by the impersonal view, which is meant to be better placed for seeing the truth.

In this paper I attempt to block the idea that the two points of view are in competition. My suggestion will be that actions are not in fact accessible from the impersonal point of view.

Two fairly immediate routes to my suggestion might be taken. One starts from denying that actions are events; the other, from denying that the explanation of action is causal explanation. Each of these denials would enable one to deny, in turn, what I do deny—that actions can be located in the impersonal world of causes. But I shall not follow either route. Indeed I start by saying why I think that actions are events (Section 2), and that reason explanation is causal explanation (Section 3). This will enable me to assemble materials for an argument that makes my suggestion plausible (Section 4). I offer some further support for it (Section 5) before I treat the two problems about agency (Sections 6 and 7).

head of Autonomy (Nagel 1986, chap. 7, Section 2), to which page references are given below). I agree with Nagel that 'the essential source of the problem is a view of persons and their actions as part of the order of nature, *causally determined or not*' (p. 110, my italics); but I leave it open whether there might be a separate threat to freedom such as would be suggested by the first sentence of this note. (In Nagel's own terms, the problem I discuss here is one about freedom: he distinguishes a question about agency, which he puts aside, from two problems about freedom, of which autonomy is the first.)

[2] The doubt I am thinking of here is what leads to eliminative materialism. But any philosopher who begins with the assumption that psychological explanation requires vindication through connection with physical science aims at such subsumption; if some such philosophers are not eliminativists that is because they do not doubt that the requirement can be met. See Section 7 below.

2. Actions as Events

We know something about the causal past of some water's boiling if we know that the water is in the kettle that Peter switched on because he wanted to make a cup of tea. Something has happened because someone wanted it to. If we see the water's boiling as an event, then we may think of an action also as an event: an action is an event that causes another, where the occurrence of the other typically amounts to the agent's having something she wanted.

Someone might allow that there is causality here, but say that only a philosopher bent upon forcing causality into the event–event model would introduce 'an action'. It is Peter with whom we credit the switching on of the kettle, it may be said; and if something about him is relevant, then it is only his wanting boiling water. This response is correct insofar as it looks back to Peter and what he wanted, and recognizes that these are not events. But it ignores the fact that Peter had to do something if the water was to boil, that wanting it to boil was not enough. There is no need to invent an item to bridge the gap between Peter's states of mind and the event of his want's being satisfied: when his want was satisfied, the gap was bridged—he switched on the kettle. Or, in an alternative idiom, there was an event—his switching on the kettle.

When it is accepted that there are actions, and that they are events, questions arise about which events they are, and how many of them there are. Not every event in whose description the name of a person features is an action; there is only an action when someone does something intentionally.[3] But since a person's intentionally doing something may be the same as her doing something else (intentionally or unintentionally), there is more to be said about the individuation of actions. For my part, I accept the view that (nearly enough) if someone did one thing by doing another then her doing the one thing was the same as her doing the other: when Peter boiled the water by switching on the kettle, his boiling the water was his switching on the kettle. On this account of individuation, the various things that people do are, many of them, the bringing about of effects of various sorts. And of course a single action can bring about a series of effects: an action of Peter's was the initiation

[3] I assume the criterion of actionhood in Davidson 1971: I take 'There is some description under which the event is intentional' to be equivalent to 'There is something the agent intentionally does'.

of a series that contained both the kettle's being on and the water's coming to the boil.

Even when this view of individuation is accepted, it may still be asked to what extremes we should take the idea that things people do allude to effects of their actions. Elsewhere I have argued that *causation* is implicit whenever we impute agency (see chaps. 1–3 of my 1980 book). Our conception of a person as an agent is a conception of something with a causal power; whether we think of a person having brought about a movement of a bit of her body or a bomb's exploding in a distant field, we should see her action as her causing something—as causing the movement, or the explosion, or whatever. This view has been challenged, because it is thought that movements of bodies must be more intimately connected with actions than is suggested by calling them effects. But the view may not be incompatible with the idea that bodily movements are parts of actions—as David Lewis has pointed out in defending *piecemeal causation* (Lewis 1986*b*, p. 173). And bodily movements need not be denied a special status in relation to agency. For we may think that our ability to make bodily movements is constitutive of our having the power that we have as agents—to initiate series of events containing some we want. An action is the exercise of such a power, and a person's actions are the events at the start of those series she initiates.

3. Reason Explanation as Causal Explanation

The previous section has been concerned for the most part with the causal future of actions. But it takes something for granted also about the causal past of a person's intentionally doing something: it assumes that in finding out what Peter wanted, we learnt something about the causal history of some events. It may seem, then, that the claim which it is the purpose of the present section to defend—that action explanation is causal explanation—has already been presupposed, and that nothing is in dispute here. But the matter is not so straightforward.

What makes it complicated is that there have been thought to be two different issues about causal explanation. We are told that there are philosophers who accept that the items alluded to in giving a reason explanation play a part in the causal past of an action, but who nevertheless deny that rational explanation is itself causal explanation.[4] Supposedly these philosophers think that if you cross the road because you want to get to the other side, then there is an explanation of your crossing in terms of where you want to get to, and there is a causal connection between the fact of your wanting to be there and your crossing, but the existence of an explanation and the existence of a causal connection are separate matters. What I mean to defend is the claim that reason explanation is causal in a sense that rules out this idea of causality and explanatoriness coming apart — the claim that reason explanation is causal-explanation (where the hyphen signals that causality and explanatoriness enter the scene together, as it were).

On the face of it, it is a strange position that these philosophers are said to occupy. For one might have thought that the best way to persuade someone that a person's having the reasons she does bears causally on what she does was to show that explanations that give people's reasons are causal-explanations. There is an argument that asks us to consider a case in which someone did something and had a reason for doing it, yet did not do it as a result of having that reason. We are asked to contrast this with the case in which we can explain her action by mentioning her reason—where she did it because she had the reason. The difference between the two cases suggests that *causation* and *explanation* are inextricable: both are introduced when we are told why someone did something — when we find the word 'because' between a statement saying what she did and a statement saying what her reason for doing it was.[5]

Why then should claims about causal connections have been thought to be separable from claims about the causal-explanatory nature of reason explanation? Presumably the answer is that we have to make allowance for those philosophers who deny that

[4] McGinn 1979, p. 26 distinguished four different theses about the explanatoriness/causal status of rational explanations. He and many others have subsequently put to work the particular (putative) distinction I am concerned with here: see below.

[5] The argument is in Davidson 1963, p. 9. Not that 'because' is everywhere a causal notion. Where action explanation is concerned, there may be more to say to ensure that causation has been at work when the explanatory claim can be made. But this is supported when it is seen (a) that the 'because' goes alongside other, recognizably causal idioms ('His belief *led* him to . . . .'; 'Her desire *moved* her to . . . .'; 'Her reason was *operative*'); (b) that the explanations rely on a network of empirical interdependences, recorded in counterfactuals ('If she had not wanted——, but had still believed that ——, then . . . .').

reason explanation is causal *tout court*.[6] They do not deny that reason explanation is explanation; so it might seem that in order to be able to contradict them, we have to isolate some 'purely causal' statements about mental states and actions which we, but not they, assent to. A prominent candidate for our endorsement is 'The primary reason for an action is its cause'.[7] Since someone might hold this without assuming any particular account of how the explanation of action works, there seems to arise the possibility of isolating it from any thesis about explanation, and thus of adopting the position that reason explanation, though it mentions causes, is not itself causal-explanation.

Well, we have seen already that support for the thesis of causal-explanatoriness may be given without assuming the availability of any 'purely causal' statements. What we should realize now is that a defence of causal-explanation need have no involvement at all with 'purely causal' statements. Indeed consideration of what goes on when action explanations are sought and found should make us very sceptical about them.

When we seek an 'action explanation', one question we usually want answered is 'Why did she do such and such thing?' We may agree that actions are events without supposing that this question is equivalent to 'Why was there an event of such-and-such kind?' Asking why *a* ϕ-d, we hope to learn something about *a*, the person; but if we asked why *a*'s ϕ-ing occurred, *a* might not be a subject of concern at all. To a question about why someone did something, an expected answer usually goes: 'She thought——', or 'She wanted——'. Philosophers' official version of an answer goes: 'She thought——*and* she wanted——'. The official version is appropriate, because someone who intentionally did something had a reason for doing it, and, having a reason, she must have believed something about what would be conducive to the satisfaction of some desire she had. When a relevantly connected belief and desire are both mentioned (e.g. 'She thought she could get to the other side by crossing and she wanted to get to the other side'), the explanation is successful inasmuch as it brings us to realize that what mattered, so far as her doing what she did is concerned, is her having had the reason she did.

[6] These are the writers to whom Davidson was responding in his 1963 article, and whom he cited there, p. 3, n. 1. And of course their view is still held by some today, e.g. Stoutland 1976.

[7] This was the thesis guaranteeing the availability of 'purely causal' statements that Davidson arrived at in his 1963. I discuss some details of Davidson's own position in the Appendix to this chapter.

It may seem only a short step from this point to speaking of reasons as 'belief–desire pairs', and to saying 'The primary reason is the cause'. But if we take this step we arrive on much less firm ground. What sort of thing is the primary reason now supposed to be? It cannot be what an agent has when she has a reason; for you may have the same reason to do something as someone else, but we are surely not to suppose that your believing and desiring something causes someone else's action. If we are to make sense of it as 'the cause', then the primary reason must be an item that there is if and only if the relevant agent believes some particular thing and desires some other (related) thing. But why should we think that there is any such item as this? Why should acknowledgement that we say something about what she believed and desired in causally explaining why she did what she did lead us to accept the existence of anything that 'the cause of her action' stands for?

We are encouraged to believe in the things at issue when we are told that the agent's belief and her desire are each of them 'token states'. Then her reason (the candidate denotation of 'the cause') is meant to be the fusion, or perhaps the intersection, of two token-states. But even if we think we know what it is for a token-state to be a cause, can we be sure that we know what it would be for this sort of thing—composed somehow from two states of the same person—to be the cause?[8] And if such a fusion (or pair, or whatever) were indeed the cause of an agent's doing what she did, how would it relate to all the other causal truths about the situation? Suppose that we could explain why Jane had done something by pointing out that she didn't think that *p*. Is there in that case a token state of her not believing that *p* that was also some part of the cause?

I do not know how one should answer these questions. The point is that we do not have to answer them if we deny that the causal-explanation view relies on the idea of discrete things combining (interacting?) in the production of action. What we rely on is only a

[8] For serious, valiant, exhaustive, but eventually abortive, attempts to make sense of the idea of causal interaction between states of persons, see W. S. Robinson 1990. Like Robinson, I think that the notion of a token-state is not unacceptable, but that it has been put to unacceptable use in philosophy of mind. My brief remarks here can only gesture towards the problems that Robinson uncovers. (Occurrences of 'state' in this paper are of two sorts: (i) those that come into descriptions of views opposed to my own, (ii) those that rely on our ordinary conception of a mental state—something a person can be in, so that a state is not a particular.)

network of intelligible dependencies between the facts about what an agent thinks, what she wants, and what she does. When we know why she did something, the fact that she did it may be seen as depending crucially on the fact that she wanted some particular thing and thought some particular thing. And the dependence is of a causal sort, of course.

Accepting that *belief* and *desire* are causal-explanatory notions, we cannot but suppose that people really do think things and want things, and that whether or not someone thinks a particular thing, or wants a particular thing, may make a genuine difference to what she does and says. But if the causal reality of *belief* and *desire* is just their causal-explanatory reality, then it need make no use of a further idea—of items inside people that we latch on to when we give action explanations.[9] Once this further idea is in place, it can come to seem that the explanatory value of *belief* and *desire* is quite unconnected with the value of those concepts in causal understanding—as if the particular contents of a particular person's beliefs and desires had nothing to do with her tendencies to do one thing rather than another. It is then that one may be led to the curious claim that 'the rational explanation of action mentions causes but is not *itself* causal explanation'.

4. Anomalousness

The philosopher most often said to be committed to this claim is Donald Davidson. The argument that he gave for monism is the focus in the present section. So far as the alleged commitment is concerned, I shall take Davidson's part: he told us why we should think that reason explanation is causal-explanation, and he has never gone back on that.[10] Another thing I shall take over from him

[9] It is a good question why people should think that recognizing the dependencies we do is not enough to ensure that we have a case of the operation of causality. Hume taught that the conception we have of necessity, as a putative ingredient of our idea of causality, is a figment, since, he said, there is no impression to which our conception corresponds. Many philosophers are happy to reply to Hume that insofar as we take necessity to be inextricable from causality, we do not take it to be an isolable, perceptible ingredient of causal transactions: searching for necessity among impressions is not the way to uncover our understanding of causation. But even when this reply has been given, the idea that our understanding of causality resides in the putative objects wherein an impression of necessity was supposed by Hume to be sought is not renounced.

[10] Many have alleged the commitment in one or another version. Smith (1984) is

is the thesis of the mental's irreducibility. Nevertheless Davidson's argument runs contrary to my suggestion that actions are not accessible from the impersonal point of view. And it is by questioning it, and attempting to diagnose a widely felt dissatisfaction with it, that I hope to make my suggestion plausible.

Davidson's famous argument uses three premisses: (1) of causal dependence, (2) of causation's nomological character, and (3) of the mental's anomalousness (see e.g. Davidson 1970/1980, p. 208). Someone who wanted to demonstrate that actions (among other mental events) are present to the impersonal point of view might use only the first two premisses. Premiss (2) says that 'events related as cause and effect fall under strict deterministic laws'; premiss (1) acknowledges (among much else[11]) that actions are related causally to other things. When the operation of strict deterministic laws is thought of as something impersonally described, then the premisses combine to secure a place for actions in an impersonal account. In this argument the presence of actions to an impersonal point of view purports to be demonstrated in the same way as the physical nature of actions purported to be demonstrated by Davidson—through their location in a law-governed world.

Davidson's own argument was different. His route to monism had to be less direct: the nomological character of causality would be of no help to him in showing that mental events are physical if it were possible to see them as law-governed even while they were conceived of as belonging to mental kinds; premiss (3), of the anomalousness of the mental, is ineliminable. This premiss relies on a 'categorial difference between the mental and the physical' which ensures that mental kinds cannot themselves be nomological kinds. In Davidson, then, the application of nomological (and thus physical) vocabulary to mental particulars is shown indirectly—

responsible for the particular formulation of the claim quoted above, at the end of Section 3. Some write as if Davidson had deliberately and explicitly committed himself to it (e.g. Lennon 1990); others as if it required argument to demonstrate his commitment (e.g. Honderich 1982). Some, like Smith, think that the alleged commitment does no damage; but most hold it against Davidson, and say that it shows that in his view the mental is epiphenomenal (e.g. H. Robinson 1982). But whatever the status or consequence of his commitment is supposed to be, an enormous volume of writing suggests that Davidson must in consistency allow that reason explanation is not causal-explanation.

[11] It is often assumed that whereas the states and events that precede actions must be treated by an argument for monism, actions themselves can be left out. But I think that it is only a prejudice about the nature of mind that leads to the idea that *being in mental states* is problematic whereas *doing things intentionally* is not.

through the involvement of the mental with causality (premiss 1) and the involvement of causality with nomologicality (premiss 2). But the argument is like the more direct one: in finding mental items to have properties of each of two sorts, where possession of one sort (mental, personal) is the ground of an argument for possession of the other sort (physical, impersonal). In Davidson, there are the properties that mental items have in virtue of which we can treat their possessors as rational, and there are those they have in virtue of which they can be seen as situated in the nomological causal network, and which ensure they are physical.

Davidson believes that properties of both sorts — rational and nomological — can be used in explanations. And this belief is one source of the widespread supposition that Davidson ought really to deny that rational explanation is causal-explanation. There is thought to be a difficulty about a single thing's possessing two causal-explanatory properties. If there were a genuine difficulty, then a nomological story about an action's occurrence would rule out the possibility of a rational explanatory story that was also causal, so that Davidson would have to reject the causal-explanation thesis. Many have said that Davidson is in truth an epiphenomenalist: that for him, mental events are, *qua* mental, inert, since it is in virtue of their physical, nomological properties that they are causally efficacious (see n. 10). But when the matter is put like this, a reply on Davidson's behalf is easily found. He can simply deny that an item can have only one causal-explanatory property. And he has explained why we should deny this: we are often in the position of taking ourselves both to know one explanation of an event's occurrence, and to be justified in believing that there is another explanatory story about it of whose details we are actually quite ignorant (see Davidson 1967). Could it not be like this where actions are concerned?[12] Perhaps the fact that there is a causal-explanatory story that we cannot tell need not interfere with the idea that we can give a rational causal-explanation.

None the less the feeling that it does interfere is widespread. If we want to understand why nomological and rational explanation, as Davidson interprets them, should be thought to conflict, then we

[12] See e.g. Davidson 1970/1980, p. 219, where he speaks of generalizations which support explanations, but which are heteronomic, i.e. not stated in a form and vocabulary that points to a finished law. For more on this, see the Appendix to this chapter.

need to remember that his conception of rational explanation was supported by considerations that are quite unaffected when the argument for monism is given. This means that the problem that so many people think they see about his retaining the causal-explanatory thesis may really be a problem about accepting the conclusion that Davidson wants us to add to the thesis. The feeling that Davidson's theses conflict may be based in a sense of conflict between the picture one gets of the operation of mental events if one accepts Davidson's version of monism on the one hand, and a picture of how we understand people. And if that is so, then the supposed difficulty for Davidson corresponds to a more general difficulty: that in attempting to view the mental impersonally, one finds that its causal efficacy is lost.

In Davidson's case, what we have to ask is why it should be accepted that there is a nomological, causal story even about the events that are actions. The Nomological Character of Causality, as it is used in Davidson's argument, says that a law lurks in any case where it is possible to rely on causal notions to make something intelligible. Can we support this even while we assume that finding people causally intelligible is a 'categorially different' matter from understanding physical causal goings on? What are the grounds for believing that rational explanations themselves mention items that can be picked out in nomological vocabulary? Well, Davidson thinks that we regularly have evidence of laws covering particular cases, and that this gives us evidence that some full-fledged causal law exists covering each and every explanation. He has said that the evidence for the operation of laws is summarized in such generalizations as 'Windows are fragile, and fragile things tend to break when struck hard enough, other conditions being right'. And he likened behavioural generalizations to generalizations like this one (see Davidson 1963/1980, p. 16). So his idea must be that our ability to frame rough-and-ready generalizations about pieces of behaviour is to be taken as a symptom that they too are governed by law. But the trouble now is that the thesis of the mental's anomalousness will seem to obstruct any full assimilation of 'behavioural generalizations' to generalizations about the breakings of windows.

The distinctive thing about rational explanations—which points to the mental's anomalousness—is that our acceptance of them relies on the 'discovery of a coherent and plausible pattern in the attitudes and actions' of a person: they are 'governed by an ideal'. In that case the special character of the mental sets answers to *Why*? questions about what people have done apart from answers to questions about why (e.g.) windows break. Davidson once said that 'our justification for accepting a singular causal statement is that we have reason to believe an appropriate causal law exists though we do not know what it is' (Davidson 1967/1980, p. 160). Well, perhaps we do take ourselves to witness the operation of physical law when we see the window break, and perhaps that is our justification for thinking that the ball's hitting it caused the window's breaking. But our justification for accepting an account of why someone did something would seem to have nothing to do with any reason we might have for believing in the world's nomological workings—not if discovery of a rational pattern is what we actually rely on, and if our aim is conformity with a rational ideal.

Even if a fully general link between 'singular causal statements' and laws could be established, it is unclear that that would help very much in an argumentative strategy for bringing mental particulars inside the scope of laws. For when an action explanation is given, it may be that there is no item said to stand to an action in the relation of 'cause' (see Section 3). If that is so, then the possibility of a single state or event's possessing two causal-explanatory properties is not something that Davidson can exploit in the present connection; if we are trying to accommodate the causal efficacy of the mental, we cannot now think of ourselves as seeking another causal-explanatory property pos sessed by some item already possessed of a nomological one. This point also may be seen as connected with the special explanatory character of the mental, in virtue of which it is irreducible and, in Davidson's sense, anomalous. An action explanation is not a reply to a question about why some event occurred, and, in revealing what an agent thought and what she wanted, it does not introduce any singular term for 'the cause'. Rather it shows a person's doing something to make sense by seeing her as (at least approximately) rational—as conforming (more or less) to norms of consistency and coherence in her thought and practice. Since its focus is how things were with *her*, it is no wonder that no 'purely causal' statement can be extracted from the explanation. The objective is to see a causally complex whole—a person—in a certain, intelligible light; and this fits ill with the idea of locating an item on which an event that happens to be an action may be seen to follow in the way things do, nomologically speaking.[13]

[13] Consider LePore and Loewer's (1987) attempted reconciliation of (*a*) mental items'

Of course Davidson himself would be the first to acknowledge that accounts of action are outside the direct reach of physical law. The present question is why physical law should be thought to reach them at all, however indirectly. In order to use the notion of a law to forge a connection between the causal-explanatory nature of a concept and the physical nature of the things it applies to, Davidson relies on a transition from the causal-explanatory to the 'purely causal'. But the connection is one that the irreducibility of the mental stands in the way of, and our inability to make the transition may be seen as a symptom of that.

My argument here can be sketchily stated by setting out the steps that Davidson needs to take:

mental → causal-explanatory → 'purely causal' → nomological → physical

Someone might start from a conception of the nomological, and look backwards, insisting that some property that the *nomological* encompasses applies to anything that has some causal-explanatory property. But then she would precisely have disregarded the special causal-explanatory character of the *mental* whose concepts have application to people; and it would be unsurprising if she seemed to reach the position that the mental is epiphenomenal. Someone else might start with a conception of the mental and try to move forwards. But the conception of the causal-explanatory she reaches at the first step provides her with no way of moving to the 'purely causal' that would take her on.

The quicker argument we considered earlier is equally affected if it aspires to bring mental states within the compass of an impersonal view. In order to see the two arguments as alike, we thought of the impersonal point of view as that from which the search for

subsumability under laws, and (*b*) mental properties' being both anomalous and causally efficacious. For these authors, the causal relevance of mental states consists in the truth of counterfactuals each to the effect of an item's being such that if it had lacked some property, then some event would have lacked some property. We find, then, that the claims that serve to underpin rational explanations make no essential mention of a person.

Thinking of the objective of propositional attitude explanation as I suggest, we must take it for granted that content is both explanatory and externally fixed (where content is that which is specified when it is said what people think or want or hope or . . .). I can only gesture here towards the idea that my remarks have wider application: that they are a response to what is widely perceived to be a problem about content.

nomological explanation is appropriate. The nature of causation itself was then supposed to take us straight from a personal to an impersonal point of view.

personal → causal → impersonal

Again there is no way to take the necessary steps. For what constitutes the irreducibility of the mental/personal is the operation of a particular standard of causal intelligibility. But if the causal features of concepts used in action explanation are just their causal-explanatory features, then they are precisely what are missing from the impersonal point of view where a different standard of causal intelligibility is in place.

We now lack any argument for subsuming actions in the impersonal world of causes. When we start from a rational explanation, no conception of the nomological can be brought into sight. It seems that the particular character of action explanation prevents actions from being present to the impersonal point of view.

5. Actions Impersonally Conceived?

Before relating this conclusion to the problems about agency we began with, I want to draw attention to what I see as a sign of its correctness, and also to some habits of thought that may obscure its correctness.

Seeing something as an action requires the identification of a person and the exercise of concepts that we put to work in understanding people. This on its own does not show that an event that is an action might not also be picked out by someone operating without such concepts as *belief*, *desire*, and *intention*. But I suggest now that someone not operating with these concepts would not in fact be able to identify an action.

Consider a particular case. Bring on to the scene not only Peter's action, and the series of events which he initiated and which the action caused, but also such events as one is likely to think of as causal antecedents of an action — neuronal firings, signals going out to the nerves, muscles contracting. In the picture is a whole collection of events leading from some happening in the depth of Peter's brain all the way to an event beyond his body in which his desire's being satisfied consists. The question to ask is: 'how much of all that we have brought on to the scene does the action consist of?' About some things, we feel certain: events in the brain quite remote from the motor system are no part of the action; events in the world quite remote from Peter's body are no part of the action. But certainty about these things gives us no exact answer where to draw the lines. Looking at the picture, we have no opinion in some cases whether this or that is a part of the action.

Of course we do know exactly what the action is: it is Peter's switching on the kettle (or whatever). But having a determinate answer from the perspective from which Peter is apparent does not give us anything determinate to say in the terms of the picture. Nor, it seems, do we lose anything by resisting the thought that there ought to be some exact answer from this point of view, or that the answer we give from our and Peter's point of view is somehow inadequate. If we are content to accept that no answer to our question can be forced upon us, that may be because there is no answer: as the picture is drawn, we start to adopt an impersonal point of view, from which it is impossible to locate actions.

A reductionist might say that scientists would be capable of returning the answer, and that it is no surprise to find that we cannot do so without further investigation.[14] But, though it is true that a reductionist is likely to have confidence that there is a definite brain-event at the beginning of the action, when it comes to a question about the end—about the action's finishing-point, as it were — even her confidence will evaporate. For the question in this case concerns the line between an action and its effect, which has always seemed to everyone to be a philosophical question — not a question for further empirical investigation, but one about how common sense and talk operate. Yet it still does not seem that there is a definite answer to it which we have immediate intuitions about.

Thoughts about actions are much less the product of intuitions than philosophers have come by habit to suppose. Of course the thought that there are actions is, in one sense, something that no one would dream of denying. But it is not in this sense that I argued, and tried to make it seem obvious, that there are actions. What a non-philosopher means when she accepts that there are actions is that the phenomenon of action is exemplified: people do things (for reasons). But she does not mean (even if it can be made obvious)

[14] In Hornsby 1981, Section 3.2, I attempted to show that the reductionist would have trouble making a plausible case anyway.

that there are events each one of which is a person's doing something. The word 'action' is ambiguous. Where it has a plural: in ordinary usage what it denotes, nearly always, are the things people do; in philosophical usage, what it denotes, very often, are events, each one of them some person's doing something. We may find ourselves with views which we can readily express in the language of action, and then, finding it obvious that there are actions, we (philosophers) assume that we have views which we can readily express in the language of events. Explanation of action is a case in point. We may move from knowing that we have an instance of 'action explanation' straight to thinking that we have an explanation of an action (event).[15]

Our picture may provide another case. If our opinions about *action* do not immediately yield anything definite to say about actions (events), then we should not have expected it to seem evident where the line comes between the action and its effects. Earlier I mentioned the view that movements of people's bodies must be more intimately connected to actions than is suggested when they are thought of as effects, and Lewis's claim that a movement of someone's body is both an effect and a part of her action (Section 2). It is supposed to be quite plain to common sense that a bodily movement is a part of an action.[16] But is this really something we are justified in feeling we are apt to be right about straight off? (Never mind for the moment whether we are right about it or not.) Certainly we know that no one moves her finger unless her finger moves; and we know that we can tell by observation what people do, and that we could not observe someone move her finger unless we saw her finger move. But we also know that these considerations alone could not suffice to show that her finger's moving is a part of her action—no more than

[15] Where we talk e.g. about 'human action' (general, no plural), this is another use again from the two I have separated. (Presumably we find this general use in 'action explanation'. So where something is an instance of action explanation, it is actually wrong to think of it as an explanation of an action in either of the two senses of 'an action' that I have distinguished.)

Dretske (1988) holds that actions are not events, but are complex causal processes. His argument is that a bit of behaviour is a complex causal process, and he assumes that philosophers had always meant a bit of behaviour by 'action'. Dretske is relying on the assumption that I am questioning: the assumption that the things we naturally say can readily be expressed as claims about actions.

[16] Presumably, though, it would be allowed that it takes some argument, or at least explication, to get someone to agree that bodily movements are effects of actions—as both Lewis and I think.

similar considerations could suffice to show that Jones's death was a part of Smith's killing him. Again we know that typically when there is an action, an agent moves her body and thereby initiates a series of events, so that something she wants comes to happen. But this consideration does not circumscribe an action, beyond showing it to be where the agent is. It is not at all clear what would definitively settle the question as to which things are parts of actions. This will not seem worrying if we are aware that there need be no more plain truths about the events that are actions than there are plain truths about action (about agency, and things people do).

The events that are actions are understandably a focus of philosophical debate; but they are not ordinary objects of scrutiny. It is important to appreciate this, because the supposition on the part of philosophers that all our naïve opinions in the area of action readily come to us stated in the language of events is one source of the presumption that actions are impersonally apparent.

6. Agency Undermined?

Thomas Nagel takes it to be evident that actions can be impersonally apparent. I turn now to the first of the two problems about agency—the one that he introduces. In his *View From Nowhere*, he assumes that we know that there is a possible picture from an 'external perspective' which includes actions in it; the 'external perspective' is supposed to provide 'an objective view of a particular person with his viewpoint [which is an internal one] included' (1986, p. 3). (I hope that it will be enough for the time being to say that the external perspective of Nagel's assumption is thus an impersonal one. I leave it to the next section to relate Nagel's external/internal or objective/subjective distinction more exactly to the impersonal/personal one.)

Nagel thinks that the threat to autonomy—to the idea that 'we are authors of our actions' (1986, p. 114)—arises when we find that our conception of ourselves as agents is ambitious: 'our capacity to view ourselves from outside . . . gives us the sense that we ought to become the absolute source of what we do' (1986, p. 118). This sense 'is not just a feeling but a belief', he says, although he suspects that it may be 'no intelligible belief at all' (1986, p. 114). But Nagel does not think that our inability to make the belief fully intelligible diminishes the threat to agency: we can have aspirations without knowing how they might be met.

There is no doubt that it can be disturbing to try to think about ourselves in the manner that Nagel suggests. And it may seem evasive, even unphilosophical, to insist that we turn from our thoughts to their verbal expression. Nevertheless I suggest that we have to look carefully at Nagel's words, and to ask in the first instance what he means by 'action'.

If 'actions' stands for the things we do, then, evidently enough, we do them; but they are not particulars, and we are not their authors or sources. If 'actions' stands for a class of events, on the other hand, there seems to be no better way to say how an agent relates to her action than to say that it is hers. The relation between agent and action is signalled by the genitive in phrases for actions — '*her* speaking'; '*a*'s opening the door'. We find here a sort of ownership; but it does not seem to be authorship. Perhaps the thought that we are authors, or sources, of our actions need not be taken literally at all.

I think we know what Nagel means, however. An agent is the source, or the author, of the events that she causes. Earlier I called actions the initiatings of series of events — as a way of trying to place them on the causal scene. Our sense of ourselves as authors is then the sense that we are responsible for the events in those series that we initiate; to hold ourselves responsible for an event is to take responsibility for initiating the series it belongs to. But our responsibility consists in the action's being ours, and not in its having been caused, or done, by us. Nagel makes it sound as if we might locate an agent and find her action set apart from her. But though we may separate the events she causes from the agent, we cannot separate her from the event that starts the series — which is her causing them.

When Nagel says that 'everything I do or that anyone else does is part of a larger course of events that no one "does", but that happens' (1986, p. 114), he entices us into thinking that we have located actions from an external viewpoint. But what a person does is not an event, and it is therefore not a 'component of the flux of events in the world'. Nagel's ways of putting things suggest that we always have aspirations, which, in fact, we only come to seem to have when the event language is used as if it expressed things that cannot be said. Perhaps Nagel is only too right when he holds that the 'difficulty' is that 'it is impossible to give a coherent account of the internal view of action which is under threat', and that we 'cannot say what would . . . support our sense that our free actions originate with us' (1986, pp. 112–13, 117). Perhaps we have said everything that we need to say when we have understood what it is to be responsible for our actions' effects.

But Nagel thinks that our conception of ourselves as agents is revealed more fully when we consider the explanation of action. 'The final explanation . . . is given by the intentional explanation of my action, which is comprehensible only through my point of view. My reason for doing it is the *whole* reason why it happened, and no further explanation is necessary or possible'. And now, thinks Nagel, the trouble is that this sort of explanation, on which our sense of agency is based, is shown to be unsustainable when we take account of the possibility of an objective view; for that view 'admits only one kind of explanation of why something happened . . . ',[17] and equates its absence with the absence of any explanation at all. Intentional explanations are shown up as inadequate, Nagel says, when we see that they 'cannot explain *why I did what I did rather than the alternative that was causally open to me*' (1986, p. 116).

Intentional explanation may in fact be more powerful than Nagel allows here. At least it seems to be more powerful if we take it to be the kind of explanation in which concepts such as *belief* and *desire* are used to make sense of people and what they do and don't do—rather than as consisting in a series of once-off occasions on which 'the' reason for something actually done is given. I might tell you why she refused the job, but leave you realizing that there is more you could learn to help you to see why accepting it was something she didn't do. It is true that there could come a point at which there is no more for anyone to say about why she did one thing rather than another, and I have to resort to 'Those were the reasons she saw in favour and against, and the reasons in favour weighed more heavily with her'. But it is not as if you would then suppose that you would understand better if only you could see that the event which is her action 'or a range of possibilities within which it falls, was necessitated by prior conditions and events' (1986, p. 115). It seems that up to a point we can meet the demands that

[17] I have extracted the word 'causal' at the ellipsis: Nagel assumes that one who admits that action explanation is not of the 'objective' kind denies that it is causal; the assumption is not compulsory.

Nagel puts on action explanation, and that beyond that point, they are of a sort that it is simply not susceptible to.[18]

The pressure of these demands is supposed to be felt when the internal and external perspectives come together. In Nagel they are brought together through an equation of his reason for doing something with the explanation why 'it' happened. ('My reason for doing it is the whole reason why it happened.') But really Nagel's reason for doing something is not an explanation of any happening. (His reason does not explain anything, although the fact that he had it may explain why he did something.) Nor is the explanation why Nagel did something itself a reason for anything. (The explanation gives his reason.) It seems that a threat to our sense of agency has been created by an illusion that we are trying to explain an event's occurrence when in fact we are trying to make sense of a person and what she did.

I may seem to be suggesting that the barrier between the external and internal explanatory schemes is a merely terminological one. The obstacles to thinking what Nagel wants us to think are created by differences of category—between actions and things done, between reasons and explanations. But I think that these obstacles mark the presence of a genuine barrier. Accounts in terms of what a person thinks and wants are fitted to provide explanations for those who share with that person a point of view on the world. When the ideal of rationality can be brought to bear on explaining something she has done, that can be seen as something delivered from the contents of her thoughts and wants. Those who seek and give 'action explanations' do not regard the matter impersonally or externally, any more than the agent herself does when she deliberates about what to do.

[18] Nagel appreciates this: 'the sense of an internal explanation persists—an explanation insulated from the external view which is complete in itself and renders illegitimate all further requests for explanation of my action as an event in the world' (1986, p. 116). But instead of taking this to show the irrelevance of the external perspective, he takes it to be another sign of the conflict.

Nagel entertains the idea that someone who insists that the external perspective be brought to bear in the domain of reasons may be using a very limited conception of what an explanation is (1986, p. 117). But he says that anyone who considers herself entitled to a broader conception is under an obligation to show why the language of belief and desire doesn't introduce 'descriptions [merely] of how it seemed to the agent'. I suspect that Nagel thinks this obligation arises because he takes the internal view to be ultimately a first-personal one. See Section 7.

7. Agency Refuted?

Nagel's problem is engendered in the first instance from within the personal view—when it seems to need to rise above itself and take on the ambitions of an impersonal view. The second problem about agency is engendered from outside—when the impersonal view seems to swamp the personal one.

The ambitions of the impersonal view are not usually seen as a problem for agency. But there must be acknowledged to be potential problems here. For there are philosophers who think that any real phenomenon, however we may actually understand it, is intelligible from an impersonal point of view. And if it could be demonstrated both that the whole truth can be told from there, and that it leaves out of account everything that is personal, then the effects would be quite devastating: at stake is the idea that anyone ever really means to do anything, or wants anything, or believes anything. These truly devastating effects are seldom contemplated, because they cannot seriously be entertained, and because those who hold the threatening metaphysical doctrine for the most part believe that it actually holds no threats—that actions and their explanation can in fact be accommodated in an impersonal view. But something slightly less devastating is more frequently contemplated, as we have seen in reactions to Davidson. His anomalous monism is thought to deprive the mental of causal efficacy: the intrusion of the impersonal view is supposed to render people's being in states of mind causally quite idle, yet somehow to leave people intelligible.

The problematic effects on our conception of ourselves would be the same whether agency was undermined, from the inside, or refuted, from without. And the idea that I am suggesting stops those effects, and ensures that there is no real threat, is the same. But different considerations show how the threat is prevented from arising in the two cases. In discussing Nagel, the strategy was to deny to the personal view the pretensions he accords to it: I tried to show its explanatory scheme as insulated from that of the impersonal view. When agency seems to face refutation, though, the ambitions of an impersonal view are called directly into question. I finish with some further explanation and defence of the idea that we may resist them.

To be satisfied with saying that actions are apparent only from what I have called the personal view, we need in the first place to be clear that this is not a view confined to a particular self. We cannot explain what someone has done, unless we know whether she has been successful in achieving what she wanted. So the point of view from which she is understood must not only be one from which she can be seen to be in states of mind representing things beyond her, but also one from which those same states of mind can be evaluated, as correct or incorrect representations. The personal point of view, then, may differ from the most 'internal' view of Nagel, of 'a particular person inside the world'.

In Nagel, it is a matter of degree to which a point of view is objective or external: 'to acquire a more objective understanding of some aspect of life or the world, we step back from our initial view of it and form a new conception which has that view and its relation to the world as object' (1986, p. 5.). Now the notion of an impersonal point of view as I have used it is related to Nagel's internal/external (or subjective/objective) dimension: when we step back sufficiently that we have detached from everything contingent to our human subjectivity, we have reached a point of view that is external enough to be impersonal. Two of Nagel's ideas, then, need not be in dispute. First, we can allow that one point of view may incorporate another: a state of affairs might impinge upon a point of view, but it be possible to take up a more external one from which that state of affairs and that point of view were both represented. (Perhaps this is what happens when, from my point of view, I understand another person's.) Second, we can allow that there is such a thing as an impersonal view: we have a conception of an objective world whose nature is independent of whatever conscious beings occupy it, and our own capacity to stand back entitles us to this. But to allow these things—that one view may subsume another, and that some things can be viewed quite impersonally—is not to grant that we can always step away from any phenomenon and retain a view of it.[19]

Some people are persuaded that we can step back from actions when they are told that we have 'a view of persons and their actions

[19] For ways to make these ideas precise, see Moore 1987. The target at the end of Moore's paper is the 'absolute conception' of reality. Belief that such a conception ought to be attainable is surely one source of the view that actions are impersonally apparent; compare McDowell 1985, p. 395. But aspirations more limited than aspirations to this putative conception are all that are required to generate the pressure that I am trying to counteract, or so at least my argument assumes.

as part of the order of nature'. The idea that actions are 'components of the flux of events of the world of which the agent is a part' combines with the idea that the flux of events in nature constitutes how things objectively are to make it seem that an impersonal view of actions is not only possible, but appropriate. But we need to consider carefully this thought that persons and their actions are part of nature. It seems right when we point out that nothing supernatural needed to happen for human beings to evolve, and that it is a natural fact about people that, for instance, they have the abilities they do, and thus a natural fact that there are actions. Such considerations ensure that a naturalistic view of ourselves is in order, and indeed that the personal point of view is itself a naturalistic one. But they do not help to place our actions in a world 'of nature' if a world 'of nature' is to be thought of as constituted independently of the conscious beings that occupy it. It is (as Kantians might say) an empirical question whether an event is such that it would exist whether or not we were present in the world. If the event is an action, the answer is 'No'. So where the world 'of nature' is not the naturalistic world in which we find ourselves, but the world as it might be anyway — whether there were any people, or whatever any person's states of mind might be—actions are no part of it. This is not a particularly shocking conclusion: our conception of the world independent of us is not a conception of the world including us.

The conclusion evidently fits with the Davidsonian thesis of the disparateness of two conceptual frameworks — that by which we render ourselves intelligible to one another, and that by which we understand what goes on as the operation of physical law. But the conclusion is equally evidently at odds with Davidson's monism. For it would be a very strange idea that, from the impersonal point of view, we employ conceptual resources which describe the world 'of nature' and which are not such as to identify actions, which, however, for all that, can be used to identify actions. We saw in Section 4 that we were left without any reason to believe in the identities that Davidson asserts. Without such reason, we have no inclination to use the quicker argument that we considered there for bringing the mental inside the scope of law. Arguments like that one simply assume that whatever principles govern our account of a world 'of nature' have universal application, in any area where we can use causal notions to make sense of something. And the suspicion arises that Davidson himself, in invoking the Nomological Character of Causality, has simply imported his own universalizing assumption about 'nature'.[20]

So we have to say that there are events that are not in the world 'of nature'. Perhaps this ontological doctrine is the stumbling-block. In addition to the feeling that it is a naturalistic world that we inhabit, there is the belief that the world 'of nature' is complete; and would it not be incomplete if it did not contain us and all the events we participate in? Someone who objects at this point may think that the cost of saying that we and our actions are not in the world 'of nature' is to render that a gappy world—with pieces missing where people and their actions should be. But she would be mistaken if she supposed that because people and their actions are absent from the impersonal point of view, the portions of space and time occupied by persons are missing too. We have to distinguish between an aspect of reality and a portion of reality. The claim about the completeness of what is accessible from the impersonal point of view is ruled out if it is the claim that every aspect of reality is present to it. But if it is a claim to survey the whole of space and time and deal with every portion of what it surveys, then nothing stands in its way. A correct account of an impersonal conception brings 'the whole world of nature' within its scope. Some portions of space-time are occupied by the bits of matter that people are composed from, and the account will deal with them, with flesh and blood, and nervous systems.[21]

There must, of course, be things to be said about how it can be that people are the sorts of being that we are, given that they are composed only from what can be scrutinized impersonally. It is in virtue not only of our occupying the position that we do in the world on which we act, but also of our being constructed as we are that we can have the cognitive and practical capacities that we do, and can, for instance, initiate series of events containing some of kinds we want. So there are questions about how nervous systems can subserve the phenomena of mentality and agency.[22] But these

[20] There is evidence that some universalizing assumption may serve for Davidson to ground his nomological principle in the ease with which he moves from 'nomological' to 'physical': compare Johnston 1985, p. 411.

[21] For the relation between the conclusion here and (*a*) present-day versions of physicalism, and (*b*) Descartes' dualism, see Hornsby 1985 and 1990, respectively.

[22] See Clark 1989 for the idea that cognitive psychology may proceed without any of the standard assumptions about connections between folk psychology and brain science.

questions are not made easier by the assumption that, to everything we speak of from the personal point of view, there attaches a piece of vocabulary apt for describing things impersonally. This assumption after all is the source of the thought that actions are swallowed up from an external perspective, and of the thought that the mental is epiphenomenal. And it is not as if the assumption on its own could do anything to integrate the personal with an impersonal point of view. Davidson himself has made this clear: in the sphere of reason-explanations, causality is 'connected with the normative demands of rationality' (Davidson 1985, p. 246).

There is then no new problem about integration when the assumption is abandoned, and actions are thought neither to be swallowed up nor deprived of genuinely causal explanations, but absent simply, from the impersonal point of view. When we see an action as a person's initiating a series of events, we recognize a type of event whose causal ancestry is understood from a personal, rational point of view, and whose causal successors come to be understood from an impersonal, perhaps scientific one. And we appreciate that causality is a concept that we may operate with from both points of view: people make a difference, and do so because their actions are events which make a difference.

Appendix

In emphasizing my real agreement with Davidson (on the causal-explanatoriness *and* irreducibility of the mental), I have ridden over some areas of disagreement. In this Appendix, I attempt to clarify these, taking in turn, (*A*) 'purely causal' statements, (*B*) the Nomological Character of Causality, (*C*) the relation between (*A*) and (*B*).

(*A*) It is assumed nowadays that we find claims such as 'Reasons are causes' or 'Beliefs and desires causally interact with one another to produce actions' to be at least as obvious as the causal-explanation thesis. Davidson's influential simultaneous defence of both the claims and the thesis (in his 1963) has probably contributed as much as anything else to the prevalence of this assumption. And in Section 3 I may have let it seem to be more surprising than it really is that separate explanatory and causal elements have been supposed to be extricable from Davidson's causal-explanation thesis. I hoped to make it clear (*a*) that the claims are in fact more dubious than the thesis, and (*b*) that if we attend to Davidson's arguments, we shall give the thesis priority. The consequence is that I have ignored Davidson's own support for claims to the effect that 'purely causal' statements about actions are available.

It is worth noting that, although 'The primary reason is the cause' is one of Davidson's own formulations, it is not obvious that he endorses actual statements that would count as instances of it. All the same, Davidson certainly does believe that we are entitled to more in the way of causal statements than the everyday 'because' ones. Whereas for some philosophers the purpose of making out our entitlement is served by talk of token states (and I addressed them in Section 3), for Davidson, it is served by arguing for the pervasiveness of events. Two of the things he said to this end seem to me inadequate. (1) He said that we may associate with a person's being in any mental state an event that is her coming to be in that state. But so long as we realize that an event that is the onslaught of someone's being in a state must plausibly be (identified with) a precisely datable event, there will not appear to be many of them. (2) He said that where we cannot find any candidate for the immediate cause of an action using psychological language, we are still 'sure that there was an event or sequence of events' (1963/1980,

p. 13). But we might accept this because we know that there is an impersonal story to be told whenever a bit of someone's body moves; in that case our acceptance again lends no support to a causal statement of the kind to which entitlement was sought—such that statements of that kind go hand in hand with truths stated when action explanations are given.

(*B*) In Section 4, I questioned whether our belief in laws can ground our belief in psychological causal-explanatory statements. Davidson never asserts that it can. What he does assert is that our ability to generalize—including our ability to generalize psychologically—grounds our belief in the operation of laws. (General statements linking mental and physical are said to be heteronomic (Davidson 1970/1980, p. 222), and the instantiations of heteronomic statements are said to 'give us reason to believe that there is a precise law at work' (1970/1980, p. 219).) Of course I should question this also: if explanations using 'believe' and 'desire' are credible even when they are not seen as nomologically grounded, why should these generalizations be thought to provide evidence for the operation of laws?

Evidently raising these questions does not prove the falsity of the Nomological Character of Causality. But it may make us wonder whether we could have a case for it where Davidson needs one most. I let the argument with Davidson rest here, because I think that we shall resist the motivation for the Nomological Character of Causality when we see the sort of principle that it is, in the context e.g. of the quicker argument which I contrasted with Davidson's in Section 4.

(C) In the schema in which the quicker argument was summed up (at the end of Section 4), personal, and impersonal, and causal might be taken as properties of facts (if one is prepared to talk in that way). Thus in thinking about that argument, one need not assume an account of causation with the specific ontological presuppositions of an account that is grounded in 'purely causal' statements. Though it is formulated in terms that make it comparable with Davidson's own, then, the quicker argument is an instance of a more general style of argument: namely, an argument from a conception 'of nature', which I address in Section 7. It rests on a universalizing assumption, that there are principles governing any area where we can use causal notions to make sense of something (see n. 20).

In the schema in which Davidson's own argument was summed

up, nomological, causal-explanatory, and mental can be understood as second-order properties. Such an understanding may reveal the indispensability of the items (states or events) to Davidson's way of thinking: these are the particulars having the properties that have the (second-order) properties. Certainly 'purely causal' statements are needed for a monistic argument like Davidson's. For unless rational-explanatory statements are seen to be concerned with the same things as laws are concerned with—with states or events or whatever—the Nomological Principle cannot do its work. (Nor can we find heteronomic generalizations of such a form as could provide us with reason for belief in laws.)

The two schematic arguments show us then that a universalizing assumption may be held in the absence of belief in 'purely causal' statements, although a conception of the 'purely causal' is needed for Davidson's own particular universal principle to be put to work. We should also notice that belief in the ubiquity of 'purely causal' statements does not introduce any universalizing assumption all by itself: someone might think that wherever there is (as we say) an action explanation, there are statements having the form but not the import of the statements needed for an argument that actions are present from the impersonal point of view. This dialectical situation explains a certain tentativeness on my part about whether we should hold that discrete items interact in the production of action. My own opinion is that we should not hold this; but, for the purposes of the argument here, it may be enough to cast the tenet in doubt. A reader is then free to accept the principle of the Nomological Character of Causality provided that its domain is restricted so that we are outside it in the rational realm (and psychological heteronomic generalizations can then lend it no support). Alternatively she is free to carry on asserting the usual 'purely causal' statements about beliefs and desires and/or associated events, provided that she now denies that there is any principle of nomologicality having application wherever statements of a 'purely causal' kind can be asserted (and psychological heteronomic generalizations then require a different attitude from that which Davidson takes towards all heteronomic generalizations).

11

The Non-Reductivist's Troubles with Mental Causation

JAEGWON KIM

1. A Bifurcated World or a Layered One?

MIND–BODY dualism in the classic Cartesian style envisages two non-overlapping domains of particulars ('substances') that are, by and large, equal in ontological standing. Mental items are thought to share a certain defining property ('thinking' or 'consciousness', according to Descartes) that excludes the defining property shared by the items on the physical side ('extension', according to Descartes). And associated with each domain is a distinct family of properties, mental properties for one and physical properties for the other, in terms of which the particulars within that domain can be exhaustively characterized. We are thus presented with a bifurcated picture of reality: the world consists of two metaphysically independent spheres existing side by side.

But not everyone who accepts a picture like this thinks that the two domains are entirely unrelated; although there are notable exceptions, such as Leibniz and Malebranche, many substantival dualists, including of course Descartes, have held that, in spite of their separateness and independence, the domains are causally connected: mental events can be, and sometimes are, causes and effects of physical events, and changes in a mind can be causes or effects of changes in a body. This means that events of both kinds can occur *as links in the same causal chain*: if you pick a physical event and trace its causal ancestry or posterity, you may run into mental events, and similarly if you start off with a mental event. It follows then that under Cartesian causal dualism there can be *no complete physical theory of physical phenomena*. For it allows physical occurrences that cannot be causally explained by invoking physical antecedents and laws alone. Any comprehensive theory of the physical world must, on Cartesian interactionism, include references to non-physical causal agents and laws governing their behaviour. We can say then that *Cartesian interactionism violates the causal closure of the physical domain*. Of course, it violates the causal closure of the mental domain as well; Cartesianism implies that no scientific theory could hope to achieve complete coverage unless it encompassed both the physical and mental realms—unless, that is, we had a unified theory of both mental and physical phenomena.

The ontological picture that has dominated contemporary thinking on the mind problem is strikingly different from the Cartesian picture. The Cartesian model of a bifurcated world has been replaced by that of a layered world, a hierarchically stratified structure of 'levels' or 'orders' of entities and their characteristic properties. It is generally thought that there is a bottom level, one consisting of whatever micro-physics is going to tell us are the most basic physical particles out of which all matter is composed (electrons, neutrons, quarks, or whatever). And these objects, whatever they are, are characterized by certain fundamental physical properties and relations (mass, spin, charm, or whatever). As we ascend to higher levels, we find structures that are made up of entities belonging to the lower levels, and, moreover, the entities at any given level are thought to be characterized by a set of properties distinctive of that level. Thus, at a certain level, we will find lumps of H_2O molecules, with such properties as transparency, power to dissolve sugar and salt, a characteristic density and viscosity, etc. At still higher levels we will find cells and organisms with their 'vital' properties, and farther up organisms with consciousness and intentionality. Beyond them, there are social groups of organisms, and perhaps groups consisting of such groups.[1] Sometimes, one speaks in terms of 'levels of description', 'levels of analysis', or 'levels of language'; the layered model is often implicit in such talk.

Thus, the world as portrayed in the new picture consists of an array of levels, each level consisting of two components: a set of *entities* constituting the domain of particulars for that level and a set of *properties* defined over this domain. What gives this array structure is the mereological relation of *being part of*: entities belonging to a given layer are mereologically composed of entities

[1] For a highly useful and informative presentation of this layered picture, see Oppenheim and Putnam 1958.

belonging to the lower levels, and this relation generates a hierarchical ordering of the levels. As earlier noted, this multi-tiered picture usually carries the assumption that there is a bottom tier, a layer of entities that have no physically significant parts.

The characterization thus far of the layered model leaves one important question unanswered: how are the properties characteristic of entities at a given level related to those that characterize entities of adjacent levels? Given that entities at distinct levels are ordered by the part–whole relation, is it the case that properties associated with different levels are also ordered by some distinctive and significant relationship?[2]

That is the crucial question answers to which have defined various currently contested positions on certain metaphysical and methodological issues including, most notably, the mind body problem. The classic positivist answer is that the distinctive properties of entities at a given level are *reducible to*, or *reductively explainable in terms of*, the properties and relations characterizing entities at lower levels. That is 'reductionism'. But reductionism has had a rough time of it for the past few decades, and has been eclipsed by its major rivals, 'eliminativism' and 'non-reductivism'. These positions agree in their claim that higher-level properties are in general not reducible to lower-level ones, but differ on the status of irreducible higher properties. Non-reductivism maintains that they can be real and genuine properties of objects and events of this world, constituting an ineliminable part of its true ontology. Eliminativism, on the other hand, holds that they are useless danglers that must be expunged from the correct picture of reality. Thus, the split between non-reductivism and eliminativism hinges on the significance of reducibility: the former, unlike the latter, rejects reducibility as a test of legitimacy for higher-level properties, and holds that such properties can form an autonomous domain, a domain for an independent 'special science' that is irreducible to the sciences about lower-level phenomena. 'Emergentism', which was influential during the first half of this century, was the first systematic articulation of this non-reductivist approach.

At first blush, the layered model may appear to hold promise as an elegant way of averting violation of the causal closure of the

[2] When the layered model is described in terms of 'levels of description' or 'levels of language', there is a corresponding question about how the descriptive apparatus (predicates, concepts, sentences, etc.) of one level is related to that of another.

physical: causal interactions could perhaps be confined within each level, in a way that respected the autonomy and closedness of the causal processes at the fundamental physical level. In particular, on the non-reductivist version of the layered model, it may be possible to view causal chains at a given level, like the properties distinctive of that level, as forming an autonomous and self-contained realm immune to causal intrusions from neighbouring levels. Moreover, this picture may not preclude the assignment of some special status to physical causation: in spite of the causal-nomological autonomy at each level, causal relations at higher levels may in some sense depend, or supervene, on the causal-nomological processes occurring at the lower levels (McLaughlin 1989, Fodor 1989)—just as, on the non-reductivist view, the irreducibility of higher-level properties is thought to be consistent with their supervenience on the lower-level properties and relations.

Let us narrow our focus on the mind–body problem. 'Non-reductive physicalism', a position that can deservedly be called 'the received view' of today, is non-reductivism applied to the mind–body case. It consists of the two characteristic theses of non-reductivism: its ontology is physical monism, the thesis that physical entities and their mereological aggregates are all that there is; but its 'ideology' is anti-reductionist and dualist, consisting in the claim that psychological properties are irreducibly distinct from the underlying physical and biological properties. Its dualism is reflected in the belief that, though physically irreducible, psychological properties are genuine properties nonetheless, as real as underlying physical-biological properties. And there is a corollary about psychology: psychology is an autonomous special science independent of the physical and biological sciences in its methodology and in the concepts and explanations it generates.[3]

As we saw, Cartesian interactionism involves violation of the causal closure of the physical, and that was one cause of its downfall. I shall argue that non-reductive physicalism, and its more generalized companion, emergentism, are vulnerable to similar difficulties; in particular, it will be seen that the physical causal

[3] There is also the position of Donald Davidson in his 'Mental Events' (1970) which accepts both physical ontological monism (usually formulated as a thesis about individual events) and property dualism of non-reductive physicalism as characterized here, while rejecting the corollary about the scientific status of psychology. Davidson's views on psychology are hinted at by the title of one of his papers on this issue, 'Psychology as Philosophy' (1974*b*).

closure remains very much a problem within the stratified ontology of non-reductivism. Non-reductive physicalism, like Cartesianism, founders on the rocks of mental causation.

2. Non-Reductive Physicalism and 'Physical Realization'

The basic ontological thesis of non-reductive physicalism confers on the physical a certain kind of primacy: all concrete existents are physical—there are no non-physical particulars, no souls, no Cartesian mental substances, and no 'vital principles' or 'entelechies'. Stated as a thesis about properties, physical primacy in this sense comes to this: all mental properties are instantiated in physical particulars. Thus, although there can be, and presumably are, objects and events that have only physical properties, there can be none with mental properties alone; mentality must be instantiated in physical systems.

There appears to be no generally accepted account of exactly what it means to say that something is 'physical'. Minimally perhaps a physical entity must have a determinate location in space and time; but that may not be enough. Perhaps an entity is physical just in case it has some physical property or other. But what makes a property a physical property? Perhaps, the best answer we could muster is what Hellman and Thompson (1975) have offered: explain 'physical' by reference to current theoretical physics. This strategy can be extended to higher-level sciences, chemistry and biology; when we reach psychological properties, however, the question as to what should be regarded as our reference scientific theories is itself an unsettled philosophical issue centrally involved in the debates about reductionism and mental causation. For mental properties, then, we must look to vernacular psychology and its characteristic intentional idioms of belief, desire, and the rest, and their intentional analogues in systematic psychology. Nothing in the discussion to follow will depend on precise general definitions of 'physical' and 'mental'.

In any case, many physicalists, including most non-reductive physicalists, are not willing to rest with the ontological primacy of the physical in the sense explained, just as many substantival dualists are not content merely to posit two separate and independent domains. Most non-reductive physicalists want to go beyond the claim that mental properties are had by physical systems; they want to defend a thesis of *primacy, or basicness*, *for physical properties in relation to mental properties*. The main idea here is that, in spite of their irreducibility, mental properties are in some robust sense dependent on or determined by physical-biological properties. This means that the property dualism of non-reductive physicalism is an attenuated dualism: it is a dualism with dependency relations between the two domains, just as Cartesian dualism is a dualism with causal connections between its two domains. For many non-reductive physicalists, therefore, irreducibility is not the last word on the mind–body relationship. The irreducibility claim is a negative thesis; non-reductive physicalists want a positive account of the relationship between the two sets of properties. Here, the catch-words are 'dependence' and 'determination'. Hellman and Thompson, who have proposed an elegant form of non-reductive physicalism, describe their project as follows:

> Of late there has been a growing awareness, however, that reductionism is an unreasonably strong claim. Along with this has come recognition that reductionism is to be distinguished from a purely ontological thesis concerning the sorts of entities of which the world is constituted. . . . Although a purely ontological thesis is a necessary component of physicalism it is insufficient in that it makes no appeal to the power of physical law. . . . We seek to develop principles of *physical determination* that spell out rather precisely the underlying physicalist intuition that the physical facts determine all the facts. (pp. 551–2)

Hellman and Thompson speak of physical facts as determining all the facts; presumably, that happens only because what objects have which physical properties (including relations) determines what mental properties these objects have.

But how do we capture this relation of determination, or dependence, in a way that escapes the threat of reductionism? Answering this question has been one of the principal projects of non-reductive physicalists in the past two decades. Two ideas have been prominent: 'supervenience' and 'physical realization'. Hellman and Thompson themselves gave an account of the determination relation that is very close to what is now commonly known as 'global supervenience': once the physical character of a world is fixed, its entire character is thereby fixed.[4] The idea that mental states are 'physically realized' (or 'instantiated' or 'implemented')

[4] For a survey of supervenience relations see Kim 1990*a*.

gained currency, in the late 1960s,[5] chiefly through an argument ('the multiple realization argument') that helped to defeat reductive physicalism and install non-reductivism in its current influential position. The reputed trouble for reductionism was that the realization is 'multiple', namely that any given mental state is realizable in a variety of widely diverse physical structures, and that this makes its reductive identification with any single physical property hopeless. The two approaches, one based on 'supervenience' and the other on 'physical realization', are not mutually exclusive: as we shall see, on reasonable readings of the terms involved the claim that mental states are physically realized arguably entails the claim that they are physically supervenient. Whether the converse entailment holds is a question that depends, among other things, on the strength of the supervenience relation involved.

Many non-reductive physicalists avail themselves of both supervenience and realization, and some do so explicitly; for example, LePore and Loewer characterize non-reductive physicalism by three principles, one of which is 'global supervenience', the thesis that 'If two nomologically possible worlds are exactly alike with respect to fundamental physical facts . . . then they are exactly alike with respect to all other facts' (1989, pp. 177–8). But they go on to say: 'The relationship between psychological and neurophysiological properties is that the latter *realise* the former'. What is it for a property to 'realize' another? LePore and Loewer explain:

> Exactly what is it for one of an event's properties to *realize* another? The usual conception is that *e*'s being *P* realizes *e*'s being *F* iff *e* is *P* and *e* is *F* and there is a strong connection of some sort between *P* and *F*. We propose to understand this connection as a necessary connection which is *explanatory*. The existence of an explanatory connection between two properties is stronger than the claim that $P \rightarrow M$ is physically necessary since not every physically necessary connection is explanatory. (1989, p. 179)

It is clear that if all mental properties are realized in this sense by physical properties, the global supervenience of the mental on the

[5] As far as I know, Hilary Putnam first introduced the idea of 'physical realization', in the early 1960s, to describe the relationship between 'logical' and 'structural' states of computing machines, extending it by analogy to the mental-physical case (see Putnam 1960). I believe that the idea really began catching on, in discussions of the mind–body problem, when it was used to formulate the influential 'multiple realization argument' in the seminal Putnam 1967 paper.

physical is assured. In fact, their Physical Realization Thesis, as we might call it, entails a stronger form of supervenience, the 'strong supervenience' of mental properties on physical ones (Kim 1984*a*).

For the purposes of my arguments in this paper I wish to focus on those versions of non-reductive physicalism that make use of 'physical realization' to explain the psycho-physical property relationship. This for two reasons: first, there are a variety of non-equivalent supervenience relations, and this makes it difficult to formulate a reasonably uniform and perspicuous argument concerning supervenience-based versions; and, second, many philosophers have been converted to non-reductive physicalism by 'the multiple realization argument' briefly alluded to earlier. In consequence, for many non-reductive physicalists, the Physical Realization Thesis is one of their early and basic commitments. It is often a sound expository strategy to formulate an argument in a stark and perspicuous fashion even if this involves making use of fairly strong premisses, and then worry about how the argument might be qualified and fine-tuned to accommodate weaker assumptions. It may well be that there are versions of non-reductive physicalism to which my considerations do not apply, at least not directly;[6] I believe, though, that they are relevant to many of the more popular and influential versions of it.

Let us return to the concept of realization. LePore and Loewer, as we saw above, explain 'realization' for properties of events; however, there is no need to confine the relation to events, and we will assume that the realization relation, without substantive changes, applies to properties of objects ('substances') as well. In any case, according to LePore and Loewer, P realizes M just in case (1) $P \rightarrow M$ holds with nomological necessity (LePore and Loewer say 'physical necessity') and (2) P 'explains' M. I think LePore and Loewer are correct in suggesting these two kinds of conditions; however, their specific conditions need improvement. Consider first their explanatory requirement: I believe the idea behind this requirement is correct, but we should look for an objective metaphysical relation between P and M, not an essentially epistemic relation like explanation; that is, we should view the explanatory relation between the two properties as being supported by a

6 In particular, Davidson's 'anomalous monism' *sans* a supervenience thesis will be largely immune to my argument. But there are other difficulties with such a position; in particular, an account of the causal powers of mental properties appears hopeless under anomalous monism. See Kim 1989*b*.

metaphysical realization relation. Here I am taking a realist attitude about explanation: if *P* explains *M*, that is so because some objective metaphysical relation holds between *P* and *M*. That *P* explains *M* cannot be a brute, fundamental fact about *P* and *M*. In causal explanations the required relation of course is the causal relation. In the case of realization, the key concepts, I suggest, are those of 'causal mechanism' and 'microstructure'. When *P* is said to 'realize' *M* in system *s*, *P* must specify a micro-structural property of *s* that provides a causal mechanism for the implementation of *M* in *s*; moreover, in interesting cases—in fact, if we are speak meaningfully of 'implementation' of *M*—*P* will be a member of a family of physical properties forming a network of nomologically connected micro-structural states that provides a micro-causal mechanism, in systems appropriately like *s*, for the nomological connections among a broad system of mental properties of which *M* is an element. These underlying micro-states will form an explanatory basis for the higher properties and the nomic relations among them; but the realization relation itself must be distinguished from the explanatory relation. Thus, my difference with LePore and Loewer in regard to their condition (2) is quite small: I agree that something like their explanatory condition should in general hold for the realization relation; however, it should not be regarded as constitutive of it.

What of the condition (1), to the effect that $P \rightarrow M$ be nomically necessary? I believe this condition is acceptable with the following proviso: in each system *s* in which *M* is physically realized, there must be a determinate set, finite or infinite, of physical properties, P_1, P_2, . . . , each of which realizes M in the sense explained, so that we may consider the disjunctive property, $P_1{}^{\vee}\ P_2{}^{\vee}$ . . . , as a nomic co-extension of *M*. Since I will not be making use of this requirement in this paper, I will not offer an argument for it here.[7]

3. Non-Reductive Physicalism as Emergentism

The non-reductive physicalism I have in mind, therefore, consists of the following theses:

[7] For reasons for requiring this see Kim (forthcoming).

1. (*Physical Monism*) All concrete particulars are physical.
2. (*Anti-Reductionism*) Mental properties are not reducible to physical properties.
3. (*The Physical Realization Thesis*) All mental properties are physically realized; that is, whenever an organism, or system, instantiates a mental property *M*, it has some physical property *P* such that *P* realizes *M* in organisms of its kind.

And we must add a further thesis that is implicit in the above three and is usually taken for granted:

4. (*Mental Realism*) Mental properties are real properties of objects and events; they are not merely useful aids in making predictions or fictitious manners of speech.

I believe that these four basic tenets of non-reductive physicalism bring the position very close to 'emergentism'—so close, in fact, that non-reductive physicalism of this variety is best viewed as a form of emergentism. I shall briefly explain why this is so (for more details, see Kim 1992).

Emergentists in general accepted a purely materialist ontology of concrete physical objects and events. For example, Samuel Alexander, one of the principal theoreticians of the emergence school, argues that there are no mental events over and above neural processes:

> We thus become aware, partly by experience, partly by reflection, that a process with the distinctive quality of mind or consciousness is in the same place and time with a neural process, that is, with a highly differentiated and complex process of our living body. We are forced, therefore, to go beyond the mere correlation of the mental with these neural processes and to identify them. There is but one process which, being of a specific complexity, has the quality of consciousness. . . . It has then to be accepted as an empirical fact that a neural process of a certain level of development possesses the quality of consciousness and is thereby a mental process; and, alternately, a mental process is *also* a vital one of a certain order. (1927, pp. 5–6)

This is, almost word for word, just what is claimed by 'token physicalism' or 'the token-identity thesis', a form of non-reductive physicalism. It is no surprise then that Alexander calls his position a version of 'the identity doctrine of mind and body'.

Both the 'layered' structure of the emergentist ontology and its fundamentally physicalist character are evident in the following passage from C. Lloyd Morgan, another leader of the movement:

In the foregoing lecture the notion of a pyramid with ascending levels was put forward. Near its base is a swarm of atoms with relational structure and the quality we may call atomicity. Above this level, atoms combine to form new units, the distinguishing quality of which is molecularity; higher up, on one line of advance, are, let us say, crystals wherein atoms and molecules are grouped in new relations of which the expression is crystalline form; on another line of advance are organisms with a different kind of natural relations which give the quality of vitality; yet higher, a new kind of natural relatedness supervenes and to its expression the word 'mentality' may . . . be applied. Vital*ism* and anim*ism* are excluded if they imply the insertion of Entelechy. (1923, p. 35)

Atoms and their mereological aggregates exhaust all of concrete existence; no 'entelechies', or any other physically alien entities, are to be 'inserted' at any point in the hierarchy of levels of existence, although new properties emerge to characterize the more complex structures of basic entities. There is no room in this picture for any concrete existent not fully decomposable into atoms and other basic physical particulars.

The emergentist doctrine that 'emergent' properties are irreducible to the 'basal conditions' out of which they emerge is familiar; to most of us, this irreducibility claim is constitutive of the emergentist metaphysical world-view. Although the emergentists' idea of reduction or reductive explanation diverges from the model of reduction implicit in current anti-reductionist arguments (see Kim 1992), the philosophical significance of the denial of reducibility between two property levels is the same: the higher-level properties, being irreducible, are genuine new additions to the ontology of the world. Alexander, for example, says this:

Out of certain physiological conditions nature has framed a new quality mind, which is therefore not itself physiological though it lives and moves and has its being in physiological conditions. Hence it is that there can be and is an independent science of psychology. . . . No physiological constellation explains for us why it should be mind. (1927, p. 8)

This idea of irreducible higher properties lies at the basis of some recent versions of emergentism, such as one promoted by the noted neurophysiologist Roger Sperry, who writes:

First, conscious awareness . . . is interpreted to be a dynamic emergent property of cerebral excitation. As such conscious experience becomes inseparably tied to the material brain process with all its structural and physiological constraints. At the same time the conscious properties of brain excitation are conceived to be something distinct and special in their own right. . . . Among other implications of the current view for brain research is the conclusion that a full explanation of the brain process at the conscious level will not be possible solely in terms of the biochemical and physiological data. (1969, p. 533–5)

For both emergentism and non-reductive physicalism, then, the doctrine of irreducible higher-level properties is the centre-piece of their respective positions; and their proponents take it to be what makes their positions distinctive and important. As net additions to the world, the emergent higher-level properties cannot be reduced or explained away; and as irreducible new features of the world, they form an autonomous domain, and, as Alexander says, make 'an independent science of psychology' possible. This is exactly what current non-reductive physicalists have been urging for over two decades: the 'special sciences' are autonomous and independent from the underlying physical and biological sciences.[8]

Let us now turn to the third basic tenet of non-reductive physicalism, the Physical Realization Thesis. This involves the claim that for a mental property to be instantiated in a system, that system must instantiate an appropriate physical property, and further that whenever any system instantiates this physical property, the mental property must of necessity be instantiated by it as well. Mental events and states require physical bases, and when required physical bases are present, they must occur. A precisely parallel thesis was part of the emergentist doctrine: the emergence of higher-level properties require appropriate 'basal conditions', and when these basal conditions are present, they must of necessity emerge. For both the non-reductive physicalist and the emergentist, physical bases are by themselves sufficient for the appearance of the higher-level properties; as Morgan says, 'no insertion of Entelechy', or any other non-physical agent, is required for the emergence of higher properties:

Since it is pretty sure to be said that to speak of an emergent quality of life savours of vitalism, one should here parenthetically say, with due emphasis, that if vitalism connotes anything of the nature of Entelechy or Elan—any insertion into physico-chemical evolution of an alien influence which must

[8] In spite of all this, there is an apparent difference between emergentism and non-reductive physicalism concerning the relationship between properties belonging to adjacent levels. As may be recalled, LePore and Loewer require that the physical ('realization') base must *explain* the mental property it realizes. However, emer-gentists will deny that the 'basal conditions' can ever constitute an explanatory basis for any property emergent from them. Much of the difference can be traced, I believe, to differing conceptions of explanation and reduction involved; for further

be invoked to explain the phenomenon of life—then, so far from this being implied, it is explicitly rejected under the concept of emergent evolution. (1923, p. 12)

And Morgan goes on to stress the necessity of physical bases for all higher-level phenomena: 'Thus, for emergent evolution, conscious events at level *C* (mind) involves specific physiological events at level *B* (life), and these involve specific physico-chemical events at level *A* (matter). No *C* without *B*, and no *B* without *A*. No mind without life; and no life without "a physical basis".' (1923, p. 15)

There is little doubt, I think, that on these three crucial tenets there is a broad agreement between emergentism and non-reductive physicalism, and that it is fair, and illuminating, to view non-reductive physicalism as a form of emergentism. It isn't for nothing that non-reductive physicalists sometimes speak of higher-level properties as 'emergent'.[9]

As for the fourth thesis of non-reductive physicalism, that is, Mental Realism, it is clear that the quotations from the emergentists that we have seen are shot through with realism about mentality. To the emergentist, emergent evolution is a historical fact of paramount importance; through the process of emergent evolution, the world has reached its present state—more complex, richer, and fuller. Most physicalists who reject reductionism also reject mental eliminativism; this realist attitude is implicit in what we have called the Physical Realization Thesis (assuming realism about the physical). And it is all but explicit in the claim, accepted by both emergentists and many non-reductivists, that psychology is a legitimate special science (unless one adopts a universal anti-realism about all science); as such it must investigate a domain of real phenomena and systematize them by discovering laws and causal connections governing them.

4. Mental Realism and Mental Causation

But just what does the commitment to the reality of mental properties amount to? What is the significance of saying of anything

details see Kim 1992. This difference, whether real or only apparent, will not affect the applicability of the main argument of this paper to both emergentism and non-reductive physicalism.

[9] e.g. Hellman and Thompson (1975, p. 555) say this: 'what may be called 'emergence' of higher-order phenomena is allowed for without departing from the physical ontology'.

that it is 'real'? Alexander supplies an apt answer, in a marvellous paragraph in which he curtly dismisses epiphenomenalism: '[Epiphenomenalism] supposes something to exist in nature which has nothing to do, no purpose to serve, a species of *noblesse* which depends on the work of its inferiors, but is kept for show and might as well, and undoubtedly would in time be abolished.' (1927, p. 8)

This we may call 'Alexander's dictum': *To be real is to have causal powers.* I believe this principle, as applied to concrete existents and their properties, will be accepted by most non-reductive physical-ists.

Emphasis on the causal role of emergent properties is pervasive in the emergentist literature. Here is a pair of revealing quotations:

Just as the holistic properties of the organism have causal effects that determine the course and fate of its constituent cells and molecules, so in the same way, the conscious properties of cerebral activity are conceived to have analogous causal effects in brain function that control subset events in the flow pattern of neural excitation. In this holistic sense the present proposal may be said to place mind over matter, but not as any disembodied or supernatural agent. (Sperry 1969, p. 533)

But when some new kind of relatedness is supervenient (say at the level of life), the way in which the physical events which are involved run their course is different in virtue of its presence—different from what it would have been if life had been absent. (Morgan 1923, p. 16)

What is striking about these paragraphs is the reference to 'downward causation': both Morgan and Sperry seem to be saying that mentality, having emerged from physical-biological processes, takes on a causal life of its own and begins to *exercise causal influence 'downward' to affect what goes on in the underlying physical-biological processes.* Whether the idea of such causation makes sense is one of the main questions I want to discuss in the balance of this paper. But let us first note what the non-reductive physicalist has to say about mental causation.

There is no question that the typical non-reductive physicalist has a strong commitment to the reality of mental causation. As we saw, our non-reductivist is not an eliminativist: why bother with mental properties unless you think that they are good for some causal work and can play a role in causal explanations? Fodor puts the point this way:

I'm not really convinced that it matters very much whether the mental is the physical; still less that it matters very much whether we can prove it.

Whereas, if it isn't literally true that my wanting is causally responsible for my reaching, and my itching is causally responsible for my scratching, and my believing is causally responsible for my saying, . . . if none of that is literally true, then practically everything I believe about anything is false and it's the end of the world. (1989, p. 77)

One could hardly declare one's yearnings for mental causation with more feeling than this! Non-reductive physicalists in general regard mental causation seriously; they have expended much energy and ingenuity trying to show they are entitled to mental causation (see e.g. LePore and Loewer 1987, 1989; Fodor 1989; Davidson, Chapter 1, above). I don't think that they can have what they want, and showing this will be my main burden in the remainder of this paper. My argument, if correct, will also show that Fodor is wrong in feeling that he could have his wishes fulfilled without having to worry about the mind–body problem—about 'whether the mental is the physical'.

Here is my plan for the remainder of this paper: I shall first show that both emergentism and non-reductive physicalism are committed to downward causation—that is, mental-to-physical causation for the mind–body case. This should be no news to the emergentist: for in a sense downward causation is much of the point of the emergentist programme. What I shall show would still be of interest, even for emergentism, since the argument will make clear that downward causation is entailed by the basic tenets of emergentism, and of non-physical reductionism. I shall then argue that the idea of downward causation is highly problematic, and perhaps incoherent, given the basic physicalist commitments.

5. Non-Reductive Physicalism is Committed to Downward Causation

It is easy to see just how downward causation follows from the basic principles of emergentism and non-reductive physicalism. First, as we have observed, the emergentist and the non-reductive physicalist are mental realists, and Mental Realism, via Alexander's dictum, entails causal powers for mental properties. In fact, whether or not they accept Alexander's dictum, most of them will want causal powers for mental properties. Now, mental properties, on both positions, are irreducible net additions to the world. And this must mean, on Alexander's dictum, that mental properties bring with them *new causal powers, powers that no underlying physical-biological properties can deliver*. For unless mentality made causal contributions that are genuinely novel, the claim that it is a distinct and irreducible phenomenon over and beyond physical-biological phenomena would be hollow and empty. To be real, Alexander has said, is to have causal powers; *to be real, new, and irreducible, therefore, must be to have new, irreducible causal powers*.

This fits in well with the autonomy thesis, alluded to earlier, concerning the science of psychology: as an empirical science, psychology must generate causal explanations of phenomena in its domain; and as an irreducible, autonomous science, the causal explanations it delivers must themselves be irreducible, representing causal connections in the world not captured by the underlying sciences. The autonomy thesis, therefore, makes sense only if causal relations involving mental events are novel and irreducible—that is, mental properties are endowed with genuinely new causal powers irreducible to those of underlying physical-biological properties.

If *M* is a mental property, therefore, *M* must have some new causal powers. This must mean, let us suppose, that *M* manifests its causal powers by being causally efficacious with respect to another property, *N*; that is, a given instance of *M* can cause *N* to be instantiated on that occasion. We shall assume here a broadly nomological conception of causality, roughly in the following sense: an instance of *M* causes an instance of *N* just in case there is an appropriate causal law that invokes the instantiation of *M* as a sufficient condition for the instantiation of *N*. There are three cases to be distinguished: (i) the property *N* for which *M* is a cause is a mental property; (ii) *N* is a physical property; (iii) *N* is a higher-level property in relation to *M*. (i) is mental-to-mental causation ('same-level causation'); (ii) is mental-to-physical causation (that is, 'downward causation'); and (iii) is a possibility if there are properties, perhaps social properties, that emerge from, or are realized by, mental properties ('upward causation').

My argument will show that case (i) is possible only if case (ii) is possible; namely, that mental-to-mental causation presupposes mental-to-physical causation. It will be clear that the same argument shows case (iii) presupposes case (ii), and therefore case (i). So suppose *M* is causally efficacious with respect to some mental property *M**, and in particular that a given instance of *M* causes an instance of M^*. But M^*, *qua* mental property, is physically realized; let P^* be its physical realization base. Now we seem to have two distinct and independent answers to the question 'Why is this instance of M^* present?' *Ex hypothesi*, it is there because an instance of M caused it; that's why it's there. But there is another answer: it's there because P^* physically realizes M^* and P^* is instantiated on this occasion. I believe these two stories about the presence of M^* on this occasion create a tension and must be reconciled.[10]

Is it plausible to suppose that the joint presence of M and P^* is responsible for the instantiation of M^*? No; because that contradicts the claim that M* is physically realized by P^*. As we saw, this claim implies that P^* alone is sufficient to bring about M^*, whether or not any other condition, earlier or later or at the same time, obtained (unless it is somehow connected with the occurrence of P^* itself—we shall recur to this possibility below). And the supposition is also inconsistent with our initial assumption that the given instance of M was a sufficient condition for that instance of M^*. Nor is it plausible to suppose that the occurrence of M^* on this occasion was somehow over-determined in that it has two distinct and independent origins in M and P^*. For this, too, conflicts with the assumption that M^* is a property that requires a physical realization base in order to be instantiated, and that this instance of M^* is there because it is realized by P^*. In the absence of P^*, we must suppose that M^* could not have been there—unless an alternate realization base had been present. In either case, every instance of M^* must have some physical base that is by itself sufficient for M^*; and this threatens to pre-empt M's claim to be the cause of this instance of M^*.

I believe the only coherent story we can tell here is to suppose that the M-instance caused M^* to be instantiated *by causing* P^*, M^**'s physical realization base, to be instantiated*. This of course is downward causation, from M to P^*, a case of mental-to-physical causation. I believe the argument goes through with 'physical realization' replaced with 'emergence' (see Kim 1992). The gist of my argument is encapsulated in the following principle, which I believe will be accepted by most non-reductive physicalists:

> (*The Causal Realization Principle*) If a given instance of S occurs by being realized by Q, then any cause of this instance

[10] This is essentially identical to the situation we face when we are given two distinct independent causes for one and the same event, each claimed to be a sufficient cause. See Kim 1989*a*.

of S must be a cause of this instance of Q (and of course any cause of this instance of Q is a cause of this instance of S).

A parallel principle stated for emergence will be accepted by many, if not all, emergentists. In any case, I think we apply this principle constantly in daily life: for example, we treat pain by intervening with bodily processes, and we communicate by creating vibrations in the air or making marks on paper. (Direct mental-to-mental causation between different individuals is generally considered disreputable and unscientific: it goes by such names as 'ESP', 'telepathy', and 'mind-reading'.)

But couldn't we avoid this commitment to downward causation by exploiting the fact that M, as a mental property, has its own physical realization base, say P? Why not say then that M's causation of P^* comes to merely this: M is physically realized by P, and P causes P^*. The more basic causal relation obtains between the two physical properties, P and P^*, and M's causation of M^* is ultimately grounded in the causal relation between their respective physical realization bases. I think this is a highly appealing picture,[11] but it is not something that our non-reductivists can avail themselves of. For the picture reduces the causal powers of M to those of its realization base P: P is doing all the causal work, and M's causation of P^*, or of M^*, turns out to be derivative from P's causal powers. Thus, M has no causal powers over and beyond those of P, and this is contrary to Alexander's dictum and the assumption that M is an irreducible property. I shall take up this point again in the next section.

What these reflections show is that within the stratified world of non-reductive physicalism and emergentism, 'same-level' causation can occur only if 'cross-level' causation can occur. It will not be possible to isolate and confine causal chains within levels; there will be inevitable leakage of causal influence from level to level.

6. What's Wrong with Downward Causation?

So does downward causation makes sense—that is, within the scheme of non-reductive physicalism? I think there are some severe

[11] This is closely similar to the model of 'supervenient causation' I have suggested in earlier papers of mine, e.g. Kim 1984*b*. It has been called 'causal reductionism' by Menzies (1988). Also see LePore and Loewer 1989.

problems. As we shall see, the tension arises out of an attempt to combine 'upward determination' with 'downward causation'. The non-reductive physicalist wants both: mentality is determined by, and dependent on, the physical, and yet minds are to have causal powers, novel causal powers that can be exercised, if my argument is correct, only by causally affecting physical-biological processes in novel ways.

Suppose then that mental property M is causally efficacious with respect to physical property P^*, and in particular that a given instance of M causes a given instance of P^*. Given the Physical Realization Thesis, this instance of M is there because it is realized by a physical property, say P. Since P is a realization base for M, it is sufficient for M, and it follows that P is sufficient, as a matter of law, for P^*. Now, the question that must be faced is this: What reason is there for not taking P as the cause of P^*, by-passing M and treating it as an epiphenomenon?[12]

I believe this epiphenomenalist solution with regard to M cannot easily be set aside: we are looking for a causal explanation of why P^* is instantiated at this time. We see that M was instantiated and we can invoke a law connecting M-instances with P^*-instances. But we also see that P was instantiated at the same time, and there is an appropriate law connecting P-instances with P^*-instances. So the situation is this: P appears to have at least as strong a claim as M as a direct cause of P^* (that is, without M as an intervening link). Is there any reason for invoking M as a cause of P^* at all? The question is not whether or not P should be considered a cause of P^*; on anyone's account, it should be. Rather, the question is whether M should be given a distinct causal role in this situation? I believe there are some persuasive reasons for refusing to do so.

First, there is the good old principle of simplicity: we can make do with P as P^*'s cause, so why bother with M? Notice that given the simultaneity of the instances of M and P respectively, it is not possible to think of the M-instance as a temporally intermediate link in the causal chain from P to P^*. Moreover, if we insist on M as a cause of P^*, we fall foul of another serious difficulty, 'the problem of causal-explanatory exclusion' (see Kim 1989*a*, 1990*b*). For we would be allowing two distinct sufficient causes, simultaneous with

[12] To be precise, we should put this in terms of instances of these properties rather than the properties themselves. In what follows, liberties of this form are sometimes taken to avoid verbosity.

each other, of a single event. This makes the situation look like one of causal over-determination, which is absurd. And *ex hypothesi*, it is not possible to regard *M* and *P* as forming a single jointly sufficient cause, each being individually necessary but insufficient. And given the assumed irreducibility of *M*, we cannot regard *M* as identical with *P*, or as a part of it. The exclusion problem, then, is this: given that *P* is a sufficient physical cause of *P**, how could *M* *also* be a cause, a sufficient one at that, of *P**? What causal work is left over for *M*, or any other mental property, to do? *M*'s claim as a cause of *P** will be weakened especially if, as we would expect in real-life neurobiological research, there is a continuous causal chain, a mechanism, connecting *P* with *P**. It is clear that the exclusion problem cannot be resolved within the framework of non-reductive physicalism.

All these considerations, I want to suggest, point to something like the following as the natural picture for the layered physicalist world: all causal relations are implemented at the physical level, and the causal relations we impute to higher-level processes are derivative from and grounded in the fundamental nomic processes at the physical level.[13] This goes perhaps a bit, but not much, beyond what is directly implied by the supervenience thesis most non-reductive physicalists accept: if, as the supervenience thesis claims, all the facts are determined by physical facts, then all causal relations involving mental events must be determined by physical facts (presumably including facts about physical causation).

Consider, then, a somewhat bald way of stating this idea:

> (*The Principle of Causal Inheritance*) If *M* is instantiated on a given occasion by being realized by *P*, then the causal powers of *this instance of M* are identical with (perhaps, a subset of) the causal powers of *P*.

In other words, higher states are to inherit their causal powers from the underlying states that realize them. Non-reductivists must reject this principle; they will say that higher-level causal powers are 'determined by', but not identical with (or reducible to) the lower-level causal powers. What our considerations have made clear is that if 'determined but not identical' means that these higher-causal powers are genuinely novel powers, then non-reductivists are

[13] There is a strong indication that Fodor e.g. accepts this sort of principle in Fodor 1989.

caught in a web of seemingly insurmountable difficulties. And I challenge those non-reductivists who would reject this principle to state an alternative principle on just how the causal powers of a realized property are connected with those of its realization base; or to explain, if no such connections are envisaged, the significance of talk of realization.

The implications of the Causal Inheritance Principle are devastating to non-reductive physicalism: if the causal powers of *M* are identical with those of its realization bases, then *M* in effect contributes nothing new causally, and *M*'s claim to be a new, irreducible property is put in jeopardy. And if, as suggested, *M* is treated as an epiphenomenal dangler from its physical realization base, with no causal work of its own to do, the next step of the argument, as mandated by Alexander's dictum, will be that *M* ought to be 'abolished'. All this seems like an inescapable lesson of Alexander's dictum.

The case for scepticism about downward causation is strengthened when we see that, as in the case of Cartesian interactionist dualism, it breaches the causal closure of the physical domain. What is worse, when we see that *P*, *M*'s realization base, is there to serve as a full cause of P^*—and this will always be the case whenever a mental cause is invoked—the violation isn't even as well motivated as it is with Cartesian interactionism.

Most emergentists will have no problem with the failure of the physical causal closure; although they may have to tinker with their doctrines somewhere to ensure the overall consistency of their position, they are not likely to shed any tears over the fate of the closure principle. For many emergentists that precisely was the intended consequence of their position. I doubt, however, that contemporary non-reductive physicalists can afford to be so cavalier about the problem of causal closure: to give up this principle is to acknowledge that there can in principle be no complete physical theory of physical phenomena, that theoretical physics, insofar as it aspires to be a complete theory, must cease to be pure physics and invoke irreducibly non-physical causal powers—vital principles, entelechies, psychic energies, elan vital, or whatnot. If that is what you are willing to embrace, why call yourself a 'physicalist'? Your basic theory of the world will have to be a mixed one, a combined physical-mental theory, just as it would be under Cartesian interactionism. And all this may put the layered view of the world itself in jeopardy; it is likely to require some serious rethinking.

At this juncture it seems highly plausible that the only solution to the exclusion problem and the problem of the physical causal closure lies in some form of reductionism that will permit us to discard, or at least moderate, the claim that mental properties are distinct from their underlying physical properties. It is this claim that forced us to posit for mentality novel and distinct causal powers, thereby leading us to the present predicament. To identify the causal powers of mentality with those of its underlying physical base is, in effect, to deny it a distinct ontological status, and consider it reduced.

But a question must leap to your mind at this point, if you are at all familiar with current wisdom in philosophy of mind: Doesn't the Physical Realization Thesis itself, given the phenomenon of 'multiple realizability', rule out any form of reductionism? Hasn't 'the multiple realization argument' (see e.g. Fodor 1974) refuted reductionism once and for all? The entrenched, almost automatic, response is 'yes' to both questions. I believe the correct answer is a qualified but firm 'no'. But defending that answer is something I must leave for another time.[14]

[14] I undertake a defence of this reply in Kim (forthcoming). For a sketch of an argument see Kim 1989*b*.

12

Explanation in Biopsychology

RUTH GARRETT MILLIKAN

I WOULD like to explore implications for the science of psychology of the thesis that the categories of intentional psychology are function categories in the biologist's sense of 'function', taking this to be a sense in which function is determined by evolutionary history rather than by current dispositions. I would like to explore, first, the general shape of the discipline that is psychology under this interpretation. What is its subject-matter? What kinds of explanations does it seek for what kinds of phenomena? Second, I would like to bring these reflections to bear on the classic question concerning in what way, if any, giving an individual's reasons for action tells of the causes of that action. I will not attempt to defend the thesis that the categories of intentional psychology are biological function categories, nor the thesis that biological function categories are carved out by reference to evolutionary history, but some clarifications of these theses, will of course, be in order.[1]

1. Teleo-Functions

To describe the biological function of an item is not to describe its dispositional capacities. It is to describe the role that its ancestors played in a particular historical process, a concrete cyclical process of birth, development, and reproduction extended over a large number of previous generations. It is to tell how earlier items involved in this historical process that are homologous to this functional item characteristically contributed to continuation of the

I am very grateful to my invaluable colleague John Troyer for his abrasive reading of an earlier draft of this essay. It has a sharper edge now, I hope.

[1] These theses are defended in Millikan 1984, 1986*a*, 1989*a*, 1989*b*, 1989*c*, 1990*a*, 1991*a*, 1991*b*.

cycle (thus helping, of course, to account for this item's existence). To say this is not to define the phenomenon of biological function. That can only be done, probably, by reference also to natural selection (see Millikan 1984, 1989*b*, 1989*c*). But I wish to call attention to the fact that the focus of the biological notion of function is on only very restricted aspects of the functional item's capacities, namely, those that have contributed over and over, in the same sort of way, to the historical cycle or chain of life.

Not every biological function of every biological item (type) is realized in every historical instance, say, in every generation. Some biological functions are very seldom performed. Still, they must occasionally have been performed, and performed in such circumstances as to weld an essential link in the historical chain of life, or they are not true functions. Consider, for example, the ability human babies are rumoured to have of instant hibernation when submerged in very cold water. Surely it is a rare baby whose life has been saved by this capacity. But there have been enough, apparently, to fix the relevant genes in the gene-pool, hence to confer a biological function on this disposition. Alternatively, if the disposition should, as a matter of fact, have no such felicitous history, but arose only as a concomitant of other functions, as a 'spandrel', then it has no biological function (see Gould and Lewontin 1979). We should also note that not every functional item actually has the dispositional capacities to perform its biological functions. Homology is not identity; members of biological function categories can be malformed, diseased, or injured (see Millikan 1984, chapter 1). We can sum these points up by saying that biological functions are 'teleo-functions' rather that 'mechano-functions'. They are biological purposes rather than activities or dispositions.[2]

2. Psychological Classification as Functional Classification; Categorial vs. Relational Functions

The position is that psychological classification is biological classification, hence proceeds by reference to teleo-function. This means that categories such as belief, desire, memory, percept, and purposive

[2] What I am here calling 'teleo-functions' I called 'proper functions' in Millikan 1984 and in most earlier papers.

behaviour are biological function categories — very broad and general ones, of course. Compare the categories limb, hormone, circulatory system, eye, visual system, etc. More contentious, the position is that such categories or types as belief-that-it-is-raining, desire-to-visit-Paris, percept-of-a-cat, and purposeful-shooting-of-a-rabbit are carved out with reference to biological functions (though in the case of beliefs, not directly according to function; see Section 9 below.) This more contentious claim presupposes two points that are not wholly familiar from a layman's understanding of biology.

The first point is that heredity does not directly dictate traits but rather patterns of interaction with the environment, thus controlling development. These interaction patterns control development not only before birth but also throughout life, so that how and what one learns is as much (and as little) dictated by heredity as is one's height and hair colour. The second point is that the homologies among items that have historically played the same biological role in a species, and the homologies among the biological roles or functions that these homologous items have performed, are often highly relational. Homologous items may differ greatly from one another, as non-relationally or categorially described, both in structure and in function, their biologically significant similarities being captured only by multiply relational characterizations. To have biological functions an item need neither have the same categorial *properties*, e.g. the same absolute structure, as items that participated in the life cycles of ancestors, nor need its *functions*, when categorially described, be functions performed by any of its ancestors. Let me try to explain this clearly, for it is crucial.

Consider the neurological mechanism responsible for imprinting in ducklings. It has the relational function of imprinting on the duckling the visual character of something related to the duckling in a certain way, namely, as that which bears the relation *mother of* to the duckling. This relational function translates into a different categorial function[3] for the individual imprinting system of each individual duckling, since the visual character of each duckling's mother is different. Taking a still simpler example, this time from the domain of artefacts,[4] consider the function of a copying

[3] In Millikan 1984 I called such categorial functions 'adapted' proper functions.

[4] In Millikan 1984 I argued that all teleology can be analysed as belonging to the causal order in accordance with patterns analogous to those that establish biological teleology in the causal order. Therefore I use examples freely from the domain of artefacts as well as biology.

machine. Its relational function is to produce something that matches whatever pattern is put into its feeder. But given something particular put into its feeder, it then has the categorial function of producing a particular pattern. Notice that it is possible that this precise categorial function is one that neither it nor any other copying machine in history has ever happened to have before.

Similarly, humans are born with the capacity to develop concepts in accordance with certain general principles that operate upon the matter of the individual's particular experiences, and we are born with the capacity, in accordance with further general principles operating upon experience, to proceed to form desires and beliefs employing these concepts. These capacities are, in the first instance, relationally described capacities, but given the particular experiences of a particular individual, the biological functions of that individual's concept-forming systems and belief-and-desire-forming systems translate into categorials. Likewise, the modifications of the nervous system that result, the instantiations of particular concepts, beliefs, and desires, have functional descriptions that are categorial. Further, these may, in many cases, be unique in history. Recall the individual mother-memory of the individual duckling, the function of which is to enable the duckling to recognize its individual mother, say, Sabatha. If the duckling has no elder siblings, then perhaps no biological device has ever had just that biological function before. This is the manner in which we speculate that belief-that-it-is-raining and desire-to-visit-Paris are distinct types carved out, in the end, by teleo-functional analysis.[5]

3. Biopsychology as a Study of Norms; The Ubiquity of Cognitive Failure

If the central categories of intentional psychology are indeed teleo-functional categories, this suggests that the core of the science of psychology should be a study of teleo-function. This core of psychology concerns the functions of the mechanisms that regulate those life-processes, those links in the life-chain from generation to generation, that are completed through the mediation of behaviours. We can call this discipline 'biopsychology'. The central concern of biopsychology is not to discover laws, neither universal

[5] For fuller discussion of these issues, see Millikan 1984, 1990*a*.

laws nor statistical laws. Indeed, with a few rather special exceptions, the biological sciences do not typically traffic in laws. They seek to understand mechanisms that contribute to the cyclical processes that constitute development, maintenance, and reproduction for the various species. But the rate of failure for many of these mechanisms is exceedingly high, especially when heavy interaction with the environment is involved. These mechanisms unfold in anything but a law-like manner. Biological functions are not, in general, reliable functions. They quite standardly go awry. Were this not the case, the world would be a marvellously populous place. The central job of the biological sciences is to describe biological norms, normative norms, not necessities or statistical averages. Indeed, these norms might better be called 'ideals'.[6] Let me detail this point as it applies, in particular, to the study of cognitive functions.

Some biological devices are such that a failure to perform their functions is immediately disastrous for the organism itself, or disastrous to its reproductive prospects. That is how it is, for example, if the heart or the kidneys fail. Equally often, however, functional failure is neither fatal nor the least bit dangerous. This may be for any of a variety of reasons. Some devices routinely get second chances, even multitudinous further chances, to perform their functions. Consider devices that regulate the performance of mating displays. Their teleo-function is to produce a display that will attract a mate, but if they fail on one occasion, they often have a chance to succeed on the next. Similarly, for predatory animals, the mechanisms that issue in food-procuring behaviours characteristically fail numerous times for every success. Many devices have functions that are redundant. They coexist with other devices that serve exactly the same functions in other ways. Thus the human system has several mechanisms redundantly devoted to cooling. These produce sweating, dilation of the capillaries, lethargy, motivate cooling-off behaviours, motivate the seeking of cooler spots, etc. Similarly, many animals have alternative means of procuring food, so that if one fails, another may succeed. Alternative ways of doing the same often take the form of mechanisms that back one another up. For example, most animals possess reflex mechanisms designed to lessen the likelihood of

[6] In Millikan 1984 I capitalized the 'N' in 'Normal' to remind that these norms are ideals rather than averages.

physical harm (ducking reflexes, fall-checking reflexes), as well as exhibiting more sophisticated behaviours with the same purpose, but they also have mechanisms for repairing physical harm should it occur. They have mechanisms for preventing the entry of noxious bacteria, viruses, etc. into the tissues, but they also have mechanisms for destroying those noxious elements that do enter—mechanisms that themselves operate on a number of levels and with considerable redundancy. The multiplicity of devices aimed at the same end attests, in these cases, to the likelihood for each that it may fail.

We should be especially ready to expect failures in the case of mechanisms, such as the cognitive systems, that help to produce behaviours. This is because in order for behaviours to serve their biological functions, hence to complete the functions of the mechanisms that regulate them, mediation by the environment is required. Biological processes, portions of the biological cycle, that behaviours initiate are processes that loop through the world outside the organism. And it is obviously a great deal more difficult for the organism to stabilize its outer environment so as to provide the necessary conditions for completion of such loops than to stabilize its inner environment so as to complete, say, its physiological functions. So there is good reason to speculate that the cognitive systems might be abundantly unreliable in the performance, at least, of one portion of their functions—that portion which, unlike, say, inference and memory retrieval (though these are surely fallible enough), is accomplished through the mediation of structures and conditions in the world outside. Common examples of such failures result, we may suppose, in the acquisition of empty or confused concepts, in acts of misidentification of objects, kinds, stuffs or properties, in the fixation of false beliefs, in the acquisition of harmful desires, and in the failure of healthy desires to become realized. For each of these mishaps may be occasioned by failure of the environment to provide the ideal conditions which are necessary, for proper functioning of the cognitive systems. (Frequently it is, as it were, the world that fails us, rather than our inner systems.)

It follows that a description of the biological functions of the cognitive systems will in no way resemble a catalogue of psychological laws. It is certainly no psychological law, for example, that our beliefs are true, though it is a (teleo-)function of our belief-fixing systems to fix true beliefs. Of course there are many biological functions that do get performed with pretty law-like regularity, such as blood circulation and eyeblink reflexes, but it is not because of their lawlike properties that these functions are of interest to the biopsychologist. Turning the coin over, the frequency and, for the most part, the harmlessness of the occurrence of false beliefs, mistaken identifications, and so forth, should not cause us to suppose that these occurrences are biologically normal. Such failures may be frequent, conceivably they are even average, but they are not biologically normal. They do not exemplify patterns that have helped to forge links in the historical life-chain. Compare the fact that being eaten by a bigger fish is the average thing that happens to little fish, but it is not on that account a biologically normal happening, relative to the little fish, nor is how little fish get eaten, as opposed to how they avoid getting eaten, a part of the ethology of little fish.

4. The Subject-Matter of Biopsychology is a Process

The biopsychologist is not like a physicist or, say, a mineralogist. The object of biopsychological study is not a chunk of matter, warm or cold, lying on the lab table waiting for its structure to be examined, for its input–output dispositions to be tabulated, or waiting to see what causes applied will produce what effects, what 'special science' laws may hold for it. Nor is the point of biopsychology to examine or speculate on details of the complex structures inside the black box, to check on the dispositions of the components, nor to examine how the little dispositions inside add up to the complex dispositions of the whole. Biopsychology is not, then, all of what has traditionally been labelled 'psychology'. There are many industrial psychologists, for example, and many psychologists who work for the advertising industry, and even the education industry, and so forth, who have reason to study certain average behavioural dispositions of people quite apart from reference to the teleo-functional aspects of these behaviours. Also, but less happily, there have been animal studies done under the flag of behaviourism that involved extreme deprivations and other abuses to experimental animals with no thought given to whether the results obtained flowed from normally functioning mechanisms or, instead, from grievous damage to the animals' insides. Similarly, the Nazis are supposed to have used Jewish prisoners to study aspects of 'physiology' with no concern about whether the effects they were observing were the result of mutilating the physiological systems or whether they were effects of normal, that is, adaptive, functioning under stress. But to study organisms in that sort of way, even for praiseworthy purposes such as the promotion of effective and efficient education, or the fostering of effective psychotherapy, is surely not the core job of the biological sciences. For example, physiologists and ethologists are usually concerned to study healthy animals rather than diseased or mutilated ones, and not because the healthy animal is the average animal. The point is not, in general, a quest for laws holding on the statistical average. Rather, the healthy animal is, indeed is by definition, the animal that is so constructed that its parts can perform each of their teleo-functions adequately, if given appropriate environmental contingencies. The healthy animal is the animal that does or could function normally in the normative sense of 'normal'.

The biopsychologist's study has little to do with averages over chunks of living matter. The subject of the biopsychologist's study is the stages of an ongoing cyclical historical process, an ongoing event in history. As such, it is not, strictly speaking, even the study of a secondary substance or of a natural kind. The chunk of matter, the exemplar of a natural kind, that is the current specimen on the table represents, if it is lucky, a partial cross-section of the target event. It represents a stage in the historical cyclical process. It is an embryo stage, an infant stage, an immature or a mature stage, on its way to the ensuing stage.

Being more precise, it represents cross-sections from a numerous set of loosely co-ordinated intertwined parallel processes, each having strands of its own, each developing through its own inner logic and at its own pace in rough harmony and interchange with the others. In the case of human cognition, for example, the various strands of the processes of perceptual learning, concept formation, the development of beliefs and desires, and of progressively more effective use of beliefs and desires through action, are roughly integrated with stages in the development of various motor skills, with many aspects of physical growth and development, and so forth. It is inevitable that certain strands of these processes should fail in the case of individual animals, and if failure is central and massive enough and redundancy in the system not sufficient to overcome it, the individual dies. The historical species, and to a lesser degree each individual animal, is like a rope with a small central core of overlapping strands running from one end to the other, the majority of strands, indeed the vast majority, being peripheral and very short where they have broken off. The biopsychologist's study concerns only the central unbroken strands of this fabric, and each fibre in these only so far as it has spun itself out in a principled historically precedented way. Such a study is not a study of substances or kinds, and not a study of averages.

5. The Organismic System Penetrates into the Environment

Because psychology is the study of processes resulting in and through external behaviour, it focuses at the point where the organism and the environment interlock, or better, merge. For there is no clear line but only the most arbitrary demarcation between the organism considered as a process and its environment. The organismic process has no skin. It is constantly sucking in matter from its surroundings and spewing it out again. Every breath is a refusal of separation from the environment. Nor are those aspects of the biological process that are cyclical in the sense of being reproduced confined within the skin. Spider webs and moth cocoons, bird nests and beaver dams, are reproduced by the genes out of environmental materials exactly as are bones, wings, and eyes. Richard Dawkins (1983) discusses the phenomenon of 'the extended phenotype' through which boundaries between biological individuals or species become blurred, the biological projects of (the genes of) one individual or species being carried out through opportunistic manipulation of the bodies or behaviours of others. And he discusses also the more obvious way in which phenotypes are extended into the environment through incorporation into the organismic system of inanimate non-body parts such as animal artefacts, and of other adaptive effects of an animal's behaviour. The extended phenotype may thus reach yards or even miles beyond the animal's body. The unity of the organismic process might better be compared, then, to that of a wave or, say, a whirlpool, than to that of an ordinary physical object. Yet it is not as close, even, as a whirlpool to being encompassed within a unit space-time worm. For example, the beaver and his dam are aspects of the same organismic system, yet they are separable both in space and in time. And the beaver's dam is also part of the systems that comprise each of his kin.

Through its behaviour, the biological system that is an animal merges into and incorporates portions of its environment. Inner mechanisms initiate processes completed by outer mechanisms, through outer structures and conditions that are either given in the environment or that have been put in place through prior behaviours of the individual or his kin. It is not just that the teleo-functions of an animal's behavioural systems are, as such, 'long armed' functions. The animal itself, considered as a system of events, extends far out into the extra-body environment. To study an animal's behavioural systems without at the same time studying the normal integration of these into the environment, without studying the loops through the environment it is the function of these systems to initiate, would be exactly like studying the digestive system without considering what normally passes through it. Digestion without food is an exact analogue of behaviour without environment. Turning to another analogue, to study behaviour abstracted from the environment would be no less absurd, and for exactly the same reason, as if one were to study the structure and function of the heart's ventricles while ignoring the existence of the auricles and of the blood that passes through. The other half of the system containing the behaviour-producing mechanisms lies in the environment in exactly the same sense that the other half of the system containing the ventricles lies in the atrium and in the blood running through.

Imagine attempting to study the inner mechanisms that produce migration in birds, or nest-building, or mating displays and female reactions to them, or imprinting in birds, without making reference to the way these mechanisms have historically meshed with the birds' environments so as to perform the functions for which they are named. More vividly, imagine attempting to study the origins of the co-ordinated motions made by the eyes and the head and the hand that effect eye-hand co-ordination while leaving completely out of account that there is, normally, a seen and felt object in the environment that mediates this co-ordination. It is equally ludicrous to suggest studying the deeper systems that produce human behaviours, for example, the systems that process beliefs and desires and intentions, etc., without considering how the environment has historically mediated performance of their functions. To understand what the ventricles do one must understand also what the auricles and the blood do and understand the relation that the ventricles ideally bear to the blood and the auricles. To understand what beliefs and desires do one must understand what the environment is doing and what relations beliefs and desires ideally bear both to one another and to the environment.

It is always possible to describe any motion that an organism makes categorially. It is possible, anyway, to describe it relative only to the organism itself rather than relative to environmental structures.[7] And to describe sufficient causes of an organism's categorially described motions, one can always begin, merely, with categorial descriptions of the organism itself plus categorial descriptions of the environmental input to the organism. From this perspective, the organism's relation to its distal environment appears causally impotent in the production of its motions. But its motions are not its behaviours. The changes in categorial structure thus traced are significant biologically, are aspects of behaviours, only in so far as changing certain categorial properties of the organism effects significant changes in the organism's relation to its environment. Good comparisons are not easy to find here but we can try this one. The dentist has no particular interest in the exact shapes and sizes of individual persons' lower jaws. That is, he has no particular interest in them disregarding their relations to the shapes and sizes of the teeth that fit into them and of the upper jaws they must match. Clearly the details of absolute structure are not significant here, but only the details of relation. The same must surely be true both for the physiological structures supporting cognitive functions and for the behaviours these help to produce. Their relations to one another and their relations to the environment are what is biologically significant, and what is, for the normal case, uniformly describable within biological theory, not their categorial properties.

From the perspective of biopsychology it should be evident both that the personal history of the organism is relevant to understanding its psychological nature and that its way of interlocking with the environment is relevant. Whether a person remembers or merely seems to remember, whether a person knows or merely believes

[7] For a discussion of biologically relevant vs. biologically irrelevant ways of describing the same behaviours, see Millikan 1993*b*.

truly, are matters of personal history, but equally are matters of whether the biological cycle is proceeding normally or whether some of its links have been forged only by luck.[8] Whether a belief corresponds to the outer world as it should or is false instead is a matter of the interlocking of the organism with its environment, but equally a matter of whether the wider organismic system, which system includes part of that environment, is normally, that is, ideally, constituted or whether it is biologically abnormal. If it is biologically abnormal, this shows, in turn, that abnormalities must have occurred in the development of the system, for insofar as the organism-environment system cycled entirely normally (which, of course, it never does) beliefs would all come out true.

6. Biopsychology is a Predictive Science if at all, then only Accidentally

These reflections on the nature of intentional psychology entail that, as a biological science, it does not aspire to be predictive. Biopsychology studies what happens when biological processes proceed normally, but the normal is neither the necessary nor always the statistically average. Prediction and control do of course play an important role under parts of the wide umbrella called psychology—I have mentioned psychological testing, human engineering, psychotherapy, etc.—but prediction and control are not required by-products of intentional psychology. Indeed, intentional attitude psychology is a rather unlikely candidate to aspire to the detailed prediction of individual human behaviours.

This is true for at least two reasons. The first is diversity among individual constitutions. For psychology to predict individual behaviours, just as a starter, babies would have to be born cognitively and affectively, indeed also physically, alike. But it is abundantly clear that different newborns, inserted into identical environments, would not behave at all alike, except under the most general and vacuous of descriptions. People are born with predispositions to different cognitive and affective styles, with different cognitive strengths and weaknesses. Non-psychological factors such as body-build, reaction time, energy level, and health also play

[8] For a compatible discussion of the nature of knowledge, see Millikan 1986*b*.

a large role in determining behaviour. Further, it is likely that many aspects of our cognitive processes are partly stochastic, hence that which among many possible solutions to a given problem an individual discovers and executes often is not governed by well-defined psychological principles at all. Surely nothing short of complete physical and chemical analysis could in fact predict the detailed behaviours of any individual. The individual is not a replica of its ancestors or of its friends. It is a bundle of heavily redundant unfolding sub-systems adapted each to the others' concrete peculiarities to form co-ordinated larger units, this in accordance with principles of co-ordination and development all of which are, as yet, subject to merest speculation. We are still trying to find out how an individual's muscles and tendons grow the right length to fit the individual's bones, let alone how the various facets of individual cognitive development and function grow into a coherent unit. But there is no reason to suppose that exactly how an individual thinks is any more governed by laws quantifying over individuals than, say, how he walks or plays tennis — or how he reacts to allergens.

The second reason that intentional psychology cannot be required to predict individual behaviours is that there is no compelling reason to suppose that all or even most of the norms that it describes are usually fulfilled. Most obvious, as has already been noted, is that the environment cannot always be relied upon to do its part in completing the functions of the cognitive systems. Because this is so obvious, it has been equally apparent to all that there could not possibly be any reliable laws of organism–distal environment interaction, certainly not for the case of humans. Hence theorists who take it that psychology's main business is to deal in laws have found it necessary to insist that a scientific intentional psychology would have to be 'narrow', that it would have to ignore the environment. But it is also likely that those portions of the cognitive functions that are carried out inside the organism are abundantly vulnerable to failure. The cognitive mechanisms seem to be paradigms of functional redundancy and layered back-up systems, commanding a variety of means to the accomplishment of the same or functionally equivalent projects. If at first you don't succeed, try another way, is a fundamental heuristic for our cognitive functions. Witness, for example, the well-documented variety of forms of compensation employed by those with brain damage. This redundancy strongly suggests the vulnerability of various cognitive techniques taken separately. It follows that there is little reason to suppose that the exact progression of anyone's inner cognitive systems could be predicted on the basis of even the most exact understanding of all types of human cognitive teleo-function, an understanding of all the biological norms involved.

Suppose, for example, that man is indeed a rational animal; that conformity to certain logical principles is a biological norm for human thought-processes. It would not strictly follow that conformity to reason was so much as a common occurrence. Reasoning could be one among other functions of the behaviour-controlling systems, one that sometimes worked and was then to the organism's advantage. It could also be one that seldom caused irreparable damage when it failed, due to redundancy and to backing by various cruder behaviour-controlling devices such as those found in the lesser animals. Indeed, remembering the way evolution works, it seems that there must at least have been a time when human reason had exactly this tentative status. It is not likely that the ability to reason well or to learn to reason well arrived all at once in a single lucky mutation. And we can raise the question of how well, in fact, the average modern human reasons. Clearly from the fact that drawing rational inferences may be a norm for the human cognitive systems it does not follow that any reliable predictions about inference patterns can be made. Even though man is a rational animal, rational psychology could remain very far from a reliable predictive science.

But a strong contemporary tradition has it that rational psychology must be a predictive science if it is to be a science at all, and that its central job is exactly to predict individual humans' behaviours. It is claimed, further, that our layman's way of thinking about intentional mental states constitutes a 'folk psychological theory', the central employment of which is to effect prediction of the behaviours of our fellows, for this is necessary in order to project our own paths through the tangle of other folks' actions. Do I maintain that it is mere illusion that we thus predict the actions of others?

No, it certainly is not an illusion that we do a lot of correct predicting concerning the behaviours of others. Most ordinary forms of social intercourse and social co-operation would be impossible if we could not. But there may be a misunderstanding over the *methods* that we typically employ for prediction. The tool that we most commonly use, I suggest, is not a theory of the inner *mechanisms* that lie behind predicted behaviours. The tool is not, for example, belief-desire theory. Most of our predictions are done with a much blunter tool—the method of brute correlation. In many cases there is, of course, some understanding of the outlines of the psychological mechanisms lying behind predicted behaviours, but our predictions do not usually rest on this understanding, either at all, or at least very deeply. They rest mainly on observations of past behavioural regularities for the individual and for the group(s) to which the individual belongs. Within fairly well-defined limits, people, especially people from the same culture, just do behave uniformly in a theatre, on the road, at the grocer's, even when recreating in the park. Most people are more likely than not to meet what others consider to be their business and social obligations, to conform to general expectations concerning what is appropriate or seemly and, very important, to do the things they have said they will do. Beyond this, we project ahead patterns observed in the past for particular individuals. Known personality traits, character traits, and habits serve as our guides. Of course such knowledge merely limits the boundaries of people's likely behaviour. It does little or nothing towards actually *determining* behaviour in its variety. But seldom do we make an attempt to predict others' behaviours in much more detail than this. How inept we actually are at predicting behaviours, even of our best friends and family members, when these behaviours are not covered by known regularities, may be illustrated by friends who become separated in a large crowd, say at a fair, each trying in vain to outguess what the other will do in an attempt at reunion.

7. Reasons and Causes

If we are rational, what that means is that rationality is a biological norm for humans, not that rationality is necessitated by special causal laws of human psychology. Compatibly, it is standard nowadays to claim (though on somewhat different grounds) that thoughts categorized in accordance with their semantics are not the sorts of things that could, even in principle, fall under causal laws. On the account of this essay, the semantic category of a thought is determined relative to its biological functions, which depend in turn upon its history, upon its place relative to certain prior events. But having a certain history is not, of course, an attribute that has 'causal powers'. Hence reasons cannot be, as such, causes. More generally, that a thing has a teleo-function is a causally impotent fact about it. Especially, it is never directly *because* a thing *has* a certain function that it performs that function or any other function. More nearly the reverse is true. The thing exists and has a certain function because things homologous to it have performed that function (better, had that effect) in the past. Moreover, here the 'because' is only partly causal, the other part is constitutive or logical.

But perhaps it will be thought that although things that have functions cannot be supposed to perform these functions either on account of having these functions or in accordance with strict causal laws, still they must perform them in accordance with *ceteris paribus* laws. Roughly, there have to be conditions under which the functional item would perform its functions since there have to have been conditions under which its ancestors did perform these functions, and the same kind of item in the same kind of conditions would do the same kind of thing again. This ignores defective members of function categories—diseased hearts, injured limbs, etc. It also ignores the fact that performance of their functions is, for many items, a relatively rare occurrence. Would we really wish to speak of *ceteris paribus* laws in cases where *ceteris* are not *paribus* most of the time? And it also ignores a third point.

Characteristically, the same function could, at least in principle, be performed by many differently constituted items. But if these items are differently constituted, if they operate in accordance with different principles, then the supporting conditions required for them to effect this function must differ as well. Brain cells performing the division algorithm require oxygen whereas computer chips require electric currents, and so forth. Similarly, the outer world conditions that support the bat's mosquito-locating abilities and those that support his mosquito-catching abilities are different from those that support the same abilities in humans. (The bat can perform in the dark on silent mosquitos; humans cannot.) The result is that there are no *ceteris paribus* laws covering all items having a certain function. For *ceteris paribus* conditions are unspecified conditions that must remain the same from case to case for the law to hold, whereas here the necessary conditions would have, precisely, to vary from case to case. A 'law' applying to all such cases could say no more than that the items falling under the law could be made, by adding different circumstances tailored specifically to each case, to perform the function. But surely anything can be made to effect anything if one adds the right intervening media, if one adds enough special enough circumstances. So any such 'law' would be empty. There are no causal laws of any kind, then, that directly concern the causal efficacy of reasons as such. The closest we could get would be *ceteris paribus* laws for human reasons, other *ceteris paribus* laws for dolphin reasons, still others for Martian reasons, and so forth.

8. Normalizing Explanations

Our argument suggests that explanation of an agent's behaviour by reference to reasons for acting is not best analysed as explanation by subsumption under causal laws. The question that arises, then, is what kind of explanation the citing of reasons for acting is, and how it can still be causal-order explanation. Intentional attitude explanations of behaviours proceed, I will argue, by subsumption of behaviours under biological norms rather than laws, and/or by noting departures from these norms and, perhaps, causes of these departures. Following Philip Pettit (1986), to whose views mine run parallel here, I call such explanations 'normalizing explanations'. The status of explanations of individual behaviours by reference to reasons concerns the relation of normalizing explanations to other forms of causal-order explanation that are, perhaps, better understood.

To explain a phenomenon by subsuming it under norms is to exhibit it as an instance of conformity to or departure from proper operation of some teleological system. A very simple form of normalizing explanation explains the occurrence of a phenomenon by reference, merely, to something whose function it was to produce that phenomenon. For example, the dishes are clean because they have been put through the dishwasher; the washing machine door is locked because the washer is not finished spinning and the door is designed not to unlock until it is finished spinning; the bear is asleep because it is winter and it is (biologically) normal for bears to sleep through the winter (see note 4 above).

In order to explain a phenomenon this way it is necessary, of course, to classify it appropriately as the outcome of a teleo-functional process, and this classifying may itself count as a simple form of explanation. What is happening? What is it doing? It's washing dishes, not making soup or just dirtying the water; it's winding a magnetic coil, not storing wire on a spool; it's resting, cooling its motor between cycles, not playing dead, or broken; and so forth.

More complex normalizing explanations tell or implicitly refer to the place an event has in a series or interdependent pattern of functions, or tell where, and perhaps why, malfunction occurred within such a series or pattern. Thus, that cog-wheel's turning in the calculator is its carrying one in a certain addition algorithm; the car went through the light because its brakes failed; the outboard stalls because there's dirt in the carburettor that gets into the needle-valve. Normalizing explanations often make reference to conditions that must be presupposed for normal operation of a device or system. Thus the outboard won't start because the spark-plugs are wet or because there's no gas in the tank, the scuba-diver passed out because it was too cold or because his tank ran out of oxygen, and so forth.

Finally, the relation between certain conditions of the functional system itself or of the environment and certain states of the system that normally adapt the system's progress to those conditions may be targeted in a normalizing explanation. Thus, the motor is racing because the heavy-load switch is on, but the load is not heavy; the washer failed to fill properly because the soap was put into the tub rather than into the dispenser, so that the rising suds tripped the water cut-off before the tub was full; the animal's winter-approaching detectors failed because it was kept indoors, which is why it is attired inappropriately, or is behaving inappropriately to the season.

9. The Normal Roles of Beliefs and Desires

Notice how natural it would be to say in the last two of these cases that the washer thought it was full when it wasn't and that the animal's system didn't know it was winter. This is because a belief or a bit of knowledge is likewise a teleo-functional item, one whose function is to adapt the containing system so that it can perform its functions under certain conditions, namely, those conditions which the belief is about. Or, being a little more precise, it is the belief-forming mechanisms that produce the adaptations, the adjustments of the organism to the environment, the beliefs. Beliefs themselves are functionally classified, are 'individuated', not directly by function but according to the special conditions corresponding to them that must be met in the world if it is to be possible for them to contribute to proper functioning of the larger system in a historically normal way. Somewhat similarly, the water switch's being off will promote the washer's tasks normally only if the condition is fulfilled that the washer is full. And the animal's winter detectors' being off will effect appropriate functioning of the animal in accordance with historically normal reasons only if winter is not yet approaching.

Explicit human beliefs, however, are much more than just biological adapters to certain environmental conditions. They are adapters that perform their tasks in a certain sort of way, namely, through participation in inference processes. A picture that I advocate but will not try to defend here (see Millikan 1984, 1986*a*, 1989*a*, 1991*b*) shows beliefs and desires as working for the organism by *modelling* (in accordance with very abstract mathematical mapping functions) the environment, modelling the organism's goals, and modelling types of environmental transitions that the organism knows how to bring about. Normal practical thinking, then, involves tinkering with these models until solutions are found that will effect transitions from the present state of the environment to various desired states. On this picture the teleo-functions of desires (which they may not very often perform), like those of blueprints, are to effect what they model, to get themselves realized. When everything goes according to norm, action guided by the models inside is action conformed to the outside world so as to issue in productive loops through the environment. This happens in accordance with explanations that, made fully general, that is fully spelled out relationally, apply perfectly generally to all successful uses of the (same capacities of the) species' cognitive systems, historical and current. Theoretical inference is then interpreted as a process whereby the internal model of the environment grows or extends itself in accordance with principles that model various logical, geometrical, and causal necessities or regularities or dependencies in the environment.

Be all this as it may, what seems quite certain is that there must exist some sort of systematic teleo-functional organization of the human cognitive systems whereby the making of good practical and theoretical inferences corresponds to normal (but perhaps not average) functioning for beliefs and desires, and whereby it is biologically normal (not average) for desires to be fulfilled, at least under certain conditions. (Why else the capacity to have desires?) Accordingly, explanations of behaviours by reference to reasons for action are normalizing explanations.

10. How Normalizing Explanations Circumscribe Causes

Why it is that normalizing explanations explain, how it is that they fall under a general theory of explanation, is too large a question for this essay. Our question here is only how such explanations connect with simpler kinds of causal explanation. One connecting link is that whatever has a teleo-function has a normal way of operating, a normal way of performing its function. For functional artefacts this may be, in part, the way the designer proposed that the function be performed; for biological devices, it is the way the function has been performed historically. An exhaustive analysis of the way, given its history, that any functional item operates when operating normally, arrives eventually at a description of normal physical structure for such a device and normal physical conditions for its operation, such that physical laws generate performance of this function given this structure and these conditions. By making implicit reference to such causal explanations, normalizing explanations may thus circumscribe quite specific physical explanations without detailing them.

Guided by Cummins (1975, 1983), we notice that the analysis of how a system normally functions may have several parts. First, the larger function or functions of the system may be analysed into sub-functions that are performed either serially or simultaneously or in some more complicated pattern of interaction. This kind of analysis Cummins calls 'functional analysis'. Cummins suggests that a functional analysis may generally be represented by a flow-chart, but of course highly parallel processes, especially those that interact to some degree stochastically, must be represented otherwise. Second, the system may be analysed into sub-systems, which may or may not correspond to discrete physical parts, each of which is responsible for a designated set of sub-functions. This kind of analysis Cummins calls 'compositional analysis'. Compositional analysis results in a description of the normal (not necessarily actual) constitution of the system by reference to parts described teleo-functionally, that is, normatively rather than dispositionally. (Here I depart from Cummins, who equates functions with dispositions.) Finally, the normal physical constitutions of the elements normally composing the system may be described, along with the surrounding physical conditions required for normal functioning, and it may be shown how these descriptions together account, in accordance with physical law, for cases of normal operation. That is, the system may ultimately be analysed into a set of physical parts and physical dispositions rather than, merely, functionally categorized parts and normal functions.[9]

By reference to the possibility of this kind of physical analysis, explanations of behaviours according to reasons for action may circumscribe physical causes. Compare explaining why a man shakes by saying that he suffers from Brown's syndrome, even though the aetiology of Brown's syndrome may not be known. Or compare explaining why a man has brown hair by saying he has genes for brown hair rather than, say, having dyed his hair, though no one knows the constitution of the gene or how it produces brown hair (cf. Block 1990).

That this is not the complete answer to how reasons circumscribe causes becomes evident, however, when we remember that devices falling in the same function category can have widely varying constitutions. For example, we do sometimes explain, say, how John managed to get the can open by noting that he finally found a can-opener, but given the enormous variety among can-openers, the various different principles on which they may work, how could such an explanation possibly do anything towards circumscribing

[9] This does not imply that, given a certain species, there is a classically understood type–type identity relation between, say, normally constituted and normally functioning beliefs and desires about *x* on the one hand, and certain physiological structures on the other. Certainly if the physical constitutions of human beliefs are typed categorially, there is no reason at all to suppose that any such identity holds. If there are bridge laws for humans that map the semantics of thoughts on to physiological structures, surely what these laws map is certain semantic relations among beliefs and desires on to physical relations among these, hence principles of logical interaction on to principles of causal interaction, not categorial meanings on to categorial physiological 'shapes'.

physical causes or types of physical processes lying behind the can's having come open? Similarly, if there really were various other creatures designed quite differently from humans and made of quite different stuffs but who still had beliefs and desires, then explanation of actions by reference to beliefs and desires without mention of the species of creature involved would seem not to circumscribe any particular kind of physical process at all.

But, looking more closely, whether it circumscribes a kind of process depends on how you type your kinds. Behind every normalizing explanation is a device or system with teleo-functions, and an item acquires a teleo-function only by having a very special sort of causal history. For example, if the cat's purr is explained as produced by a purr-box, an organ especially designed, in the smaller cats, to produce purrs, then we know that the purr-box itself has resulted, ultimately, from the operation of prior purr-boxes in ancestor cats which produced purrs, these purrs somehow having survival value, contributing an essential link, at least occasionally, to the historical cat-chain. Thus a salient cause of the purr is a series of prior purrs. Of course when the functions referred to by normalizing explanations are described categorially though they are actually derived from relational functions, no such simple analysis applies. Still, to assign to any phenomenon a place in a functional system is to claim that it has emerged from a very special kind of causal-historical process, a kind that defines functionality. It is to distinguish its particular type of causal origin quite sharply from other aetiological patterns.

13

Who's in Charge Here? And Who's Doing All the Work?

ROBERT VAN GULICK

> Tom raised the canteen to his lips because he believed it still contained some water and he was very thirsty.
>
> Greta chose her tomatoes carefully, picking only those that looked the reddest; because Henrik was colour-blind he was unable to help her.
>
> Little Sonja pushed away the toy rabbit the day-care worker held out to her; she wanted her own brown teddy bear and nothing else would do.

THERE is nothing exceptional about such explanations and the everyday situations they describe. In each case a common-sense or folk psychological explanation of someone's behaviour is offered that explains why someone acted as he or she did by appeal to one or more of the person's mental states and their mental properties. Tom put the canteen to his lips *because* of his belief and *because* his belief had the propositional content that it did—that there still was water in the canteen. Greta picked the tomatoes that she did *because* of the visual experiences they had produced in her and *because* those visual experiences had the qualitative property of being phenomenally red—a property none of Henrik's visual experiences has. Little Sonja rejected the fluffy rabbit *because* of her desire and *because* that desire had a particular toy as its intentional object—her own brown teddy bear.

Though the overwhelming majority of philosophers and ordinary folk find such explanations informative and predictive (with San

An earlier version of this paper was presented at the conference on Mental Causation held at the Centre for Interdisciplinary Studies (ZIF), University of Bielefeld, Bielefeld, Germany in March 1990. I am grateful for useful criticisms from Jaegwon Kim,who commented on the paper at that conference. I have also benefited from suggestions offered by the editors of this volume.

Diego PDP-tensor-network-neuro-eliminativists as the notable exceptions (Churchland 1981, Churchland 1986)) there is somewhat less unanimity of opinion about how the word 'because' is to be interpreted in such explanations. Due in part to the work of Donald Davidson (1963) in the 1960s, the dominant view among Anglo-American philosophers has been that the 'because' in such explanations must be read as involving a causal relation. Beliefs and desires cause the behaviours that they rationalize. There are philosophers who deny this, e.g. Daniel Dennett (1987) and Jonathan Bennett (1990), but it remains the majority view, and since I count myself within that majority I will accept it as a working assumption; my concern will be with the difficulties that supposedly result from adopting the causal interpretation.

It is misleading, however, to speak of *the* because in the relevant explanations; each of them contains at least implicitly a double occurrence of 'because'. Tom raised the canteen to his lips because of his belief *and* because his belief had the intentional content that it did. Such explanations appeal both to mental states or events and to mental properties. If both of these 'becauses' are to be interpreted causally then what is being claimed about the event of Tom's raising the canteen to his lips is both that it was caused (at least in part) by the event of his having a certain belief and that that belief's having the intentional content that it did was causally relevant to (or causally responsible for) its producing the sorts of effects that it did. This may seem to be an unsurprising claim, one that accords well with our common-sense or folk intuitions. Surely if Tom's belief had had a different content, e.g. that the canteen was empty or that it contained poison, its effects on his behaviour would have been quite different.

However common sense rarely suffices to prevent a good philosophical fight, and there has been of late quite a debate about whether the mental properties invoked in such explanations—e.g. the content of Tom's belief or the phenomenal properties of Greta's visual experiences—can be *causally relevant* or *causally potent* properties. To quote Jerry Fodor (1989) there has been an 'outbreak of epiphobia', a widespread fear of mental property epiphenomenalism, that is a fear that mental properties are causally irrelevant or inert. The worry is that even if mental events such as believings or desirings have causal effects (including external behavioural effects) they do not do so in virtue of having the mental properties that they do. In particular, content-properties and phenomenal properties are alleged to be causally impotent. The view is sometimes combined with the token-identity thesis that every mental event-token is identical with some physical event-token. There is just one ontology of events possessing both physical and mental properties. However, with respect to causal potency, the mental properties are distinctly disadvantaged; indeed they are completely excluded from affecting any token event's causal powers or causal relations; those are determined solely by its physical properties.

Mental-property (MP) epiphenomenalism is an unintuitive and not very attractive hybrid. Yet a variety of arguments may seem to force us to it. The relevant arguments are diverse both in the principles on which they base their claim and in the range of mental properties they allege to exclude from causal relevance.

To get a sense of the options, consider four arguments. They are all a bit sketchy, but they present a fair sample of the sorts of arguments that have been offered of late. Some like A1 appeal to a necessary connection between causality and strict laws (Kim 1984*b*, Sosa 1984).

A1. The Strict Law Argument

1. An event *C*'s having the property *F* can cause an event *E* to occur (or cause *E* to have the property *G*) only if *E* has property *G* and there is a strict law which subsumes *C* and *E* in virtue of *C*'s being *F* and *E*'s being *G*.
2. *Anomalism of the Mental*: There are no strict laws involving mental properties.

∴ 3. *C*'s having a mental property *M* can neither cause the occurrence of any event *E* nor cause an event *E* to have a property *G* (from 1, 2).

∴ 4. Mental properties are not causally potent; they cannot affect nor explain an event's having the effects that it does (from 3).

∴ 5. Mental properties are not causally relevant; they are epiphenomenal (from 4).

A related but distinct argument A2 appeals not to the alleged strictly nomic nature of causality but rather to the overriding role of physical properties in determining causal relations thereby excluding mental properties from playing any causal role (Kim 1989*a*, 1989*b*.)

A2. The Exclusion Argument

1. *Token Physicalism*: Every mental event-token (i.e. every event-token having mental properties) is identical with some physical event-token (i. e. some event-token having physical properties).
2. The causal powers of a physical event-token are completely determined by its physical properties.
3. *The Nonreducibility of the Mental*: Mental properties are neither identical with nor reducible to physical properties.

∴ 4. A mental event-token's mental properties do not even partially determine its causal powers (from 1, 2, 3).
∴ 5. Mental properties are not causally potent (from 4).
∴ 6. Mental properties are not causally relevant; they are epiphenomenal (from 5).

Both A1 and A2 are intended to establish that all mental properties are causally impotent, but other arguments aim at a more modest conclusion excluding only some proper subset of mental properties from causal relevance. Some like A3 attempt to show that so-called wide intentional properties are not causally potent (Fodor 1987).

A3. The Argument from Lack of Individual Supervenience

1. The wide content properties of a person's mental states do not supervene on her intrinsic or individualistic properties (i.e. on those properties that she would share with any molecule-for-molecule duplicate of herself).
2. The causal powers of a person's mental states supervene on her intrinsic or individualistic properties (she has a given causal power if and only if any molecule-for-molecule duplicate of her would also have that power).

∴ 3. A mental state's causal powers must be completely determined by some set of properties other than its wide content properties (from 1, 2).
∴ 4. A mental state's wide content properties do not even partially determine its causal powers (from 3).
∴ 5. Wide content properties are not causally potent (from 4).

∴ 6. Wide content properties are not causally relevant; they are epiphenomenal (from 5).

Arguments such as A3 are sometimes extended to draw a further conclusion about psychological method and the proper mode of individuating states in a scientific psychological theory. One might hope to reach such conclusion through such added steps as 7–9.

Extension of A3

7. Psychological explanations (at least those of the sort produced by a psychology of cognitive or intentional processes) are causal explanations.

∴ 8. Thus the states and processes appealed to in such psychological explanations should be type-individuated in terms of their causal powers (from 7).

∴ 9. Our psychological theories of cognitive or rational processes should not individuate states in terms of their wide content properties (from 5, 8).

I have explained elsewhere my disagreements with A3 (see Van Gulick 1989). In short, I argue contrary to Fodor that many causal powers relevant to psychology, such as whether or not an organism is able to pick up information, need to be individuated widely, i.e. in a way that individuates causal powers within contexts not across contexts. By analogy, think of a comparison with respect to the causal power of being camouflaged between two molecularly identical groups of lizards living in very different natural environments. They might differ greatly in how well their identical colouring camouflaged them and allowed them to avoid detection and predation. For at least some biological purposes it would be correct to classify the two groups of lizards as having different causal powers.

I suppose that I should also lay my cards on the table by saying that I do not find any of these arguments sound or convincing; nor do I think they could be made such merely by remedying the defects in my admittedly sketchy formulations. Indeed I am sceptical that there are any sound arguments for MP-epiphenomenalism since I am inclined to believe that position is false. Nonetheless, I think there are things to be learned by examining the arguments listed above.

Let us thus turn our attention then to A1, the Strict Law Argument. Such arguments have been used in the attempt to show that Donald Davidson's anomalous monism (1970) is committed to MP-epiphenomenalism, a result which his critics believe he would find unwelcome. Most philosophers (myself included) follow Davidson in accepting premiss 2, which denies that there are any strict laws involving mental properties; so let's concede it.

The more problematic premiss is 1. Why should subsumption under a strict law be a necessary condition for causality? Davidson claims that two events can be related as cause and effect only if there is some strict law that subsumes them. But that, as Brian Mclaughlin (1989) has pointed out, is a somewhat different claim than our premiss 1. McLaughlin has argued that Davidson's requirement, which he terms 'the Principle of the Nomological Character of Causality' (or the 'Causality Principle', for short) does not imply that *only* strictly nomic properties are causal, i.e. it does not imply what he calls the Exclusion Principle: events are causally related *only* in virtue of falling under strict laws.

McLaughlin's position is something like this. The Principle of Causality requires that if two events are related as cause and effect there must be a strict law that grounds that relation, but it does not exclude the possiblity that the causal relation between them may also be grounded by some other relation not involving a strict law. He attempts to make the proposal plausible by analogy with other sorts of grounding relations. One can be a resident of the Federal German Republic (BRD) only if one is a resident of one of its states, but that does not imply that being a resident of a given state is the only relation that can ground the property of being a resident of the BRD; it might for example be grounded by being a resident of the city of Bielefeld. The fact that one cannot be a resident of Bielefeld without being a resident of a state of the BRD does not make it any less true that Ralf's being a resident of Bielefeld makes it the case that he is a resident of the BRD. Unfortunately McLaughlin doesn't give any comparable examples involving the multiple grounding of causal relationships. Still, I think he has shown that premiss 1 is not entailed by Davidson's principle that causally related events must be subsumed by some strict law.

None the less, one might find premiss 1 an independently plausible principle; Ernest LePore and Barry Loewer seem to do so in their own exegetical defence of Davidson's position (1987, 1989). But why might one do so? I think in at least one respect it appeals to that old rationalist 'verity', the Principle of Sufficient Reason. Laws qualify as strict laws in virtue of meeting two conditions: (1) being exceptionless and (2) being part of closed comprehensive theory. It is the former of these two that appeals to the Principle of Sufficient Reason. If all we know about two events *C* and *E* is that they fall under a law which allows for exceptions, we do not know why *C* was followed by *E* on this occasion. Whatever property of *C* satisfies the antecedent of the relevant law cannot have sufficed for *C*'s causing *E*, since the existence of exceptions to the law acknowledges that there are other *C**s that are just like *C* in having that property but which none the less fail to produce similar effects. Of course, in everyday singular causal statements we often appeal to causes that do not universally and necessarily produce effects of the sort we wish to explain in the particular circumstance. We may say that lighting the match caused the explosion while knowing that most match-lightings do not produce explosions. Such singular causal statements merely focus attention on what is taken to be one part of a complete explanation with the balance of the causal factors left unspecified or implicitly understood. What the Principle of Sufficient Reason seems to require is that we could not have a complete causal explanation of why an event *E* occurred unless the antecedent conditions specified were strictly sufficient for the production of *E*. Thus premiss 1 may seem to place a plausible requirement on causal relations—at least with respect to the exceptionless aspect of strict laws.

None the less I remain sceptical about the claim that two events can be causally related only if there are properties of the first that are nomically sufficient for the production of the latter. I will have more to say about my reasons below when we consider the role played by causal laws in our cognitive economy. For the moment let me just note that what might have seemed obvious to Leibniz in 1690 should not seem obvious to us in 1990, nearly seventy years after the advent of quantum mechanics, with its apparent demonstration of the irreducibly statistical nature of physical interactions at the micro-physical level. That an event *C* of a given type should produce an effect *E* on one occasion and that another event *C** physically indistinguishable from *C* in all respects should none the less fail to produce any event similar to *E* may strike us as odd and perplexing, but it should not strike us as impossible given the empirical indications that such situations are not only possible but actual.

However, even if one were inclined to concede that causes must be nomically sufficient to produce their effects, one need not accept premiss 1. One might try to explicate nomic sufficiency in a way that does not demand subsumption under strict laws. Indeed that is just the move made by Jerry Fodor (1989) in his recent attempt to deal with the 'outbreak of epiphobia'. He clearly accepts the nomic sufficiency demand on causality, 'the notion of causal responsibility of the mental that your intuitions demand is that *M*s should be a nomologically sufficient condition for *B*s. Accept no substitutes, is what I say. I'm not, however, exactly sure how to convince you that this is indeed what your intuitions cry out for' (Fodor 1989, p. 72).

However, Fodor does not accept the claim that only strict laws can provide the required nomic sufficiency; he maintains that it can be provided as well by hedged or *ceteris paribus* laws in cases in which the law's *ceteris paribus* conditions are satisfied along with its antecedent.

> Suppose it's true that causes need to be covered by laws that necessitate their consequents; it doesn't follow that they need to be covered by *strict* laws. Hedged laws necessitate their consequents in worlds where their *ceteris paribus* conditions are satisfied. Why then should mental causes that are covered by hedged intentional laws with satisfied antecedents and satisfied *ceteris paribus* conditions require further covering by a *strict* law of physics? (Fodor 1989 pp. 74–5.)

I think it would be wiser to cut off support for premiss 1 a step earlier by denying that causality requires nomic sufficiency, but Fodor offers an alternative basis for rejecting premiss 1 to those who share his acceptance of the nomic sufficiency requirement. His alternative may succeed, but it is not without potential problems. Let me list three possible difficulties.

1. Do all the properties of psychology (or of the other special sciences) that Fodor wishes to rescue from epiphenomenalism figure in non-strict laws of the form 'If *F* then *G ceteris paribus*'? Or are there some that occur only in laws that merely specify that *F*s affect the probabilities of *G*s in a less than deterministic fashion? If there are any causal laws of the latter form, it will not be possible to achieve nomic sufficiency by simply adding the satisfaction of the *ceteris paribus* conditions to the satisfaction of the antecedent; such laws contain no *ceteris paribus* clauses. (Fodor might well deny that any such laws would count as causal laws.)

2. There may be many cases in which it is impossible to tell whether the *ceteris paribus* clause of a non-strict law is satisfied except on the basis of whether or not the specified effect occurred; indeed there may be no way of saying just what counts as satisfaction of the *ceteris paribus* clause except by appeal to the occurrence or non-occurrence of the effect. There is thus a danger of trivializing the claim of nomic sufficiency with respect to such laws; all one may be saying is that in all the worlds in which *F*-related conditions sufficient for producing a *G* were satisfied, *G*s occurred.

3. A third line of criticism is raised by Barry Loewer and Ernest LePore (1989, which appears with Fodor's 1989). In brief they argue as follows. Let *c* and *e* be any two events that are subsumed by a *ceteris paribus* law *F*s cause *G*s, whose *ceteris paribus* conditions are satisfied with respect to *c* and *e*. There must then also be a fundamental law of physics that subsumes *c* and *e*. To hold otherwise, they argue, would be to allow that there are causal relations that do not supervene on basic physical properties and laws. But once we acknowledge that there is such a strict physical law subsuming *c* and *e*, like a young cuckoo in the nest of a robin, it 'greedily' grabs all the causal potency for itself. As they put the point,

> The fact that *F*s cause *G*s is a causal law is a result of the basic causal laws and the way in which *F*s supervene on physical facts. So the real locus of causal powers are the physical properties. *F*, so to speak, gets carried piggyback on physical properties and it is mere appearance that possessing *F* determines *c*'s causal powers. The basic physical properties and laws determine both the causal relations among events and the non-basic causal laws. It is merely an appearance that the non-basic causal laws determine causal relations among events. (LePore and Loewer 1989, p. 187.)

Since this is a version of what we have called the Exclusion Argument, it may be appropriate to shift our attention to our own version of that argument, A2. However, before doing so, let's take stock of how things stand with respect to A1. Our critical focus has been entirely on its problematic first premiss, about which three things have been shown:

> First, premiss 1 is not equivalent to Davidson's principle of the nomological principle of causality, nor is it entailed by that principle.

Second, premiss 1's plausibility depends on the assumption that causality requires nomic sufficiency, and that assumption is open to challenge (e.g. by appeal to quantum mechanics).

Third, even if one accepts the nomic sufficiency requirement on causation, it may not be necessary to accept premiss 1, if there is a way for the requirement to be satisfied by less than strict laws (e.g. by non-strict laws with satisfied *ceteris paribus* clauses).

I should note that I also have some reservations about the later stages of A1, especially about the move from the claim that mental properties are not causally *potent* to the claim that they are not causally *relevant*. But since those very same steps recur in A2, let us put off considering them until later.

What then of A2, the Exclusion Argument? Here I think we get much closer to the heart of the problem; unlike the strict law argument, the Exclusion Argument does not rely upon any special account of what is required for two events to be causally connected. It relies instead on two widely held physicalist views expressed by its first and second premisses: first, that all events are physical events, and second, that the world of the physical constitutes a closed causal system. Saying just what's wrong with the Exclusion Argument is much harder than criticizing the Strict Law Argument. It has no obvious point of vulnerability; nothing comparable to premiss 1 of the Strict Law Argument. A direct frontal assault is unlikely to breach its fortifications. To see where it goes wrong, we shall have to dig more deeply into the question of causal relevance in the hope of undermining the hidden foundations of the argument.

Given my non-reductionist sympathies with its third premiss (Van Gulick 1985, 1992), I am prepared to accept all three of its premisses. Thus critical attention must focus on the inferences drawn from those premisses. Before undertaking our deep dig into the question of causal relevance, let's make a quick reconnaissance of the three inferential steps in the argument that we might hope in time to undermine.

As Loewer and LePore (1989) note with respect to a similar argument, its fourth step does not follow deductively from its premisses (1–3) unless one adds a further premiss to exclude the possibility that an event's causal powers might be over-determined. For as long as over-determination is possible, an event's causal powers might be partially determined by its mental properties even if those powers were completely determined by its physical properties. Loewer and LePore do not pursue over-determination as a way of undercutting the argument. They argue that mental properties can contribute to an event's causal powers (or relations) only in a derivative sense which makes their contribution dependent on an underlying physical explanation and that any other form of over-determination would be inconsistent with physicalism (p. 188). On their view an event's mental properties do nothing more than appear to determine its causal powers. ('Who's in charge here?') All the real determination is going on down below on the physical level. ('Who's doing the work here?') Thus the over-determination, as well, remains mere appearance.

I don't see how one can adequately assess the possibility of over-determination until one is clear about the sense in which an event's properties are supposed to determine its causal powers, and I don't think that is yet clear. We have yet to do our deep digging. So it will be best to leave the question of over-determination open for now and set it to one side until later.

The inference from 4 to 5 in our version of the Exclusion Argument is similarly enthymematic. The suppressed premiss is that a property of an event is causally potent only if it at least partially determines the event's causal powers. It is this principle that Loewer and LePore choose to challenge. They offer an alternative notion of causal potency in terms of subjunctive conditionals which would allow a property of an event to count as causally potent even if it failed to determine any of the event's causal powers (or relations). Borrowing a term from Terence Horgan (1989), they call the relevant relation 'quausation' (as in *C qua F* causes *E qua G*) and define it as follows:

<*c*,*F*> is quausally related to <*e*,*G*> iff *c* and *e* occur and are respectively *F* and *G* and there is some time before the occurrence of *c* at which these two conditionals obtain: (1) if *c* were to occur and be *F* then that would cause an event *e* to be *G*; (2) if *c* were to occur and not be an *F* then it would not cause an event which is *G*. (Loewer and Lepore 1989, p.189.)

They explain the idea behind the account as follows: 'In the possible worlds which are most similar to the actual world at time *t* at which property *F* is instantiated by event *c*, *c* causes an event which is *G* and in worlds in which *c* fails to instantiate *F* it also fails to cause a *G*' (LePore and Loewer 1989, p. 189).

Their endorsement of quausation as a way of rescuing the causal potency of mental properties is tentative and hedged by a worry about whether or not quausation is sufficiently strong a relation to rebut epiphenomenalism. Their worry is well-founded since I think their quausation relation clearly won't avoid epiphenomenalism. Consider a simple example involving non-mental properties. Imagine we are preparing a chemical mixture TTT that becomes explosive when its molecular configuration is altered by successive heating and cooling, call the relevant configuration BAM. Imagine further that TTT turns blue when and only when it goes into the BAM configuration. A match is dropped into the blue BAM TTT and it explodes. Question: Was the blueness of the TTT into which the match was dropped causally potent or epiphenomenal with respect to producing an explosion?

It seems clear that that it was epiphenomenal. The TTT's being blue and its exploding were both causal consequences of its being BAM, but its exploding was not a consequence of its being blue. However, on Loewer and LePore's account of quausation, the fact that the match dropping was a dropping into blue TTT does turn out to be quausally related to its effect being an explosion. In the nearest worlds in which a match is dropped into blue TTT, explosions occur, and in the nearest worlds in which matches are dropped into non-blue TTT, explosions do not occur. But surely the causally potent property here is being BAM not being blue, which is just an epiphenomenal side-effect of being BAM with respect to the explosive power of TTT .

Loewer and LePore may reply that they never intended to exclude such cases from their stripped-down version of causal potency. But such a reply would only confirm that their version of causal potency is too weak to ward off the threat of epiphenomenalism.

Thus if we wish to block the inference from 4 to 5 of the Exclusion Argument, in hope of avoiding its final epiphenomenal conclusion 6, we will need to find a more robust notion of causal potency, but one that none the less stops short of restricting the range of causally potent properties to those that (at least partly) determine the causal powers of events that possess them. I am not optimistic that one can be found.

We come then to the last inferential step in the argument—the move from 5 to 6, which, like its predecessors, relies on an implicit assumption, in this case the assumption that only causally potent properties are causally relevant. The notion of causal relevance obviously requires some explication. Causally relevant properties might be limited to those that contribute to an event's having the causal powers that it does. So interpreted 6 says little, if anything, more than what is already stated by 5. But one might also interpret 'causal relevance' so that a property was causally relevant if it were appropriate or useful to invoke it in the context of a causal explanation. Read in this latter way, the inference from 5 to 6 becomes open to dispute, since it is far from obvious that only causally potent properties can be usefully invoked in causal explanations.

Having completed our reconnaissance of the the argument's inferential links, we can put off our deep digging no longer; we shall have to take hold of our theoretical shovels and begin our excavation.

Let us begin by asking the following question, 'What sorts of things are causal laws, that is what is their ontological status?' I think it's important to ask this question because at times in the mental causation literature there seems to be an almost theological realism about causal laws. The causal relation between two events is said to be 'grounded by the existence of a causal law' or that 'event *c* caused event *e* *because* it is a causal law that *F*-events cause *G*-events'. This makes causal laws seem like independent entities over and above the world of events and properties with the power to command events into conformity with their strictures. God said, '*Fiat lux*—let there be light' and there was light. Bodies of matter *must* attract each other gravitationally with a force inversely proportional to the square of their distance *because* were they not to do so they would violate the inverse square law. One might almost conjure up a comic version of Socrates' imagined confrontation in the *Crito* with οἱ νομοί (the laws), who berate him for contemplating disobedience. I don't suggest that any of the parties to the mental causation debate really hold such a view, but only that a subtle and perhaps unconscious tendency to reify causal laws seems implicit in much of what gets said about the way in which laws *make it the case* that one event caused another.

How then should one view causal laws and laws of nature in general? Laws are counterfactual sustaining statements (or sentences) in theories, perhaps those which appear in the simplest most comprehensive theories satisfied by the spatio-temporal totality of our world (Lewis 1980, postscript). I will not attempt to define with necessary and sufficient conditions what makes a given statement in such a theory a law; what matters for present purposes is that laws are statements or sentences in our theories of the world, not independent items among the furniture of the world itself. And what in turn are theories? They are organized systems of representation that can be used to structure our cognitive processes and guide our action. And we must not forget this action-guiding function; we are not pure intellects but agents who must choose, plan, decide, and act to survive. I offer no definition of what makes a theory; I only want to emphasize that theories and the laws they contain are cognitive constructs and that as such they are to be assessed pragmatically in terms of the roles they are designed or expected to fulfil.

What then is the function of causal laws in our cognitive economy? How are they expected to contribute to the organization of thought and the guidance of action? The answer is a familiar one and in a quick and simple way might go like this:

> We are biological organisms with needs, goals and wants. Our ability to succeed in their satisfaction is enhanced by possessing an accurate representation of the environment with which we must interact to achieve those results. In addition to possessing means by which we can pick up information about our present situation and store information picked up in the past, we must be able to make reliable predictions about the future and form plans of action that will enable us to determine or at least influence how the future will develop.

Causal laws provide us with a means of making such projections and of forming such plans of action. Like all laws of nature, they provide us with principles of connection within our representation(s) of the world, establishing connections that mirror stable recurrent patterns in the represented world. As causal laws they specifically single out the independent variables in such patterns, the levers that can and must be pushed to produce desired changes. One cannot alter the height of a flag-pole by altering its shadow despite the symmetric lawful covariance of the two parameters (Bromberger 1966). All of this I take to be true and obvious. I restate such platitudes only because I believe they are sometimes lost sight of in the debate about mental causation. (Remember, I warned you that undermining the Exclusion Argument would require an indirect attack.)

Given their cognitive role, what sorts of causal laws would it be useful to include in our representation of the world? Ideally one would like to have laws that were simple, reliable, and precise, that related properties that were determinate, easily detected, and important to our interests. However, such ideal laws are rarely available, and we must instead accept trade-offs among these various and often competing desiderata.

In constructing causal explanations, precision must often be sacrificed in the face of pragmatic constraints on what we can detect or comprehend. The micro-physical explanation of why my car stopped when I pressed the brake pedal or of why Tom's belief caused him to bring the canteen to his lips might indeed have a precision not possessed by automotive or intentional explanations of those same sequences of events. And the laws invoked in the micro-physical explanation might be strict laws while those in the alternative explanations are not.

Automotive and intentional explanations may be less precise and reliable, but they have their own advantages and virtues. Most importantly they are available *in practice*. They relate properties we are readily able to detect and that are relevant to our interests, and their explanation of how those properties interact is one we can survey and comprehend.

The importance of this last point should not be underestimated. As Hilary Putnam (1975*c*) illustrated in his peg-in-the-hole example, a *deduction* of a description of an effect from a description of its cause does not necessarily count as an *explanation* of why the effect occurred if the deduction is in practice incomprehensible and hides what is relevant about the causal transaction in a wealth of irrelevant details. Any other object with the same cross-section as the peg and some micro-structure or other that made it rigid under motion would just as easily pass through the hole. Thus our explanation of the peg's passing through the hole need not, indeed it should not, bring in all the particular micro-physical facts about the specific peg that underlie its being rigid and being of the size and shape it is. Explanations that are not pitched at the right level of abstraction fail to classify events into the similarity classes relevant to our predictive needs.

A proponent of mental property epiphenomenalism might reply as follows:

> I agree with everything you say about causal *explanations*. They have an important pragmatic dimension which will frequently require us to do our explaining in terms of more abstract higher-order properties including intentional and other mental properties. But the point at issue is whether or not mental *properties* are *causally potent*, i.e. whether or not they determine even partially the causal powers of events that have them. And that is an independent question (since causal explanations need not appeal only to causally potent properties). The fact remains that in each case in which explanatory appeal is made to mental properties, it is still the underlying physical properties that are doing the real causal work; mental properties only appear to determine an event's causal powers.

This reply may sound plausible, but it brings us back to the central claim of the Exclusion Argument and our dispute with Loewer and LePore: that is, why should we accept the claim that it is only the underlying physical properties that are really doing any causal work?

Consider an example involving refraction. Imagine three pairs of transparent optically conducting media (*A*/*B*, *C*/*D*, and *E*/*F*) with the following optical densities: *A*: 1.2; *B*: 1.5; *C*: 1.32; *D*: 1.65; *E*: 1.36; and *F*: 1.7. The three pairs of media will have the same refractive index since the optical densities of their members are all in a ratio of five to four. Consider then three cases in which rays of light pass from *A*, *C*, and *E* respectively into *B*, *D*, and *F*. If the angle of incidence is the same in the three cases, so too will be the angle of refraction since for all three pairs the sine of the angle of incidence will be equal to 1.25 × the sine of the angle of refraction.

Why is the ray of light bent as it is in each case? Is it because the ratio of optical densities is 4 : 5 in each pair, or must we say that the real reason the *A*/*B* pair bent the ray *x* degrees is different from the reason the *C*/*D* pair also bent it *x* degrees? Indeed, the defender of the Exclusion Argument may well argue that the real explanation must be in terms of the particular micro-physical transactions between each specific pair of media and the light ray passing through them. It will not suffice to say that the light ray was bent as its leading edge passed from a medium having an optical density of

1.5 into another having an optical density of 1.25 and was thus slowed down before its trailing edge was similarly slowed. The defender of the Exclusion Argument must reject such an explanation as too abstract to provide an account of the causally potent properties. One must at least descend to the the physical structures of the two media and how those structures interact with passing photons. For even if we compare the passage of light from *A* to *B* with the passage of light from *G* to *H* where *G* like *A* has an optical density of 1.5 and *H* like *B* has one of 1.25, the underlying microstructures of the respective pairs of media may be quite different and their optical densities may result from very different interactions with photons.

If the proponent of the Exclusion Argument takes such a hard line, he will have to concede that none of the properties of the special sciences are causally potent. Not only will mental properties turn out to be epiphenomenal but so will neurological properties, geological properties, and even biochemical properties. Even many properties of physics proper, such as having a given optical density, will turn out not to be causally potent. As numerous authors have noted (e.g. Fodor 1989), if the sense in which mental properties are epiphenomenal makes them no worse off than biochemical properties, then what's the big deal? Why should psychological properties have to meet a higher standard for causal potency than biochemical, geological, or optical properties? The point is well taken, and if that were the best one could say in response, it might none the less suffice to allay worries about the epiphenomenalism of the mental.

However, I believe more can and should be said. For the epiphenomenalist is still being allowed to claim a special privileged status for fundamental physical properties with respect to causal potency; on his account they remain causally potent in a sense not shared by the properties of the special sciences (except perhaps in those cases in which a special science property can be identified with an underlying basic physical property—i.e. in those cases in which the property just is a basic physical property which also has a special science name). At the risk of seeming a demagogic leveller (hardly an attractive option in this post-Marxist era), I propose that the solution to this inequality is not to find a way of giving special science properties (including mental properties) the status claimed for physical properties but in showing that physical properties have no such special status; it's not a matter of raising the status of special science properties but of exposing the pretension of the the specialness of the physical. (The physicalist emperor has no clothes.)

Here's how the story goes. Special science explanations work because they classify objects and events so that they share predictable causal roles; they pick out recurrent, stable (if sometimes less than strictly deterministic) patterns of order in the world. Sometimes this is because the classification is explicitly based on causal role (e.g. being a catalyst or a recessive gene), and at other times it is because the classification is based on features that guarantee a given causal role (e.g. being a certain sequence of nucleic acids or an atmospheric temperature inversion). (Which of the two best fits intentional classification is left as an exercise for the reader.)

Physical explanations work for the same reason; physical classifications also group objects sharing common causal roles (e.g. being a electron with 1/2 negative spin). So far so good—equality. The champion of the physical will reply that the causal roles associated with special science classifications are entirely derivative from the causal roles of the underlying physical constituents of the objects or events picked out by the special sciences. Once again we will be told that it is the physical properties that are doing all the real work.

This is not quite true, however. The events and objects picked out by the special sciences are admittedly composites of physical constituents. But the causal powers of such an object are not determined solely by the physical properties of its constituents and the laws of physics, but also by the organization of those constituents within the composite. And it is just such patterns of organization that are picked out by the predicates of the special sciences.

In a way this is just a reminder that physical outcomes are determined by the laws of physics together with *initial boundary conditions*. Special science predicates pick out stable recurring sets of such boundary conditions (or equivalence classes of such boundary conditions). By doing so they isolate a level of causal order and regularity in the natural world. (An aside: this need not entail that special science properties are reducible to physical properties for a variety of reasons. There may, for example, be opened-ended possibilities for multiple physical realization. And perhaps more importantly the criteria for applying special science predicates may be anchored in our discriminatory cognitive abilities in ways that make them sufficiently indeterminate to prevent any exact match-up with precisely specified sets of physical properties (Van Gulick 1985 , 1992).) Thus we can say that the causal powers of a composite object or event are determined in part by its higher-order (special science) properties and not solely by the physical properties of its constituents and the laws of physics.

'Not so fast', cries the champion of the physical in reply; 'in any given instance this pattern or organization, these boundary conditions of which you speak will be nothing more than a strictly physical arrangement of matter in time and space. To treat the pattern as something over and above its strictly physical instantiations would be an exercise in Platonic reification. Surely predicates, like those of the special sciences, that merely pick out such patterns don't pick out anything that's real in a causally relevant sense; what's real and causally relevant are simply the actual instantiations of such patterns, and they are entirely physical. Special science predicates are at best convenient shorthand abbreviations for referring to such physical instantiations; they should not be understood as referring to real and causally potent properties.'

But why should we not regard these patterns as real and causally potent? Consider what might be said on behalf of their reality.

1. Such patterns are recurrent and stable features of the world.

2. Many such patterns are stable despite variations or exchanges in their underlying physical constituents; the pattern is conserved even though its constituents are not (e.g. in a hurricane or a blade of grass).

3. Many such patterns are self-sustaining or self-reproductive in the face of perturbing physical forces that might degrade or destroy them (e.g. DNA patterns).

4. Such patterns can affect which causal powers of their constituents are activated or likely to be activated. A given physical constituent may have many causal powers, but only some subset of them will be active in a given situation. The larger context (i.e. the pattern) of which it is a part may affect which of its causal powers get activated. (For example, the activity of a reagent can be affected by the presence of a catalysing enzyme that forms a composite with the reagent.) Thus the whole is not any simple function of its parts, since the whole at least partially determines what contributions are made by its parts.

5. The selective activation of the causal powers of its parts (4) may in many cases contribute to the maintenance and preservation of the pattern itself (2, 3).

Taken together these five points illustrate that higher-order patterns can have a degree of independence from their underlying physical realizations and can exert what might be called downward causal influences without requiring any objectionable form of emergentism by which higher-order properties would alter the underlying laws of physics. Higher-order properties act by the *selective activation* of physical powers not by their *alteration*.

With respect to such patterns and their underlying physical constituents, we can ask the first question posed in my title: 'Who's in charge here?' Given 1–5 above there is a very real sense in which the constituents of the pattern are organized as they are because of the pattern. It is because of the existence and persistence of the pattern that the particular constituents of its instances were recruited and organized as they are. Moreover, many such patterns may be (all but) inevitable features of our world. They are among the stable states of order; because of their persistence and self-sustaining character, if given enough time they naturally emerge from the disorderly flux of nature. Their existence is far from accidental.

Still, the champion of the physical might reply that even if such patterns are inevitably occurrent stable features of our world, they are so only because the world has the physical order that it does. The order of higher-level properties or patterns is entirely dependent on and derivative from the world's underlying physical order. Once again the primacy of the physical looms in impending triumph.

But perhaps the threat is more apparent than real. Though I can't prove it, I strongly suspect this claim of dependency on the physical is false or at least misleading. Let me explain. The standard thought experiment to demonstrate dependence on the physical is try to imagine a possible world just like the actual world in all physical respects but differing in respect of some higher-order property, for example in some mental property. The standard response is that no such worlds are possible, and I am not now inclined to dispute that intuition.

I am more inclined to deny that this is the right test or the only test relevant to determining whether the order among higher-level patterns is dependent on physical order. One might also try to imagine possible worlds in which many of the laws of physics are different than they are in this world but in which many of the same higher-order patterns are present. Indeed one might try to imagine worlds containing nothing that one would count as physical but that none the less shared patterns of higher-order organization with our world.

To make my abstract speculation just a bit more concrete, consider the patterns associated with acquiring, possessing, and exploiting information, patterns that are pervasive throughout at least the biological portion of our world (though I believe they are in fact more widespread). One might turn to Fred Dretske's work for some account of how to explain such informational relations (see e.g. Dretske 1981, 1988). One would immediately notice that to bake such an informational cake one needs only very simple ingredients (Dretske's metaphor). One needs lawful covariance and perhaps causal connections, but there is no requirement that such lawful or causal connections be physical connections. In some possible worlds they might well be non-physical connections.

I am now ready to state my conjecture. In most if not all of the neighbouring worlds that are like our world in having some lawful or causal order but which do not contain any physical matter, patterns exist that are very much like the patterns associated in our world with acquiring, possessing, and exploiting information. Such patterns are all but inevitable consequences of the tendency of worlds over time to settle into patterns that are self-sustaining and self-preserving. If my conjecture is correct, then there is a sense in which even in our world the order of higher-level patterns is not dependent on the physical order of our world. It is a much more pervasive order that simply manifests itself in our world in physical realizations. (How's that for multiple realization?)

Still the champion of the physical might argue that physical properties and laws still enjoy an ontologically privileged status with respect to causality. Higher-order properties are simply stable recurring patterns of organization, nothing more—no matter how inevitable or widespread they are through the space of worlds. Our physicalist champion might go on to argue that physical properties are causally potent in a way that no such pattern ever is. Special science laws or explanations merely pick out higher-order patterns that are present in projectable, counterfactual-sustaining regularities in the world; that is, they describe a level of organization at which the world exhibits systematic order. But physical explanations are not mere descriptions of order; they tell us why things actually happen. And physical properties are not mere stable recurrent patterns; they are the basic stuff of which all the patterns are made.

I believe we should view any such claim with scepticism. I proposed earlier that we produce equality between physical and special science causal explanations by stripping physical explanations of their allegedly special status. Now is the time to try to do so. What properties of the physical world might one suppose to be more than mere recurrent patterns? Being a proton? Being an electron with 1/2 positive spin? Being a quark with a particular colour, charm, and strangeness?

Though it is a question whose answer requires more knowledge of physics than I possess, I believe it could be shown that all physical properties that enter into strict exceptionless laws are themselves nothing more than stable self-sustaining recurrent states of the quantum flux of an irreducibly probabilistic and statistical reality. If cosmologists are to be believed (and I believe them), our universe settled into these patterns very early on, some time within the first three minutes after the Big Bang. But their antiquity does not alter their status.

They are highly stable patterns whose interrelations approximate deterministic regularities to a very high degree. Or perhaps, turning the question the other way round, one could say the transition functions representing their interaction in our model of that level of reality are highly deterministic. (You have to watch out for that latent theological realism). I think we are often bewitched by their deterministic rigour, which produces in us an illusion of dealing with more than just a representation of some aspect of the organization of space-time. We feel we are dealing with something more tangible, something more real and objective. Their determininsm seduces us into seeing physical properties as determining the sequence of events in a way that no other properties do. But the fact that the transition functions in our model of the physical are deterministic in the mathematical sense certainly does not entail that the properties they model play a unique (or even a special) role of any metaphysical sort in determining the temporal organization of the world.

I suppose that by now we've been digging long enough. So let's climb up and see where we may have undermined the fortifications of the Exclusion Argument.

First, I think we can see that the link from 3 to 4 is weakened by what we have uncovered about the roles played by higher-order properties. The over-determination option now looks more promising. The complete physical descriptions which determine the causal powers of all the world's events according to 3 will have to include complete specifications of physical boundary conditions. Since higher-order properties are sets of recurrent boundary conditions, complete physical descriptions will have to refer to the instantiations of any such properties. But they will lack the conceptual resources to represent them as instantiations of the relevant higher-order properties. What we will get instead is an opaque and disorderly representation that in no way makes perspicuous the higher-order property that is being instantiated or the systematic relations that it bears to other higher-order properties.

Special science explanations refer to the same property instantiations, but do so in a perspicuous representation that makes clear how the temporal sequence of events is structured by those higher-order patterns. We have seen that such patterns and their interrelationships can enjoy a substantial degree of independence from their particular physical instantiations and perhaps even from physical instantiation altogether. Thus we can accept the global supervenience reading that makes 3 plausible, without having to accept 4 on any reading that treats mental or higher-order properties as not playing their own role in structuring the sequence of events.

We have two models of the world which cannot be reduced in the sense that there are no well-ordered complete translation functions from one to the other—a gap which results in part because of the ways their respective concepts are anchored in our specific discriminative and cognitive capacities. But both models can be satisfied by the same world even in those respects in which they model the causal structure of the world. And each model can have its own pragmatic strengths and weaknesses.

Given the causal roles played by higher-order patterns (which as we have seen are not really any different than those played by physical properties, such as being a bottom quark), there is no reason to make the inferential step to 5 and its claim that mental or higher-order properties fail to be causally potent in any sense that physical properties are potent. Thus there would be no reason to reach the epiphenomenal conclusion of 6 or to deny that mental properties are causally relevant in the most robust sense.

Thus fell the walls of Jericho, or at least I hope they cracked.

PART III

Content

14

Some Content is Narrow

FRANK JACKSON AND PHILIP PETTIT

ONE way to defend narrow content is to produce a sentence of the form '*S* believes that *P*', and show that this sentence is true of *S* if and only if it is true of any duplicate from the skin in, any doppelganger, of *S*. Notoriously, this is hard to do. Twin Earth examples are pervasive.[1] Another way to defend narrow content is to show that only a narrow notion can play the causal explanatory role we require of content in a properly scientific psychology or cognitive science. Notoriously, this is hard to do. The considerations—methodological solipsism, the principle of autonomy, or whatever—invoked to show that a broad notion of content cannot play the required causal explanatory role are open to serious objection.[2] Moreover, this approach is not an argument for the existence of narrow content as such. It is an argument that content had better be narrow.

In this paper we offer a defence of narrow content which makes no (well, almost no) reference to Twin Earth examples or to contentious doctrines about which ways of taxonomizing mental states are right for a scientific psychology. We would like to think that our argument will be found relatively non-controversial. We see it as simply drawing out and making explicit the commitment to narrow content implicit in doctrines about making sense of human

The central idea in this paper was prompted by discussions with Martin Davies, David Braddon Mitchell, David Lewis, John Bigelow, and Robert Pargetter. They should not be held responsible.

[1] Two seminal papers are Putnam 1975*a*, and Burge 1979. For a general introduction and further references see the introduction to Pettit and McDowell 1986.

[2] For the considerations see e.g. Stich 1983, chap. 8, and Fodor 1987, chap. 2; for the responses see e.g. Burge 1986*a*, and Jackson and Pettit 1988. A simple example where the broad causally explains behaviour is: 'The chicken is following the dog because it imprinted on the dog'.

behaviour familiar in the writings of, most particularly, Daniel Dennett and Donald Davidson.[3] However, as will emerge, the narrow content we will be defending is a truth-conditional notion of content which figures in folk psychology. And even (the increasingly beleaguered) defenders of narrow content have of late been conceding that their narrow content is neither a folk notion, nor a truth-conditional notion of content (although they insist that it is closely connected to folk, truth-conditional notions). In particular, the view that all truth-conditional content is (and must be, otherwise it would not 'hook on to the world') broad has become the conventional wisdom.[4] This paper is an attempt to turn back the clock. We will argue that certain points about the way we folk predict human behaviour, about the nature of our solution to the problem of predicting human behaviour, commits us to the existence of narrow, folk, truth-evaluable content. Unlike many extant arguments for narrow content, it will be no part of the argument for narrow content that there is anything 'wrong' from an explanatory point of view with broad content. Also, the sense in which the narrow content we will be defending is folk is that it figures in our everyday understanding of believers and desirers. For all we say, there may, or there may not be, English sentences naturally available to human subjects to express beliefs with these contents. Fred's abilities to discriminate, identify, and re-identify things with a certain shape may show that he believes that something has that shape, and yet he may have no (public-language) word for the shape; and of course animals are in this situation all (or nearly all) of the time.[5]

[3] See e.g. Davidson 1974*a*, and Dennett 1981. The way we put matters is perhaps closest to Stalnaker 1984. We do not suggest that Davidson, Stalnaker or Dennett would agree with what we find implicit in their doctrines. Indeed, we take it that Stalnaker 1989 is taking a position opposed to the one we defend here.

[4] Thus Dennett's 1982 defence of narrow content is, like Fodor's 1987, chap. 2 defence, explicitly a defence of a non-truth-conditional notion of content. Its link with a truth-conditional notion is that it determines a function from context to truth-conditional content. See also Devitt 1990. For evidence of the extent to which the view that we are opposing has become conventional wisdom, see Davies's 1990 review of McGinn 1989, and Fodor's 1991*a*, p. 6.

[5] We emphasize the point to make it clear that we leave open the possibility that the contents we discuss are not folk in the sense that they may not be contents which lend themselves to direct expression in the language of the folk. Some will want to express this contrast as one between what are described as personal and sub-personal beliefs. For a related contrast see the distinction between merely intentional contents and thought contents in Pettit 1992.

The first part of the paper is concerned with the folk problem of predicting behaviour. The second part of the paper is concerned with how the solution to the folk-predictive problem commits to narrow content. The paper concludes with some replies to objections.

1. The Folk Problem of Predicting Behaviour

A. Finding Patterns in Behaviour

Suppose I want to predict how someone's body will move on some specified occasion or under some specified conditions: where do I start? One place to start would be with what is going on inside her as described in the language of medical science. If I know enough about her internal neurophysiology, I will be able to predict what will happen in certain muscle fibres, and from knowledge of what will happen in certain muscle fibres along with information about how the fibres link up to various bones, and the like, I will be able to predict how her body will move.

Nevertheless, we do not have to start from what happens inside a person. We do quite a reasonable job of predicting behaviour going by what is observable about people from the outside. Even with this highly restricted database we can do much better than chance. We can call the problem of predicting behaviour going by what is externally observable alone, the folk problem of predicting behaviour. For what the folk in general know about human behaviour is indeed pretty much restricted to what can be known without dissection; and when it does go beyond what can be known without dissection, it is not of great value in predicting what movements a person's body will make. The facts that the blood circulates and that the brain is very important to mental life are nowadays common knowledge, and certainly help predict the movements a body will make in certain circumstances, but they are not of crucial significance in predicting behaviour. (Otherwise Aristotle, who did not know either fact, could not have predicted successfully what movements people's bodies would make.)

We have remarked that we have in fact solved the folk problem of predicting behaviour in circumstances, but how did we do it? We can start by asking what constitutes the externally available evidence we use to solve the folk problem of predicting behaviour. The obvious answer is: certain observed facts about what is sometimes called raw behaviour, the physical movements our bodies make described as such, rather than, for instance, the movements described in terms of the language of intentionally characterized action. For it is the raw behaviour which we more immediately perceive through the way that it impinges on our sense organs.

But now we face a well-known problem. What we need in order to predict behaviour in circumstances are past patterns; interesting projectable generalizations about what happened when, that are to be found in the historical behavioural data. What else could we reasonably use? But patterns in the raw behavioural data are hard to find. The behaviour of human beings is incredibly diverse. When the wind blows, trees generally do much the same thing; and when the wind blows harder, they do much the same, only more so. It is easy to find projectable patterns going by external data about the behaviour of trees when the wind blows. However, there are enormously many different ways that a human body may move when the wind blows. A person's body may move in such a way that she ends up encased in a jumper, or behind a wind break, or inside a house, or with her back towards the wind, or with her hand holding a string attached to a kite, and so on and so forth. What is more, there are many different bodily movements that put a body inside a jumper, behind a wind break, inside a house, back to the wind, or on the end of a string.

This problem is most familiar perhaps from discussions of functionalism. Michael Devitt, criticizing traditional formulations of functionalism which describe the inputs and outputs in purely physical terms, argues:

> What psychological laws explain is not behaviour described as neural impulses, as mere bodily movements, or as any other brute physical event. These descriptions are at the wrong level, the level of psychological *implementation*. The level that yields the interesting generalizations of psychology requires that the behaviour be described as an action. This goes against the demands of old-fashioned reductionism, but so much the worse for that reductionism. Functionalism often seems not to have fully grasped its own message about explanatory levels. . . .the ones [the properties] appropriate for outputs are not brute-physical. (Devitt 1990, p. 393.)

Similarly, Robert Van Gulick (1990, p. 125, our emphasis) remarks that 'such disparate outputs as nodding one's head, raising a hand, or uttering 'yes' get classed together only on the basis of all being taken as *gestures of assent* by the community of subjects', and Jerry Fodor (1982, p. 102, our emphasis) says that 'we have. . . no notion of behavioural systematicity at all except the one that makes behaviour *systematic under intentional* description'.

Should we follow these leads and retreat from raw behaviour to actions, behaviour described in intentional terms, in our search for the needed generalizations? We think not. Actions are bodily movements caused in the right sort of way, or more precisely, an action occurs if and only if a bodily movement caused in the right sort of way occurs. The fact that philosophers have found it so hard to specify precisely what 'the right sort of way' comes to does not justify holding that actions are some sorts of emergent entities. The fact that the total story about a person's actions supervenes on total information about movements, internal causes, and surroundings, tells us that actions are not emergent. Thus, to know that something is an action is to know about the internal aetiology of certain behaviour (and maybe in addition about social setting, community conventions, and the like, if it is an action like signing a cheque). But the folk problem is how to predict behaviour starting from the outside. We would be begging the question to start by describing the data available to the folk in terms of internal aetiology.

We can put the central point this way: to turn to intentional descriptions of behaviour is in effect to 'go internal'. But we cannot go internal to find the patterns and generalizations we folk need to get started. Rather, we have to find the patterns at the behavioural, external level first, and then maybe we can proceed to go internal to explain the patterns we have discovered, and so describe our data in the language of intentional action. When Robinson Crusoe saw Man Friday's footprint in the sand, the fact that it was Man Friday's footprint was, and had to be, his conclusion; where he finished up, not where he started from. Of course, when we see someone behaving in a certain way, we often find an intentional description like 'signalling a taxi', the immediately natural one to apply; we, that is, see the behaviour as signalling a taxi. Similarly, experts on the fossil record often see a fossil as the fossil of some long extinct insect. They do not say to themselves, 'That fossil is of such and such a shape. We have shown that such and such a shape is best explained as laid down by such and such a long-extinct insect.' Nevertheless, it is the 'raw' fossil and not the fossil under some highly historical description which is their datum.

To avoid possible misunderstanding, we should emphasize that our point is independent of the debate in the philosophy of action about the reference of compound singular terms like 'my intentionally annoying Fred yesterday'. On some views such terms do not refer to a compound of internal state and caused behavioural response, but rather to something entirely internal (a willing, perhaps); and on other views such terms refer to something constituted by, not identical with, an internal state and a behavioural response (in the same way that it is sometimes held that a jug is constituted by but not identical with the sum of its parts). But the epistemological point made above turns on the point that in order to know that I intentionally annoyed Fred yesterday, you need to know about internal aetiology of behaviour, and this point is independent of how the debate about the reference of terms designating actions should be resolved. Here is a simple illustration which brings out the independence of the epistemological issue from the issue about reference. In order to know that that object over there is the President's hat, you need to know, among other things, something about the President as well as something about the hat. But it does not follow from this that the term 'the President's hat' designates a compound entity containing the President as a part. Indeed, the most plausible view is that the term designates the hat alone.

In any case, there is a way to make patterned sense of the apparent chaos of raw bodily movement. It is to attend to what effects bodily movements have on the situations subjects find themselves in. It is to attend to what a subject's bodily movements in a given situation achieve. We remarked earlier that when the wind blows a tree will behave in much the same way on different occasions, but that with people it is far more complicated. When the wind blows their bodies move in a whole host of different ways. Nevertheless, there is a pattern to be discerned in this enormously diverse collection of bodily movements: very many of them have the effect that the person ends up out of the wind. And this is a pattern we can note without first describing things in intentional terms. The pattern is there in the brute physical movements themselves.

When we say that the pattern is there in the bodily movements themselves, we do not mean that the pattern is intrinsic to the movements. The pattern is discerned by noting the effects that the bodily movements have on situations subjects find themselves in. A student of human behaviour sets us the following problem: find the pattern in Fred's behaviour consequent on Mary's entering the room. We focus on the relatively intrinsic features of Fred's bodily movements and get nowhere. There is no pattern in the movements *per se*. Then we notice that though the various movements on the various occasions are very different, they very often have the same effect on Fred's situation. As a result of them, on many occasions he ends up in the same half of the room as Mary. The penny drops. We then know the projectable generalization governing Fred's behaviour on Mary's entering the room.

We suspect that opposition to the commonsensical view that raw behaviour is our data for projecting behaviour in circumstances from past to future has been engendered by confusing the question of whether our data are facts about raw behaviour with the question of whether our data are those facts about raw behaviour which are central to taxonomizing raw behaviour *qua* raw behaviour. Two bits of elbow-bending may be grouped together as items of behaviour by the student of raw behaviour, by the physiotherapist, by the student of how muscular contraction issues in limb movement, but may consistently be grouped apart by the folk seeking projectable generalizations concerning behaviour in circumstances. The crucial point about one bit of elbow-bending may be that it brings beer near a mouth, so that the generalization that works for the folk in this case is: when a person enters a pub, expect behaviour that brings beer near mouth; whereas the crucial point about the other is that it wards off a fly, so that the generalization to project in this case is: when out in the bush, expect behaviour that leads to the departure of flies.

B. Improving the Generalizations

What we are saying is that the folk patterns in behaviour, the patterns suitable for projecting going by observation of past behaviour in situations, are to be found by looking at the effects of the behaviour in those situations. Now we can effect a dramatic improvement in our predictions of behaviour by considering not just the effect a piece of behaviour would actually have, but in addition what effect it *would have were things thus and so*. Sometimes we find the pattern in Fred's behaviour not by noting that his behaviour in fact brings him near Mary, but by noting that his behaviour would have brought him near Mary had things been thus and so. Mary enters a maze. Fred's behaviour brings him nowhere near Mary. We solve the puzzle by noting that had Mary ended up where one might well have expected she would, Fred's behaviour would have brought him near to Mary. A salient pattern in Ivan's behaviour is that it leads to his becoming richer, but there are some notable exceptions. We make sense of the failures by noting that his behaviour on those occasions would have made him richer had things been thus and so, and things being thus and so is how one, or at least Ivan, might well have expected them to be. In sum, to cut a long, familiar story short, we find the projectable patterns by using belief-desire psychology, by using the intentional stance, to put the matter in Dennett's 1979, 1981 terminology. The salient pattern externally available to solve the folk-predictive problem is: people behave in such a way that had their beliefs been true, then their desires would have been satisfied.

We take it that it is not really open to dispute that we are able to capture projectable generalizations concerning behaviour in the terms of belief-desire psychology. We do it every day, and it works. Based on past observations of you and others similar to you, I have opinions about what you believe and desire, and about what you would believe and desire were such and such to happen. I use these opinions to predict what you will do were such and such to happen. And the fact of the matter is that my predictions are right far more often than could possibly be explained by chance.

There is, of course, a great deal that is very much open to question. How exactly do we use behavioural data to arrive at hypotheses concerning a person's beliefs and desires; how determinate are these hypotheses; how important is it that we are language-using creatures; to what extent do we have to presuppose rationality, and so on and so forth (see e.g. Davidson 1974, Lewis 1974, and Dennett 1981). But we mention these highly debatable matters in order to emphasize what we take not to be debatable: belief-desire psychology captures projectable patterns in behaviour. If it did not, our success in using it would be a miracle, and it isn't. (We also take it as obvious that we make a still better fist of finding the patterns if we use not simply belief and desire hypotheses but instead degree of belief and strength of desire hypotheses. We will, however, neglect this complication here. Similarly, we neglect complications arising from belief *de se*; see e.g. Lewis 1979.)

C. Describing Patterns in Terms of Possibilities

We can describe Fred's Mary-directed behaviour in terms of possibilities. There are many ways Fred's body might have moved. For each of these ways, there is how things would be were Fred's body to move in that way. Fred's behaviour is Mary-directed in the sense that, as a rule, his body moves so as to realize one of the ways where he is near Mary.

Similarly, we can describe the way belief-desire psychology captures the patterns in human behaviour in terms of possibilities. Associated with what a person believes at a time is a set of possibilities, the set compatible with what she believes, the set containing all the ways things might be for all she believes. To say this is not to say that belief is a relation to a set of possibilities. It is to say that belief effects a partition between the possibilities compatible with it and the possibilities incompatible with it. Whether it does this because that is what belief is, or because belief is, say, a relation to an internal sentence in the language of thought, and that sentence effects the partition by virtue of the fact that there are possibilities in which the sentence is true and possibilities in which the sentence is false, is another question. All we are using is the everyday fact that one way of giving pertinent information about what you believe is by specifying the various ways things might be for all you believe (see Lewis 1986*a*, p. 28). Similarly, associated with what a person desires at a time is a set of possibilities, the possibilities she would prefer to be actual. The way belief-desire psychology captures the projectable patterns in raw behaviour can now be described in terms of possibilities, as follows. Among the various possible ways that a subject's body might move at a time, a subject tends to move in such a way that had any one of the possibilities associated with her beliefs been the way things actually were, then one of the ways associated with her desires would have been actual. Had any one of the believed possibilities been actual, one of the desired possibilities would have been actual. We predict behaviour in circumstances by projecting these patterns.

Incidentally, this approach does not work if you take individual beliefs. You have to think in terms of big, conjunctive beliefs. Suppose someone says that they have found the pattern in Bruce's behaviour in terms of belief-desire psychology thus: Bruce believes there is beer in the fridge and desires beer, and that is why his body moves towards the fridge. The trouble with this story as it stands is that the possibilities consistent with there being beer in the fridge are vastly too diverse for the rule 'Bruce's body will move in such a way that had any one of the beer-in-the-fridge possibilities been actual, Bruce would have actualized a possibility where there was beer in him' to be of any use at all. The rule won't effect any worthwhile reduction in the number of possible bodily movements. You have, instead, to work with the possibilities associated with a belief like: there is beer in the fridge and the fridge is four feet in front of me and there is no lock on the fridge and the beer is cold and I can traverse the distance from here to the fridge safely and so on. Only by working with a big belief do we cut down the diversity of the possibilities consistent with the belief sufficiently for the rule to give a prediction worth having about the movements Bruce's body will make.[6]

Does this concession mean that what we are putting forward as the way the folk can bring order to the apparent chaos of bodily movement is very different from belief-desire psychology as employed by the folk? We would not normally complain at an explanation of Bruce's behaviour that simply cited his belief that there is beer in the fridge and his desire for beer. However, we cannot take this evidence at face value. We all know that Bruce believes that bodily movement is fatiguing and that Bruce desires not to be fatigued. That combination would seem to lead to the opposite prediction that Bruce will not move towards the fridge, or indeed move at all. The folk know how to solve this problem. They tell us about trade-offs. They tell us that Bruce believes that a certain movement will bring him beer and that it will bring him fatigue, and that Bruce desires beer and fatigue more than no beer and no fatigue. But this is simply the first step away from individual beliefs and desires in their explanations and towards big beliefs and big desires. The folk know implicitly that they have to work with big, conjunctive beliefs and desires.

[6] Why not handle the problem by changing the predictive rule to: Bruce's body will move in such a way that for at least one possibility consistent with his belief, it is true that had it been actual, he would have ended up with beer inside him? Because such a rule is consistent with: Bruce's body will move in such a way that for at least one possibility consistent with his belief, it is true that had it been actual, he would have ended up without beer inside him.

2. The Derivation of Narrow, Folk, Truth-Conditional Content

We have rehearsed how to find predictively useful patterns in behaviour in circumstances in terms of the possibilities associated with a person's beliefs and desires. How does what we have rehearsed commit us to narrow, folk, truth-conditional content? The commitment to folk, truth-conditional content is relatively straightforward, and we will deal with this part of the story first.

A. The Commitment to Truth-Conditional Content

We can find patterns in behaviour in terms of sets of possibilities associated with a person's beliefs and desires. But surely sets of possibilities associated with a person's beliefs and desires are among the kinds of thing one might properly mean by the content of what they believe and desire, particularly when these sets enable us to predict behaviour in circumstances. For, as already observed, such sets tell us something very important about what a person believes and desires. Maybe it is not the only thing you might properly mean by the content of what they believe and desire. 'Content' is a recently prominent term of art and may well mean rather different things to different practitioners of the art. However, the sets of possibilities we have been talking about are one thing you might properly mean by the term. But content in terms of sets of possibilities is automatically truth-evaluable. It comes out true precisely if the content set of possibilities contains the way things actually are.

B. Is Predictive Content a Folk Notion?

Let's call the sets of possibilities associated with beliefs and desires 'predictive content'. This highlights the facts that we are not here committing ourselves to there being exactly one notion of content (maybe there are other notions which would need to be marked by differently prefixing the term 'content'), and that we introduced the notion as a way of predicting behaviour in circumstances (but we will see later that the notion is not merely predictive). Predictive content counts as folk on two grounds. First, there is the point that it is a piece of common sense, as well as a piece of Stalnaker or Lewis theorizing, that sets of possibilities are individuatively associated with beliefs and desires. It is common currency to explain how you would like things to be in terms of rankings of the various possibilities, and how you take things to be in terms of how likely various possibilities are.

Secondly, the projectable patterns that we have been remarking can be described in terms of sets of possibilities associated with beliefs and desires are patterns in behaviour in circumstances discernible by the folk. The story is in terms of such happenings as Mary's entering the room, Fred's moving near Mary, the wind's blowing, the putting on of jumpers, and so on and so forth. We did not need to use the language of neuroscience, of peripheral stimulations, of retinal activations, or anything of that kind. We were not in the business of identifying a concept foreign to the folk and then arguing that, for whatever reason, the concept was needed in mature cognitive science, properly scientific psychology, or whatever. We were simply spelling out something which is an implicit part of common-sense theory about people's behaviour. The patterns we described in terms of possibilities associated with belief and desire are not news to the folk. They use them implicitly all the time in predicting behaviour. All that is unfamiliar to them is the jargon and the theoretical articulation.

C. *Is Predictive Content Narrow?*

Opponents of individualism in psychology in general, and of narrow content in particular, frequently argue the case against individualism by urging that our understanding of central psychological concepts is tied to our interactions with what goes on around us described as such—that is, described as what goes on around us. Their claim is that, as a matter of principle, you cannot tell the psychological story in terms of how things are at and inside the skin. Here is how Burge puts this kind of position:

> philosophy of psychology must do justice not only to the mechanistic elements in the science. It must also relate these to psychology's attempt to account for tasks that we succeed and fail at, *where these tasks are set by the environment*. . . . The most salient and important of these tasks are those that arise through relations to the natural and social worlds. A theory that insists on describing the states of human beings *purely* in terms that abstract

from their relations to any specific environment cannot hope to provide a completely satisfying explanation of our accomplishments . . . (1986*a*, pp. 44–5)

This kind of position is sometimes put by saying that a psychological state's 'ecological job description' is essential to it.

A natural thought is that the content we have been talking about, predictive content, is non-individualistic and so broad. The folk-predictive problem we have been talking about was framed in terms of predicting how subjects interact with their surroundings, of predicting how Fred will behave in future when Mary enters the room, of predicting what a person will do when the wind blows. And the kinds of predictions we got were predictions of how the subject's behaviour would change his or her situation described in environmental terms—Fred will end up in Mary's half of the room, the person in the wind will end up out of the wind, or whatever. We were talking very much in terms of 'relations to the natural and social worlds'. Predictive content's job description clearly falls into the ecological category.

It is, however, important to distinguish two anti-individualistic doctrines, doctrines which, it seems to us, sometimes get conflated: one says that some given central psychological property cannot be explained individualistically; the other says that the property does not supervene on how the subject is from the skin in: it is, that is, not necessarily shared by doppelgangers.

Predictive content is certainly non-individualistic in the first sense. It can only be explained by reference to a subject's interactions with his or her surroundings. It is like the concept of water solubility. If you do not understand the connection between being water-soluble and behaving in a certain way on being put in water, you do not understand what water solubility is. Although as a matter of fact (and perhaps as a matter of necessity) there is some internal state of a water-soluble substance which is responsible for the behaviour definitive of being water soluble, if what you know is confined to that internal state, you do not know that the substance is water-soluble. Nevertheless, any internal duplicate, any doppelganger, of a water-soluble substance is itself water-soluble. Hence, water solubility is not a non-individualistic property in the second sense; being water-soluble is a narrow property in the official sense defined in terms of supervenience on internal nature. The explanation of how it is that water solubility is not non-individualistic in the second sense is, of course, that (*a*) it is the totality of potential interactions with water which matters for being water soluble, not which of the totality are actual, and (*b*) if *X* and *Y* are internally identical substances, the totality for *X* is one and the same as the totality for *Y*. Or consider a predicate like 'if *x* were near a tiger, *x* would start to run away from the tiger'. Is it individualistic? You might say no on the ground that what makes the predicate true of some *x* is in part how the world is (it is non-individualistic in the first sense), or you might say yes on the ground that, necessarily, if it is true of *x* then it is true of any doppelganger of *x* (it is not non-individualistic in the second sense).

We can put the distinction in terms of possible worlds as follows. To be individualistic in the first sense is to be inter-world narrow, where a property *P* of *x* is inter-world narrow if and only if in every possible world any doppelganger of *x* has *P*. To be individualistic in the second sense is to be intra-world narrow, where a property *P* of *x* is intra-world narrow if and only if in every possible world where *x* has *P* any doppelganger of *x* has *P*.[7] Being water-soluble is not inter-world narrow. A doppelganger of sugar in a world where the laws are relevantly different need not be water-soluble. But being soluble is intra-world narrow: within a possible world, internal duplicates are duplicates with respect to whether or not they are soluble, and so to find a substance which is internally exactly like sugar but which is not water-soluble, you must move to a different possible world. Or, equivalently, when we said that being water soluble supervenes on internal nature, we should in strictness have said that it supervenes on internal nature plus laws.[8]

Our argument will be that while all predictive content is obviously not individualistic in the first sense, some predictive content is individualistic in the second sense. Some predictive content is intra-world narrow—there are predictive contents such that, necessarily, doppelgangers in the same possible world share them. But predictive content is never inter-world narrow. My doppelganger in a world with very different laws may well have

[7] McGinn 1989, chap.1, distinguishes strong externalism from weak externalism. We think that his distinction is related to the distinction between inter- and intra-world narrowness thus: strong externalism says that no content (or no content of such and such a kind if it is a restricted version of strong externalism) is intra-world narrow; weak externalism says that no content (or no content of such and such a kind if it is a restricted version of weak externalism) is inter-world narrow.

[8] We are indebted here to David Armstrong.

states with totally different predictive contents. Does this mean that we are not really going against the conventional wisdom that all folk, truth-conditional content must be broad? For perhaps all that is meant is that such content cannot be inter-world narrow, not that it cannot be intra-world narrow. However, the arguments that folk, truth-conditional content must be broad rest on claims about how certain (actual) causal links between the head and the world are essential for truth-conditional content, and about how context (Is it water or XYZ that surrounds me? Is it that cup or this cup that is before me?) and one's linguistic community affect truth conditions. And arguments like these are arguments that content can vary without supposing any change in the laws of nature, or in general any change that is 'big' enough to require supposing a change in possible world.[9] They are, therefore, arguments that folk, truth-conditional content cannot be intra-world narrow. In any case, our defence of the narrowness of predictive content is a defence of the intra-world narrowness of predictive content.

Our argument that some predictive content is narrow (understood from here on in the intra-world sense) turns on two facts: one is that we folk are committed to the robustness of solutions to the problem of predicting behaviour for a person *S*; the other is that for any historical solution to the folk problem of predicting behaviour, there is an ahistorical solution.

By a robust solution we mean a solution which would not be exposed as being based on the misleading appearance of a pattern in a biased sample, by the acquisition of any actual or possible new data concerning what a person does or would do in circumstances. We dream of knowing everything of the form: were such and such to happen, then Fred's body would move thus and so; we dream, that is, of a complete solution to the folk-predictive problem in the form of a huge raft of subjunctive conditionals whose antecedents are detailed specifications in folk terms of possible circumstances (were Mary to enter the room when Fred was in the room and the lights were on and Fred's leg was not broken and. . .), and whose consequents are about bodily movements described in common-sense, environmental terms (Fred's body moves so that he is nearer beer. . .), a huge raft of subjunctive conditionals of the form '$C_i \rightarrow B_i$'. What we actually have in practice is a tiny selection from this

[9] As many have noted, Twin Earth need not be (and typically is not supposed to be) in a different possible world from Earth.

complete solution, a tiny selection which constitutes our observations that C_i & B_i for some i; a selection which displays patterns, projectable generalizations, capturable as we have seen in terms of certain hypotheses about belief and desire framed in terms of sets of possibilities. (When seeking a pattern for a given individual, we will of course have collateral information of value, most particularly to do with observed truths of the form C_i & B_i for other creatures, including ourselves.)

Now, in using our pattern to predict behaviour in circumstances, we commit ourselves to its being a robust pattern. For to hold that the pattern we have discerned is misleading, is a flukey pattern whose deceptiveness would be revealed if only we had the full picture, is precisely to hold that we are not entitled to project the patterns we discern in our database. Our practice of projecting the belief-desire patterns we discern in our fellows from past to future commits us to believing that there is a robust solution in terms of the possibilities associated with belief and desire to the folk-predictive problem—a solution which would survive learning all there is to know about how a person's body would move were such and such to happen. And what is more, we are committed to holding that this survivor solution, though no doubt vastly more detailed than our solution, is an improvement and detailing of our pattern, not a demonstration that the pattern we discerned was a misleading appearance arising from a biased sample. For you cannot properly project a pattern from a sample at the same time as holding that by the lights of the very best possible evidence, the pattern you project is quite the wrong one to project. Perhaps it is—that is the hostage to fortune inductive projection gives—but you must in consistency hold that this unpleasant possibility is unlikely. Here is a simple example to help make the point clear. A machine is printing out numbers on a tape. I observe just the sequence: 1,2,3,4, and I predict that the next number produced by the machine will be 5. I cannot, consistently with this prediction, hold (*a*) that the most likely sequence to have preceded my observation is: 1,2,3,4,1,2,3,4, 1,2,3,4, and (*b*) that had I observed that fuller sequence, then the right prediction for me to make would have been that the machine would next print out a 1.

In arguing that we are committed to there being a robust solution, we are not suggesting that we are committed to there being exactly one robust solution. For all we have said, there might be a number of robust patterns. Davidson and Dennett (most particularly) have made us sensitive to the possibility that not only might there be no single best belief-desire hypothesis covering what we have actually observed of a person's behaviour, there might be no single best belief-desire hypothesis covering the totality of actual and possible observations of a person's behaviour. If this happens, there will be more than one robust solution in terms of the possibilities associated with belief and desire to the folk-predictive problem. But that there is at least one robust pattern is all we will need here.

It might now appear a simple matter to derive our result that some, indeed all, predictive content is narrow. Robustness says that at least one belief-desire pattern is there in the complete raft of subjunctive conditionals saying how a person would behave in such and such a situation. But if *X* and *Y* are doppelgangers, then the complete raft for *X* is one and the same as the complete raft for *Y*. The movements that *X*'s body would make were *X* in such and such a situation are the very same as the movements *Y*'s body would make were *Y* in such and such a situation. But predictive content captures the belief-desire patterns. So the predictive contents of *X*'s beliefs and desires must be the same as those of *Y*. (If there is more than one belief-desire pattern that fits the full raft *X* and *Y* have in common, and there is no non-arbitrary way to choose between the patterns, then *X* and *Y* share predictive contents in the sense that the range of contents each of which is an admissible, but none of which is a determinately correct, candidate to be a predictive content associated with their beliefs and desires is the same for each.)

You might complain that I and my Twin Earth doppelganger do not behave in the same way in the same situations. I drink water; he drinks XYZ. I reach for that cup; he reaches for this cup. But that is to misunderstand what is meant by 'the same situations' here. It means what Stich (1983, p. 165) has in mind when he talks of 'replacement'. If I were replaced by my Twin Earth twin, it would be true that he would drink water, and would be true that he would reach for the very same cup as I in fact reached for. The argument does not turn on the fact that doppelgangers in fact behave in the same way—something which is only true at the level of raw movement so described—it turns on the fact that they would in every situation behave in the same way, and that is true both in the sense that their raw movements are the same and in the sense that the way these raw movements would affect their environmental orientations is exactly the same. Their movements are, that is, the same in just the sense we saw to be crucial for detecting the belief-desire patterns. In a certain situation, Fred moved towards Mary. Had Fred been replaced by Fred's twin in that very situation, Fred's twin would have moved towards Mary. In this lies the force of the claim that predictive content is narrow. It is this which makes it so hard to see how the best belief-desire pattern (or set of equally good patterns if indeterminacy threatens) could be different for Fred and twin Fred.

But now we need to note a lacuna in the derivation of narrow content from robustness just given. Doppelgangers' behaviour in situations will differ in historical properties. It might be true that if Fred had been in situation *S*, he would have moved for the third time towards Mary, but not true that had twin Fred been in situation *S* he would have moved for the third time towards Mary. Twin Fred has never met Mary, so had he been in *S*, he would have moved towards Mary for the first time. It can be tempting to rule out such differences as irrelevant to psychology. This is Stich's approach. He introduces the notion of an 'autonomous behavioural description', a description which 'if it applies to an organism in a given setting, then it would also apply to any replica of the organism in that setting' (Stich 1983, p. 167), and argues that psychology only needs to concern itself with autonomous descriptions. This would rule out properties like moving towards Mary for the third time or selling one's car (Stich's own example), because instantiating them depends on history—to sell a car (legally) you have to have entered into a certain transaction in the past—as well as on setting (current setting, that is, which is what Stich has in mind). The trouble with this view is that the only reason he gives, and could give, for supposing that autonomous descriptions are all psychology needs is that systematic generalizations of behaviour do not usefully employ non-autonomous descriptions. This seems simply false. Very few people touch a hot stove twice; a cat behaves very differently on the second occasion of meeting a young child; and so on. Historical, and so non-autonomous, properties can play a major role in explaining and systematizing behaviour. Certainly, from our perspective here, you could not possibly rule out historical properties. Noting them can reveal a behavioural pattern apt for projection into the future.

What is true is something different. Whenever there is a belief-desire pattern manifest in behaviour in situations which can be captured using historical descriptions, there is a belief-desire pattern which can be captured without using historical descriptions; indeed, can be captured using autonomous descriptions alone. This is because history does not act at a distance; causation is local. Consider the behavioural pattern: when children come close to a hot stove for the second time, their bodies slow down. The stove will have the property of having been come across previously, and this very fact will be part of the causal explanation of the observed behaviour. But it will also be true that this historical fact will work via some feature the stove possesses at (or just prior to) the time the avoidance behaviour occurs. There will be something about the stove—an autonomous feature of the stove—which marks it out for the child as having been previously encountered. This means that whenever we can predict the child's behaviour by appeal to the fact of the previous encounter, we can in principle also predict the child's behaviour in terms of an autonomous feature. Or think of a machine programmed to respond when presented with an object of the same shape as it was presented with previously. Any response to the fact that a presented object is the same shape as one previously presented to it, is also a response to the fact that the presented object is some particular shape together with the fact that a previously presented object was that particular shape. The local nature of causation tells us that whenever there is a belief-desire pattern capturable in non-autonomous terms, there is a belief-desire pattern capturable in autonomous terms.

We can now repair the argument for narrow predictive content. The crucial point is that robustness tells us that the best autonomous belief-desire pattern (or patterns) for Fred and twin Fred must be the same, and so that the predictive contents which describe those autonomous patterns, the sets of possibilities associated with Fred and twin Fred's beliefs and desires which bring projectable order to behaviour in situations as described autonomously, must be the same for Fred and for twin Fred. So the conclusion we get is that there exists narrow, predictive, folk, truth-evaluable content, but not that all predictive content is narrow, or, still less, that all content is narrow.

Although the predictive content which brings order to the autonomous belief-desire patterns must be narrow, it does not follow that sentences in English ascribing content using only autonomous descriptions have narrow truth-conditions. If it is true that Fred moves towards Mary in a certain situation, then it will be true that twin Fred would do so in that situation. But it is not the case that 'Fred believes that —— Mary ——' is true if and only if 'Twin Fred believes that —— Mary ——'. Twin Fred will, by virtue of failing to have the appropriate (actual) causal links to Mary, lack any beliefs truly reportable by sentences in our mouths using the name 'Mary'. There will, of course, be an explanation of why it is true that twin Fred would move towards Mary. Fred and twin Fred are reactively sensitive to the very same properties—the properties that underlie Fred's capacity to identify and re-identify Mary—and these 'Mary-distinctive' properties will figure in the predictive contents which make projectable sense of the autonomous patterns Fred and twin Fred have in common. But that is another question. Moreover, it is very much an open question whether or not Fred or twin Fred have words for the 'Mary-distinctive' properties. Think of the familiar problem of verbalizing one's responses to gestalts, or think of how hard it can be to say exactly how you are able to identify a person as someone you have met before.[10]

3. On Two Objections

It might be objected that content is explanatory as well as predictive. Perhaps we have shown that there exists something folk, narrow, and truth-evaluable, which is associated with belief and desire and has predictive value. But in order for a notion to count as an interesting notion of content it must, in addition, have explanatory value. Merely predictive content is not content.

We reply that the existence of patterns good for prediction effectively ensures explanatory value in certain kinds of cases, and the case of predicting human behaviour by noting belief-desire patterns is one of these cases. Suppose that you see a robot successfully negotiate a minefield. The robot is not being controlled by a human operator, or by another robot. We have a pattern: getting through a minefield successfully. Suppose that we project it into the future; that is, we predict that the robot will make it

[10] One author, P. P., inclines to the view that narrow, predictive content is generally sub-verbal. The other author, F. J., is more optimistic about our powers to express narrow content in English, while granting that a great many of the sentences we naturally use to ascribe beliefs and desires have broad truth-conditions.

through minefields in future trials, and suppose that the robot does indeed successfully negotiate minefields on a regular basis.

Can we offer anything by way of explaining the robot's success? We can. The probability that the robot makes it through minefields by chance is extremely small. We do not have to look inside the robot in order to be confident that the robot (*a*) registers the location of the various mines, that is, the mines' locations causally impinge on the robot leaving some kind of enduring trace which carries the information as to the whereabouts of the mines, and (*b*) whatever it is that drives the robot accesses this information and employs it to steer the robot away from the mines. And now we can explain the success of the robot: it gets through minefields because it stores information about the whereabouts of the mines and this information controls the movements of the robot. Of course, it would be nice to able to say a lot more. How does it store the information, how is the systematic co-variance between internal nature and the location of mines secured, and how does the robot's drive-train access the information appropriately? But to have far less than ideal explanatory value is not to have no explanatory value.

The same goes for the belief-desire patterns that solve the folk-predictive problem. The very fact that they hold tells us a great deal about what information from our surroundings is received, stored, and influences our bodily movements. And in projecting the patterns, we take all this for granted. It is obvious that Fred receives, stores, and utilizes information about Mary's whereabouts. And in predicting Fred's future responses to Mary's arrivals and departures, we take all this for granted. But that is to say that the contents we use to describe the belief-desire patterns in solving the predictive problem—predictive contents, as we are calling them—have explanatory as well as predictive value.

When we say that it is obvious that Fred receives, stores, and utilizes information about Mary's whereabouts, we do not mean that it is obvious *no matter what else we might know*. If we discovered that the robot which made its way through the minefield was in fact radio-controlled by a human operator, what would then be obvious would be that the information about the whereabouts of the mines was stored in the human operator. Similarly, if we consider a science-fiction case where Fred turns out to be controlled by radio transmissions from Mars, the obvious hypothesis about the locus of the information reception, storing, and utilization will become that it takes place on Mars and not in Fred. But as a matter of fact we know more than enough about the human beings who display the belief-desire patterns to know that the receiving, storing, and utilization takes place inside them.

Here is another way in which extraneous information about Fred might undermine what would, in the absence of that information, be the explanatory hypothesis demanded by our success in predicting his behaviour. We present Fred with a number of complex chess positions. Each time he comes up with an excellent suggestion for the next move. Presented with a position *P* he makes excellent response *R*. What feature of *P* prompts his response? In view of the fact that he makes an excellent response each time, the obvious hypothesis is that it is the feature of *P* responsible for the response *R* being excellent. Perhaps *P* contains a certain imbalance in the distribution of white pawns, and it is this imbalance along of course with other matters, like the rules of chess, which (*a*) is responsible for *R* being an excellent response, and (*b*) causes Fred to make *R*. But the hypothesis that Fred's responses are generated by the properties of the positions that make them excellent responses could be defeated. Perhaps we discover that Fred has somehow coded all the positions he could possibly be presented with. He has a unique tag for each, and he has simply learned off by heart, say from a table provided by an expert chess-player, an excellent response for each tag. In that case he is no good at chess. He is good at memorizing chess positions, and that is not the same thing. His defect is that he does not know what makes one of his excellent responses an excellent one. He responds to the tag in each case, but the nature of the tag is not what makes the response an excellent one. That is why forgetting which tag goes with which position would be such a disaster for his performance at chess (or, for that matter, why he would be quite unable to handle even minor changes in the rules of chess).

We mention these two ways in which the obvious explanatory hypotheses arising from predictive success might be undermined in order to highlight the fact that, by and large, we know that these sorts of things are not happening with our fellow human beings.[11] By and large the obvious explanatory hypotheses about the

[11] The two ways are variations on cases described in Block 1981*a* and Peacocke 1983.

information we store, retain, and access, though not the various speculations about how we do it, are known to be true. That is how predictive content is also explanatory content.

Secondly, it might be objected that the account of content being defended here is simply a revival of the Lewis–Stalnaker view that the content of belief is a set of possible worlds, and that this view is known to face an overwhelming objection. It entails that when *P* and *Q* are true in just the same worlds, that is, are logically equivalent, *S* believes that *P* if and only if *S* believes that *Q*. And a moment's reflection on belief in mathematical theorems and on failures of logical omniscience shows that this view is absurd (see e.g. Field 1978).

We reply that it is one thing to say that *S* believes that *P* if and only if *S* has the belief attitude to the set of *P*-worlds; quite another to say that an important fact about what I believe can be captured in terms of sets of possibilities. And it is only the latter which this paper employs. It was to emphasize this that we talked of the set of possibilities associated with what I, or Fred, believes. All we need is the fact that if I tell you which are the open possibilities and which are the closed possibilities as far as I am concerned about what will happen tomorrow, I tell you something important about what I believe concerning tomorrow.

4. Summary

We humans can predict behaviour in circumstances going on generally available external evidence. We have, that is, solved the folk-predictive problem. We must have solved it by using facts about raw behaviour, but how can order be brought to the chaos of raw behaviour? The answer is to look on behaviour as determining a function from one set of possibilities, the set associated with what the agent believes, to another set, the set associated with what the agent desires. These sets are properly describable as a species of folk, narrow, truth-evaluable content: they are folk because the story is all in terms that are common currency; they are truth evaluable because they are sets of possibilities, counting as true precisely if they contain how things actually are; and they are narrow because provided they are the sets we need to solve that part of the folk-predictive problem which can be framed in autonomous terms, the sets which solve the problem for a given agent must be the same as the sets which solve the problem for any doppelganger of that agent—otherwise the solution is no solution.

15

Object-Dependent Thoughts: A Case of Superficial Necessity but Deep Contingency?

H. W. NOONAN

AN *externalist* (or anti-individualist) is one who holds that the psychological states possible for a subject are not independent of the state of the world outside his skin.

One version of externalism is the Evans–McDowell doctrine of 'object-dependent' or 'Russellian' thoughts: thoughts about a particular concrete object, or objects (other than the thinker and the time of the thought), which are possible for a thinker only if he stands in some relation to that object, or those objects—a relation perhaps appropriately thought of, in Russellian terms, as one of 'acquaintance' (see Evans 1982 and McDowell 1984, 1986).

My own view is that externalism is a correct doctrine, but that the Evans–McDowell doctrine of object-dependence is mistaken. In what follows I shall first set out the argument which convinces me of the incorrectness of the object-dependence doctrine and distinguish it from an argument frequently put forward in the literature against externalism in general. (For reasons that will become apparent I shall henceforth refer to the former argument as the *Two List Argument* (TLA) and to the latter argument as *the argument for the causal redundancy of externally individuated contents* or, for short, as the *Causal Redundancy Argument* (CRA).) Granted this distinction, however, it might still seem that the former argument, i.e. the Two List Argument, if cogent at all, must be as effective against externalism generally as against object-dependence in particular. In fact, I believe, the Two List Argument is as effective against some other forms of externalism as it is against object-dependence. In particular, I think that it is as effective against the versions of externalism defended by Tyler Burge (1979 and 1982*a*) as it is against object-dependence. But I do not think that it is inconsistent with externalism generally. I shall try to establish this point by reflecting on the case of the brain-in-the-vat (BIV).

Next I will draw out the implausible epistemological consequences of object-dependence (and the Burgean versions of externalism inconsistent with the TLA) for the scope and limits of a priori knowledge (in this context: knowledge obtained independently of empirical investigation of the external world).

The subsequent sections of the paper will be devoted to analysing and briefly responding to the Burgean Twin Earth arguments for externalism and I shall indicate how these arguments can very easily be modified to yield arguments for object-dependence. In fact, I believe, there is a sense in which these arguments are correct and object-dependence has to be acknowledged. However, in my view, in any particular case its status is not, as its defenders believe, that of an a priori knowable conceptual necessity, but rather that of a merely *a posteriori* knowable Kripkean *metaphysical* necessity, and as such, I shall tentatively suggest, it is, in a sense due to Gareth Evans (1979), only a *superficial* necessity, but a *deep* contingency.

1. The Two List Argument

I turn first therefore to my own argument against object-dependence. According to Evans and McDowell, object-dependent thoughts include those singular thoughts we express with demonstratives and proper names (in this context a thought is singular, whether or not it is object-dependent, when it is both apt to express reference to an individual and has a content differing from that of any purely general thought), and one of their central arguments for the existence of object-dependent thoughts is the indispensability, in the psychological explanation of intentional action, of reference to such singular thoughts. Against this, I shall argue that reference to object-dependent thoughts is never required for the satisfactory psychological explanation of action, and hence that either there are no singular thoughts reference to which is essential to the adequate psychological explanation of action (which, I think, is untrue) or those singular thoughts, reference to which is essential to the adequate psychological explanation of action, are not object-dependent.

The thesis I wish to defend I shall call the *Redundancy Thesis*. Let us call an explanation of an action in which the only psychological states referred to are object-independent an 'OI explanation' of the action. Then the Redundancy Thesis states that:

> Whenever an action is directed towards a concrete, contingently existing object, other than its agent, in the sense that it is intentional under a description in which there occurs a singular term denoting that object, then an adequate OI psychological explanation of it is available under a (possibly distinct) description in which occurs a term denoting that object.

The Redundancy Thesis does not actually deny the existence of object-dependent thoughts. But to acknowledge that such thoughts must be redundant in the psychological explanation of action is to retreat to a position significantly weaker than that of Evans and McDowell. In fact if (so-called) object-dependent thoughts are established as redundant in the adequate psychological explanation of action, this is surely a reason to regard them as not, properly speaking, 'thoughts' or 'psychological states' at all, but rather as complexes consisting of psychological states plus certain external factors. The contention that there are object-dependent thoughts is trifling if it is merely an insistence on categorizing certain complex states of affairs, composed of psychologically explanatory psychological states plus external factors which do not have to be cited in psychological explanation, as 'psychological states' or 'thoughts'. But Evans and McDowell do not intend anything trifling.

The basic argument for the Redundancy Thesis, the TLA, proceeds as follows. Suppose I kick a cat, and suppose my action is intentional under a description in which occurs a term denoting that cat. Then there will be an adequate psychological explanation of my action under that description. Now let us suppose, for *reductio*, that this action is a counter-example to the Redundancy Thesis. Then there will be no adequate OI psychological explanation of it under any description in which occurs a term denoting the cat. That is, any adequate psychological explanation of it under such a description will make reference to certain object-dependent psychological states which would not exist if the cat did not exist. Imagine now a second situation in which, from my point of view, everything is the same, but in which, in fact, I am hallucinating a cat. Since this is so I presumably lash out at the cat I believe to be within kicking distance in exactly the same way as in the first situation. The difficulty for the opponent of the Redundancy Thesis is now to explain why I do so. For if the first, veridical, situation was a counter-example to the Redundancy Thesis, some of the object-dependent psychological states I was in in that situation, reference to which was essential to the explanation of my action there, are not present at all in the second, hallucinatory situation. Moreover, my hallucination in the second situation does not make it possible for me to think anything I was not able to think in the first, veridical, situation: it does not, that is, make available to me any content, or component of content, which was unavailable to me in the first situation. Hence the contents of my psychological states in the hallucinatory situation are a subset *X* (a proper subset if the set of my psychological states in the veridical situation contains any object-dependent thoughts about the cat, but certainly a subset) of the contents of my psychological states in the veridical situation. That is, if we draw up two lists, the first a list of the contents of my psychological states in the veridical situation and the second a list of the contents of my psychological states in the hallucinatory situation, *the second list will mention nothing not already mentioned in the first list*.

The opponent of the Redundancy Thesis is thus faced with a dilemma: he must either deny that the behaviour of deluded HN in the hallucinatory situation is rationally explicable by reference to his contentful psychological states, or he must acknowledge that reference to a proper subset, *X*, of the thought contents available to non-deluded HN suffices to explain deluded HN's action. Obviously, he cannot accept impalement upon the first horn of this dilemma, hence he must choose the second. But this is a fatal concession for him to make. For if the subset of contentful psychological states common to deluded HN and non-deluded HN suffices to explain the former's action, it must suffice to explain the latter's action too, since *the actions are identical*—each, that is, *makes exactly the same bodily movements*.

The opponent of the Redundancy Thesis might now protest: The actions are not the same, though the bodily movements are, for deluded HN lashes out wildly into thin air, whilst non-deluded HN kicks a cat, and these are certainly quite different actions (as the cat would be the first to agree). But this point is ineffective, for the only difference between the actions of deluded HN and those of non-deluded HN is a relational one: each lashes out, but deluded HN makes contact with nothing, whilst non-deluded HN makes contact with a cat. What makes non-deluded HN's action a kicking of a cat then, is simply: the presence of a cat. Thus if, as by supposition is being conceded, non-deluded HN's action, non-relationally described, can be explained by reference to that subset *X* of his total contentful psychological states whose contents he shares with deluded HN, then his action under the relational description can also be explained by reference to *X*, together with a description of the surrounding circumstances (i.e. the presence of a cat) which ensure the success of the action. However, if this is so the supposed counter-example to the Redundancy Thesis collapses. But then, since this example is typical of the situation in which an agent acts on a demonstratively identified object, it follows that no such situation could present a counter-example to the Redundancy Thesis. But such situations, it would seem, contain the most promising possible counter-examples to the Redundancy Thesis. If such counter-examples cannot be found in the case of action on demonstratively identified objects they can surely be found nowhere. That is, there can be no object-dependent thoughts reference to which is non-redundant in the psychological explanation of action.

(The defender of object-dependence might still wish to debate the point. For he might say, the fact that the set of non-object-dependent psychological states possessed by non-deluded HN suffices to explain his action does not mean that that set of psychological states is what explains his action.[1] Consider a case in which a worker on a chocolate-packing assembly-line forms the desire *to eat the next chocolate* (*whatever it is*) *that passes in front of him*. He then sees the next chocolate that passes before him—a particularly inviting one—and forms the distinct desire *to eat that chocolate*. He promptly does so. What explains his action is his desire *to eat that* (*visually presented*) *chocolate*, which causally pre-empts his previously formed desire *to eat whatever chocolate next passes in front of him*. Nonetheless, the latter desire would have caused him to eat the chocolate if it had not been causally pre-empted. He would have eaten the chocolate, therefore, even if the desire which actually explained his action had not been present. Now, Martin suggests, object-dependent thoughts might have a similarly causally pre-emptive role in the psychological explanation

[1] I owe this point to Michael Martin.

of action. That is, they might causally pre-empt the set of non-object-dependent psychological states which would have caused the very same action if the object-dependent thoughts had not been present. If this analogy were a good one it would rescue a sense in which object-dependent thoughts might, consistently with the TLA, be non-redundant in the psychological explanation of action. But I do not think that the analogy is a good one. For what makes the idea of causal pre-emption intelligible in the story of the chocolate-eater is that either one of the two desires mentioned might have been present in the absence of the other. But it is not intelligible that non-deluded HN might have an object-dependent thought about the cat whilst lacking the (explanatorily relevant) non-object-dependent thoughts which he shares with deluded HN (to appreciate this point it is crucial to recognize that the non-object-dependent thoughts common to deluded HN and non-deluded HN need not all have exclusively descriptive contents—they might have demonstrative contents also).[2] This reinforces the point that so-called object-dependent 'thoughts' are best thought of as complexes of psychologically explanatory psycho logical states plus external factors which do not have to be cited in psychological explanation.)[3]

2. The Two List Argument and the Causal Redundancy Argument Contrasted

This, in outline, is the Two List Argument against object-dependent thoughts, conceived as non-redundant elements in the psychological explanation of action. I now wish to distinguish this argument from the more general Causal Redundancy Argument. The TLA concludes that:

[2] See my 1991 article for elaboration of this point.

[3] As Alfred Mele pointed out to me, doubt might still remain. For consider a case in which HN hallucinates a cat and, as it happens, one is right there where he hallucinates one. Hence he kicks a cat, but not intentionally, it seems. Perhaps, then, object-dependent thoughts are required for intentional action in some cases? I lack the space to deal with this point now, but I respond to it in my 1991, where I argue that what distinguishes this case from the standard case of action on veridical perception is a lack of knowledge on the agent's part, but that, since the very same thing can be the object of knowledge and the object of belief, this gives no support to the idea that object-dependent thoughts are required to explain action in the veridical case.

> *if object-dependent thoughts exist they are redundant in the psychological explanation of intentional action.*

Another way to put this is to say that object-dependent thoughts, even if they exist, must *lack psychological reality*. The more general CRA concludes that:

> *insofar as thought content is externally individuated, reference to it is redundant in the causal explanation of action.*

Despite the fact that both arguments make play with the notion of explanatory redundancy, they are, as we shall see, quite distinct.

The line of thought lying behind the more general CRA goes as follows. We can distinguish, in general, between those features of an event which are *causally relevant* to its causal interactions with other events and those which are not. Thus, as Dretske (1989, p. 1) writes:

> Meaningful sounds, if they occur at the right pitch and amplitude, can shatter glass, but the fact that those sounds have a meaning is irrelevant to their having this effect. The glass would shatter if the sounds meant something completely different or if they meant nothing at all. This doesn't imply that the sounds don't have a meaning, but it *does* imply that their having meaning doesn't help explain their effects on the glass. To know *why* the glass shattered you have to know something about the amplitude and frequency of the sounds, properties of the sounds that are relevantly involved in their effect on the glass.

Or as Sosa explains:

> A gun goes off, a shot is fired and it kills someone. The loud noise is the shot . . . in a certain sense the victim is killed by the loud noise. But not by the loud noise as a loud noise, only by the loud noise as a shot, or the like. . . . the loudness of the shot has no causal relevance to the death of the victim. Had the gun been equipped with a silencer the shot would have killed the victim just the same. (1984, pp. 277–8)

This distinction between causally relevant and causally irrelevant features of an event (relative, that is, to a particular causal transaction) is a familiar one. But now, the CRA proceeds (in the words of Colin McGinn 1989, p. 133): 'causation is local, proximate and intrinsic: the features of the cause that lead to the effect must be right there where the causal interaction takes place.' Suppose my sunburn leads to cancer and eventually to my death. Then, of course, it is a change in the condition of my skin which is caused by an external object—the sun—which causes my death. But that change in the condition of my skin would have caused my death even if it had not been brought about by the rays from the sun. It is not *because* my sunburn is *sun-burn* that it has the causal powers it in fact has. Similarly, if I perform a certain action because of my knowledge that *p*, it will be true that my knowledge that *p* causes me (in conjunction with other beliefs and desires) to act in that way, but it will not be because my state of mind is one of *knowing* that *p* that I act in that way, for my belief would have caused the same action (in conjunction with the same beliefs and desires) even if, because the external facts were different, it had not been knowledge at all but mere belief.

In the same way, then, it seems that if a psychological state with an externally individuated content causes an agent to act in a particular way, it will not be because of its external relations (in terms of which it is individuated), but because of its local, internal features. If, for example, my belief that that cat is dangerous has an externally individuated content then, whilst the explanation of my lashing out may make reference to that belief, that is, that belief may be a cause of my action, it will not be because it has the externally individuated content that it has that the belief has the effect it does, for it would have had the same effect, in virtue of its internal features, no matter how it was caused.

This, in sketchy outline, is the Causal Redundancy Argument. The argument has, of course, been much discussed in the literature and there seem, broadly speaking, to be two possible responses available to the externalist. First, he may grasp the nettle, accept that it is not because of their externally individuated contents that psychological states cause behaviour, but emphasize that it is consistent with this that psychological states with externally individuated contents are causes of behaviour (just as sunburn is a cause of cancer) and also consistent with it that such states have to be referred to if behaviour is to be given an adequate psychological explanation. Alternatively, he may resist the argument and try to explain a sense in which, despite the considerations outlined, externally individuated contents are causally relevant features of psychological states with respect to their causation of behaviour. (In this endeavour he may begin from the point, emphasized in Heil and Mele 1991, that it is consistent with the argument outlined that the agent's internal state, in virtue of which he acts as he does, would not have been the same if his external circumstances had been different, just as my skin would not have undergone the cancerous change if I had not been over-exposed to the sun.)

Obviously, this second response is preferable if it can be developed successfully, but if not I think that it would not be absurd for the externalist to adopt the first, nettle-grasping, response. However this may be, what I want to emphasize is the distinctness of the CRA from the TLA.

To see that these arguments are distinct it suffices to notice that, as already stated, the CRA does not imply that states with externally individuated content are redundant in the psychological explanation of action. It does not imply, that is, that whenever an action is explained by reference to a psychological state with externally individuated content, the action could have been explained without reference to that psychological state (so individuated), *but still in a manner that would have counted as the giving of a psychological explanation*. To assume that this is possible is to assume that narrow psychological states (in Putnam's sense) are always available to explain actions whenever it is customary to offer explanations in terms of externally individuated, or broad, contents—and this, of course, is a substantial assumption. By contrast, the TLA does imply that whenever an action is explained by reference to an object-dependent content, the action could have been explained without reference to that content *but still in a manner that would have counted as the giving of a psychological explanation*.

The sense in which the TLA, if successful, establishes the redundancy of object-dependent thoughts, then, is stronger than the sense in which the CRA, if successful, establishes the redundancy of externally individuated contents. This is why I suggested earlier that the nettle-grasping response was a possible reaction to the latter argument. But this is not so in the case of the former argument. For, as already said, if a subset of (so-called) psychological states is demonstrated to be redundant in the psychological explanation of action, this is surely reason to regard them as not, properly speaking, psychological states at all (like knowledge, which is best regarded not as a psychological state, but as a complex consisting of a psychological state (belief) plus certain external factors—not because its status as knowledge is causally irrelevant in action explanation, but because it does not have to be cited, as such, in the psychological explanation of action at all).

3. The Two List Argument and Externalism

But if the TLA establishes the redundancy of object-dependent contents in a sense stronger than that in which externally individuated contents are established as redundant (if they are) by the more general CRA, and indeed, as I believe, establishes their redundancy in a sense which the believer in object-dependence cannot accept without trivializing his position, this is only because the TLA rests on assumptions which the CRA does not need. It is for this reason that I said previously that I believed that the TLA was consistent with externalism.

Recall the case of HN and the cat-kicking. It will be evident on reflection that application of the TLA to this case rested on three crucial assumptions:

(1) that *no content or component of content is available to deluded HN which is unavailable to non-deluded HN*, hence that deluded HN's contentful psychological states are a subset of those of non-deluded HN;
(2) that *only reference to contentful psychological states need figure in the psychological component of action explanation* (or, alternatively, that the very same non-conceptual items could be present in both cases);
(3) that *an adequate psychological explanation of an action under a non-relational description, together with a description of the surrounding circumstances in which that action constitutes an action answering to some relational description, provides an adequate psychological explanation of it under the relational description*.

The second and third of these assumptions are general propositions about the psychological explanation of action, but the first assumption is different: it is an assumption about the particular case. In this case, I think, it is clearly correct. How could deluded HN be capable of thinking anything which non-deluded HN is incapable of thinking? What would this thought be? What would it be a thought about? Why would it be an impossible thought for non-deluded HN? But assumption (1) does not generalize unproblematically in the way that would be required if the TLA were to be a threat not just to the doctrine of object-dependence, but to externalism in general.

It is this point I now wish to elaborate. It will be helpful first of all to see how the first assumption does generalize unproblematically sufficiently far to allow the conclusion that not only demonstrative thoughts, but also those thoughts we express with proper names of individuals, and names of natural kinds, are not object-dependent. Reflection on the case of the BIV will highlight, by contrast, the obstacles in the way of generalizing this assumption sufficiently far to threaten externalism generally.

The assumption in question is in fact quite complex. It is the assumption that corresponding to the situation of non-deluded HN there is a counterfactual situation in which a deluded counterpart exists *who intentionally performs an action which is identical with non-deluded HN's action* (*non-relationally described*) *though having available no content or component of content unavailable to non-deluded HN*.

Now let us consider a case in which the candidate for an object-dependent thought is one expressed with a proper name. Suppose that at a philosophy conference I choose to attend one rather than the other of two alternative afternoon sessions. Why do I do so? Well, the reason is that I think that that particular session is to be addressed by a famous philosopher (and the alternative is to be addressed by an unknown). Why do I think this? Because I believe that the speaker is to be Christopher Peacocke and I believe that Christopher Peacocke is a famous philosopher.

If, then, the thought I express with the sentence 'Christopher Peacocke is to address the session' is an object-dependent one, we have a case in which an object-dependent thought is essential to the psychological explanation of action. However, it seems clear that, supposing this to be the actual situation, we can imagine a counterfactual situation in which CP does not exist, but in which I have a deluded counterpart who also makes such a choice at a conference and has no content or component of content available to him which is unavailable to the actual HN in the CP-containing world. For we can imagine a situation in which CP does not exist but a group of hoaxers set out to convince the philosophical world that there is such a person, producing books, articles, etc. under his name. In such a situation I might be capable of having every thought that I am actually capable of having—except of course for the supposed CP-dependent thoughts in question—and need not be capable of having any thoughts I am actually not capable of having (for why should the absence of CP from the world make a richer psychological life possible for me?), and I might, acting perfectly rationally by my lights, choose to attend the first of the two sessions for exactly the same reasons as in the actual situation.

Since this is an entirely typical case of an action explained by a thought which would be expressed by the use of a proper name, it seems that we must conclude that not only demonstrative thoughts but also the thoughts we express with sentences containing proper names of individuals are not object-dependent—or else are redundant in the psychological explanation of action.

But if the TLA succeeds in this case it seems evident that it must also be capable of being employed equally successfully against the Burgean thesis that the thoughts we express with names of natural kinds, like water and arthritis, are object-dependent (here, of course, the notion of an object is the wide Fregean one). For it seems clear in these cases that a deluded HN, not acquainted with water or arthritis (nor with a substitute—XYZ or tharitis) might act in a way that is identical with the way non-deluded HN acts when his action is non-relationally described and might be rational in doing so, by his lights, though no content or component is available to him which is unavailable to non-deluded HN.

With these cases in mind, however, let us now turn to a consideration of externalism in general, which, I wish to claim, cannot be refuted by the TLA.

The basic consideration in favour of externalism I take to be the Wittgensteinian one (elaborated by Putnam in the early pages of his 1981). The intrinsic qualities of a mental state or event cannot determine what extra-mental events that mental state or event represents, or what features it represents them as having, any more than the intrinsic qualities of a physical occurrence can determine what it represents. For example, the intrinsic qualities of a mental state can no more constitute it as a thought of Winston Churchill than the intrinsic qualities of a pattern of lines on paper can constitute that pattern as a picture of Churchill or a sentence about Churchill. Only its relations to something outside itself can determine the representationality of a representation, whether it be a mental item or a physical item.

Of course, even if this Wittgensteinian line of argument establishes the truth of externalism, it leaves all the details to be filled in. But it seems clear that, however the details are filled in, any version of externalism worthy of the name must be incompatible with the supposition that *a BIV, whose brain-states throughout its history are identical with mine, will, no matter what its external circumstances, have psychological states identical with mine*.

The question is, then, whether the TLA is consistent with rejection of this supposition. I think that it is. The TLA would not be consistent with rejection of this supposition if it forced us to accept that any contentful psychological states of embodied HN not possessed by envatted HN were redundant in the psychological explanation of his (embodied HN's) intentional actions. But we are not forced to accept this unless we can think of envatted HN as *intentionally performing actions which are identical with embodied HN's actions (non-relationally described), though having available no content or component of content unavailable to embodied HN*.

However, it is by no means obvious that we can think of envatted HN in this way. For one thing it is not obvious that we can regard envatted HN as possessing any psychological states at all (so that his difference from embodied HN might merely come down to the fact that the latter possesses, whilst he lacks, a mental life). Secondly, even if we ought to regard envatted HN as possessing psychological states, it is not evident that we can regard him as intentionally performing any actions which are identical with embodied HN's actions (non-relationally described). In the original case of HN and the cat-kicking, it was plausible to describe deluded HN in this way because he did something of which he had non-observational knowledge—namely, lashed out with his foot—which in non-deluded HN's context constituted kicking a cat. But it is not obvious how we can ascribe non-observational knowledge of any such actions to a brain in a vat. For we do not, as embodied beings, have non-observational knowledge of the activities of our own brains (non-relationally described). Thirdly, even if these objections can be answered, it is not obvious why, if we can ascribe contentful psychological states to envatted HN, we cannot regard him as possessing contentful psychological states with contents not available to embodied HN (as Putnam (1981) puts it, not contents concerning brains and vats, but rather concerning brains and vats 'in-the-image'). For, of course, the external relations of his brain-states are quite different from those of embodied HN. (The defender of object-dependent thoughts could, of course, say the same of deluded HN in the case of HN and the cat-kicking, and I gave no argument to the contrary, but in this case the claim would be completely implausible.)

I conclude, then, that the argument I gave against object-dependence cannot be used equally well against externalism conceived more generally.

4. Externalism and the Possibility of A Priori Knowledge

I turn now to the implausible epistemological consequences of the object-dependence doctrine and the Burgean versions of externalism for a priori knowledge, in particular, for our non-empirical knowledge of the contents of our own psychological states.

The basic implausibility can be expressed straightforwardly. Commonsensically we think that we can acquire knowledge of the contents of our psychological states antecedently to acquiring knowledge of the existence of any particular external objects. But, if this is correct, and if the object-dependence doctrine or Burgean externalism is also correct, we can move from such knowledge, by a priori reflection, to knowledge of the existence of particular external objects. This, however, seems wholly implausible, as a little thought about particular examples will bring out. How could I deduce a priori, simply from knowledge of what is going on in my own mind, the existence of a particular cat, or Christopher Peacocke, or water (H_2O), or arthritis?

The defender of object-dependence or Burgean externalism might agree about this implausibility and respond to the problem by denying that our thought contents are capable of being known by us antecedently to our acquiring knowledge of the existence of any particular external object. But this would be a desperate move (and certainly one Burge himself would not wish to make), with nothing to recommend it apart from the fact that it would enable him to reject the possibility of acquiring knowledge of the existence of particular external objects by a priori reflection on the contents of his own psychological states.

To drive this point home, it helps to note that to accept that we can acquire knowledge of our thought-contents antecedently to acquiring knowledge of the existence of particular external objects, does not commit one to regarding our (second-order) beliefs about our (first-order) thought contents as infallible. Nor does it commit one to regarding our first-order thoughts as self-intimating—such that whenever we have them we are aware that we have them. Not that infallibility and self-intimation are in any obvious conflict with object-dependence or Burgean externalism. For insofar as object-dependence or Burgean externalism specify conditions necessary for the possession of first-order thoughts, they also, of course, implicitly specify conditions necessary for second-order thoughts about those first-order thoughts. But infallibility fails only if cases are possible in which one has a second-order thought to the effect that one has a first-order thought with a certain content when one does not. But if one has the second-order thought it cannot be that one fails to have the first-order thought because the external conditions for its possession required by object-dependence or Burgean externalism are not satisfied: they must be satisfied, otherwise one would not be capable of the second-order thought. Nor is the idea that first-order thoughts are self-intimating evidently incompatible with object-dependence. For, if a first-order thought is to fail to be self-intimating, it must first of all be possessed, and hence whatever conditions for its possession object-dependence or Burgean externalism require must be satisfied. But then object-dependence or Burgean externalism provide no reason for denying that its subject will also have a (second-order) belief to the effect that he does have the (first-order) thought in question (see also Heil 1988).

The fact is, then, that the defender of object-dependence or Burgean externalism can give no good reason for denying that our thought-contents are capable of being known by us antecedently to our acquiring knowledge of the existence of particular external objects. He cannot suggest that to accept this commits one to accepting the theses of infallibility and self-intimation, and even if he could, he can give no reason why these theses should not be accepted.[4]

Thus the only course open to the defender of object-dependence or Burgean externalism is to accept that we can move from antecedently acquired knowledge of our thought contents, by a priori reflection, to knowledge of the existence of particular external

[4] This conclusion is also drawn by Burge in his 1988, which I have found most helpful.

objects. But this is just the implausibility with which we initially confronted him.

The conclusion must be that, however the defender of object-dependence or Burgean externalism chooses to wriggle, he is bound to adopt a position incompatible with our common-sense views on the scope and limits of a priori knowledge.

But, it may be said, whilst this is a point that can fairly be made against object-dependence and Burgean externalism, it is not a point which can be made by a self-avowed externalist. For exactly the same commonsensical argument can be brought against externalism in general. Namely that, if it is correct, one will be able to deduce a priori from mere knowledge of the contents of one's thoughts, that an external world exists. But one obviously cannot make any such a priori deduction. Hence externalism must be incorrect.[5]

I agree that logically the two arguments—against object-dependence and Burgean externalism on the one hand, and against externalism in general on the other—are on a par. But the difference lies in the extent of their conflict with common sense. It is simply bizarre to think that a priori reflection on the contents of one's mental states, which can be known antecedently to any knowledge of the existence of particular external objects, can enable one to conclude to the existence of such particular objects as that cat, or Christopher Peacocke, or water (H_2O), or arthritis. It is not bizarre, even if it is a little surprising, that reflection on the contents of one's mental states, which can be known antecedently to knowing the existence of an external world, can enable one to conclude to the existence of an external world.[6] It is the specificity of the knowledge of the external world which object-dependence and Burgean externalism make available to a priori reflection, rather than the mere fact that it is knowledge of an external world, which creates the unacceptable conflict with common sense.

5. The Case for Object-Dependence

So much then for reasons for thinking object-dependence and Burgean externalism to be unacceptable doctrines. Unfortunately,

[5] This argument is brought against externalism by McKinsey 1991, to which this Section is greatly indebted.

[6] Of course, Putnam's argument against scepticism in his 1981 takes precisely this form. I take it to be a sound argument.

however, matters cannot be left at this point. For as I noted at the outset, there are seemingly powerful arguments for these doctrines, which indeed seem to suggest that we have no choice but to accept them.

The arguments I have in mind here derive from Burge, elaborating on the earlier work of Putnam on Twin Earth. The arguments of Putnam and Burge are, of course, very familiar, but, in order to appreciate the way in which Burge's arguments seem to support his versions of externalism, and object-dependence, it will be important to be clear exactly how they proceed, what their official targets are, and how they differ.

Putnam's main target is a position determined by two propositions which he takes to be implicit in traditional theories of meaning: (i) that 'what is in the head', i.e. not externally individuated, determines meaning and (ii) that meaning determines reference. In conjunction propositions (i) and (ii) entail that 'what is in the head' determines reference, and it is this contention which Putnam attacks with his Twin Earth arguments. Now, since Putnam is not intending to attack a straw man, proposition (ii) of his target position must be understood as asserting, not that meaning by itself determines reference, but merely that meaning together with *how things are*, or *the actual state of the world*, determines reference. (For even in the case of a description wholly devoid of indexicality, like 'the first dog ever born at sea', it is obviously false that its meaning determines its reference independently of how things are.) Consequently, in order for his argument to be relevant to his target position, the Twin Earth Putnam writes about must be located (as Putnam makes perfectly explicit) not in another possible world, but somewhere in the actual world.

Given that this is so, while Putnam's arguments are appropriate ones for him to bring against his target position, and do in fact, I believe, refute it (establishing, as Putnam says, that indexicality extends beyond the obviously indexical expressions at least to natural-kind terms), they provide no grounds (despite suggestions from Putnam to the contrary) for accepting externalism in general, or object-dependence in particular.[7] The 'contribution of the

[7] Putnam's view that natural-kind terms have an indexical element has been disputed. However, it is not refuted by the fact that the 'water'-utterances of a space-traveller from earth to Twin Earth would not shift their reference immediately on touch-down—nor would his utterances of the indexical description 'my wife'. Nor is it refuted by the fact that his 'water'-utterances would change their reference after he had settled on Twin Earth for a while—so would his utterances of the indexical

environment' does not have to be taken into account to explain the fact that I and my distant doppelganger refer to different substances — H_2O and XYZ — when we use the term 'water', any more than it has to be taken into account to explain the fact that he and I refer to different people when we use the pronoun 'I' or the description 'my wife'. Nor can it be concluded from Putnam's Twin Earth arguments that my 'water'-thoughts would be unavailable to me in an environment in which water was absent — any more than it can be concluded that the thoughts I express with sentences containing the description 'my wife' would be unavailable to me in an environment in which my wife did not exist. In general, Putnam's Twin Earth arguments go no way at all to establishing the environmental dependencies required for externalism in general or object-dependence in particular.

Burge's arguments, however, are a different matter. They are explicitly aimed at establishing externalism, and, in consequence, for Burge's purposes, I and my doppelganger on Twin Earth cannot be distinct people, as we must be in Putnam's arguments, and so Burge's Twin Earth has got to be, not a distant planet in the actual universe, but a *counterfactual earth*. Burge's arguments are intended to show that both the physical and social environment of a thinker can enter into the individuation of his thought-contents. He argues for the first of these contentions in his 1982*a* and for the second in his 1979. The pattern of argument is the same in both cases.

In his 1982*a* Burge makes use of Putnam's Twin Earth thought experiment with 'water'. Everything is the same as in Putnam's discussion except, of course, that Twin Earth is now a counterfactual earth. On the counterfactual Earth the substance which is present in the seas and rivers is not H_2O but a superficially similar substance XYZ. This is known to the scientific community on the counterfactual earth, just as the fact that the substance in the seas and rivers is H_2O is known to the scientific community on the actual earth. But there are some users of the term 'water' on the

description 'my best friend'. Anyway, even if we have to accept that 'water' is non-indexical and hence that its meaning is different on earth and Putnam's actual Twin Earth, it does not follow that its meaning has to be different on earth and counterfactual Twin Earth. The reason why its meaning has to be different on earth and actual Twin Earth, if its reference is different and indexicality is not involved, is that indexicality is the only thing that can account for a difference of reference given constancy of meaning in different actual world contexts. However, identity of meaning cannot guarantee identity of reference across possible worlds even for wholly non-indexical expressions.

counterfactual earth who are ignorant that what they refer to by this term is XYZ, and who could not, unaided, distinguish XYZ from H_2O. The counterfactual Adam is such a person. Similarly, the actual Adam is ignorant that what he refers to as 'water' is H_2O, and he could not, unaided, distinguish H_2O from XYZ. However, there is no doubt that the counterfactual Adam and the actual Adam do refer respectively to XYZ and H_2O when they employ the term 'water' since they use this term deferentially to their respective scientific communities, who are aware of the difference. The counterfactual Adam and the actual Adam thus refer to different substances when they use the term 'water', the actual Adam to water, the counterfactual Adam not. Consequently, while the actual Adam has a multitude of beliefs about water to which he could give expression using the term 'water', the counterfactual Adam may have no beliefs about water, and certainly has none he could give expression to using that term. That is, none of the beliefs he could give expression to using that term are ones which it would be correct to ascribe to him in sentences in which that term occurred transparently.

It is important to note that so far this is all entirely consistent both with individualism and with the contention that the correct account of the way the term 'water' functions is given by the traditional theory of meaning targeted by Putnam: that reference differs between a counterfactual and an actual situation can show neither that the term in question is implicitly indexical nor that the user of the term is in any different psychological state in the counterfactual situation from that which he is in in the actual situation. (Both points can be seen by reflecting again on 'the first dog ever born at sea'. This is not an indexical description, but its reference will differ as used in different possible situations. However, it would be absurd to regard this as entailing that its user in such different situations will be in different psychological states, will be thinking different things—as opposed, that is, to thinking about different things.)

But Burge goes further. The counterfactual Adam, he claims, does not even have any beliefs which it would be correct to ascribe to him in sentences in which the term 'water' occurs obliquely, or at least, none to which he himself could give expression using the term 'water'. But now, what is his ground for this contention? It cannot merely be, as we have seen, that the counterfactual Adam's thoughts are not thoughts about water, i.e. about what in the actual world is the referent of the term 'water'. It might equally be the case that he has no thoughts about the first dog ever born at sea, i.e. about what in the actual world is the referent of the description 'the first dog ever born at sea', but this would not debar us from ascribing to him thoughts in sentences in which that description occurred obliquely, e.g. 'Adam believes that the first dog ever born at sea was brown'.

In fact, however, Burge's contention about counterfactual Adam seems right. For it may be that there is water on counterfactual earth; it is just that it is not where it is on the actual earth and is not the referent of the counterfactual term 'water'. But then, if we allow that the counterfactual Adam does have *de dicto* beliefs about water (beliefs in whose description we would use the term 'water' obliquely) we get into conflict with the compelling principle that if '*A* believes that *X* is *F*' is true with respect to a possible world, *A*'s belief in that world must be about the referent of '*X*' with respect to that world. (Thus, for example, if '*A* believes that the first dog ever born at sea was brown' is true with respect to a possible world *w*, then *A*'s belief in *w* must be about the referent of the description 'the first dog ever born at sea' with respect to *w*—which need not be the same, of course, as its referent with respect to the actual world and may be nothing (if no dog in *w* was the first ever born at sea).)

The reason why this principle compels us to say that the counterfactual Adam does not have *de dicto* beliefs about water is that the referent of 'water' with respect to counterfactual earth is the same as its referent with respect to the actual earth. This is because 'water' is a rigid designator (in its actual use). Thus we see that the crucial assumption underpinning Burge's argument is that natural-kind terms are rigid designators, that is, that their referents with respect to any possible world are the same as their referents with respect to the actual world. But given that this assumption is correct his argument does seem compelling.

The same is true of Burge's arguments in his 1979. Here Burge supposes that the actual Adam and the counterfactual Adam are in identical physical environments and, in particular, suffer from the same afflictions. But on the actual earth the physicians, to whom the actual Adam uses the term deferentially, use 'arthritis' to refer to arthritis, i.e. an ailment that only afflicts the joints; whilst on the counterfactual earth the physicians, to whom the counterfactual Adam uses the term deferentially, use it to refer to a variety of ailments, including some that do not affect just the joints. Consequently, the counterfactual Adam, unlike the actual Adam, has no beliefs with respect to arthritis, i.e. what in the actual world is the referent of 'arthritis', or, at least, none he could express using the term 'arthritis', and so, since 'arthritis' is a rigid designator in its actual use, whose referent with respect to any counterfactual situation is identical with its actual referent, the counterfactual Adam does not have any *de dicto* beliefs about arthritis he could express using that term. That is, none of the beliefs the counterfactual Adam has to which he could give expression using the term 'arthritis' are such as to make true, with respect to counterfactual earth, any belief sentence of the form 'Adam believes that arthritis is *F*'.

Burge's arguments thus establish, I believe, that a sentence of the form '*A* thinks that *X* is *F*', in which '*X*' is a natural-kind term (and hence a rigid designator) occurring obliquely, can be true with respect to a possible world only if *A*'s thought in that world is one about the actual world referent of the term '*X*'.

This is not yet Burgean externalism, but we are now not far off. For we need only add the assumption that a belief, in a counterfactual situation, can be about a natural kind in the actual situation only if that natural kind exists in the counterfactual situation, to arrive at the required contention about existential dependence.

Furthermore, now that we have seen how it is crucial to Burge's pattern of argument that the term occurring obliquely in the content clause of the thought ascription be a rigid designator, it is easy to see how it can be extended to thought ascriptions in which proper names of individuals occur obliquely — thus apparently establishing object-dependence.

Suppose some children find a strange-looking creature wandering around the outskirts of their home, make friends with it, and give it the name 'ET'. Suppose now that this is the actual situation and imagine a counterfactual situation in which everything seems exactly the same, but in which in fact it is another creature from the stars the children encounter, a distinct but indistinguishable member of the species. Then it is obvious that in this counterfactual situation, in which although ET exists the children never meet him, they will have no *de re* thoughts about him. Moreover, since 'ET' is a proper name, i.e. a rigid designator, in its actual use, no *de dicto* thought ascription, in which the term 'ET' occurs obliquely, will be true with respect to this situation. Thus it will be false, for example, with respect to this situation, that Eliot believes that ET wants to phone home, since in order for this to be true it would have to be the case that Eliot's belief was a belief about the actual world referent of 'ET'.

The same point can be made by considering the extension of Kripke's (1979) case of puzzling Pierre made by Lewis (1981). According to Kripke's story, Pierre has never been to London but he has heard much about the place and on that basis believes that London is pretty. Lewis now imagines a counterfactual situation in which Bristol, rather than London, is called 'London' (in consequence of its beautification by Sir Ogdred Londers), in which Pierre's informants were all talking about Bristol, and in which Pierre's qualitative beliefs about London (in the actual world) are all true of Bristol. In this counterfactual world Pierre's beliefs are not about London, but about Bristol. Moreover, despite the fact that Pierre's narrow psychological states are the same in this world as in the actual world, it is false that he believes that London is pretty. For, in order for the *de dicto* belief ascription 'Pierre believes that London is pretty' to be true with respect to this counterfactual world, it would have to be the case that Pierre's belief was a belief about the referent of 'London' with respect to this world, which, since in its actual use 'London' is a rigid designator, is identical with its referent in the actual world. Since Pierre's belief is not about the actual world referent of 'London', therefore, it cannot be ascribed to him using the name 'London', even in an oblique occurrence.

Thus we arrive at the conclusion that thought ascriptions of the form '*A* thinks that *X* is *F*', where '*X*' is a proper name of an actually existing individual occurring obliquely in the content clause of the thought ascription, can be true with respect to a counterfactual situation only if *A*'s thought in that situation is a thought about *X*, which can only be so if *X* exists in that situation. Object-dependence thus seems to be established.

6. Superficial Necessity and Deep Contingency?

But, I argued earlier, object-dependence is an incorrect doctrine, so we have an apparent contradiction. In the remainder of the paper I wish to suggest a possible line of resolution.

One's first thought is that all that Burge's argument establishes is that it is a necessary condition of the truth of '*A* thinks that *X* is *F*', where '*X*' is a rigid designator of a kind or individual, that *X* exists. Hence that such a sentence's role is not merely to ascribe a thought to a subject but also to assert his relation to an object which the thought concerns.

There are cases in which this is true. In particular, it is true of sentences of the form '*A* thinks that that *F* is *G*', in which a thought about a demonstratively identified individual is ascribed to a subject. Such a sentence can be true only if the contained demonstrative expressions have reference. But this is entirely compatible with the view that demonstrative thoughts—the thoughts expressed with sentences whose subjects are demonstratives—are not object-dependent. For the function of such sentences is not to ascribe a demonstrative thought to a subject but to assert that an object, identified demonstratively by the utterer of the sentence, is one about which the subject is thinking—and it is left unspecified by the sentence how the subject is thinking about the object.[8]

If sentences of the form '*A* thinks that *X* is *F*', where '*X*' is a proper name of an individual, or a name of a natural kind, could be regarded in the same way, the Burgean arguments would thus be entirely compatible with the rejection of object-dependence and Burge's own versions of externalism. But, it seems to me, they cannot be regarded in the same way. For we are willing to regard as literally true *de dicto* belief ascriptions about non-existent natural kinds, e.g. ambrosia and unicorns, and non-existent individuals, e.g. Zeus and Santa Claus; and we could not do so if we regarded it as a necessary condition of the truth of '*A* believes that *X* is *F*' that *X* exist.

The apparent contradiction between the earlier arguments against object-dependence and the Burgean arguments for object dependence thus remains. In order to approach the suggestion I wish to make about this it will help first of all to recall the conclusions of the arguments against object-dependence.

The first argument, the Two List Argument, was to the effect that object-dependent thoughts would be redundant in the psychological explanation of action, would lack psychological reality. The

[8] Burge would, I think, agree. He has made it clear in several places that he is opposed to the Evans–McDowell position on demonstrative thought, e.g. in his 1986*b* and 1988.

thoughts we express with proper names and natural-kind terms, however, do not lack psychological reality and so cannot be object-dependent. That is, they must be identical with thoughts which are not object-dependent.

The second argument against object-dependence was simply that its defender was faced with a choice between two epistemological hotspots: he could either deny that first-personal knowledge of thought contents was possible antecedently to knowledge of the existence of particular external objects (the frying-pan) or he could claim that knowledge of the existence of particular external objects was capable of being acquired by a priori reflection on the contents of one's own psychological states (the fire). But whether he chose the frying-pan or the fire his position would be in flagrant contradiction with common sense.

This second argument against object-dependence, however, now suggests an obvious way to deal with the problem facing us. For the dilemma presented only confronts the defender of object-dependence if he holds that the dependence of thought content on the external world is a conceptual necessity and thus knowable a priori. If he maintains instead that it is a Kripkean metaphysical necessity, knowable only *a posteriori*, then his problem is resolved. Now I do not think that this is the way in which the defenders of the doctrine of object-dependence typically conceive their position, but, I wish to suggest, it represents the only hope we have of reconciling the case against object-dependence with the Burgean case in its favour.

I do not have space to develop this point in detail, but I shall finish by briefly sketching out the way in which it might proceed.

The actuality operator and descriptions 'rigidified' by it have been a focus of much recent work. This work demonstrates how attention to features of the actuality operator can yield satisfying explanations of (at least some) examples of the necessary *a posteriori* and (at least some) examples of the contingent a priori, and motivates a distinction between *superficial* necessity/contingency and *deep* necessity/contingency (see, particularly, Evans 1979).

Now, if we consider sentences of the form '*A* believes that the actual *F* is *G*', we can see that there is no necessary incompatibility, after all, between the Burgean arguments for object-dependence and the arguments against object-dependence I gave earlier in the paper. For the sense in which the Burgean arguments establish the object-dependence of thoughts about natural kinds and individuals is that they establish the truth of certain *modal* assertions: for example 'No one *could* believe that London was pretty if London did not exist'. In the same sense, however, if the (actual) *F* exists, the belief that the actual *F* is *G* is object-dependent. Given that there is indeed such an object as the actual *F*, no one *could* believe that the actual *F* was *G* unless that object existed. But the sense in which this is true corresponds merely to the superficial necessity (in Evans's sense) ascribable to the assertion: 'If *A* believes that the actual *F* is *G*, the actual *F* exists'.

However, this is entirely compatible with its being possible for *A* to know, antecedently to acquiring any knowledge of the external world (and, in particular, any knowledge that there is such an object as the actual *F*), that he does believe that the actual *F* is *G*. For to know this all *A* has to know is that he believes that the *F* is *G*, since the non-modal assertions (1*B*) '*A* believes that the actual *F* is *G*' and (1*B′*) '*A* believes that the *F* is *G*' say exactly the same thing.

Nor, of course, does the object-dependence of the belief that the actual *F* is *G* (given the existence of the actual *F*) entail that it will be possible for *A* to move by a priori reflection from his knowledge that he believes that the actual *F* is *G* to knowledge that the actual *F* exists. Such a move would be possible only if the object-dependence in question was a matter of conceptual necessity. But it is not.

Finally, the object-dependence of the belief that the actual *F* is *G*, in the sense in which it has been established, is compatible with that belief being psychologically real, i.e. a non-redundant factor in psychological explanation. For it is compatible with the belief that the actual *F* is *G* being identical with a belief which is not object-dependent and is uncontroversially psychologically real, namely, the belief that the *F* is *G*. And here, of course, the apparent conflict with Leibniz's Law is merely apparent.

To sum up, it is possible to maintain without contradiction that the beliefs we express with sentences containing proper names and natural-kind terms are: (*a*) object-dependent (in a sense to be explained in terms of superficial necessity), (*b*) psychologically real, (*c*) available to their subjects as items of a priori knowledge, but (*d*) not such as to make it possible for their subjects to acquire by a priori deduction from them specific knowledge of the external world. It is possible to maintain this because there are beliefs, namely those we express with sentences containing rigidified descriptions of the form 'the actual *F*', which possess exactly these four properties. But with these hints I must finish.

16

Abilities, Concepts, and Externalism

ERNEST SOSA

TRADITIONALLY the mind and its contents are thought *internal* to the subject. Thoughts, feelings, and experiences are considered entirely disparate and independent from the concrete, contingent surroundings *external* to the subject. Such internalism is presupposed in the Cartesian meditations that founded modern philosophy. According to this view, one's mind (with its contents) neither *involves* nor *depends upon* anything external. Consider the states constitutive of having a mind with certain contents, constitutive of one's experiencing, feeling, and thinking in certain ways at a given time. According to internalism no such state is *constituted* essentially by anything external, and every such state *depends* simply on the intrinsic properties of the subject whose state it is, and is *determined* wholly by these.

This view has come under increasing scrutiny and doubt in recent decades and years, and a persistent opposition has formed under the banner of *externalism*. The externalists challenge both parts of mental internalism. For them the mind is *both* environment-constituted or environment-involving *and* environment-determined (and supervenes at least in part on aspects of the environment external to the subject). What follows takes up one aspect of this controversy.

Some of the material in this paper was presented in a SOFIA conference at the University of Buenos Aires, and a paper that complements this one will appear in the proceedings of that conference, edited by Enrique Villanueva, as 'Between Internalism and Externalism'. The commentators on that occasion were Donald Davidson, Ronald DeSousa, and Alejandro Tomasini. Some of this material was also used for a talk at the Scepticism Conference held at the University of Rochester in 1989. The commentator on that occasion was Earl Conee. Later versions were presented at Duke University and as the 1991 invited talk for the meetings of the Georgia Philosophical Society. Others with whom I have discussed these matters include David Armstrong, James Dreier, John Gibbons, John Heil, Jaegwon Kim, David Martens, David Sosa, James Van Cleve, and Robert Welshon. My warm thanks to all those mentioned.

Suppose the existence of a brain in a vat with a syntactic command of English to rival that of a normal speaker, and with a rich stream of 'sensa': i.e. inner goings-on intrinsically just like the inner goings-on in a normal one of us, caused by brain stimulations in just the way such goings-on are caused in us. Such an envatted brain need only be plugged into a skull appropriately—i.e. connecting the right portion of it to the right bit of detached tissues and/or nerves in the skull—in order for the entity thus constructed to be as indistinguishable from a normal human being as is one twin from another. True, the creature would be wrong about lots of particular questions having to do with its past history, and so on, but on its grasp of concepts, on its general beliefs and desires, and on the receptivity of its behaviour to explicative and predictive rationalization, it might exactly as well be one of us—or so it is very plausible to believe.

Though intrinsically indistinguishable from ours, nevertheless the envatted brain can be no seat of our normal thought or representation, or so externalists would have us believe, when they deny that the vat-brainers can think about or represent trees or any other such externalia. What is the argument? Different externalists argue somewhat differently, though there is a strong family resemblance.

1. Putnam, Brains in a Vat, and the Wittgensteinian Argument

Putnam's argument, to begin, sets out from the fact that, though brains in a vat have no sense organs, they do have

> *provision* for sense organs; that is, there are afferent nerve endings, there are inputs from these afferent nerve endings, and these inputs figure in the 'program' of the brains in the vat just as they do in the program of our brains. . . . But the fact that they are conscious and intelligent does not mean that their words refer to what our words refer. The question we are interested in is this: do their verbalizations containing, say, the word 'tree' actually refer to *trees*? More generally: can they refer to *external* objects at all? (Putnam 1981, p. 12.)

Putnam answers his own questions in the negative, denying the envatted brains any ability to refer either to trees (by 'tree') or to anything external (by anything). Here is his argument:

> If these brains think about, refer to, represent trees (real trees, outside the vat), then it must be because of the way the 'program' connects the system

of language to *non-verbal* inputs and outputs. There are indeed such non-verbal inputs and outputs in the Brain-in-a-Vat world (those efferent and afferent nerve endings again!), but we also saw that the 'sense-data' produced by the automatic machinery do not represent trees (or anything external) even when they resemble our tree-images exactly. . . . How can the fact that, in the case of the brains in a vat, the language is connected by the program with sensory inputs which do not intrinsically or extrinsically represent trees (or anything external) possibly bring it about that the whole system of representations, the language-in-use, *does* refer to or represent trees or anything external? . . . The answer is that it cannot. (1981, p. 13)

Later Putnam summarizes his claim by saying that 'one cannot refer to certain kinds of things, e.g. *trees*, if one has no causal interaction at all with them' (1981, p. 16).

If Putnam left his point at that, it would be little more than dogma: the dogmatic claim that *only* if one has actual causal interactions with a kind of thing may one represent such things. But Putnam offers further support for his view, by appeal to what he calls 'a very abbreviated version of Wittgenstein's argument in *Philosophical Investigations*', which runs as follows:

We have seen that possessing a concept is not a matter of possessing images (say, of trees—or even images, 'visual' or 'acoustic' of sentences, or whole discourses, for that matter) since one could possess any system of images you please and not possess the *ability* to use sentences in situationally appropriate ways (considering both linguistic factors—what has been said before—and non-linguistic factors as determining 'situational appropriateness'). A man may have all the images you please, and still be completely at a loss when one says to him 'point to a tree' even if a lot of trees are present . . . . [No] matter what sort of inner phenomena we allow as possible *expressions* of thought, . . . it is not the phenomena themselves that constitute understanding, but rather the ability of the thinker to *employ* these phenomena, to produce the right phenomena in the right circumstances. (1981, pp. 19–20)

There is a large gap, however, between this 'Wittgensteinian' argument and Putnam's lemma that one can understand or grasp the concept of a tree only if one has actual causal interactions with trees. What seems required in order to close the gap is the following assumption:

(*P*) One has the *ability* to respond in situationally appropriate ways *vis-à-vis* trees only if one has actual causal interactions (past, present, or future) with trees.

But can't a round marble have the ability to roll down an incline even if it never rolls? The whole question now is that of allowable abstraction from *actual* situations appropriate for manifesting an ability. One might be unable to pick out trees *in the dark* (visually anyhow, in total darkness). Even in the dark one can still have the abilities constitutive of possession of the concept of a tree, however, even given the 'Wittgensteinian' argument above. What rules out a similar view of the envatted thinker? Why not say that the envatted thinker does have the required abilities; he only needs the right circumstances in order to manifest them. Connecting his brain appropriately in a suitable body is like turning on the lights (or waiting for daybreak). *Then* we shall see how easily and accurately the thinker can pick out trees. (Why judge the bodiless brain to be the seat of such abilities? Why deny the brainless body a similar right? For the same reasons, presumably, why we view the *embodied* brain, and not the surrounding body, as such a seat.)

2. Davidson's Externalism

Putnam is not alone in his externalism. Davidson writes:

> As Hilary Putnam put it, 'meanings ain't in the head'. The point is that the correct interpretation of what a speaker means is not determined solely by what is in his head: it depends also on the natural history of what is in the head . . . . [In] the simplest and most basic cases words and sentences derive their meaning from the objects and circumstances in which they were learned. A sentence which one has been conditioned by the learning process to be caused to hold true by the presence of fires will be true when there is a fire present; a word one has been conditioned to hold applicable by the presence of snakes will refer to snakes. (1989, p. 164)

Here again it seems possible to distinguish two factors: (*a*) the natural history of the disposition, and (*b*) the disposition itself. The conditioning process that leads one to be disposed to say 'Fire!' or 'Snake!' in the right circumstances is one thing; the disposition thus acquired another. It is possible or at least conceivable that the very same disposition might have been acquired in some other way; for that matter, it might have been innate. Perhaps the salient factor for understanding the sentence or word and for grasping the concepts involved is possession of the relevant abilities or dispositions, *however acquired*.

In another paper, Davidson adds:

Suppose lightning strikes a dead tree in a swamp; I am standing nearby. My body is reduced to its elements, while entirely by coincidence (and out of different molecules) the tree is turned into my physical replica. My replica, The Swampman, moves exactly as I did; according to its nature it departs the swamp, encounters and seems to recognize my friends, and appears to return their greetings in English. It moves into my house and seems to write articles on radical interpretation. No one can tell the difference. But there *is* a difference. My replica can't recognize my friends; it can't *recognize* anything, since it never cognized anything in the first place. It can't know my friends' names (though of course it seems to), it can't remember my house. It can't mean what I do by the word 'house', for example, since the sound 'house' it makes was not learned in a context that would give it the right meaning—or any meaning at all. Indeed, I don't see how my replica can be said to mean anything by the sounds it makes, nor to have any thoughts. (1987, pp. 443–4)

Recall Putnam's position. Our brains are encased in skulls, and connected to sense organs, limbs, etc. Brains intrinsically identical to ours might by cosmic coincidence have been envatted and always in causal isolation from other external things, while coinciding with ours in all biographical intrinsic detail. For Putnam the words and images and other goings-on in the minds of such envatted brains would not represent what the intrinsically identical items represent in ours.

Already in 'The Meaning of Meaning' (1975*a*) Putnam had argued that meaning depends on context. Thus the word 'water' for us earthians means H_2O, but for Twin Earthians it means XYZ, since on Twin Earth XYZ takes the place in the scheme of things occupied on earth by H_2O, including the causal relations with users of the word 'water'.

Davidson for his part writes:

I am, as I said, persuaded that Putnam is right; what our words mean is fixed in part by the circumstances in which we learned, and used, the word. Putnam's single example (water) is not enough, perhaps, to nail down this point, since it is possible to insist that 'water' doesn't apply just to stuff with the same molecular structure as water but also to stuff enough like water in structure to be odourless, potable, to support swimming and sailing, etc. . . . The issue does not depend on such special cases nor on how we do or should resolve them. The issue depends simply on how the basic connection between words and things, or thoughts and things, is established. I hold, along with Burge and Putnam, if I understand them, that it is established by causal interactions between people and parts and aspects of the world. The *dispositions to react differentially to objects and events thus set up are central to the correct interpretation of a person's thought and speech*. (1987, p. 450; my emphasis.)

This last seems both true and important. Indeed such dispositions seem central not only to the interpretation of someone's speech and thoughts but to the very existence of such speech and thoughts as the speech and thoughts that they are. Having a disposition to discriminate white objects, for example, is partially constitutive of possession of the concept of white (*as* the concept of white), which in turn is required for having the thought that snow is white.

But from the fact that such dispositions are normally acquired through certain causal interactions with the external surroundings, it does not follow that they *must* be acquired that way. The Swampman is a counter-example, and the brain in a vat provides another (if it is just like one of ours and would perform swimmingly when plugged appropriately into one of our skulls).

Much of what Davidson says about the Swampman remains true. The Swampman can't recognize Davidson's friends, or much of anything particular, and it can't remember particular things like Davidson's house. But in all general respects it is a match for Davidson as thinker and agent. It certainly has the dispositions required for discriminating colours, shapes, etc., and for behaving intelligently given its perceptible surroundings. What is more, we would do as well by applying belief-desire explanations and predictions to the Swampman, as we would have done had Davidson survived in its place. Accordingly, it seems plain that the Swampman is a thinker and agent, all right, even though its beliefs about its past history, etc., are mostly false. (Here we can understand massive falsehood, apparently, and this may be a place where the Principle of Charity should yield to the Principle of Humanity.)

3. Abilities and Concepts

I want to take seriously the emphasis by Wittgenstein, Putnam, and Davidson on abilities or dispositions as a key to understanding our grasp of concepts and hence as a crucial part of what enables us to have contents for our beliefs. Davidson speaks of 'dispositions to react differentially to objects and events', and Putnam speaks of 'the ability of the thinker . . . to produce the right phenomena in the right circumstances'.

Dispositions and abilities are constituted by conditionals according to the following model, where 'ϕ' represents the ability or disposition:

Nec.: (x has ϕ iff if x were in C, it would emit behaviour B)

(According to Webster, to 'behave' is 'to act, function, or react in a particular way'. In this very general sense, which I am adopting, any response, any reaction by anything will count as 'behaviour'.) My claim does *not* entail that every such conditional defines an ability or disposition. It may be that only conditionals satisfying certain further requirements constitute 'abilities'. I am claiming only that *if* ϕ is an ability possessed by x then there will be *some* C and B such that the following is true:

Nec.: (x has ϕ iff *if x were in C, it would emit behaviour B*)

Thus consider the dispositional property that a round marble has of being a 'roller', defined as:

Nec.: (x has (the disposition of) being a roller iff if x were released at the top of an incline, it would roll)

And let's abbreviate the form of conditional involved as:

$Cx \rightarrow Bx.$

Such a conditional is normally true only relative to certain presupposed circumstances. Thus consider the conditional about rolling—i.e. if x were released at the top of an incline, it would roll—abbreviated as:

$REx \rightarrow ROx.$

When this is true of a basketball on the surface of the Earth, its truth is relative to the rigid sphericity of that basketball and the downward pull of gravity. If the basketball were flat or if it were in a spaceship, the conditional would not be true of it.

Let's define now the 'grounds' of a true conditional of the form $Cx \rightarrow Bx$ as conditions $G_1, \ldots, G_n$, holding of x, such that:

$Cx \;\&\; G_1x \;\&\; \ldots \;\&\; G_nx \rightarrow Bx$

is true in *all* circumstances, but

$$G_1x \mathbin{\&} \ldots \mathbin{\&} G_nx \rightarrow Bx$$

is *not* true in all circumstances; nor is any other such conditional that weakens the antecedent (without importing independent subject-matter): e.g.

$$Cx \mathbin{\&} G_2x \mathbin{\&} \ldots \mathbin{\&} G_nx \rightarrow Bx.$$

The grounds of such a conditional will often include both grounds *intrinsic* to the object involved (e.g. the rigid sphericity of the basketball) and grounds *extrinsic* to the object (e.g. the presence of gravitational pull exerted by a nearby massive body). Let's now combine *all* extrinsic grounds into G_Ex and all intrinsic grounds into G_Ix. Then the grounds of $Cx \rightarrow Bx$ will be G_Ex and G_Ix, so that:

$$Cx \mathbin{\&} G_Ex \mathbin{\&} G_Ix \rightarrow Bx$$

is true absolutely and in *all* circumstances. Consider now the true conditional

(*) $Cx \mathbin{\&} G_Ex \rightarrow Bx$

(where, in the case of the basketball, we leave out of the antecedent all reference to the intrinsic state of the basketball: e.g. whether it is inflated or flat, etc.). This conditional (*) does in some sense *involve* matters extrinsic to the item of which it is true (e.g. the basketball) for it involves a relationship to an *incline*, *rolling*, *a massive external body*, etc.—all matters extrinsic to the item in question (the basketball). And yet conditional (*) is *concurrently determined* to hold of an item *x* simply in virtue of G_Ix, which is something purely intrinsic to *x* (e.g. the basketball's being rigidly spherical). It is determined to hold of x by G_Ix in a sense entailing that:

> In any factually or counterfactually possible world, if an item *x* had G_I, the following would be true of *x*: $Cx \mathbin{\&} G_Ex \rightarrow Bx$.

Consider again the Wittgenstein–Putnam–Davidson view of understanding (or of grasped concepts) as constituted by abilities or dispositions, where these are viewed as constituted in turn by appropriate conditionals: conditionals about how one would respond in certain circumstances, conditionals of the form: $Cx \rightarrow Bx$. Clearly these conditionals will *involve* the environment external to the subject. But will they also be *concurrently determined* by matters external to the subject? Consider externalism about one's mental contents and about the abilities constitutive of one's grasp of the concepts which enable one to have such mental contents. Is such externalism right not only about what such contents and abilities involve but also about what concurrently determines them?

The answer, it seems to me, is: 'It depends'. Suppose the conditional that constitutes the ability in question has the form: $Cx \rightarrow Bx$. And suppose it applies to someone and has grounds $G_E x$ *and* $G_I x$. Clearly in that case the externalist is right not only about involvement but also about concurrent determination. For in that context ($Cx \rightarrow Bx$) is true of that subject x *partly* in virtue of something intrinsic to x, namely $G_I x$, and partly in virtue of something extrinsic to x, namely $G_E x$. It is only the two acting *jointly* that concurrently determine the truth of the conditional and the possession of the ability.

On the other hand, if the conditional $Cx \rightarrow Bx$ has only intrinsic grounds $G_I x$, then the externalist would be right *at most* about involvement and not about determination (assuming at least one of [Cx] or [Bx] does involve something external).

We need not insist that *all* acceptable psychological properties, including all grasped concepts and appropriate contentful states derive from conditionals of such maximum abstraction from the external environment. Compare:

(C2) If *b* were released at the top of an incline, then *b* would roll down that incline.

(C3) If *b* were at the top of an incline, and acted on by a downward resultant force along the incline's surface, then *b* would roll down that incline.

Assume that C3 successfully abstracts from all external conditions, so that the holding of C3 with respect to *b* at a time *t* would depend only on *b*'s having a certain internal character—e.g. being rigidly spherical. Then the property expressed by C3 is determined by the intrinsic character of *b*. However, there is also the property expressed by C2, and possession of *that* property is *not* determined just by the intrinsic character of *b*. It requires also the holding of certain external conditions. There is no apparent reason to require either that all appropriate psychological concepts, including those of all content-ful states, must be of the same sort as C2, or that all must be of the same sort as *C*3. With this more permissive view, we avoid once again, now in another way, both extremes on the mental, and remain between internalism and externalism.

We take a middle course by combining the following two views:

(*a*) Abilities may constitute possession of concepts while constituted in turn by certain conditionals. And these conditionals may *involve* the external ineliminably (*involvement externalism*) while holding merely and wholly in virtue of the intrinsic character of the subject of whom they hold (*concurrent determination internalism*).

(*b*) There may well be two kinds of such concept-constitutive abilities, and two corresponding kinds of underlying conditionals: (i) There may be environment-dependent (or environment-determined) abilities, constituted by conditionals that hold not just in virtue of how it is inside the relevant subject but also in virtue of how it is outside, in the environment. And (ii) there may be environment-*in*dependent (or environment-*un*determined) abilities, constituted by conditionals that do hold simply in virtue of how it is inside the relevant subject.

4. An Externalism of Concepts as Abilities

What, more specifically, are abilities? Capacities are distinguished from abilities presumably by features of the constitutive conditionals. As a baby Chris Evert already had the *capacity* to play great tennis but not yet the ability. At that time it was true of her that if she underwent a long period of appropriate training then, at the end of that period, but not before, she would have the *ability* to play great tennis. And this ability at t is itself constituted by conditionals like: if she were at t to play against almost any other woman who ever played, she would be likely to win (with each at their peak, and so long as their actual intrinsic physical constitutions remained unaltered, and the conditions of play were normal, etc.)

Suppose, again, possession of a concept is just having a more or less complex ability, including perhaps a whole cluster of subabilities. Thus having a concept of a certain colour may not only include an ability to discriminate things with that colour, but may also require the ability to operate with a vocabulary of colours, responding appropriately with, say, 'blue' to the sky (in relevant circumstances), with 'white' to snow, with 'green' to grass, etc.; and *also* assenting to 'The sky is blue', etc., to 'No surface is blue and white all over', and so on. And possession of the concept of a certain colour may also include, finally, the ability to point to things with that colour; for example, having the concept of blue may require that, when in appropriate circumstances, you are asked to point to the 'blue' things before you, you do so (so long as the light is good, they are not too far removed, there are no obstructions, and so on).

If we think of matters in the ways just considered, then it is hard to see how, independently of chemical theory, two people could possibly have different concepts of 'water' simply because one is always on earth (with H_2O and no XYZ) and the other is always on Twin Earth (with XYZ and no H_2O). For it would seem that their pertinent abilities would be indistinguishable.

So long as we stick to the ability conception of concepts, therefore, the usual earth/Twin Earth cases will not show that it is possible for intrinsically indistinguishable subjects to possess different concepts, that concepts do not supervene upon, are not concurrently determined by the intrinsic constitution of the subject. For, as we have seen, abilities can be the same even with very different causal aetiologies.

Interestingly, however, it is possible to argue in favour of externalism even on the basis of an ability view of concept-possession. And the externalism thus supported is not just an externalism of concept 'specification' but is rather an externalism of what concurrently determines the possession of a concept. According to this externalist view one's possession of a concept may be determined in part by the character of one's external environment, so that, in a different environment, one may have *different* concepts, even though one may remain quite the same in every intrinsic respect. Thus, planet environments may so differ that intrinsically identical subjects may nevertheless differ in abilities depending on which planet they inhabit. Their eyes may be identical, perhaps, while the lighting conditions differ in such a way that discriminative abilities differ. (And, for simplicity, let's disregard the other senses.) For example, our corresponding abilities to discriminate shapes at a few paces in prevailing light may differ widely. As a consequence, our shape concepts may differ significantly, though of course they would still be concepts of the same 'sort' in some natural sense: they would all be shape concepts. Nevertheless, intrinsically identical subjects would have *different* shape concepts, which means that what concepts one possesses does *not* supervene on, is not concurrently determined by, one's intrinsic properties.

Of course it is true that for every such environment-dependent ability possessed by a subject there is a corresponding environment-*in*dependent ability or 'ability', which must also characterize that subject. And this latter ability would no doubt supervene on (be concurrently determined by) the intrinsic character of the subject and nothing else. Still, though there is always such an individualistic ability, there are *also* the environment-*dependent* abilities, which are not just individualistic, but supervene on environment-individual combinations.

Externalism, therefore, does not have to be causal, but may rest wholly on a view of concepts as abilities. Intrinsically identical people may yet have different concepts, because they differ in relevant abilities.

Take again, for example, two planets which differ in lighting conditions: Sunny and Foggy. The Sunny people and the Foggy people are intrinsically indistinguishable molecule for molecule. And yet, because of the environmental difference, they have different concept-constitutive abilities, with the result that important differences distinguish the shape concepts of the Sunny people from those of the Foggy people. For example, the Sunny people can easily discriminate certain circles from similar ellipses at six paces when outside at noon, but the Foggy people are unable to make that discrimination at six paces when outside at noon.

What makes abilities the same or different is not easy to say in general. Nevertheless, the examples used here seem somewhat plausible cases where abilities differ in ways that are relevant to what concepts are possessed, given our present assumption that concepts are constituted by abilities. If wider divergences are required before difference of concepts will be granted, we could perhaps appeal to further distorting influences in the respective media of the two planets, such that despite the intrinsic indiscernibility of the respective dwellers, they fail to share certain colour concepts. For the sake of the example, let's suppose that colours are objective features of middle-sized physical objects to which we have access through our eyesight and our visual experience, but properties which are there in the objects at a given time *t* independently of whether they are at *t* in a dark room, and independently of whether anyone sees them. And suppose moreover that colours are features of objects which are like primary qualities at least to the extent that they are not to be analysed in terms of the responses of normally sighted subjects who observe them in certain favourable conditions. Given these assumptions, it might turn out that objects which are objectively polka-dot blue and yellow are perceived by the dwellers of Shady as quite like grass in colour, whereas dwellers of Sunny see them as different from grass, since grass is homogeneously green, whereas these objects are polka-dot blue and yellow. And in that case should we not say that the concept of green possessed by the dwellers of Foggy is different from that possessed by the dwellers of Foggy? We might even want to say that the concept of 'green' that the Foggy people have is in a way inadequate, since it classifies polka-dot blue and yellow things together with bona fide green things like grass. And yet if the Foggy people are brought to Sunny they will of course be just as proficient as the Sunny people in discriminating green things from polka-dot blue and yellow ones.

Still it may be argued that Putnam, Burge, and Davidson are right in postulating further dimensions of externalism. For, it may be held, concepts are *not* constituted just by abilities. That is to say, possession of a concept is not just constituted by possession of an ability, no matter how complex. Even Davidson's Swampman lacks the most elementary colour and shape concepts, since it has never encountered any colours or shapes in its experience.

It must of course be granted that perfect twins Mary and Jane might know, respectively, perfect twins Paul and Dick; and that the discriminative and other abilities, and perhaps even the *general* beliefs and memories, constitutive of Mary's concept of Paul may be matched exactly by such abilities, beliefs, and memories possessed by Jane and constitutive of Jane's concept of Dick; while, nevertheless, Mary's concept is a concept of Paul, not of Dick, and Jane's concept is a concept of Dick, not of Paul.

Even if we grant that example, as I believe probably we should, there is still room to disagree on how it should be viewed. One way, for example, is to regard one's concept of Jane as involving an appropriate causal relation to Jane specifically, as in the causal theory of names. But another way is to consider a parallel to the concept of oneself that each of us employs. Paul has a concept of himself and Dick has a concept of himself. And these are constituted by abilities and perhaps beliefs and memories which may happen to match perfectly point for point. Yet Paul's concept is a concept of himself and Dick's is a concept of himself, and they are of course different people. On this view we distinguish *concepts* from their *objects*, and allow that a shared concept (of oneself) may have different objects as you move from possessor to possessor of that concept (e.g. from Paul to Dick).

Similar disagreements may arise concerning natural kinds, such as H_2O and XYZ, and even concerning colours and shapes. For properties may also be regarded as 'objects' that may or may not 'fit' certain concepts in our heads. And now the same options arise: Do we view such 'fitting' as constituted at least in part by a special causal relation linking the property in question to the subject whose concept it fits? Or do we view it rather by analogy to the way one fits one's concept of oneself: e.g. the way I fit my concept of myself by simply being able to use a first-person pronoun appropriately, and being the one to whom my uses of that pronoun would refer?

These are of course much debated issues about *de re* versus *de dicto* belief, and about proper names and natural-kind terms. Here I have touched on such issues only tangentially. For it has been my main objective rather to explore the consequences for the externalism/internalism debate of a view of concepts as fully constituted by abilities, which are in turn to be viewed as constituted by subjunctive conditionals.

5. A Broader Distinction

The internalism/externalism distinction in the philosophy of psychology is a special case of a much broader distinction applicable in metaphysics more generally and also in ethics and epistemology. Consider just the following list: secondary qualities, faculties, virtues, powers, and dispositions generally. In each case we may think of ϕ—of the secondary quality, faculty, virtue, power, or disposition—as necessarily equivalent to a conditional, so that the following sort of analysis will hold:

(*A*) Nec. (x has ϕ iff: if x were in C, x would emit behaviour B)

And consider now the following questions.

(*a*) *Re* secondary qualities: Do things lose their colour in the dark?
(*b*) *Re* faculties: Does one's eyesight get worse in the dark? In a fog?
(*c*) *Re* powers and dispositions: Do bodies get lighter when they are moved to the moon?

Concerning the properties involved in each case, externalism of such properties would answer the corresponding questions in the affirmative, while internalism would answer them in the negative. Thus a certain externalism of secondary qualities would say that things *do* lose their colour in the dark, whereas the corresponding internalism would say that things *do not* lose their colour in the dark. And so on for the other cases above.

As (*a*), (*b*), and (*c*) suggest, the distinction between internalism and externalism is not just a matter of whether the property or the family of properties in question is reducible to conditionals about how *x* would behave in certain conditions. This is not enough, for the truth or falsity of such conditionals might itself be relative to a presupposed environment—in such a way that the truth of such a conditional is determined not just by the intrinsic character of *x* but also by the character of the external environment.

6. Conclusion

Regarding *some* psychological abilities and related contents of beliefs (experiences) internalism is right on concurrent determination though wrong on involvement. In making such a claim I assume willingness to abstract as much as possible from presupposed actual conditions in understanding the pertinent conditionals (which give content to the Wittgensteinian, Davidsonian, or Putnamian dispositions constitutive of one's possession of concepts). For such a view concepts are not possessed in virtue of the *actual* character of the subject's environment—even though such possession is constituted by a battery of dispositions. For these dispositions are in turn a matter of abstract conditionals *defined* in terms of environment-involving inputs and outputs, but depending for their truth on no external grounds concerning *x*'s environment, past, present, or future, at the moment when *x* has such a disposition. Our view is in this sense 'between internalism and externalism': it accepts analysis-, or definition-, or involvement-externalism, but accepts also, in at least some cases, dependence-, or supervenience-, or determination-internalism.

And there is moreover a further respect in which we do well to avoid both extremes concerning the basis of mental content, and in which we do well to avoid both radical internalism and radical externalism. For abilities come in two relevant varieties: some are environment-dependent, others environment-independent. Environment-dependent abilities are constituted by conditionals which are true not just in virtue of the intrinsic nature of the one with the ability, but in virtue also of some feature of the environment, at least in part. Environment-independent abilities are instead constituted by conditionals which load the required features of the environment into their antecedents, so that they can be true simply in virtue of the intrinsic character of the one with the ability. Finally, if possession of concepts *is* constituted by abilities, as in the Wittgenstein–Putnam–Davidson view, there is no evident reason to suppose that all such concept-constitutive abilities must be environment-dependent, nor is there any to suppose that they must all be environment-*in*dependent. The best course for the abilities view of concepts is therefore at present the middle course which avoids both internalism and externalism, even just on the question of determination, on the question of what it is in virtue of which we have our concept-constitutive abilities, and in virtue of which we satisfy the required ability-constitutive conditionals.

Appendix: Burge on the Width of Content

That meanings and contents lie at least in part outside the head is a view most vigorously and radically propounded by Tyler Burge, who adopts Putnam's examples and arguments about the externality of meaning, adds some of his own, and draws conclusions even more radical than Putnam's. What follows details some of my doubts about Burge's reasoning.

Suppose $Adam_{te}$ is Adam's counterpart on Twin Earth, where XYZ takes the place of H_2O. And let Adam believe that there is water nearby. Does $Adam_{te}$ hold such a belief? Burge thinks it 'intuitively obvious that he does not' (1982*a*, p. 109). And he argues that

> two broad sorts of consideration back the intuition. One is that it is hard to see how $Adam_{te}$ could have acquired thoughts involving the concept of water. . . . There is no water on Twin Earth, — no H_2O, only XYZ that is potable, flows downhill, etc.; so he has never had any contact with water. . . . The point is that none of their terms even translates into our (non-indexical) word 'water' . . . . [In addition,] . . . a second consideration . . . backs the intuition that $Adam_{te}$ lacks attitudes involving the notion of water . . . . There is no water on Twin Earth. If $Adam_{te}$ expresses attitudes that involve the concept of water a large number of his ordinary beliefs will be false — that *that* is water, that there is water within twenty miles, . . . and so forth. But there seems no reason to count his beliefs false and Adam's beliefs true (or vice versa). Their beliefs were acquired and relate to their environments in exactly parallel and equally successful ways. (1982*a*, p. 110)

Suppose I am Adam and I believe there is an apple before me. Can $Adam_{te}$ hold the corresponding belief which he would express by saying 'There is an apple before me', with that sentence having in his utterance the same meaning it has in mine? Someone might have the intuition that he cannot, and might offer two broad sorts of consideration in support of that intuition. One is that it is hard to see how $Adam_{te}$ could have acquired the concept of *me*, of myself. I am not on Twin Earth, so he has never had any contact with *me*, with myself. The point is that none of their terms translates into our terms 'me' or 'myself'. In addition, a second consideration backs the intuition that $Adam_{te}$ lacks attitudes involving the notion of myself. There is no myself on Twin Earth (since I am not and never have been there). If $Adam_{te}$ expressed attitudes that involve the concept of myself, a large number of his ordinary beliefs will be false — that this is myself, that he could find *me* within twenty miles, and so forth. But there seems no reason to count his beliefs false and my beliefs true (or vice versa).

Such reasoning involving the terms 'me' and 'myself' is obviously fallacious, precisely because these terms are indexical. Accordingly, Burge's reasoning needs to assume that the term 'water' is not indexical. Clearly aware of this, Burge is at pains to defend the assumption. Hence he argues in detail against Putnam's suggestion that natural-kind words like 'water' are indexical (Putnam 1975*a*, pp. 229–35). His case rests on the following two arguments:[1]

Burge's First Argument (*BA I*)[2]

1. Indexical terms vary their extension (from context to context or token to token).
2. 'Water' does not vary its extension.
3. 'Water' is not an indexical.

Burge's Second Argument (*BA II*)[3]

Consider:

[1] The first of which appears on p. 103, and the second on p. 104, of Burge 1982*a*.

[2] Quoting from Burge 1982*a*, p. 103:
Putnam gives the customary explication of the notion of indexicality: 'Words like "now", "this", "here", have long been recognized to be *indexical* or *token-reflexive* — i.e. to have an extension which varied from context to context or token to token' (Putnam 1975, pp. 233–4). I think that it is clear that 'water', *interpreted as it is in English*, or as we English speakers standardly interpret it, does not shift extension from context to context in this way. (One must, of course, hold the language, or linguistic construal, fixed. Otherwise, every word will trivially count as indexical. For by the very conventionality of language, we can always imagine some context in which our word — word form — has a different extension.) The extension of 'water', as interpreted in English in all non-oblique contexts, is (roughly) the set of all aggregates of H_2O molecules, together, probably, with the individual molecules. There is nothing at all indexical about 'water' in the customary sense of 'indexical'.

[3] Quoting from Burge 1982*a*, p. 104:

(*Dw*) 'Water' *means* 'stuff that bears the same-liquid relation to the stuff we call 'water' around here.'

1. If Adam visited Twin Earth and (still speaking English) called XYZ 'water' by means of some utterance *u*, and (*Dw*) above is correct, then Adam's utterance *u* would be true.
2. But there is no water on Twin Earth, and '. . . there is no reason why an English speaker should not be held to this account when he visits Twin Earth'.
3. Hence, (*Dw*) above is *incorrect*.

A third argument is also offered (Burge 1982*a*, p. 105) but it is effective only against a very special form of the indexical view of natural-kind terms, unlike *BA I* and *BA II*, variants of which would be applicable to widely different forms of the indexical view. Thus *BA II* could be applied not only to (*Dw*) but also to the following:

(*Dw′*) 'Water' means 'stuff that bears the same-liquid relation to the transparent, potable, colourless, odourless liquid that flows in these rivers and out of these taps, etc.'

However, neither *BA I* nor *BA II* is effective against *Dw′*, which may be seen as follows.

Against *BA I*, its first premiss is false. Thus the indexical term 'We thinking beings' and 'We existing entities' do not vary their extensions from context to context or token to token.[4] Moreover, to hold with the second premiss that 'water' does not vary its extension from earth to Twin Earth is just to beg the question against the indexical account. (And the question would be begged similarly even on a more complex Kaplanian account of what it is for something to be an indexical, one that involved the distinction between character and content, and held indexicals to have constant character across possible worlds even when the corresponding

One might . . . [arrive at] the notion that 'water' *means* . . . 'stuff that bears the same-liquid relation to the stuff we call "water" around here'. But this cannot be right. . . . For if Adam and his colleagues visited Twin Earth and (still speaking English) called XYZ 'water', it would follow on this meaning explication that their uses of the sentence 'Water flows in that stream' would be true. They would make no mistake in speaking English and calling XYZ 'water'. For since the extension of 'here' would shift, occurrences on Twin Earth of 'stuff that bears the same-liquid relation to the stuff we call "water" around here flows in that stream' would be true. But by Putnam's own account, which is clearly right on this point, there is no water on Twin Earth. And there is no reason why an English speaker should not be held to this account, when he visits Twin Earth.

[4] In defining what makes a term indexical, one would need to be sensitive to a distinction between basic indexicals—such as 'I' or perhaps 'We'—and derivative

contents varied, perhaps widely. Whether 'water' has such character, being equivalent to 'stuff of the same natural kind as this transparent, potable, odourless, etc., liquid', is then just too close to the question of whether 'water' is an indexical, being in fact just the same question. Anyone who views 'water' as equivalent to 'stuff of the same kind as this *F* stuff', or the like, will of course think that 'water' does have a constant Kaplanian 'character', one that determines quite possibly different contents relative to different possible speakers or occasions of use. There seems not to be enough logical space here to permit even a gesture of an interesting argument.)

Against *BA II*, the indexical view can hold both (*Dw'*) *and* (1) *and* (2). In particular, from our standpoint on earth we *can* as indexicalists about 'water' hold that indeed there is no water at all on Twin Earth, even though our Twin Earthian counterparts speak the truth when *they* say 'There is water on Twin Earth', as does even an earthian visitor to Twin Earth. Compare the fact that we can as indexicalists about 'we' hold that we are not at all on Twin Earth, even though our Twin Earthian counterparts speak the truth when *they* say 'we are on Twin Earth'.

indexicals—perhaps 'We thinking beings', perhaps 'water'. And we must be careful about the sort of variation of extension that defines indexicality, if indexicality is to be defined by reference to such variation. 'Actually varies in extension' would seem to tie the fortunes of indexicality to such contingencies as how many speakers there are to say 'I'. 'Could vary in extension' seems better, with the *could* extending quite far through the realm of possibility.

References

Achinstein, P. (1979), 'The Causal Relation', *Midwest Studies in Philosophy*, 4: 369–86.

Alexander, S. (1927), *Space, Time, and Deity*, ii, 2nd edn., London: Macmillan.

Aristotle, *Nicomachean Ethics*, in W. Ross (ed.), *Works of Aristotle*, ix, London: Oxford University Press, 1915.

Audi, R. (1971), 'Intentionalistic Explanations of Action', *Metaphilosophy*, 2: 241–50.

—— (1973), 'The Concept of Wanting', *Philosophical Studies*, 24: 1–21.

—— (1980), 'Wants and Intentions in the Explanation of Action', *Journal for the Theory of Social Behaviour*, 9: 227–49.

—— (1985), 'Rationalization and Rationality', *Synthese*, 65: 159–84.

—— (1986), 'Acting for Reasons', *Philosophical Review*, 95: 511–46.

—— (1989), *Practical Reasoning*, London and New York: Routledge.

—— (1992), 'Ethical Naturalism and the Explanatory Power of Moral Concepts', in Wagner and Warner (1992).

Baker, L. (1987), *Saving Belief: A Critique of Physicalism*, Princeton, NJ: Princeton University Press.

—— (1989), 'On a Causal Theory of Content', *Philosophical Perspectives*, 3: 165–86.

—— (1991*a*), 'Has Content Been Naturalized?' in Rey and Loewer (1991): 17–32.

—— (1991*b*), 'Dretske on the Explanatory Role of Belief', *Philosophical Studies*, 63: 99–111.

Beckermann, A., Flohr, H., and Kim, J. (1992) (eds.) *Emergence or Reduction? Essays on the Prospect of Nonreductive Physicalism*, Berlin: De Gruyter.

Bennett, J. (1988), *Events and Their Names*, Indianapolis: Hackett.

—— (1990), *Linguistic Behaviour* (2nd. edn.), Indianapolis: Hackett.

Bieri, P. (1992), 'Trying Out Epiphenomenalism', *Erkenntnis*, 36: 283–309.

Binkley, R., Bronaugh, R., and Marras, A. (1971) (eds.), *Action, Agent, and Reason*, Toronto: University of Toronto Press.

Block, N. (1981*a*), 'Psychologism and Behaviorism', *Philosophical Review*, 90: 5–43.

—— (1981*b*) (ed.), *Readings in Philosophy of Psychology*, ii, Cambridge, Mass.: Harvard University Press.

—— (1990), 'Can the Mind Change the World?' in Boolos (1990): 137–70.

Bolton, N. (1979) (ed.), *Philosophical Problems in Psychology*, London: Methuen.

Boolos, G. (1990) (ed.), *Meaning and Method: Essays in Honor of Hilary Putnam*, Cambridge: Cambridge University Press.

Bromberger, S. (1966), 'Why-Questions', in Colodny (1966): 86–111.

Brown, S. (1974) (ed.), *Philosophy of Psychology*, London: Macmillan.

Burge, T. (1979), 'Individualism and the Mental', *Midwest Studies in Philosophy*, 4: 73–121.

—— (1982*a*), 'Other Bodies', in Woodfield (1982): 97–120.

—— (1982*b*), 'Two Thought Experiments Reviewed', *Notre Dame Journal of Formal Logic*: 23, 284–93.

—— (1986*a*), 'Individualism and Psychology', *Philosophical Review*, 95: 3–46.

—— (1986*b*), 'Cartesian Error and the Objectivity of Perception', in Pettit and McDowell, (1986): 117–36.

—— (1986*c*), 'Intellectual Norms and the Foundations of Mind', *Journal of Philosophy*, 83: 697–720.

—— (1988), 'Individualism and Self-Knowledge', *Journal of Philosophy*, 85: 649–65.

—— (1989*a*), 'Individualism and Causation in Psychology', *Pacific Philosophical Quarterly*, 70: 303–22.

—— (1989*b*), 'Wherein Is Language Social?' in George (1989): 175–91.

Capitan, W., and Merrill, D. (1967) (eds.), *Art, Mind, and Religion*, Pittsburgh: University of Pittsburgh Press.

Castañeda, H.-N. (1967), 'Indicators and Quasi-Indicators', *American Philosophical Quarterly*, 4: 85–100.

Churchland, P. M. (1981), 'Eliminative Materialism and the Propositional Attitudes', *Journal of Philosophy*, 78: 67–90.

Churchland, P. S. (1986), *Neurophilosophy*, Cambridge, Mass.: MIT Press.

Clark, A. (1989), *Microcognition*, Cambridge, Mass.: MIT Press.

Colodny, R. (1966) (ed.), *Mind and Cosmos: Essays in Contemporary Science and Philosophy*, Pittsburgh: University of Pittsburgh Press.

Crane, T. (1991), 'All the Difference in the World', *Philosophical Quarterly*, 41: 1–25.

Cummins, R. (1975), 'Functional Analysis', *Journal of Philosophy*, 72: 741–60.

—— (1983), *The Nature of Psychological Explanation*, Cambridge, Mass.: MIT Press.

Davidson, D. (1963), 'Actions, Reasons, and Causes', *Journal of Philosophy*, 60: 685–700; reprinted in Davidson (1980).

—— (1967), 'Causal Relations', *Journal of Philosophy*, 64: 691–703; reprinted in Davidson (1980).

—— (1969), 'The Individuation of Events', in Rescher (1969): 216–34.

—— (1970), 'Mental Events', in Foster and Swanson (1970): 79–101; reprinted in Davidson (1980).

—— (1971), 'Agency', in Binkley *et al.* (1971): 3–25; reprinted in Davidson (1980).

—— (1973), 'The Material Mind', in Suppes *et al.* (1973): 709–22; reprinted in Davidson (1980).

—— (1974*a*), 'Belief and the Basis of Meaning', *Synthese*, 27: 309–23; reprinted in Davidson (1984).

—— (1974*b*), 'Psychology as Philosophy', in Brown (1974): 41–52; reprinted in Davidson (1980).

—— (1980), *Essays on Actions and Events*, Oxford: Clarendon Press.

—— (1984), *Inquiries Into Truth and Interpretation*, Oxford: Clarendon Press.

—— (1985), 'Replies to Essays X–XII', in Vermazen and Hintikka (1985): 242–52.

—— (1986), 'Knowing One's Own Mind', *Proceedings of the American Philosophical Association*, 60: 441–58.

—— (1987), 'Problems in the Explanation of Action', in Pettit *et al.* (1987): 34–49.

—— (1989), 'The Myth of the Subjective', in Krausz (1989): 159–72.

Davies, M. (1990), 'Review of Colin McGinn, *Mental Content*', *Mind and Language*, 5: 243–8.

Dawkins, R. (1983), *The Extended Phenotype*, New York: Oxford University Press.

Dennett, D. (1973), 'Mechanism and Responsibility', in Honderich (1973): 159–84; reprinted in Dennett (1979).

—— (1979), *Brainstorms*, Brighton: Harvester Press.

—— (1981), 'Three Kinds of Intentional Psychology', in Healy (1981): 37–61; reprinted in Dennett (1987).

—— (1982) 'Beyond Belief', in Woodfield (1982): 1–95; reprinted in Dennett (1987).

—— (1987), *The Intentional Stance*, Cambridge, Mass.: MIT Press.

Devitt, M. (1990), 'A Narrow Represenational Theory of Mind', in Lycan (1990): 371–98.

Dretske, F. (1981), *Knowledge and the Flow of Information*, Cambridge, Mass.: MIT Press.

—— (1988), *Explaining Behavior: Reasons in a World of Causes*, Cambridge, Mass.: MIT Press.

—— (1989), 'Reasons and Causes', *Philosophical Perspectives*, 3: 1–15.

Evans, G. (1979), 'Reference and Contingency', *The Monist*, 62: 161–89.

—— (1982), *The Varieties of Reference*, ed. J. McDowell, Oxford: Clarendon Press.

Ewert, J.-P. (1987), 'Neuroethology of Releasing Mechanism: Prey-Catching in Toads', *Behavioral and Brain Sciences*, 10: 337–405.

Feigl, H., Scriven, M., and Maxwell, G. (1958) (eds.), *Concepts, Theories, and the Mind–Body Problem* (Minnesota Studies in the Philosophy of Science, 2), Minneapolis: University of Minnesota Press.

Field, H. (1978), 'Mental Representation', *Erkenntnis*, 13: 9–61; reprinted in Block (1981*b*).

Fodor, J. (1974), 'Special Sciences, or the Disunity of Science as a Working Hypothesis', *Synthese*, 28: 97–115.

—— (1981*a*), *Representations: Philosophical Essays on the Foundations of Cognitive Science*, Cambridge, Mass.: MIT Press.

—— (1981*b*), 'Special Sciences', in Fodor (1981*a*): 127–45.

—— (1982), 'Cognitive Science and the Twin Earth Problem', *Notre Dame Journal of Formal Logic*, 23: 98–118.

—— (1987), *Psychosemantics*, Cambridge, Mass.: MIT Press.

—— (1989), 'Making Mind Matter More', *Philosophical Topics*, 17: 59–80.

—— (1991*a*), 'A Modal Argument for Narrow Content', *Journal of Philosophy*, 88: 5–26.

—— (1991*b*), 'You Can Fool Some of the People All of the Time, Everything Else Being Equal: Hedged Laws and Psychological Explanations', *Mind*, 100: 19–34.

Føllesdal, D. (1985), 'Causation and Explanation: A Problem in Davidson's View on Action and Mind', in Le Pore and McLaughlin (1985): 311–23.

Foster, L., and Swanson, J. (1970) (eds.), *Experience and Theory*, Amherst, Mass.: University of Massachusetts Press.

George, A. (1989), (ed.), *Reflections on Chomsky*, Oxford: Basil Blackwell.

Ginet, C. (1990), *On Action*, Cambridge: Cambridge University Press.

Goldman, A. (1970), *A Theory of Human Action*, Englewood Cliffs, NJ: Prentice-Hall.

Gould, S., and Lewontin, R. (1979), 'The Spandrels of San Marco and the Panglossian Program', *Proceedings of the Royal Society of London*, 205: 281–8.

Grunbaum, A. and Salmon, W. (1988) (eds.), *The Limits of Deduction*, Berkeley, Calif.: University of California Press.

Gunderson, K. (1975), *Language, Mind, and Knowledge* (Minnesota Studies in the Philosophy of Science, 7), Minneapolis: University of Minnesota Press.

Hare, R. (1952), *The Language of Morals*, Oxford: Clarendon Press.

—— (1984), 'Supervenience', *Aristotelian Society Supplementary Volume*, 58: 1–16.

Harman, G. (1985), 'Moral Explanations of Natural Facts—Can Moral Claims Be Tested Against Moral Reality?' *Southern Journal of Philosophy*, 24 (Supplement): 57–68.

Haugeland, J. (1983), 'Phenomenal Causes', *Southern Journal of Philosophy*, 22 (Supplement): 63–70.

Healy, R. (1981) (ed.), *Reduction, Time, and Reality*, Cambridge: Cambridge University Press.

Heil, J. (1988), 'Privileged Access', *Mind*, 97: 238–51.

—— (1992), *The Nature of True Minds*, Cambridge: Cambridge University Press.

—— and Mele, A. (1991), 'Mental Causes', *American Philosophical Quarterly*, 28: 61–71.

Hellman, G., and Thompson, F. (1975), 'Physicalism: Ontology, Determination, Reduction', *Journal of Philosophy*, 72: 551–64.

Hempel, C. (1988), 'Provisos: A Problem Concerning the Inferential Function of Scientific Theories', in Grunbaum and Salmon (1988): 19–36.

Honderich, T. (1973), (ed.), *Essays on Freedom of Action*, London: Routledge and Kegan Paul.

—— (1982), 'The Argument for Anomalous Monism', *Analysis*, 42: 59–64.

—— (1988), *A Theory of Determinism: The Mind, Neuroscience, and Life Hopes*, Oxford: Clarendon Press.

—— (1990), *Mind and Brain*, Oxford: Clarendon Press.

—— (1991), 'Better the Union Theory', *Analysis*, 51: 166–73.

Hook, S. (1960) (ed.), *Dimensions of Mind*, New York: New York University Press.

Horgan, T. (1989), 'Mental Quausation', *Philosophical Perspectives*, 3: 47–76.

Hornsby, J. (1980), *Actions*, London: Routledge and Kegan Paul.

—— (1981), 'Which Physical Events are Mental Events?' *Aristotelian Society Proceedings*, 81: 73–92.

—— (1985), 'Physicalism, Events, and Part-Whole Relations', in LePore and McLaughlin (1985): 444–58.

—— (1990), 'Descartes, Rorty, and Mind-Body Fiction', in Malachowski (1990): 41–57.

Jackson, F., and Pettit, P. (1988), 'Functionalism and Broad Content', *Mind*, 97: 381–400.

Johnston, M. (1985), 'Why Having a Mind Matters', in LePore and McLaughlin (1985): 408–26.

Kenny, A. (1970), (trans. and ed.), *Descartes: Philosophical Letters*, Oxford: Clarendon Press.

Kim, J. (1979), 'Causality, Identity, and Supervenience in the Mind–Body Problem', *Midwest Studies in Philosophy*, 4: 31–49.

—— (1984*a*), 'Concepts of Supervenience', *Philosophy and Phenomenological Research*, 65: 153–76.

—— (1984*b*), 'Epiphenomenal and Supervenient Causation', *Midwest Studies in Philosophy*, 9: 257–70.

—— (1985), 'Psychophysical Laws', in LePore and McLaughlin (1985): 369–86.

Kim, J. (1987), ' "Strong" and "Global" Supervenience Revisited', *Philosophy and Phenomenological Research*, 48: 315–26.

—— (1988*a*), 'Explanatory Realism, Causal Realism, and Explanatory Exclusion', *Midwest Studies in Philosophy*, 12: 225–39.

—— (1988*b*), 'Supervenience for Multiple Domains', *Philosophical Topics*, 16: 129–50.

—— (1989*a*), 'Mechanism, Purpose and Explanatory Exclusion', *Philosophical Perspectives*, 3: 77–108.

—— (1989*b*), 'The Myth of Nonreductive Materialism', *Proceedings of the American Philosophical Association*, 63: 31–47.

—— (1990*a*), 'Supervenience as a Philosophical Concept', *Metaphilosophy*, 21: 1–27.

—— (1990*b*) 'Explanatory Exclusion and the Problem of Mental Causation', in Villanueva (1990): 36–56.

—— (1992), ' "Downward Causation" in Emergentism and Nonreductive Physicalism', in Beckermann, Flohr, and Kim (1992): 119–38.

—— (forthcoming), 'Multiple Realization and the Metaphysics of Reduction'.

Krausz, M. (1989) (ed.), *Relativism: Interpretation and Confrontation*, Notre Dame, Ind.: University of Notre Dame Press.

Kripke, S. (1979), 'A Puzzle about Belief', in Margalit (1979): 239–83.

Lennon, K. (1990), *Explaining Human Action*, London: Duckworth.

LePore, E., and McLaughlin, B. (1985) (eds.), *Actions and Events: Perspectives on the Philosophy of Donald Davidson*, Oxford: Basil Blackwell.

—— Loewer, B. (1987), 'Mind Matters', *Journal of Philosophy*, 84: 630–42.

—— —— (1989), 'More on Making Mind Matter', *Philosophical Topics*, 17: 175–91.

Lewis, D. (1973), 'Causation', *Journal of Philosophy*, 70: 556–67; reprinted in Lewis (1986*b*).

—— (1974), 'Radical Interpretation', *Synthese*, 23: 331–44; reprinted in Lewis (1983).

—— (1979), 'Attitudes *De Dicto* and *De Se*', *Philosophical Review*, 88: 413–543; reprinted in Lewis (1983).

—— (1980), 'A Subjectivist's Guide to Objective Chance', in Jeffrey 1980: 263–93; reprinted in Lewis (1986*b*).

—— (1981), 'What Puzzling Pierre does not Believe', *Australasian Journal of Philosophy*, 59: 283–9.

—— (1983), *Philosophical Papers*, i, New York: Oxford University Press.

—— (1986*a*), *On the Plurality of Worlds*, Oxford: Basil Blackwell.

—— (1986*b*), *Philosophical Papers*, ii, New York: Oxford University Press.

Lycan, W. (1990) (ed.), *Mind and Cognition: A Reader*, Oxford: Basil Blackwell.

MacDonald, C., and MacDonald, G. (1986), 'Mental Causes and Explanation of Action', *Philosophical Quarterly*, 36: 145–58.
McDowell, J. (1984), '*De Re* Senses', *Philosophical Quarterly*, 36: 281–94.
—— (1985), 'Functionalism and Anomalous Monism', in LePore and McLaughlin (1985): 387–98.
—— (1986), 'Singular Thought and the Extent of Inner Space', in Pettit and McDowell (1986): 137–68.
McGinn, C. (1979), 'Action and its Explanation', in Bolton (1979): 20–42.
—— (1989), *Mental Content*, Oxford: Basil Blackwell.
Mackie, J. (1974), *The Cement of the Universe*, Oxford: Clarendon Press.
McKinsey, M. (1991), 'Anti-Individualism and Privileged Access', *Analysis*, 51: 59–68.
McLaughlin, B. (1985), 'Anomalous Monism and the Irreducibility of the Mental', in Le Pore and McLaughlin (1985): 331–68.
—— (1989), 'Type Epiphenomenalism, Type Dualism, and the Causal Priority of the Physical', *Philosophical Perspectives*, 3: 109–35.
Malachowski, A. (1990), *Reading Rorty: Critical Responses to* Philosophy and the Mirror of Nature *(and Beyond)*, Oxford: Basil Blackwell.
Malcolm, N. (1968), 'The Conceivability of Mechanism', *Philosophical Review*, 77: 45–72.
Margalit, A. (1979) (ed.), *Meaning and Use*, Dordrecht: Reidel.
Mele, A. (1992), *Springs of Action*, New York: Oxford University Press.
Menzies, P. (1988), 'Against Causal Reductionism', *Mind*, 97: 551–74.
Millikan, R. (1984), *Language, Thought and Other Biological Categories*, Cambridge, Mass.: MIT Press.
—— (1986*a*), 'Thoughts Without Laws: Cognitive Science with Content', *Philosophical Review*, 95: 47–80. Reprinted in Millikan 1993*a*.
—— (1986*b*), 'Naturalist Reflections on Knowledge', *Pacific Philosophical Quarterly*, 65: 315–34. Reprinted in Millikan 1993*a*.
—— (1989*a*), 'Biosemantics', *Journal of Philosophy*, 86: 281–97. Reprinted in Millikan 1993*a*.
—— (1989*b*), 'In Defense of Proper Functions', *Philosophy of Science*, 56: 288–302. Reprinted in Millikan 1993*a*.
—— (1989*c*), 'An Ambiguity in the Notion "Function"'. *Philosophy and Biology*, 4: 172–6.
—— (1990*a*), 'Truth Rules, Hoverflies, and the Kripke–Wittgenstein Paradox', *Philosophical Review*, 99: 323–53. Reprinted in Millikan 1993*a*.
—— (1990*b*), 'Seismograph Readings for *Explaining Behaviour*', *Philosophy and Phenomenological Research*, 50: 807–12.
—— (1991*a*), 'Speaking up for Darwin', in Rey and Loewer (1991): 151–64.
—— (1991*b*), 'Compare and Contrast Dretske, Fodor, and Millikan on Teleosemantics', *Philosophical Topics*, 18: 220–39.
—— (1993*a*), *White Queen Psychology and Other Essays for Alice*, Cambridge, Mass.: MIT Press.

Millikan, R. (1993*b*), 'What is Behavior?' in Millikan (1993*a*).
Moore, A. (1987), 'Points of View', *Philosophical Quarterly*, 37: 1–20.
Morgan, C. (1923), *Emergent Evolution*, London: Williams and Norgate.
Nagel, T. (1986), *The View from Nowhere*, Oxford: Clarendon Press.
Noonan, H. (1991), 'Object-dependent Thoughts and Psychological Redundancy', *Analysis*, 51: 1–16.
Oppenheim, P., and Putnam, H. (1958), 'Unity of Science as a Working Hypothesis', in Feigel *et al.* (1958): 3–36.
Peacocke, C. (1983), *Sense and Content*, Oxford: Clarendon Press.
Pereboom, D., and Kornblith, H. (1991), 'The Metaphysics of Irreducibility', *Philosophical Studies*, 61: 131–51.
Perry, J. (1983), 'Castañeda on "He" and "I" ', in Tomberlin (1983): 15–42.
—— (1990), 'Self-Notions', *Logos*, 11: 17–31.
Petrie, B. (1987), 'Global Supervenience and Reduction', *Philosophy and Phenomenological Research*, 48: 119–30.
Pettit, P. (1986), 'Broad Minded Explanation and Psychology', in Pettit and McDowell (1986): 17–58.
——(1992), *The Common Mind: From Intentional Psychology to Social and Political Theory*, Oxford: Clarendon Press.
—— and McDowell, J. (1986) (eds.), *Subject, Thought, and Context*, Oxford: Clarendon Press.
—— Sylvan, R., and Norman, J. (1987) (eds.), *Metaphysics and Morality*, Oxford: Basil Blackwell.
Plato, *Phaedo*, trans. R. Hackforth, Cambridge: Cambridge University Press, 1955.
Post, J. (1987), *The Faces of Existence: An Essay in Nonreductive Metaphysics*, Ithaca, NY: Cornell University Press.
—— (1990), *Metaphysics: A Contemporary Introduction*, New York: Paragon House.
Putnam, H. (1960), 'Minds and Machines', in Hook (1960): 138–64; reprinted in Putnam 1975*b*.
—— (1967), 'Psychological Predicates', in Capitan and Merrill (1967): 37-48.
—— (1975*a*), 'The Meaning of "Meaning" ', in Gunderson (1975): 131–93; reprinted in Putnam (1975*b*): 215–71.
—— (1975*b*), *Philosophical Papers*, ii, Cambridge: Cambridge University Press.
—— (1975*c*), 'Philosophy and Our Mental Life', in Putnam (1975*b*): 291–303.
—— (1981), *Reason, Truth, and History*, Cambridge: Cambridge University Press.
—— (1988), *Representation and Reality*, Cambridge, Mass.: MIT Press.
Quine, W. (1973), *The Roots of Reference*, La Salle, Ill.: Open Court.
Quinn, W. (1986), 'Truth and Explanation in Ethics', *Ethics*, 96: 524–44.

Rescher, N. (1969) (ed.), *Essays in Honor of Carl G. Hempel*, Dordrecht: Reidel.

Rey, G., and Loewer, B. (1991) (eds.), *Meaning in Mind: Fodor and His Critics*, Oxford: Basil Blackwell.

Robinson, H. (1982), *Matter and Sense*, Cambridge: Cambridge University Press.

Robinson, W. (1990), 'States and Beliefs', *Mind*, 99: 33–51.

Rumelhart, D., and McClelland, J. (1986), *Parallel Distributed Processing: Explorations in Microstructure of Cognition*, i and ii, Cambridge, Mass.: MIT Press.

Sayre-McCord, G. (1989), 'Functional Explanations and Reasons as Causes', *Philosophical Perspectives*, 3: 137–64.

Schiffer, S. (1991), 'Ceteris Paribus Laws', *Mind*, 100: 1–17.

Segal, G. (1989), 'The Return of the Individual', *Mind*, 158: 39–57.

Silvers, S. (1989) (ed.), *ReRepresentations: Readings in the Philosophy of Mental Representation*, Dordrecht: Kluwer.

Smith, P. (1984), 'Anomalous Monism and Epiphenomenalism: A Reply to Honderich', *Analysis*, 44: 83–6.

Sosa, E. (1984), 'Mind–Body Interaction and Supervenient Causation', *Midwest Studies in Philosophy*, 9: 271–81.

Sperry, R. (1969), 'A Modified Concept of Consciousness', *Psychological Review*, 76: 532–6.

Stalnaker, R. (1984), *Inquiry*, Cambridge, Mass.: MIT Press.

—— (1989), 'What's in the Head?', *Philosophical Perspectives*, 3: 287–316.

Stich, S. (1983), *From Folk Psychology to Cognitive Science: The Case Against Belief*, Cambridge, Mass.: MIT Press.

Stoutland, F. (1976), 'The Causation of Behavior', in *Essays on Wittgenstein in Honor of G. H. Von Wright* (*Acta Philosophica Fennica*, 28): 286–325.

—— (1985), 'Davidson on Intentional Behavior', in LePore and McLaughlin (1985): 44–59.

Sturgeon, N. (1985), 'Harman on Moral Explanations of Natural Facts', *Southern Journal of Philosophy*, 24 (Supplement): 69–78.

Suppes, P., Henkin, L., Moisil, G., and Joja, A. (1973) (eds.), *Proceedings of the Fourth International Congress for Logic, Methodology, and Philosophy of Science*, Amsterdam: North-Holland.

Tolman, E. (1948), 'Cognitive Maps in Rats and Men', *Psychological Review*, 55: 189–208.

Tomberlin, J. (1983) (ed.), *Agent, Language, and the Structure of the World*, Indianapolis, Ind.: Hackett.

Van Gulick, R. (1985), 'Physicalism and the Subjectivity of the Mental', *Philosophical Topics*, 13/3: 51–70.

—— (1989), 'Metaphysical Arguments for Internalism and Why They Don't Work', in Silvers (1989): 151–60.

Van Gulick, R. (1990), 'Functionalism, Information, and Content', in Lycan (1990): 107–29.

—— (1992*a*) 'Nonreductive Materialism and Intertheoretic Constraint', in Beckermann, Flohr, and Kim (1992): 157–79.

Vermazen, B., and Hintikka, M. (1985) (eds.), *Essays on Davidson: Actions and Events*, Oxford; Clarendon Press.

Villanueva, E. (1990) (ed.), *Information, Semantics, and Epistemology*, Oxford: Basil Blackwell.

Wagner, S., and Warner, C. (1992) (eds.), *Naturalism: A Critical Appraisal*, Notre Dame, Ind.: University of Notre Dame Press.

Woodfield, A. (1982) (ed.), *Thought and Object: Essays on Intentionality*, Oxford: Clarendon Press.

Index